Out of Many, One People

CARIBBEAN ARCHAEOLOGY AND ETHNOHISTORY

L. Antonio Curet, Series Editor

Out of Many, One People

The Historical Archaeology of Colonial Jamaica

Edited by
James A. Delle, Mark W. Hauser, and Douglas V. Armstrong

THE UNIVERSITY OF ALABAMA PRESS
Tuscaloosa

Typeface: Minion

Library of Congress Cataloging-in-Publication Data

Delle, James A.
Out of many, one people : the historical archaeology of colonial Jamaica / James Andrew Delle, Mark W. Hauser, and Douglas Armstrong.
p. cm. — (Caribbean archaeology and ethnohistory)
Includes bibliographical references and index.
ISBN 978-0-8173-1726-3 (cloth : alk. paper) — ISBN 978-0-8173-5648-4 (paper : alk. paper) — ISBN 978-0-8173-8530-9 (electronic) 1. Jamaica—Antiquities. 2. Archaeology and history—Jamaica. 3. Excavations (Archaeology)—Jamaica. 4. Historic sites—Jamaica. 5. Jamaica—History, Local. 6. Material culture—Jamaica—History. 7. Plantation life—Jamaica—History. 8. Slaves—Jamaica—Social life and customs. 9. Jamaica—Social life and customs. I. Hauser, Mark W. II. Armstrong, Douglas V. III. Title.
F1875.D45 2011
972.92—dc22

2010045986

Front Cover: Marketplace, Falmouth, Jamaica, by Adolph Duperly, *Daguerian Excursions in Jamaica* (Kingston, Jamaica, 1843). Courtesy of the National Library of Jamaica.

Contents

Illustrations

FIGURES

TABLES

Preface

One of my reflections on growing up in colonial Jamaica was the absence of our history. The little that was readily available came mainly in the form of anecdotes from older family and community members. There was little evidence of the past, tangible or intangible, that was not of colonial vintage. However, to be realistic, this colonial status was how most of the society was structured from 1655 to 1962.

The formation of the Institute of Jamaica in 1879 under Governor Anthony Musgrave has allowed us to retain artifacts and historical documentation over the past 130 years. These otherwise might have disappeared. The institute, its divisions, and its offspring, such as the National Library, the National Gallery of Jamaica, the Afro Caribbean Institute, and the Jamaica National Heritage Trust, have all contributed to the retention of material cultural remains and recording the intangible heritage that are so important to a people. To these institutions we must also add Jamaica Welfare and its descendants, the Jamaica Cultural Development Commission and the Social Development Commission, recognizing them for their role in preserving the intangible heritage of Jamaica.

The work of these institutions was enhanced with the advent of the University College of the West Indies, now the University of the West Indies, which was founded in 1948. Its ongoing research over the past decades has added much to our knowledge of ourselves, of our history, and of our culture. Seminal work was undertaken and published and inter alia became texts for schools. With this support the succeeding post-independence generations began to learn some of the history of its peoples, its society, and its raison d'être. This has resulted in a much more focused society with an understanding of its past. The emerging nation status of a country in the twentieth century demanded that its people have a sense of who they are, recognizing that they are in fact the sum of their past.

Today we have more complete data on the great variety of the origins of the Jamaican people. These people came from South America (the Taino), Europe (the

Spanish beginning with Columbus and then the English captured the island), and Africa (some early arrivals came with the Spanish). The English began with the importation of the Irish ancestors who came as indentured labor. They were followed by the Africans who came as enslaved labor. They were joined by the Scots also as indentured labor. After emancipation in 1838 Indian, Chinese, German, and African indentured laborers were brought over. In the interregnum, as the economy grew, those who had been persecuted in their host countries came to seek a better way of life. These people included Jews who originated from the Iberian peninsula and Huguenots from Catholic Europe. Later came Arab Christians from the collapsing Ottoman Empire.

These are the origins of the people of Jamaica. This melting pot of cultures and ethnicities gave rise to the national motto "Out of Many, One People." To understand all the nuances and social variances and to explain the further meanings of the motto, scholars have dealt deeply, but there is a real need for more to be undertaken. How the people of Jamaica settled, their lifestyles, the prevailing conditions at those times, the cultures they brought and the residues that prevail, the various sociopolitical landscapes, and the socioeconomic platforms are all meat for the continuing grinder of research.

This volume of essays is yet another set of work that has been undertaken to research the varied and unfolding rich heritage of the Jamaican people. These essays speak to the painstaking efforts of the research undertaken and to the interpretations of this research. They uncover more of the storied past, laying more groundwork for understanding the Jamaican people's past, present, and future. The essays collected here lay down challenges for further work on understanding the variety of cultures and races that make up the present society. The findings are not just for the Jamaican people; they are important for the host communities from which the forbears came, helping them understand how, when, and why their fellow men, women, and children were brought to this island home, Jamaica. These essays aptly cover the ground to allow the collection to use the Jamaican motto as its title.

It has been my pleasure to have contributed from the periphery, to have helped influence the energies that have been set to work to do the archaeology, to do research, and to publish these interpretations that continue to add credibility to the motto and now the title *Out of Many, One People.*

Ainsley Henriques
Former Chairman
Jamaica National Heritage Trust

Out of Many, One People

1
Introduction
Historical Archaeology in Jamaica

Mark W. Hauser, James A. Delle, and Douglas V. Armstrong

The largest and wealthiest of Britain's former Caribbean colonial possessions, Jamaica has long been a major locus of inquiry into the archaeology of the colonial experience. This volume assembles for the first time the results of nearly three decades of historical archaeology in Jamaica. Spanning four hundred years of Jamaica's colonial history, the essays in this volume consider topics ranging from the late fifteenth-century settlement of Jamaica's north coast by the Spanish, through the seventeenth-century establishment of what was once the world's wealthiest colonial entrepôt, to the eighteenth-century fluorescence of slave-based plantation agriculture, to the post-emancipation hopes and dilemmas arising in the aftermath of the nineteenth-century abolition of slavery. Through their work on Jamaica, which Christopher Columbus reputedly described as "the fairest isle eyes have seen," the archaeologists represented here have explored in microcosm the material realities of colonialism as experienced throughout the New World.

Jamaica's national motto, "Out of Many, One People," expresses a deep understanding of the diverse heritage of the population that emerged during the colonial period, a concept that has been carried over in the breadth of archaeological research conducted in Jamaica. The island nation projects a rich diversity of cultural settings and a corresponding set of archaeological remains from contact period sites linked directly to Columbus and early Spanish settlers, to the complex of colonial forts and urban settlements associated with the late seventeenth-century maritime trading center at Port Royal that was devastated by an earthquake in 1692, to an array of plantation sites relating to the British colonial period and tied to a complex set of social and economic structures built upon the labor of enslaved Africans. Jamaica's colonial history did not end with the abolition of slavery, however, and an increasing number of archaeological projects have focused on post- and extra-slavery contexts.

In this introductory chapter, we frame the historical archaeology of Jamaica through an outline of the primary temporal and topical themes that have shaped the history of the island nation. In so doing, we provide a condensed history of the colonial experience on the island, providing a context for the historical archaeological explorations that follow in the subsequent chapters.

The Archaeology of History in Colonial Jamaica

The year that Columbus first landed on Jamaica, 1494, marks the beginning of Jamaica's colonial history. Certainly it is not the beginning of the story of the Jamaican people, nor is it the likely end of the story of indigenous people on the island they called Xamaca. Rather it is the year in which the long and complex story of European colonialism, African labor, and creole life began in Jamaica. The goal of this volume is to explore the history of Jamaica through archaeological engagement with the materials and landscapes left to us by past peoples resident on this island; these material realties are reflected, revealed, and created by the artifacts, buildings, and landscapes shaped through the productive capacities, inventiveness, and perseverance of twenty generations of Jamaica's people. We hope to show through the material record that these Caribbean people cannot be defined solely through structures of inequality or resistance to colonial abstractions. While it is quite evident that social and economic inequalities have existed and continue to do so, by closely reading the material record of the indeterminacies of everyday life archaeologists can interpret and better understand the complexities inherent in the quotidian experiences of colonialism.

While there have been a number of traditional histories written about the colonial experience in the Caribbean, and of Jamaica in particular, we believe that this is the first attempt to pull together a narrative history of the island using material culture as a point of departure. The authors in this volume follow James Deetz's definition of material culture as the aspects of the natural environment that have been impacted by and in turn have shaped human agency (Deetz 1977). Material culture in Jamaica can be as dramatic as the leg irons used by planters to shackle a laborer or as unassuming as a clay pot found in the burned remains of the governor's mansion. Material culture reveals a level of tangible evidence that we can use to complement, confront, and sometimes confound the documentary record. We recognize that material culture introduces its own kinds of silences (Morrison and Lycett 1997; Cobb 2005), largely due to the sometimes arbitrary nature implicit in the exercises of typology, classification, and interpretation. However, material culture studies can give active voice to those who might seem passive in the documentary evidence, whether they be the indigenous peoples confronted by Columbus, the Africans enslaved by the British to work on sugar and coffee plantations, the sailors who made intra-island trade possible, the free and enslaved artisans who created the material realities of the Jamaican world, or the South Asian contract laborers transported across an empire to ensure the production of cheap sugar for the world market. While not necessarily going as far as calling it a democratic form of evidence as Leland Ferguson (1992) would have us do, the analysis of material culture can, in the best of worlds, expand our understanding of the past.

What enables us to mitigate silences in the documentary record and the arbitrary nature of material identification and interpretation is the archaeological perspective of scale. Ultimately archaeology is the study of the distribution of material culture in time and space. It looks at how these two axes are shaped by and continue to shape human interaction. After all, it is important to note that historical processes that make archaeological interpretations methodologically possible—such phenomena as the mass production of goods, large volume consumption, and occasional choice (agency)—are also our primary problematics, or at least questions of concern. From the perspective of archaeology, when we look at the history of Jamaica, we see continually unfolding processes transforming both the social structures of the island and the material lives of the colonizing and colonized people of the "fairest isle."

Early Colonial Jamaica, 1494–1692

While most casual observers consider Jamaica to be part of the Anglo-sphere of the colonial British West Indies, the island was a Spanish colonial possession for over 150 years. The colonial history of Jamaica begins with the fifteenth-century arrival of the Spanish, who claimed possession of the island and its indigenous people until 1655, when Jamaica was wrested away by the British. Columbus claimed Jamaica for the Spanish Crown when he landed on the island's north coast in May 1494. While Columbus was famously marooned on Jamaica for a year, it was not until 1509 that Sevilla la Nueva, the first permanent Spanish settlement on Jamaica and the first Spanish capital, was established near the modern town of St. Ann's Bay, on Jamaica's north coast. While much of the early historical archaeology on Jamaica focused on trying to locate and define early Spanish sites, the results of those efforts were sparsely reported. Fortunately, Robyn P. Woodward's studies of Sevilla la Nueva provide an important picture of social and economic systems from the early days of colonial settlement of the region (Woodward 1988, 2006a, 2006b).

Woodward's contribution to this volume (chapter 2) synthesizes her extensive research into this first capital of colonial Jamaica. Her study of a sixteenth-century mill site at Sevilla la Nueva explores the transferal of Spanish feudal systems of agricultural production to Jamaica. As was the case in more famously Spanish possessions like Hispaniola, on Jamaica the indigenous population was put to work

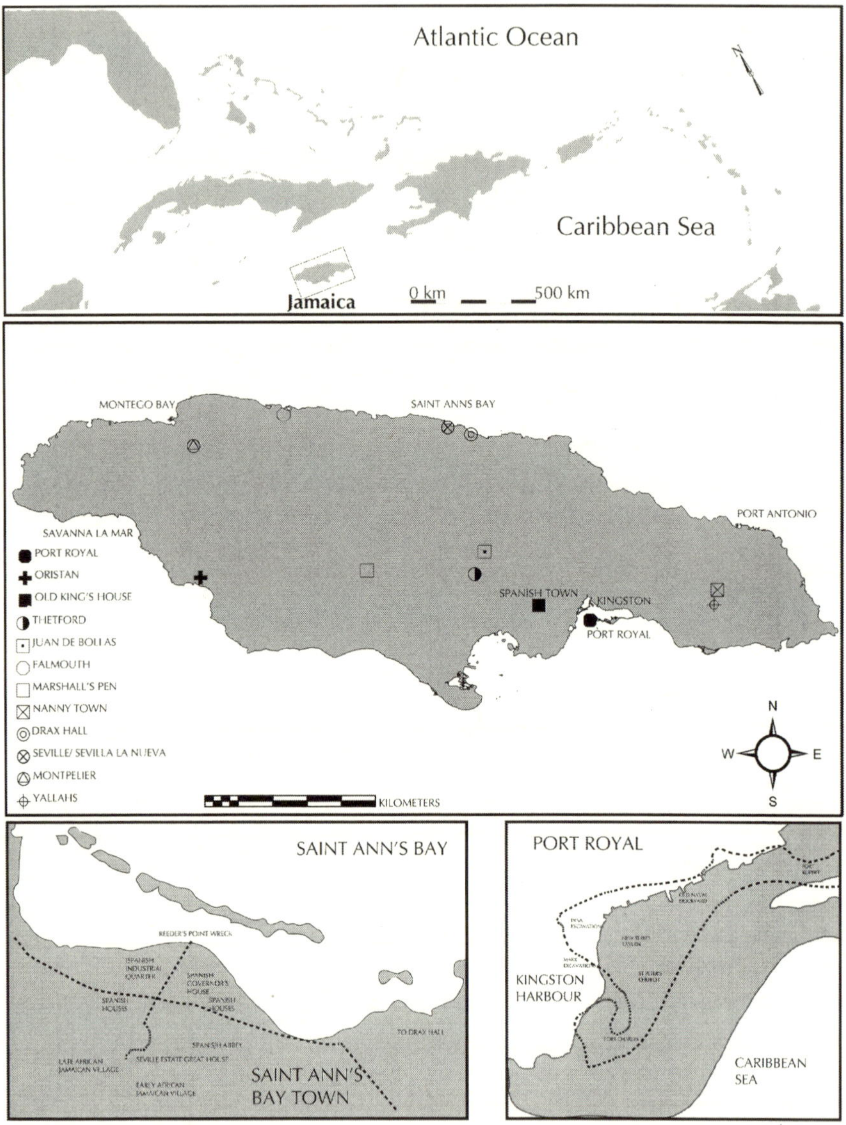

Figure 1.1. Locator map of Jamaica showing archaeological sites discussed in this volume. Insets include details of archaeological excavations conducted in Port Royal and St. Ann's Bay. Artwork by Mark W. Hauser.

sharecropping land patented by the crown to Spanish landlords. Their crops were processed in a central milling operation located in the town. The mill and related settlements at Sevilla la Nueva project a center of craftspersons, artisans, and agricultural producers (Woodward 2006a). It is important to note that although Sevilla la Nueva never reached the prominence of La Isabella on Hispaniola, sculptors in Jamaica were similarly trained to produce statuary and architectural detailing to provide symbolic capital for the Catholic Church and colonial administrators of Jamaica.

Woodward's research explores the beginning of many institutions that played a pivotal role in Jamaica's later economic and social development. Shortly after New Seville's establishment we see the beginning of the effect of the *asiento*, the legal framework that established crown approval for the importation of enslaved Africans into Spain's New World possessions. Africans were first brought to Jamaica during the sixteenth century. In 1513 Juan de Esquivel, complaining about the lack of indigenous labor, requested that the king permit him to bring three enslaved Africans to Jamaica (Cundall and Pietersz 1919:1). It was thus the Spanish that introduced African slavery to Jamaica.

Spanish governors continued to administer colonial Jamaica from Sevilla la Nueva until 1534, when the seat of power was moved from the north coast to the south coast. In that year the new colonial capital was established in Villa de la Vega, known to this day as Spanish Town. In 1540 the crown granted Jamaica to the descendants of Christopher Columbus. As a personal estate of the Columbus family, the island remained relatively underdeveloped throughout the late sixteenth and early seventeenth centuries. As the empires of the Aztec and Inca were folded into the Spanish Empire, the crown shifted interest away from the agricultural colonies of the Caribbean to its wealthier holdings on the Spanish Main—Mexico, Central America, and Andean South America. Spanish settlement remained relatively sparse on the islands, though Jamaica was utilized to provision ships' crews with fresh water, cured pork, and a kind of cassava bread called bammy.

The Spanish occupation of Jamaica ended on May 10, 1655, when British admiral William Penn and general Robert Venebles, unable to conquer Hispaniola, landed at Passage Fort on the western shore of Kingston Harbor; within a day they secured a Spanish surrender of the island of Jamaica. While some of the Spanish settlers escaped to nearby Cuba, others stayed and fought an internecine guerilla war from the Juan de Bolas hills, located in today's parish of St. Catherine. Commanding a small guerilla force and supplied by Cuba, Don Cristobal Arnaldo de Ysassi struggled against the British for several years. In a remarkable historical moment, formerly enslaved laborers of the Spanish who had run away into the hills of St. Catherine—known as Maroons—aided the Spanish effort against the British. Indeed, much of the early success of de Ysassi has been attributed to the tactical skill and charismatic ability of Juan de Bolas, the Maroon leader. Two pitched battles were fought—at Ocho Rios in 1657 and Rio Nuevo in 1658. It was only in 1660 that de Ysassi was finally defeated when Juan de Bolas and his Maroon guerillas abandoned the Spanish to side with the English.

While British control of Jamaica was not fully consolidated until 1694, when a French effort to seize the island was repulsed, the defeat of de Ysassi and the alliance of the Maroons allowed English and native-born creole settlers to concentrate on establishing Port Royal, one of the most important colonial settlements in the seventeenth-century Caribbean. Located in the western Caribbean, along one of the largest natural harbors in the western hemisphere, the English settlement at Port Royal was one of the most important commercial centers in Anglophone America. While Spanish Town continued to be the political seat of the island, considerable settlement and investment occurred in Port Royal, perched at the end of the Palisadoes, a sandy spit protecting Kingston Harbor (Pawson and Buisseret [1975] 2000).

Given Jamaica's proximity to Cuba, Hispaniola, and the Honduran and Miskitu coasts, British colonial power was concentrated there, as Port Royal grew into one of the largest transshipment ports for enslaved Africans in the western Caribbean. Concomitant with the growth in legitimate trade was a growth in contraband, privateering, and piracy. Nuala Zahedieh estimates that 1,500 residents of Port Royal were engaged in privateering, out of a population of 8,500–9,000 (1986). The cosmopolitan population of Port Royal had mostly come from other Caribbean colonies where the land had already been claimed and prospects were limited. Seventeenth-century Port Royal was home to peoples of African descent (including creoles from Barbados and Nevis), English, Scottish, Welsh, Irish, Spanish Jews, and Gypsies (Burton 1999:15), 5,000 of whom were freemen recruited from the older West Indian colonies of St. Kitts, Nevis, and Barbados (Watts 1987:216). Since sugar production required significant technological and financial investment, the early poor settlers set up less economically intensive agricultural concerns, including small-scale ranches (known in Jamaica as pens), as well as cotton and cocoa plantations, which required less infrastructural investment than sugar (see Dunn 1972:149).

At 11:43 A.M. on June 7, 1692, an earthquake struck the island of Jamaica. This massive quake wrought many changes to the island's geography, including a landslide that buried a plantation at Judgment Cliff in the parish of St. Thomas. The Palisadoes strip, mostly made of sand, experienced a geological effect known as liquifaction; some two-thirds of the city of Port Royal slumped into Kingston Harbor as a result of the earthquake. While the destruction of Port Royal is commonly used to separate Jamaica's early colonial period from the later plantation period—a convention we use here—it is simplistic to assume that the cataclysmic earthquake was the primary determinant in shifting Jamaica's economy away from trade and into plantation production. Certainly, as Pawson and Buisseret ([1975] 2000) have noted, by the time the earthquake struck, Port Royal was already in a state of economic decline. Indeed, if any causality is to be ascribed to the earthquake it is that it hastened the city's decline and the shift of the island's economic basis from commercialism to agro-industry. Indeed, as Douglas V. Armstrong highlights in his discussion of Seville Plantation (see chapter 5), the Hemmings family had already established their sugar plantation in St. Ann's Bay by the time the earthquake struck.

The earthquake that destroyed Port Royal created something of a Pompeii effect—a moment of time was captured for archaeologists when the city was destroyed. The attraction of the "Sunken City" has fostered a considerable amount of archaeological research in Port Royal for the early colonial period, ranging from amateur investigations focused on the "pirate port" to intensive and systematic investigations seeking to recover and re-create the seventeenth-century port city landscape. Most notable among this research was a multiyear project conducted by Donny Hamilton of Texas A&M University and the Institute of Nautical Archaeology. Hamilton's project resulted in a number of articles focusing on the merchants and craft producers of Port Royal, as well as theses and dissertations specializing in specific sets of material culture (McClenaghan 1988; Gotelipe-Miller 1990; Franklin 1992; Heidtke 1992; Darrington 1994; Hailey 1994; Trussel 2004; C. Smith 1995; H. DeWolf 1998; Fox 1998; Winslow 2000).

In chapter 3, Marianne Franklin discusses research she conducted in Port Royal. Rather than focusing on the kinds of material culture only relatively few would have had—porcelain and pewter—Franklin examines iron tools, a form of material culture all of the inhabitants would have required. Through an examination of over one hundred wrought-iron tools recovered from several underwater excavations, Franklin highlights the growth and fluorescence of Port Royal as a mercantile city. Franklin points out that both fine and crudely crafted tools show that demographic growth and demand for tools to support the population outstripped local merchants' ability to meet that demand through the importation of prefabricated tools.

In chapter 4, Maureen J. Brown summarizes her findings on the archaeological materials recovered from Anthony Priddy's excavation at the New Street Tavern. As is the case with all social institutions, taverns in the seventeenth- and eighteenth-century Atlantic world reflected the cultures from which they derived and the settings in which they operated. Emergent class and social status in the seventeenth and eighteenth centuries stimulated the development of consumerism in colonial contexts like Jamaica. The use and display of material goods purchased in public spaces provided a powerful channel for the communication of symbolic and cultural capital at least among the merchant classes of Port Royal. The cosmopolitan nature of Port Royal and the variegated interests of the merchant and artisan classes of the city are reflected in the material culture recovered from the New Street Tavern site.

The destruction of Port Royal in the earthquake of 1692 represents a symbolic, if not material, shift in the colonial identity of Jamaica. As the eighteenth and nineteenth centuries progressed, that identity was defined primarily by Jamaica's place as the wealthiest of Britain's sugar colonies, wealth that was created simultaneously from the labor of enslaved Africans and the seemingly unending demand for the addictive products of tropical agriculture: sugar, rum, and coffee.

The Plantation and the African Atlantic, 1692–1838

Jamaica's colonial transition from dependence on transshipment and trade to agro-industrial production was gradual, never exclusive, and driven by a massive forced migration of enslaved African labor into Jamaica. The colonial economy was similarly not one-sided; as Eric Williams has argued, and Richard Sheridan, Sidney Mintz, and others have corroborated, the profits that investors, absentee planters, and bankers made from their sugar estates in Jamaica, Barbados, and Antigua provided capital, systematic know-how, and emergent markets crucial to the development of European industrialization. In addition to the economic impact enslaved laborers had on the island, they also brought with them ways of doing things, cultural knowledge that shaped the material and social landscapes of Jamaica. Not surprisingly, much of the historical archaeological research into eighteenth- and early nineteenth-century Jamaica has focused on these economic and cultural processes.

It is not the goal of this volume to equate slavery or the plantation with the history of Jamaica. It is, however, important to highlight that by the end of Queen Anne's War in 1713, an event that formalized the European spheres of control in the Caribbean, the plantation had become the dominant economic institution in Jamaica and African slavery the social foundation of its success. By the middle of the eighteenth century, the sugar industry was the cornerstone of Jamaica's economy (Sheridan 1965, 1968, 1973:215, 1976), and slavery was the primary organizing principle of labor (Williams 1970:136). Hundreds of thousands of enslaved laborers fueled an economic system whose backers attempted to minimize the input costs; the success of the slave trade and the drive to minimize the cost of labor are both reflected in the horrific demographics of the slavery era. Trevor Burnard calculates that 1,083,369 Africans were transported to be sold in Jamaica; Barry Higman relates that the enslaved population of the British West Indies experienced negative natural increase prior to the abolition of the slave trade in 1807 (Burnard 2001:13; Higman 1995:72). The population was in a continual state of decline, fostering dependence on the continuous importation of forced labor.

This slave economy effected lasting structural change in the social milieu of the West Indies. Richard Dunn claims that "[t]he plantation system lasted without significant alteration throughout the eighteenth century, continued in modified form even after enslaved laborers were freed in the nineteenth century, and still survives in large measure in Jamaica, Barbados, and the Leeward Islands" (1972:334). Sidney Mintz (1985) has argued that the sugar plantation provided a model for emergent European industrialization and, through the production of sugar, made available a cheap source of calories for the emerging industrial working class. The plantation system also created a context in which enslaved peoples of African descent refashioned the world they were entering using organizing frameworks brought from West Africa and applying them in new contexts, yet the plantation was a regime that required strict structural control over the daily lives and economic world of the people who provided the plantation's labor.

The planters, in laying out estates, building mills devoted to processing, and placing villages to house the workers, were preoccupied with streamlining the costs of production. The French encyclopedist Denis Diderot published his *Encyclopédie* between 1751 and 1772, in which he outlines and illustrates an eighteenth-century version of a "how-to" on various trades and industries. Among his descriptions was an illustration of a sugar plantation, which describes every industrial detail from sugar processing to the layout of an estate. As Diderot observed, in Jamaica, a typical sugar estate was composed of what some archaeologists would consider elite space; both overseers' houses and Great Houses for resident or even absentee proprietors created, at least from the planters' perspective, the physical and symbolic center of the sugar plantation. Other landscape elements included the industrial works where sugar, coffee, or other commodities were rendered from their raw state into an exportable form. The plantation landscape also included agricultural fields in which the crops were grown. The enslaved workers in Jamaica lived within their own spaces, in houseyards located both in villages and in dispersed areas on plantations, and on small farm plots located on the plantation. Known as provision grounds, these latter fields were the locus of domestic production for the enslaved. The slave regime of Jamaica required that the enslaved produce food for themselves and their families; any surplus production was theirs to keep or sell.

Of incredible importance to the historical archaeology of Jamaica has been the systematic focus on the houseyard, the domestic space of the enslaved on plantations. The definition of the houseyard as the primary unit of analysis within Jamaican plantation villages began with Armstrong's pioneering work at Drax Hall (1991a) and Higman's analysis at Montpelier (1998). Armstrong's later work at the Seville Estate, located on the ruins of Sevilla la Nueva, which developed in the eighteenth century as a sugar plantation, further refined the houseyard as an analytical unit. Seville was not Jamaica's largest estate, nor was it the most profitable, but it may be a very good representation of an average sugar plantation in eighteenth-century Jamaica. In chapter 5 of this volume, Armstrong provides an overview and analysis of research conducted on the eighteenth-century component at Seville between 1987 and 1992. This research focused on the shifting landscape of the sugar estate especially as it relates to the several laborers' villages in which the enslaved workers of Seville lived. Armstrong's work demonstrates that the landscape of the villages was dynamic, both temporally as the nature of settlements at Seville changed over time and socially. Armstrong has clearly demonstrated that we cannot assume that the spatial organization and internal use of space within plantation communities was static; instead, the landscapes of plantation slavery must be considered as dynamic sociospatial phenomena.

One poorly understood sector of the Jamaican economy was the local transshipment of agricultural and manufactured goods produced by planters and local artisans. Many plantations shipped their produce from their own docks to larger wharves for transatlantic transport to Great Britain; goods coming in from Europe would also find their way to the plantations through local sea trade. As has been noted by many scholars, in the eighteenth century Kingston became an important metropolitan center in the Caribbean, second only to Havana in size and population (Burnard 2002:225), and for several generations played a central role in the shipment and transshipment of imported luxury goods to both Spanish and Anglophone America (Pares 1956:33). This trade relied on large ports and oceangoing ships like those arriving in Kingston Harbor. Kingston and the island's smaller ports also were home to a significant small boat trade using sloops that plied cabotage ports on both the north and south coasts of Jamaica. This inter- and intra-island trade played a crucial, if undervalued, part in Jamaica's economy; some have calculated that in the late eighteenth century the regional trade in provisions made up as much as 20 percent of Jamaica's exports (Sheridan 1968:55; 1976), as Jamaican beef and other foodstuffs made their way to smaller, sometimes remote British, French, and Spanish islands (Burnard 2002:227).

In chapter 6 Gregory D. Cook and Amy Rubenstein-Gottschamer examine the archaeological legacy of this trade through a summary of research conducted on a shipwreck in St. Ann's Bay known as the Readers Point wreck. Throughout the early colonial period, and indeed well into the eighteenth century, the mercantile system set up by the various European powers strictly limited trade between the Caribbean islands. While smuggling between islands had always been rampant, legitimate traffic in goods and livestock was sanctioned by the Free Port Act of 1766, which legalized inter-island trade in the hope of drawing more hard currency into the Jamaican economy. The resulting traffic employed small boats like the Readers Point wreck (Cook 1997). While there is no direct evidence that this specific wreck took part in contraband trade, sloops like this one were largely responsible for both the sanctioned and illegal inter-island trade under way in the eighteenth and nineteenth centuries. Cook and Rubenstein-Gottschamer discuss evidence that shows this ship probably moved goods between Jamaica and North America and thus was involved in regional trade.

While the coastal trade played a crucial part in the development of the colonial

West Indian economy, the core of the system was based on plantation agriculture. More than a locus of production, the plantation was a sociospatial phenomenon that shaped the everyday lives of the people who lived and worked on them. During the eighteenth and early nineteenth centuries, the logic of the plantation labor system, built as it was on enslaved labor, had at its core the constant threat of violence. The Jamaican slave system created a brutalizing social reality deeply layered with power and power relations. In chapter 7, James A. Delle explores how landscapes were created not only to reflect but to create and reinforce social power. Drawing on the work of the post-structuralists, Delle argues that plantation landscapes at various scales of analysis were shaped by and in turn shaped the power dynamics of plantation Jamaica.

Enslavement and Maroonage in Jamaica

In Jamaica, as elsewhere in the colonial world, many chose to escape from their bondage and the demands of the plantation by creating sovereign communities. In Jamaica, those who fought for and created their own independence are known as Maroons. In chapter 8, Candice Goucher and Kofi Agorsah examine the Maroon experience on Jamaica within the context of broader Maroon studies. In their chapter they discuss not only how the Maroons established distinct cultural identities but also how they interacted with fellow descendants of the African diaspora. For example, their discussion of the Reeder's Foundry excavation, conducted near Morant Bay in the parish of St. Thomas, explores the role that skilled slaves, Maroons, and free Africans had in influencing metal iron technology on the island. The foundry opened in 1772 and continued to operate for ten years. Rather than being passive craftspeople adopting European technologies, the artisans John Reeder employed were selected especially for their skill in African-derived iron smelting and smithing. While it is important to keep in mind that the Caribbean plantation was in essence a factory in the field through which Europeans experimented with regimentation and piecework later found in the industrial centers, we must also remember that the technology for some of the vital workings of the state were built with skills learned by artisans in Africa.

The Jamaican people were not an undifferentiated mass. Even under the harsh regime of slavery, intellectual and cultural expressions flourished in both town and country. Beginning with the pioneering research of Elsa Goveia in her path-breaking *Slave Society in the British Leeward Islands* (1965), much of Jamaican historiography (and Anglophone Caribbean historiography more broadly) has focused on the African Jamaican society that emerged from the plantation system. Much of this research has been an attempt to reconstruct the economic, legal, and social contexts under which the enslaved labored and lived. As such, and again in many ways derived from methodological cues anticipated by Goveia, this work focuses on the analysis of laws, economic transactions, and contemporary accounts of Jamaican society.

The internal economy controlled by the enslaved has proved a particularly fascinating line of research. One unanticipated result of the provisioning system, which recognized that the foodstuffs grown by the enslaved on their provision grounds legally belonged to them, was the development of a sophisticated market system in Jamaica that included independent acquisition, marketing, and production among the enslaved (N. D. Hall 1977, [1980] 1991, [1985] 1991, 1994; Bush 1981, 1990, 1996; Simmonds 1987, 2004; Beckles 1989, 1991, 1999; Tomich 1993; Boa 1993; see also Gaspar and Hine 1996; Hall 1989). The internal economy also presaged a Caribbean peasantry rooted in the houseyard and market (D. Hall 1959; Mintz [1974] 1992; Craton 1982; Trouillot 1988). The independent production by enslaved laborers on provision grounds and the exchange of those goods were activities on the margins of the planters' figurative and material control (Pulsipher 1986, 1990, 1991, 1994; McKee 1999; Pulsipher and Goodwin 1999) yet provided the enslaved with the means to establish some measure of cultural and economic sovereignty over their lives, despite the horrific conditions of slavery.

Significant to our understanding of the Jamaican internal market system is the analysis of independent production among enslaved laborers that largely shaped the economic and material landscapes of the island. This independent production was connected in part through a series of reciprocal exchanges on the plantation through which enslaved workers would sometimes sell their produce to the estate for cash (Delle 1998, 2002). The island was traveled by itinerant traders called higglers, who themselves were sometimes enslaved; legal and illegal street markets existed in nearly every significant Jamaican town. Markets can be viewed as "a symbolic offensive against the established order" (Beckles 1991:32) inhabited by "fettered entrepreneurs" practicing a nascent and alternate form of capitalism (see Beckles 1989, 1991). Consequently, the informal markets can be viewed as a locus of interaction where the enslaved could transgress the social and geographic boundaries imposed by the plantation. It is important to keep in mind Sidney Mintz's admonition that "slaves who plotted armed revolts in the marketplaces had first to produce for the market, and to gain permission to carry their produce there" (1971:321). The markets did not negate the economic structures with which they intersected. Rather the markets were a space where people caught in the indeterminacies of everyday life forged and broke friendships, created solidarities and expressed rivalries, and, on occasion, organized armed resistance to the inequities of the colonial system.

In chapter 9, Mark W. Hauser discusses the importance of independent production within the local economy. In his analysis of Jamaica's famous Linstead Market and the production and circulation of local coarse earthenware known as yabbas,

Hauser considers not only how markets formed and how goods were exchanged, purchased, traded, and consumed over wide distances but also the fields of social relations through which commodities like ceramic pots moved. In these fields of social relations there was room, to a certain extent, for the enslaved and freed peoples of African descent in Jamaica to fashion and refashion their identities as producers and consumers of locally produced goods.

One of the most fascinating examinations of the material manifestations of the internal differentiation that resulted from both the hierarchy of the plantation and the social movement arising from local economies has been conducted by Matthew Reeves at the Juan de Bolas and Thetford estates in the parish of St. Catherine. While Thetford and the results from excavations at its works represent the hierarchy associated with sugar estates, Juan de Bolas followed a different regime of labor associated with coffee estates.

In chapter 10, Reeves highlights how the different organizing principles of labor required by sugar and coffee production had significant impacts on the material wealth an enslaved laborer could garner. Indeed, while enslaved laborers did have access to goods through a series of markets, this access was dramatically shaped by the structures and impositions of the plantation system. As Reeves's work demonstrates, the establishment of markets and consumer activities did not precipitate social or economic equality among the enslaved.

The productive capacity of Jamaica's plantation economy often overshadows the commercial success of the local producers, consumers, and higglers that made the internal economy work. However, Jamaicans, both free and enslaved, were not only purchasing locally produced goods. They were caught in a much larger web of commodity flow that was oceanic in scale. Indeed, beginning in the eighteenth century we begin to see a phenomenon in the material record of enslaved communities. For the first time, imported goods began to dominate local economies; factory-produced goods are far more ubiquitous on archaeological sites than locally produced goods (Hauser 2008; Delle 2009). Mass-produced goods, including ceramics, quickly entered the colonial markets, eventually replacing locally produced yabbas. One could excavate a contemporaneous plantation in the Caribbean, tenement in Boston, and trading fort on the South African coast and in all likelihood most of the eighteenth-century materials would be similar if not identical.

This is in part due to the innovations in the industrial technologies of commodity production that occurred in Great Britain, which allowed for the cheap production of a truly astonishing volume of mass-produced goods. However, the change in consumer behavior also resulted from innovations in the distribution and marketing of these goods, as the eighteenth century witnessed the simultaneous disciplining of production and consumption (Mintz 1985) and the emergence of a consumer revolution. However, we must bear in mind that just because people were purchasing the same goods does not mean that they were consuming them in the same way. Indeed, it could be argued that many people caught up in this oceanic web of commerce might have been acquiring unfamiliar things but adapting them to their own symbolic understanding of the material world, and thus may well have been consuming them in traditional or familiar ways far different than the use intended by the factory supervisors.

This is especially the case for the enslaved in Jamaica. Where we see the greatest evidence of these transformative processes of material acquisition is in the markets and the purchasing of imported goods in reference to the "consumer revolution" of the eighteenth century. In chapter 11, Jillian E. Galle examines the acquisition of goods imported from Europe and the role they might have played in nonverbal communication and social networking among the enslaved. After all surveillance, both overt and implicitly understood, served to suppress communication among the enslaved. Galle considers that buttons, as a class of artifact, share a degree of functional and stylistic ubiquity in the life of the enslaved in both Jamaica and Virginia. More important, they are a potential reservoir for the display of ideas such as identity and solidarity. While the ability for the enslaved in Jamaica to purchase "nonessential" goods was markedly depressed in comparison to Virginian enslaved laborers, creating regional variation, Galle argues that this variation has less to do with expressions of antecedent cultural practices and more with the structuring of everyday life that predatory capitalism and emergent globalization had on the enslaved.

It is a historical irony that what enabled the independent production and acquisition of wealth among the enslaved was also a function of the oppression inherent in plantation societies. Planters were required by law to provide a plot of land for the enslaved to produce their own provisions. Indeed, while dependent on these grounds for their minimal livelihood, the enslaved were able to sell surplus to the plantation or in the local markets. The provision grounds through which the enslaved were required in their "free time" to grow the foodstuffs required to sustain themselves were also places set apart from the industrial core of the plantation and could be spaces of their own. While the enslaved did not own these plots of land, they did have legally established *ususfructus* and legally possessed the products of their labor. This relationship between land, labor, and capital produces one of the most interesting ironies of slave society. While the provision grounds provided potential agency and sometimes respite from the regimes of plantation life, they also bounded the enslaved to the plantation upon which they labored. As Trevor Burnard has noted in his discussion of Thomas Thistlewood's diaries (2004), the enslaved were sometimes hesitant to run away from the grounds through which they garnered a livelihood and material wealth.

These historical ironies came to a head in the Baptist War of 1831. As one of the last rebellions in the Anglophone Caribbean in which enslaved laborers participated, this struggle highlights one of the great ironies of slaveholding Jamaica.

Barry Higman (1998:227) has noted that the rebellion was led by slaves who had accumulated a degree of economic and symbolic capital. While the enslaved were dispossessed of property, the very success of the plantation economy depended on the enslaved amassing material wealth that ultimately put the planters at financial and political risk. Although deeply embedded within a stratified global economic system, enslaved laborers had their own hierarchies within their own communities. To a certain extent these statuses were derived from the exigencies of birth and familiarity of the social relations of the island. Patrick Bryan notes that there was perceived difference between creole and African-born enslaved laborers (2000:17; see also Delle 2000a, 2009). There were also distinctions based on occupation, skill, and in some cases the personal charisma of the laborers themselves. Some laborers worked in the fields for most of their lives; others worked as domestic servants, artisans, or cooks (Delle 2008, 2009). As Doug Armstrong and Mark Fleischman have noted in their analysis of human burials from Seville Estate (1993, 2003), special treatment was given to some laborers thought to have special access to the supernatural. Finally, these internal hierarchies were also in part the result of the organization of labor on the plantation itself.

The End of Slavery

Jamaica's slave-based plantation system was legislated out of existence by the British Parliament. In 1807, the first blow to the system came with the legal abolition of the Atlantic slave trade. A generation later, in 1833, Parliament passed the Abolition Act, which called for the (near) immediate abolition of slavery in the British Empire. The plan enacted called for a period of partial freedom, known as the apprenticeship system, under which able-bodied men and women were required to work for their previous masters weekly for thirty-five hours; any time worked beyond that was not required and needed to be compensated with wages. Initially enacted to last for eight years, the apprenticeship system was abolished in Jamaica in 1838, establishing full emancipation for the population of Jamaica. With the inception of apprenticeship in 1834 and emancipation in 1838, a new economic order arrived on the shores of Jamaica. This order, also founded on ideological contradictions and implicit inequality, was different in one crucial way. It recognized, in legal ways, the principles of liberty espoused by French philosophers such as Rousseau and bought into ideas of a free market of labor as promoted by Adam Smith. Indeed, the foundations of nineteenth-century emancipation in the Americas were poured in the liberal rationalism of eighteenth-century Europe and Britain. While the altruistic and humanitarian impulses of abolitionists such as John Wesley in England cannot be underestimated, emancipation was also achieved through the cold calculation by some that the slave system on which the sugar industry was based was no longer economically sustainable (Williams [1944] 1994).

Of course emancipation was only the final blow to the slave society upon which planters depended. Jamaica was rocked by sometimes violent resistance to slavery, including insurrections like Tacky's War in 1760 and the Maroon wars that were fought throughout the eighteenth century. The island's largest slave insurrection, known alternatively as the Christmas Rebellion, the Emancipation War, or the Baptist War, in which tens of thousands of enslaved workers rose up in 1831 to destroy plantation buildings and kill white planter families, has been credited as the catalyst that drove Parliament to abolish colonial slavery (Beckles 1982; Blackburn 1988; Holt 1992). Other forms of more subtle resistance to the brutalizations of slavery were experienced throughout the West Indies (Fergus 2006), including an influx of Moravian, Methodist, and Baptist missionaries in the early nineteenth century who sought to bring the gospel, as well as literacy, to the enslaved (Delle 2001; Turner 1998). The cessation of the legal slave trade, as well as growing resistance to the slave system in Jamaica and Great Britain, created social, economic, and legal setbacks to the planters' interests. Each event stimulated change in the organization and implementation of slave laws. Legislatively, the planters were successful in linking the island colony's well being to their own so that when emancipation did finally arrive in 1838 several measures were put in place to ameliorate the "hardship" experienced by the planter class. The apprenticeship system was created to help planters prepare for a post-slavery labor force and to "educate" the enslaved in the logic of wage labor. Parliament provided twenty million pounds to compensate the planters for the capital loss of chattel slaves upon emancipation. Finally, there was a facilitation, through the mechanism of imperial infrastructure, of the mass migration of new indentured labor from various points in Africa and especially South Asia to compensate for the anticipated, and actualized, labor shortages brought on by the newly emancipated workers' abandonment of plantation labor. In the 1840s and 1850s tens of thousands of contract laborers were brought to Jamaica from West Africa and the Indian subcontinent to work on the island's plantations.

Scholars have often identified the rural labor force of Jamaica as a peasantry fully realized in the social framework of colonial Jamaica through emancipation (Mintz 1978, 1985; Marshall 2003). Indeed, there were forces at work that attempted to consolidate the rural folk of Jamaica into an undifferentiated labor force. The religious bodies of Jamaica, including the Moravian, Baptist, and Methodist missions, established villages on land adjacent to plantations. Through this system of mission villages the religious bodies acted as agents for the labor force in order to collectively bargain for wages. In theory, this was supposed to provide ameliorative measures for the formerly enslaved workers. It ultimately failed as a strategy and acted to depress wages (see Delle 2001; Turner 1998). Despite the collaboration of the missionaries, Jamaican planters suffered from chronic labor shortages in the years following emancipation.

One solution to the labor shortage was the introduction of contract labor. The use of South Asian (and, to a lesser degree, West African) indentured contract labor on Jamaican plantations was part of a larger strategy first described by Woodville Marshall as the "Push and Pull Hypothesis" (2003). Essentially, the use of cheaper contract labor was used to undermine the Afro-Jamaican bargaining position and allowed planters to successfully depress wages. Whether through the reduction in Afro-Jamaican wages or through the cheaper use of contract laborers (disparaged in Jamaica as "coolies"), the plantation system was able to persevere for several decades with dependent laborers, either the newly imported "coolies" or the formerly enslaved agricultural laborers, who had few places to turn for employment. While it might be tempting to consider the newly arriving contract laborers as "scabs" or collaborators with the planter class, Verene Shepherd has pointed out that the stories that brought them to Jamaica are themselves wrought with multiple acts of violence and were embedded in systems of colonial inequality (1993, 1995).

These new migrants contributed to the cultural and material development of the social landscape of nineteenth- and twentieth-century Jamaica. In chapter 12, Kenneth G. Kelly, Mark W. Hauser, and Douglas V. Armstrong explore these contributions in their analysis of an East Indian house at the Seville Estate. When slavery ended in 1838, planters and plantation managers across Jamaica were faced with a major challenge: how to keep labor present on the plantation so that sugar could continue to be profitably produced. The managers of Seville, like many other Jamaican planters, brought in East Indian contract laborers to supplement the available pool of workers near the estate. The East Indians established a residence near the earlier abandoned village at Seville and thus were socially and spatially segregated from the Afro-Jamaican creole population working the estate. As Shepherd (1995) has pointed out, in many ways the relationship between East Indians and creole Jamaicans is one in which the intersection between race and class is apparent between members of the laboring population; these social processes were not acted out only between labor and capital. As such the variation we see in the assemblage from the East Indian house, when compared to the assemblages from the Afro-Jamaican houses, must be considered in light of management strategies, consumer choice, and the inscription of distinctive cultural patterns that embody identities within the laboring class. This research also enables us to reconsider Seville not only as a plantation labor site or an early Spanish settlement. Rather we can think of it as a shared landscape in which the tensions arising out of nineteenth-century labor politics, processes of othering, and the naissance of the concept of national identity are transcribed onto plantation landscapes.

Plantations, whether run with enslaved or contract labor, required a host of ancillary economic industries. Indeed the work of Verene Shepherd, Barry Higman, and others has highlighted the fact that while the planting class successfully defined the fate of the island through the success of the colonial sugar industry, the island's economic base was far more diverse than would appear at first blush. Although the average sugar estate contained more than 1,000 acres (Higman 1988), the majority of property holders owned less than 500 acres; rather than produce tons of sugar to export into the metropolitan economy, a class of small planters cultivated provisions to meet local and regional demand for foodstuffs and other agricultural commodities.

Though it was theoretically possible for a plantation to have its equity fully accessible, its proprietor to be free of bad debts, and to be a self-contained and fully self-sufficient enterprise, such was rarely the case. The more common reality for eighteenth-century planters was characterized by constant debt, purchasing necessary supplies on margin or on the presumed value of commodity futures, juggled books, and transactions anticipating some of the most complex and creative accounting practices to emerge in the twentieth century. Plantation-era Jamaica was a place where talented (or ruthless) young men could create wealth and opportunity far outreaching the limited prospects available in England. The opportunities of Jamaica were personified by Thomas Thistlewood, a famous Jamaican diarist and infamous slave master. Thistlewood was one of many British-born men of modest means who came to Jamaica in search of a fortune (Burnard 2004). While it would be virtually impossible for a poor immigrant to rise to the level of sugar planter, the colonial economy required a host of ancillary economic activities including raising beef and other livestock on cattle pens (Shepherd 1986), iron smelting, and legal work; the local economy required bankers, merchants, blacksmiths, and sailors. Men like Thistlewood were able to rise to higher social positions by taking advantage of the opportunities provided by these ancillary industries.

Throughout the eighteenth and early nineteenth centuries, the production and sale of colonial agricultural commodities was protected by government regulation, an economic formulation sometimes called "mercantilism"; laws like the Free Port Act of 1766 were necessary to allow for the movement of goods in a highly regulated economy. In 1846, British mercantilism was dealt a deathblow when the Sugar Duties Act was passed in London. The new law ushered in a more liberal free trade system, ending a series of market preferences for British West Indian sugar and allowed the entry of non-British sugar into the market. The sugar industry experienced significant decline, as the Jamaican planters could not compete with other sugar-producing cartels (Delle 1996, 1998). The new legislation also further exacerbated inequalities in Jamaica. The planters, facing increasing economic difficulty, began to assess higher rents on houses and the provision grounds still used by the emancipated workers. As it became increasingly difficult to maintain livelihoods through estate employment tensions rose, eventually leading to a violent confrontation between Afro-Jamaican workers and the white political establishment. On October 11, 1865, Paul Bogle, a deacon from the small hamlet of Stony Gut, near the town of Morant Bay, led a group of protesters advocating for a man arrested for trespassing on an estate (Bryan 2000; Delle 1998). The demonstration quickly turned violent; public buildings, including the parish courthouse, were destroyed, and several local politicians were killed by the protesters. This event has been long cited as a turning point in British rule over Jamaica. In the aftermath of the Morant Bay Rebellion, home rule was abolished and Jamaica became a crown colony. While the crown curtailed local political power, the event can also be interpreted as one of the first steps taken by the Jamaican people to assert and establish their right of independence from colonial rule.

Conclusion

Patrick Bryan has stated that the history of Jamaica is on the one hand universal and on the other unique (2000:92). In many ways the story of Jamaica is an all-too-familiar tale of a post-colonial nation struggling to move beyond the intellectual and economic bonds that tied it down with dependent relationships to its colonial masters. It is also a country that has produced social movements like Rastafarianism, art forms like reggae, and intellectuals who have inspired both redemptive and radical politics worldwide.

In many ways it is difficult to disentangle Jamaica's history from the history and repercussions of African slavery. However, the history of colonial Jamaica neither begins nor ends with plantation slavery. This volume explores a variety of archaeological sites and addresses a number of topical issues relevant to the archaeological history of colonial Jamaica. Part 1 of the volume is dedicated to the early colonial period. The chapters in this section examine the early Spanish period at Sevilla la Nueva and the development of the first major British settlement at Port Royal. Part 2 addresses the complexities of the plantation system, examining its development and its ancillary economy in the eighteenth and nineteenth centuries, as well as the development of Maroon communities as sovereign entities in the interior. Part 3 focuses on the development of Jamaican society, examining the everyday life of Jamaican people and addressing the development of the island's internal marketing system, consumer behavior among enslaved people, ceramic-making traditions among African people in Jamaica, and the lives of South Asian immigrants brought to work the plantations after the end of slavery. Together the chapters in this volume paint a complex and fascinating picture of life in colonial Jamaica and demonstrate the power and importance of archaeology on the island.

The contributions to this volume, taken both individually and collectively, represent a sample of the scope of historical archaeology conducted in Jamaica. While the past three decades have produced a wide variety of projects that have tackled a number of thematic issues and temporal moments, much still needs to be done. Most of the historical archaeology conducted on Jamaica has focused on the period preceding 1850. The late nineteenth and twentieth centuries witnessed a number of events crucial to the cultural and historical development of Jamaica, many of which could be examined archaeologically. For example, the United Fruit Company created a virtual world monopoly in the banana trade; their worldwide dominance in bananas began in Jamaica, yet little work has been done on the archaeology of banana production. In the twentieth century, rapid urbanization and the development of large-scale industrial production of bauxite (a raw material used in aluminum production) shifted the nature of Jamaican settlement and culture. The late nineteenth and twentieth centuries witnessed the development of broad social movements, including trade unions, political parties, and a number of revitalization movements, some religious, like Myalism, others overtly political, like Rastafarianism. Many of these movements sought to end the lingering effects of slavery and colonialism. Although the colonial era ended when Jamaica achieved independence from Britain in 1962, the struggles against the legacies of colonialism continue. While many of these historical phenomena may be difficult to study archaeologically, some may prove to be very fertile ground for the further practice and development of historical archaeology in Jamaica. Despite more than three decades of work on the small island nation, the archaeological heritage of Jamaica still has much that needs to be explored.

I

THE ARCHAEOLOGY OF THE EARLY COLONIAL PERIOD

2

Feudalism or Agrarian Capitalism?

The Archaeology of the Early Sixteenth-Century Spanish Sugar Industry

Robyn P. Woodward

Introduction

The history of European settlement in the Caribbean is intrinsically linked to the history of tropical agricultural products. Europeans have harvested coffee, cacao, tobacco, ginger, and spices over the past five hundred years, but none of these crops was ever as important as sugar (Mintz 1985:46). To date, historical and archaeological research has focused only on the late seventeenth- to nineteenth-century French, British, Dutch, and Portuguese sugar plantations and their associated slave villages in the Caribbean and Brazil; attempts by the Spanish to establish sugar estates in the sixteenth century have been largely ignored (Wolf and Mintz 1957; Dunn 1972; Fraginals 1976; Keith 1977; Galloway 1980, 1985; Schwartz 1985; Ramirez 1986; Armstrong 1990:76; Pulsipher 1991; Pulsipher and Goodwin 2001; Delle 1994; Goodwin and Sanders 1998; LeRoux 1998; Kelly 2004).

Within the broader framework of sugar production and its history on a global scale, my study focuses on the archaeology, analysis, and interpretive reconstruction of the early sixteenth-century sugar mill and industrial quarter in the town of Sevilla la Nueva, the first Spanish capital of Jamaica.

Archaeological excavations and historical research demonstrate that the sixteenth-century mill at Sevilla la Nueva was a water-powered mill set within the urban confines of an early colonial administrative and trading center (Woodward 2006a). Analysis of the unique assemblage of material culture from this feature reflects the industrial nature of the site but also provides insight into the cultural and social identities of those who worked there.

These industrial features provide a material framework from which it is possible to make wider inferences about the labor strategies and models of production that the Spanish employed in their early attempts at capitalism. Using both historical and archaeological data, I suggest that during the early decades of the sixteenth century, the Caribbean sugar industry was not uniformly prefigured as large-scale plantation production based entirely on slave labor (Deerr 1949, 1:119; Wallerstein 1974:43, 88–90; Mintz 1977:255, 1985:53, 82–83; Blackburn 1997:137–38; Moya Pons 1999:68–70).

My research also assessed the mill within the context of both the landscape in which it is situated and the Atlantic network, of which it was an integral part. When one considers the diverse social, economic, and governmental structures framing almost every aspect of early Spanish colonial experience, it is obvious the mercantile interests were always a prime concern. From a theoretical perspective, I interpreted this mill and the archaeology of the early sixteenth-century sugar industry within the paradigm of Wallerstein's (1974) world system, focusing in particular on the transition between feudalism and capitalism. Wallerstein's world-system approach was based in part on Marx's claim that "capital derived from commercial exploitation of colonial possessions was both the prime solvent of European feudalism and the sources of its capitalist successor" (Duplessis 1997:10–11). In particular, he believed that the emergence of the capitalist system was based on three fundamental developments: the territorial expansion of Europe beyond its shores; the development of variegated methods of labor control for different products and different zones of the world economy; and the creation of relatively strong state bureaucracies in the metropolitan centers or core states of the world economy (Wallerstein 1974:15; Stern 1988:829). His geographically based concepts of core, semi-periphery, and periphery are particularly pertinent to our understanding of the early development of the Spanish colonial empire wherein the mercantile wealth concentrated in Seville funded the voyages of exploration and invested in the development of colonial ventures that opened up new markets of exchange. This involved the production and export of agricultural commodities such as sugar and the purchase of cheap goods from the periphery zones (the Atlantic islands and the New World territories) to sell to the developed markets in Europe (core states) at a profit (Woodward 2006a:257).

Historical Context of Sugar Production in the Mediterranean

From sugar's introduction into the Mediterranean in the eighth century, and certainly with the development of larger feudal manorial estates in the Crusader states of the twelfth century, the production of sugar was an industrial process. The investigation of the archaeological remnants of the early sixteenth-century Caribbean sugar industry must consider how these Mediterranean antecedents structured the industry's physical remains as well as its social and economic organization.

During the nine hundred years in which sugar was produced around the Mediterranean, the techniques used to cultivate and mill cane to produce sugar remained remarkably similar despite the vast differences between the cultures and societies engaged in the industry. However, there were pronounced differences in the social and economic institutions that were developed to support and expand the industry during this period, in particular in the organization of resources, labor, and landholdings (Galloway 1977:182; Woodward 2006a:31). Table 2.1 demonstrates how each phase of the productive process in Europe during the late medieval period utilized varying modes of labor including independent farmers, tenant peasantry, sharecroppers, and temporary wage labor. Slavery was never a substantial part of the Mediterranean rural economy during the late medieval period. Slaves served primarily as domestic servants or worked as artisans in handicraft production and therefore were a fixture of the urban societies of the region (Silva 1996:79). Further, Table 2.1 demonstrates that while elements of a plantation model such as rural estates with their own mills and the use of slaves as mill labor had appeared at various times during the three hundred years preceding the European colonization of the New World, the first true example of plantation production, with slaves being used for both agricultural and mill labor, occurred on the island of São Tomé off the west coast of Africa, where sugar production started less than a decade before the industry began in the Caribbean.

Colonial expansion into the Atlantic began in the fifteenth century and was carried out by Portugal and Castile. Given that the Portuguese island of Madeira was uninhabited and the Canary Islands that belonged to Castile were sparsely inhabited, the Iberian kingdoms colonized the Atlantic islands with settlers of mixed social classes, most of whom grew varying quantities of sugar in their kitchen gardens along with other crops.

Therefore, during the fifteenth century European sugar production maintained its democratic nature as long as the independent or tenant farmers continued to grow sugar cane that was later processed by others (Wallerstein 1974:105). As long as labor was plentiful, sharecropping was preferred to coerced or slave labor, as it was more profitable for the mill owner. Areas that adopted slavery for sugar production did so only when local labor sources proved insufficient (Cyprus) or nonexistent (São Tomé).

In the sixteenth century, however, African slaves were incorporated into the labor force on the Atlantic islands but were used only in the milling operations, as estate owners continued to hire free labor to plant and cut cane (Fernández-Armesto 1982:82). The manner of colonization and structure of the sugar industry on Madeira and the Canary Islands in the fifteenth and sixteenth centuries provided the immediate prototype for early sugar producers in the Spanish Antilles. This model was the structured alternative to plantation production based solely on slave labor (Fernández-Armesto 1982, 1987; Schwartz 1985).

Table 2.1 Summary of Labor and Production Modes in the Medieval Mediterranean and Atlantic Islands Sugar Industries

	Levant Islamic	Levant-Christian	Cyprus	Sicily, Spain, Islamic	Sicily, Medit., Spain, Christian	Andalusia 14–15th Century	Andalusia 16th Century	Madeira 15th Century	Madeira 16th Century	Canary Islands Late 15th–16th Century	Morocco	São Tomé
Model of Labor on Agricultural Estates												
Independent farmers	X			X		X		X	X	X		
Tenants on large estates	X	X	X	X	X	X	X		X	X		
Wage laborers							X	X	X	X		
Sharecropping	X							X	X	X		
Corvée			X				X					
Slavery			X						X*	X*	X	X
Milling Arrangements (if known)												
Rural mills	X	X	X	X	X	X	X	X	X	X		X
Urban/ Village mills	X		X	X	X	X	X	X	X	X		
Model of Colonization												
Aristocratic		X	X		X		X	X				X
Democratic	X			X		X		X	X	X		

Note: *Denotes limited use of slaves in mill operations only.

The History of Spanish Sugar Production in the Caribbean

Columbus introduced sugar to the Caribbean in 1494; however, it did not become a major industry until the gold fields on Hispaniola started to decline. The Spanish Crown promoted the establishment of sugar and ranching estates as a means of extracting continued revenue from the region and retaining colonists on the island (Ratekin 1954; Galloway 1980). Documents suggest the authorities in Spain envisioned a sugar industry based on the same economic model that had proved so successful in Madeira and the Canary Islands, which featured mixed labor strategies and a separation between the agricultural and processing operations (I. Wright 1919:414). However, social and economic pressures in the Spanish Antilles differed from those in the Atlantic islands.

In the Caribbean the seemingly limitless amounts of land available for sugar production altered the Mediterranean and Atlantic pattern of agriculture based on small independent holdings or tenancies that could be worked by family members (Galloway 1985:338). By the middle of the sixteenth century successful sugar estates in the Caribbean were two hundred acres in size and included a mixture of kitchen gardens, livestock, cane fields, and their own mills (Ratekin 1954:14). In order to take advantage of the larger, well-watered land on the islands, planters needed more labor. However, in the Spanish Antilles after the collapse of the indigenous population they faced stiff competition for the increasingly scarce number of Indian workers initially from the mining industry and later from the production of other market-oriented crops such as ginger.

The development of sugar estates or even mill operations was not a short-term proposition; both required time and capital before they could return a profit from one's investment. It was estimated that in order to import mill equipment, ceramic sugar molds, skilled sugar technicians, and, after the Indian population declined, slaves from Africa, colonists needed to invest a minimum of 10,000 to 15,000 gold ducats (Ratekin 1954:8). Labor and shipping costs in the Antilles were considerably higher than those on the Atlantic islands. Therefore, the development of the sugar industry in the Caribbean could not have taken place without the capital generated from the initial mining activities and, more important, the financial support of the Genoese banking community and the Spanish Crown (Ratekin 1954; Pike 1966). Members of the established colonial elite had access to capital in the form of state-supported loans for the construction of mills and the purchase of African slaves to replace Indian workers. Thus the democratic nature of the sugar industry on the Atlantic islands, which allowed all members of society to participate in some manner, failed to develop in the Spanish Antilles. By the mid-sixteenth century sugar cane was instrumental in creating a slave-owning aristocracy who had the power to influence local, regional, and colonial policy (Ratekin 1954; Galloway 1980).

Despite being over-regulated and suffering from a chronic shortage of capital, skilled sugar technicians, slave labor, and cargo vessels to transport the finished product to European markets, the Spanish sugar industry in the Caribbean expanded steadily until 1570 (Chaunu and Chaunu 1957:104). After this date, sugar production declined rapidly due, in part, to competition from less labor-intensive activities such as ranching and ginger production on the islands and mining in Central and South America (I. Wright 1915, 1916, 1919; Ratekin 1954; Pike 1966; Andrews 1978). Further, in the final decades of the sixteenth century, Spanish authorities did little to protect their own domestic market from cheaper sugars being produced in Brazil (I. Wright 1916:757; Moya Pons 1999:73, 76). It was the authorities in Santo Domingo, however, that dealt the final blow to their own sugar and cattle industries on Hispaniola in 1605–6, for in an effort to curb the rampant contraband trade, they forced the abandonment of towns, ranches, and plantations on the north and western coasts of the island, including the major sugar ports (Galloway 1980:68).

Spanish Jamaica

Lacking alluvial gold deposits, Jamaica was not settled until 1509 when Juan de Esquivel, the first governor, arrived with eighty colonists. The Spanish built their capital of Sevilla la Nueva on the north coast of the island and focused on establishing agricultural and ranching properties in the area to produce supplies for local and regional markets (see Figure 2.1). In 1513 Esquivel reported that the land had been planted with both corn and sugar cane (Padrón 2003:54). The first sugar mill on the island, however, was built by Francesco de Garay, the second governor, who arrived on Jamaica in 1515. To accurately interpret the archaeology of Garay's mill, one must first understand the character of this dynamic individual.

Garay was a successful entrepreneur and capitalist. He initially came to the Caribbean in 1494 as a member of Christopher Columbus's second expedition to the region and quickly struck it rich in the gold fields of Hispaniola (Floyd 1973:137; Weddle 1985:97). Garay established a number of business ventures on Hispaniola, engaged in Indian slave trading in the Bahamas, and led an unsuccessful attempt to capture the island of Guadeloupe from the Carib Indians. Before returning to Spain in 1513, he also held senior government positions in Santo Domingo and built a substantial stone house in that city (Weddle 1985:97). In late 1514 Garay was appointed as the second governor of Jamaica by King Ferdinand, but before retuning to the Indies to take up this position he entered into a five-year agreement with his royal patron with regard to the economic development of the island (I. Wright 1921:73). Records show that he purchased two lateen-rigged caravels to transport new colonists, livestock, and African slaves to the island in 1515 (Pike 1966:56; Weddle 1985:98). Always in search of a new business opportunity, he negotiated and obtained a license in 1517 for the settlement of Panuco, a yet unexplored region of the Yucatan (Padrón 2003:60). In 1519 Garay not only renewed his agreement with the king for their business ventures on Jamaica, he dispatched a deputy on the first of two reconnaissance voyages along the coast of Panuco. Restless by nature, and hearing about Cortez's success in Mexico in an area that he knew to be part of his license, Garay left Jamaica in 1523 to uphold his claim on the mainland but died in Mexico City in 1524 (Padrón 2003:60).

Despite Garay's apparent lack of commitment to the island, Jamaica was very prosperous under his administration. One of his first official acts after arriving in Jamaica was to undertake an accurate census of the island's Indian population to determine the number of native laborers available for distribution to the colonists under the Spanish system of *encomienda*. Although this report has not survived, it is understood that in his capacity as *repartidor*, he redistributed a number of Taino laborers to other officials as well as to the new royal *estancias* (farms), in which he was a partner (Padrón 2003:150). These farms are listed by name but not by location in later court documents, as are the names of the *estancieros* (farmers) who worked as overseers on these properties in what is believed to have been some form of tenancy arrangement (Wynter 1983:116). During his tenure Garay also established two more towns on the island, Oristán on the south coast and Melilla, twelve to fourteen leagues east of Sevilla la Nueva. Finally, he provided his two ships to convey locally produced goods and agricultural supplies to regional markets, organized the island's textile industry, and was in the process of building a second sugar mill prior to his departure to the Yucatan (Weddle 1985; I. Wright 1921).

Medieval Sugar-Milling Technology and the Mill at Sevilla la Nueva

Spanish documents from the early sixteenth century refer to two types of mills used in the production of sugar in the New World. A *trapiche* or edge-runner mill was the earliest and most basic device used. It consisted of a wheel-shaped grinding stone set upright on a round stone or plaster-lined brick basin with a low lip to prevent juice from running out. Animal or human power would have been used to turn the grinding stone. The second type of mill was the larger, more efficient *ingenio* or water-powered mill that required both the channeling of water and the construction of a sunken under-house or wheel pit to accommodate a waterwheel.

In 1701 Sir Hans Sloane, a noted physician and collector of natural history who at the time was in the employ of the English governor of Jamaica, described the remains of Garay's mill in the following manner: "There was formerly here one great Sugarwork at a pretty distance, the Mill whereof went by Water, which was brought from Miles thither. The Axeltree of this is to be seen intire at this day. This Town is now Captain Hemming's Plantation" (1707–25:lxvi).

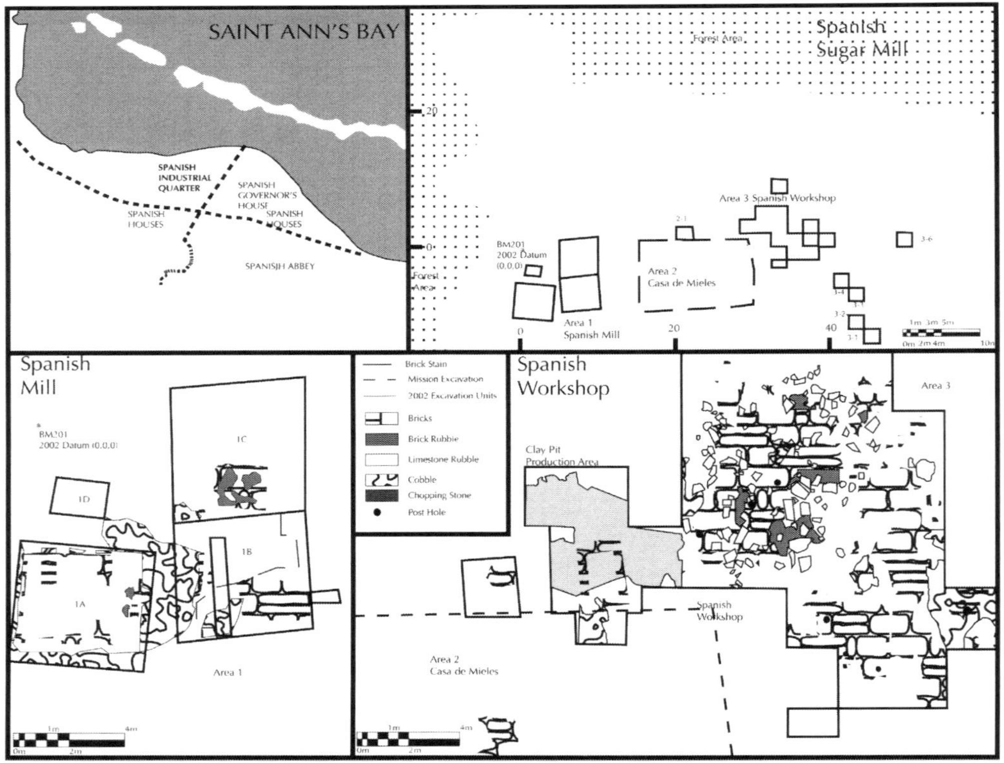

Figure 2.1. Spanish-period Sevilla la Nueva. *Clockwise from upper left:* location of known Spanish-period features at Sevilla la Nueva; overall site map of the 2002 excavation of the Spanish sugar mill site, depicting the four areas of the industrial quarter; plan view of the workshop area; plan view of the sugar mill showing Units 1-A, 1-B, 1-C, and 1-D. Artwork by Mark W. Hauser, based on illustrations by Robyn Woodward.

Despite this description and the fact that Garay's will stated he built an *ingenio,* the previous two investigators of Sevilla la Nueva interpreted the subterranean brick-lined feature found in the northwest quarter of the site in 1968 as a *trapiche* (Cotter 1970; López y Sebastián 1986). After reviewing both contemporary illustrations and detailed descriptions of architectural features found at archaeological excavations of medieval sugar production facilities in Cyprus and Spain and various water-powered mills in Britain, I believe the archaeological evidence recovered in 2002 reflects Sloane's descriptions of the Spanish mill on Hemming's Seville Estate as being a water-powered mill and not a *trapiche* (Woodward 2006a:215).

As the subterranean plaster- and brick-lined feature in Unit 1-A is divided into four parts by three semicircular brick arches, I concluded that this was a wheel pit of a Vitruvian or vertical-wheeled water mill rather than the horizontal wheeled mill, which would have had an unobstructed wheel chamber or under-house (Figure 2.2). The light buff-colored alluvial sand and gravel present in Unit 1-D differed significantly from the darker brown sandy clay matrix that covered all the other features of the industrial quarter and demonstrates that a water course, either natural or constructed, flowed north through the wheel pit before emptying into St. Ann's Bay. As a result of previous excavations, all evidence of artificial channeling or mill-races had been destroyed, thereby making it difficult to determine whether this was an overshot or breast-shot water mill.

The three large arches in the center of the wheel pit are semicircular in shape and do not have an abutment or plinth at their base. In the bottom of the wheel pit, the distance between the *intrados* (interior of the curve of the arch) is 3.01 meters and 3.47 meters from the *extrados* (exterior curve of the arch). Rather than using gauged arch construction for the three large arches, the mason achieved the desired curvature by inserting wider wedges of mortar between the bricks on the *extrados* and almost no mortar on the *intrados.* The estimated height of the arches at the top of the keystone would have been half the diameter of the arch, or approximately 1.7 meters. Two narrow wheels would have been mounted in parallel fashion on a single wheel shaft and sandwiched between the three arches, which would have acted as wheel emplacements. The action of these wheels would have created considerable torque on the main wheel shaft, which could be negated by running the axle through support or shaft bearings mounted on the top of each arch. The top of the arches and all evidence of these bearings have been lost.

The only surviving brick facing walls in the wheel pit are found in the forty-centimeter spaces on either side of the center arch. These bricks were set in a regular course pattern and were covered with lime plaster. Lime plaster was a common waterproof sealant for wheel pits or water channels on sixteenth-century Spanish sugar estates in the Canary Islands (Fernández-Armesto 1982:98). The missing west wall of the wheel pit and central sections of the arches were probably part of the rubble described as "collapsed walls" in the 1968 field notes of Charles Cotter,

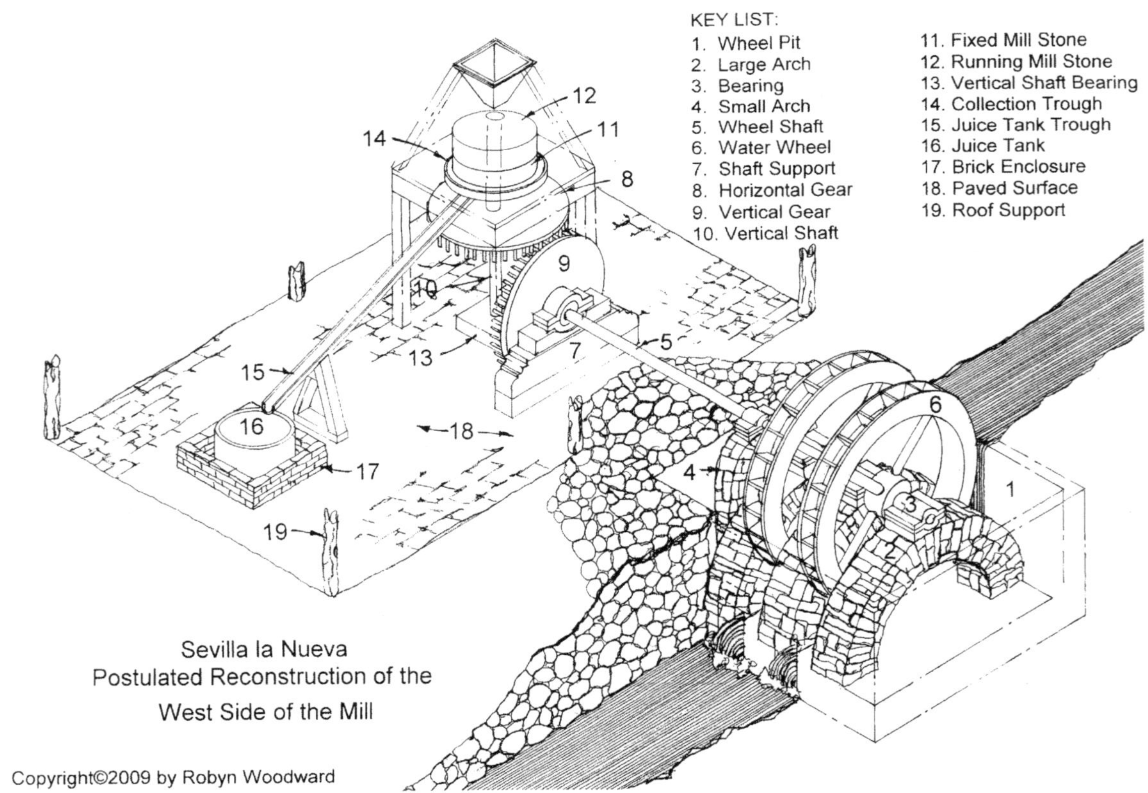

Figure 2.2. Postulated reconstruction of sugar mill at Sevilla la Nueva.

the avocational archaeologist who originally found and excavated this feature (Cotter n.d.:116).

The east wall of the wheel pit forms the west wall of the actual mill. This was a substantial drystone wall constructed of coarse rubble with larger stones at the bottom and smaller ones on the top. Large sections of lime plaster still adhered to the face of this wall. The extant wall was 1.2 meters in height but presumably stood higher as some of the larger cobbles had been dragged across the brick pavement in the adjoining pavement in Unit 1-B. In the center of this drystone wall is a small arch that is in line with the center of the three larger arches in the wheel pit. It, too, must have acted as a mount for an axle/shaft support bearing at the point the axle passed into the mill.

The dry-set brick pavement immediately east of the wheel pit (Unit 1-B) would be the *Casa de Prensas* or mill house where the millstones and offset gears for turning the millstones would have been located. A line of bricks, set on end, face the interior of the two-meter-thick drystone cobble wall that separates the wheel pit from the mill house. This may be the interior wall facing of the mill building. The mill house would typically have been a covered structure. The outer edges of this brick pavement together with the wall footings, postholes for vertical wall supports, and corner posts to support the roof of this structure, if they existed, have disappeared due to post-occupation disturbances.

The roughly square (1.80 m × 1.85 m) feature north of the mill house floor in Unit 1-C was identified as the juice tank. This structure had a brick floor and brick walls on all four sides, with a gap of 60 centimeters on the northeast corner. The extant south wall was six to eight bricks in height and the floor level of this feature was 65 centimeters below the level of the mill house floor. An ax and a stone block with cut marks were found by the juice tank, suggesting that sugar cane was chopped near this feature.

There were only a few fragments of roof tile found at the mill; these may have been used to channel cane juice rather than serving as a structural element. Further, none of the mill buildings at Sevilla la Nueva had wall footings or perimeter post molds, indicating at best they were open thatched sheds—temporary in nature—as compared to the permanent cut-stone or brick structures found in the Mediterranean or even at the contemporary Villoria mill on the neighboring island of Hispaniola (Mañón 1978).

Sugar production at Sevilla la Nueva in the early sixteenth century would have been a two-part process consisting of first milling and then pressing sugar cane in a beam press prior to the boiling and crystallization of the juice. This was typical of sugar production from the ninth to the beginning of the seventeenth century (Galloway 1980). The location of the beam press and boiling house for the mill complex are as yet unknown.

The technology for mills, prior to the introduction of cast iron machinery in the nineteenth century, was timber based. The Spanish had access to a wide variety of local hardwoods that were infinitely suitable for the construction of waterwheels, axles/driveshafts, and gears. The presence of the ruined Spanish mill and a wooden "axle tree" were noted by Sir Hans Sloane when he visited the Seville Estate in the 1690s (1707–25:lxvi). The reconstructed plan of the mill at Sevilla la Nueva demonstrates that Garay built an *ingenio,* which was the standard technology of medieval sugar production. In anticipation of the volume of sugar that could be grown in the immediate environs of the town, Garay chose to build a larger, more efficient mill capable of producing 12,000 *arrobas* of sugar or 150 tons versus a smaller and less efficient *trapiche.* Not knowing if the lands he had claim to in Mexico would provide better business opportunities than his estates in Jamaica, he did not immediately invest in the construction of a permanent facility with stone walls and tiled roofs; instead, he chose to build a rather temporary production facility of thatched sheds. Thus, if the sugar industry surrounding Sevilla la Nueva had not proved viable, Garay could have easily moved the majority of his mill equipment to a new location.

Industrial Quarter

Previous excavations had uncovered large quantities of broken cone-shaped sugar molds and a section of brick pavement in the center of the site (Area 2; see Figure 2.1). This feature has been interpreted as the location of the *Casa de Mieles* and/or the *Casa de Purgar* or purging house, where the boiled cane juice would have been poured into molds to crystallize. Excavations of a twelfth-century sugar mill in Jordan and eighteenth-century estate inventories from Barbados demonstrate that if the molds were set into the top of flat-bottomed syrup jars, these jars would have been present in roughly the same proportions as the conical molds (Brooks 1983:12; LaGro and Haas 1992). The absence of these corresponding flat-bottomed ceramic syrup jars at Sevilla la Nueva suggests the cone molds were set into wooden racks, thus saving the expense of importing additional industrial ceramics from Spain. In the absence of syrup pots, the sugar technicians could have reused other forms of earthenware shipping containers such as olive jars or made wooden casks to collect and store molasses. Cotter did find large quantities of Early Style olive jars in the vicinity (Woodward 1988, 2006a; Cotter n.d.).

During the course of our excavations in 2002 and 2004 two additional workshops were discovered north and east of the sugar mill complex. The first of these was a mason's or sculptor's workshop. Eventually covering more than twenty-five 2-m^2 units, the brick floor of this feature was covered with chips of limestone, deposits of limestone stucco, and fragments of bas-relief decoration, architectural moldings, and three-dimensional sculptures. The material was destined for an abbey that was under construction at the time the settlement was abandoned (Woodward 2006a:200–206).

A second feature, located just north of Area 2 was identified as a brick maker's workshop as it consisted of a square, brick-walled clay pit surrounded by massive amounts of jumbled adobe bricks. The large quantities of lime plaster found at the mill and Governor's Fort suggest there must have also been a limekiln in the industrial quarter.

As there were no mining activities on the island, archival sources suggest that the Spanish employed the Taino Indians in the cultivation of cotton and the production of textiles for the regional market. The discovery of a single spindle whorl south of the mason's workshop suggests that textile production might also have taken place nearby.

More significant, however, to date no evidence of domestic dwellings, domestic activities, or middens of faunal material have been found in the vicinity of the mill and workshops. In 2004, evidence of two Spanish houses was found several hundred meters south and east of the industrial quarter.

Material Culture from the Mill and the Industrial Quarter

The archaeological investigation of the industrial quarter at Sevilla la Nueva provides an opportunity to enhance our understanding of the early colonial experience by examining the material life and industrial practices of sugar technicians, artisans, and their Indian workers. The majority of the material culture (67.3 percent) found in association with the features in the industrial quarter are the by-products of the activities carried on there: sugar production, brick making, production of limestone building blocks, and architectural decoration (see Table 2.2).

Sixty-eight percent of the ceramics from the industrial quarter were cone-shaped sugar molds, an unglazed industrial ceramic used specifically in the production of sugar (Woodward 1988:94–99, 2006a:155–62). All the sugar molds at Sevilla la Nueva were thick-walled, wheel-thrown, hard-fired vessels imported from Europe. While they appear to be of similar size, the variations in both rim treatment and the manner in which the basal drip hole was made demonstrate the lack of quality control in this early phase of mass production.

Only 736 sherds (13.8 percent) of the assemblage can be classified as Spanish domestic ceramics, and the majority of this material consists of fragments of Early Style olive jars, which also could have been used in an industrial setting. The paucity of Taino material in the industrial quarter as compared to contemporary assemblages from Spanish domestic sites elsewhere in the region is notable (Willis 1976; Ewen 1987; McEwan 1995; Deagan 1988, 1995; Deagan and Cruxent 2002a, 2002b). Given the absence of personal effects, faunal remains, and a defined area for food preparation within the confines of the industrial quarter, the archaeo-

Table 2.2 Combined Totals of Material Culture from the Industrial Quarter from Cotter's and the 2002 Excavations

Description	Number of Artifacts	Percent of Assemblage
Activity Related		
Sugar molds	2,295	43.1
Sculptural limestone	1,100	20.6
Subtotal	3,395	63.7
Tools		
Chopping block	1	< 0.01
UI iron/stone tool	1	< 0.01
Spindle whorl	1	< 0.01
Hatchet	1	< 0.01
Lithics	654	12.3
Subtotal	658	12.3
Structural Hardware Building Supplies		
Lead sheeting	2	0.04
Nails	63	1.2
Iron fragments	86	1.6
Roof tiles	49	0.9
Slate	3	0.06
Subtotal	203	3.8
Weapons		
Lead balls	2	0.06
Domestic		
Majolica	51	1
Lead-glazed wares (misc.)	134	2.5
Olive jar (storage)	491	9.2
Unglazed Spanish ceramics	50	1.0
Taino ceramics	282	5.3
New Seville ware	5	0.1
Unidentified ceramics	10	0.2
Subtotal	1,023	19.3
Clothing		
Metal buckle	1	0.02
Personal		
glass beads	15	0.3
Zemi	1	0.02
Faunal		
Bones/teeth	25	0.5
Total	5,323	100

logical evidence suggests that the workers were eating in the vicinity of their workplace but not cooking or living there. In addition to the small amounts of Taino ceramics, a zemi and large amounts of lithics provide the main body of evidence for the Indian workers mentioned in archival sources. Unlike the contemporary Valloria sugar mill on Hispaniola, there is no evidence of African workers at this mill (Mañón 1978).

The Physical and Social Reconstruction of the Industrial Landscape of Sevilla la Nueva

The sugar mill and assorted workshops were industrial features situated within the urban confines of the principal port and administrative and market center of Spanish Jamaica. The construction of an urban mill, which serviced the surrounding farms, rather than a rural facility on a plantation illustrates that the initial sugar production in Jamaica was modeled after the industry in Iberia and the Atlantic islands where independent farmers brought their cane to a centrally located mill for processing. Further, urban mills were a persistent, albeit not universal, feature of the medieval Mediterranean sugar industry. It is important to note that at Sevilla la Nueva, the industrial quarter is separated from the administrative and residential section of the town (Woodward 2006a:237). During the early modern period in Europe there was a tendency to separate workspace from residential space with urban precincts (Mangan 1994:271). While the separation of industry from residential and administrative centers was not formally mandated until 1573 for Spanish towns in the Americas, the practice may have been implemented much earlier as the first settlement in the New World, La Isabela, had a separate artisans' quarter (Deagan 1995; Deagan and Cruxent 2002b; Woodward 2006a:229).

The location of the mill and workshops reflects the intentional organization of space and influences both the productive processes and organization of labor in the community. These industrial features were not the dominant feature that influenced the spatial patterning of the town. However, within the industrial quarter, the sugar mill, built parallel to the watercourse, was the dominant industry that influenced the organization of adjacent activities (Woodward 2006a:214). The spatial distribution of the sugar factory runs parallel to the stream, creating a linear landscape that enabled the Spanish to maximize the efficiency of the enterprise by organizing their labor force into groups with tightly prescribed tasks that could be easily supervised. The temporary nature of the mill structures and efficient arrangement of the production processes enabled Garay to minimize costs and thereby maximize profits from this aspect of his many island business ventures.

The Spanish first came to the north coast of the island because they knew there was abundant, well-watered land suitable for the production of foodstuffs and sugar. However, there were a number of other environmental determinants that influenced the location of Garay's sugar mill and the other industrial activities within the settlement, including their close proximity to the port. In the Caribbean the trade winds always blow from the east-southeast. It has been noted during the excavations of other sixteenth-century Spanish settlements in the region that as at Sevilla la Nueva, polluting activities were located downwind of the residential and administrative areas (Willis 1976:31; Deagan and Cruxent 2002b). Native labor was obviously viewed by the Spanish as one of Jamaica's natural assets. The three known Taino Indian villages on the hills surrounding St. Ann's Bay would have provided ample coerced Indian labor via the *encomienda* for the various agricultural, industrial, and domestic activities of the Spanish settlement.

Conclusion

The persistence of Mediterranean cultural traditions and technologies, which are the processes of the *longue durée,* are reflected in the material culture, production technologies, and agricultural practices that the Spanish brought to the New World. The linear arrangement of work processes, however, foreshadows the emerging social and economic structures of European capitalism, which would eventually define the New World sugar industry (Woodward 2006a:247).

Born out of a series of social, political, and economic crises during the late fourteenth century, the modern capitalist world system was an economic, not a political, entity that began to replace European feudalism by the mid-fifteenth century (Wallerstein 1974:15). It was assumed at the outset of this project that the production and international trade in sugar were important parts of this system.

From its inception the initial construction and ownership of the only sugar mill on the island by the governor had feudal dimensions. The entitlements in Garay's partnership agreement with the king conferred heredity title to land and powers that were normally withheld from other conquistadores (Stevens Arroyo 1997:137; Padrón 2003:55). Jamaica's economy in the early decades mirrored that of feudal Europe in that subsistence needs and small regional markets were the primary focus (Woodward 2006a:263). Profits were small and obviously not enough to entice Garay into making a permanent commitment to the island. Due to the lack of supply ships from Spain, self-sufficiency and subsistence, hallmarks of the feudal economy, were important aspects of early Jamaica, where independent farmers were assisted by tribute labor, not imported slaves (Wallerstein 1974:91; Mangan 1994:27).

In his administrative capacity Garay controlled the distribution of land and Indian labor on the island. This gave him enormous social power within the community, because without Indian labor another individual's ability to develop profitable agricultural or productive enterprises rapidly diminished.

Indian labor was distributed through the *encomienda*, which was a feudal institution based on a system of bonded labor. Originally, the *encomienda* was framed by a seigniorial land-based system in Iberia where the peasants of the former Islamic kingdoms were tied to the estates of the Christian nobility (Wynter 1983:124; Romano 1999:55). It was a reciprocal, although asymmetrical, relationship based on extra-economic compulsion rather than hiring free wage labor to produce goods. However, the intensity and scale of mercantile exploitation of the Caribbean were unlike anything in the feudal economy of pre-capitalist Europe and beg further examination before we consign this mill to being part of a wholly feudal enterprise (Stern 1988:841).

Wallerstein (1974:121) points out that there were three major distinctions between production utilizing serfs in the Middle Ages and the *encomienda* of sixteenth-century Hispanic America. The first is "the difference between assigning part of the surplus and assigning most of the surplus" to the market. Second, there is the distinction between production for the local market and the world market. Third, there is the difference between the exploiting classes merely spending the profits of their enterprise versus being motivated to maximize and reinvest them. Further, Wallerstein (1974:127) contends that the relations of production that define a system are the relations of production of the whole system, which he suggests were the hallmarks of European world economy by the sixteenth century. Skilled work in the core countries was performed by free wage labor, whereas coerced labor was used in the peripheral areas. The combination thereof is the essence of capitalism.

In the case of the early sixteenth-century Caribbean sugar industry, the only market for the product was the international one as the population was too small to support a robust internal or regional economy for luxury items (Galloway 1985:336). Therefore, almost all the sugar grown in Jamaica was surplus and consigned to the export market. Finally, Garay did not spend his profits on consumables alone; he reinvested them in other agricultural enterprises and the construction of a second mill.

In the early decades of the sixteenth century it appears that the sugar industry in the New World retained the mixed labor strategies of the Atlantic industry as coerced Indian labor assisted independent and tenant farmers and worked in the mills alongside European technicians (Woodward 2006a:261). Capital from Spain was invested in land, mills, and the construction of ships that connected the productive enterprises on the periphery to the metropolitan centers of Europe. As this asymmetrical relationship between Spain and the Indies matured, sugar production in the Caribbean became an integral part of the capitalist world economy.

During his tenure Garay was the only member of the colony with sufficient means to construct and operate a mill. This enabled him to monopolize sugar production. Further, the mill anchored the colonists to the land close to Sevilla la

Nueva and made them his dependents. Despite his apparent lack of commitment to the long-term development of Jamaica, his entrepreneurial drive and profit motives, two essential characteristics of capitalists, are an evident force in structuring both the economic and social relations of Sevilla la Nueva (Stern 1988:833; Woodward 2006a:268).

In the early sixteenth century, the colonists in the Indies had myriad systems for the production of sugar from which to choose as they began to build the industry that would later define the landscape and demographics of the region (Woodward 2006a:266).

Garay's enterprise at Sevilla la Nueva is in many ways analogous to the fifteenth and early sixteenth centuries' system of production favored in the semi-peripheral zones of the Kingdom of Granada, Madeira, and the Canary Islands as it featured a mill built on the outskirts of an urban center that was operated by the wealthiest landowner of the community. He derived his income from his own cane fields as well as from processing cane belonging to other cultivators. And as on the Atlantic islands, the labor strategy included wage laborers, sharecropping, and slavery (Woodward 2006a:267).

This urban mill illustrates the persistence of medieval modes of labor and work processes in the Antilles that results, at least for a short time, in variability in the models of production and labor in the early sixteenth-century Caribbean sugar industry.

While sharecropping clearly made a brief appearance in the Spanish Antilles prior to the collapse of the indigenous population, in the Americas unlike the Atlantic islands, there was always a new frontier to colonize that offered even the poorest settlers an opportunity to better their social and economic standing. Once the mineral wealth of New Spain and South America became a factor, the ability to subject Spanish colonists to sharecropping or other feudal peasant-based labor systems became futile. The successive collapse of the indigenous population left the sugar industry on the Caribbean islands with an insufficient labor supply. Therefore, by the middle of the sixteenth century, Spanish producers were forced to import slave labor, as had the planters on Cyprus and later São Tomé, when faced with the same dilemma a century before.

3

Port Royal and Jamaica

Wrought-Iron Hand Tools Recovered as Archaeological Evidence and the Material Culture Mentioned in Probate Inventories ca. 1692

Marianne Franklin

Introduction

In this chapter, I examine a collection of over one hundred wrought-iron hand tools recovered from five archaeological excavations undertaken upon the sunken city of Port Royal, Jamaica, (c. 1692) in conjunction with information on craftsmen, slavery, and trade from contemporary probate inventories from the parish of Port Royal (1686–94) in order to better understand everyday life in a flourishing seventeenth-century Caribbean mercantile trade center. The chapter brings together information from an increasingly diverse and expanding number of contemporary archaeological excavations, interpretations, and publications in order to focus on Jamaica's role as a major Caribbean port that linked the Old World to the New.

For our purposes here, a tool is defined as a hand-worked instrument used to perform a task or necessary to practice a vocation. Tools have been described as "human benefactors of the most primary sort" since they "increase and vary human power; they economize human time; and they convert raw substances into valuable and useful products." Recognized as the instruments of human progress, tools can provide important artifactual insight when trying to understand the inner workings of any culture (E. Sloane 1964:6). Tools recovered from an archaeological site may yield important information about the society that used them.

The Wickedest City on Earth

Historical documents portray seventeenth-century Port Royal, Jamaica, as the bustling maritime trade center of the Caribbean. The town was situated on the tip of a sand spit that protected a large, deep, natural harbor. Once a haven for pirates, privateers, and buccaneers whose plunder of enemy ships in Caribbean waters was sanctioned in exchange for the protection of British interests, Port Royal was once awarded the description of the "wickedest city on earth."

By the last decade of the seventeenth century, Jamaica was completing a switch from an economy established on small and diverse agricultural acreage to an increasingly larger plantation economy based mainly on sugar, slaves, and the related products of molasses, muscovado, and rum (Bridenbaugh and Bridenbaugh 1972; Dunn 1972). Other Jamaican-grown goods exported included parcels of cocoa, cotton, ginger, and indigo. Dye wood was harvested along the Central American coast and brought to Jamaica for reexport. Imported trade goods arrived in Port Royal from both sides of the Atlantic. The slaves that fueled the plantation economy were brought from Africa. England and Ireland supplied such commodities as wine, fruit, beef, pork, cheese, butter, flour, fabric, clothing, ironwork, pitch, tar, and rope. New England merchants shipped foodstuffs, spars, barrel staves, and hoops to the island (Taylor 1686–88:505).

Port Royal was the only recognized port of entry for the island of Jamaica in the late seventeenth century; thus, all goods that were legally traded passed though the crowded wharves and warehouses of colonial Port Royal (Claypole 1984:95). Pivotal in a triangular trade route linking the Old World to the New, Port Royal had by the beginning of the 1690s achieved recognition for its role as a mercantile capital.

Port Royal, as seen in a 1690 reconstruction drawing made by British architect Oliver Cox, was a bustling metropolis on the edge of a deep and protected harbor. Situated in a limited space, the town expanded upward and outward to the brim. In *Multum in Parvo or Taylor's Histori of His Life and Travels in America and Other Parts or Taylor's Life and Travels 1686–1688,* Port Royal and its inhabitants are vividly described. The houses generally had yards and often porches but there cannot have been much room for gardens or trees. Taylor extolled the fashionable brick mode of construction: Port Royal houses were generally four stories high, cellared below, with tiled roof, glazed sash windows, and a cook room set off by itself in a backyard. Taylor particularly admired the opulent merchant's Exchange, a stone gallery adjoining the parish church, which was graced by Doric pillars and a twisted balustrade. Here, elegantly shaded, Port Royal's grandees met to transact their affairs. But the raw side of life was also very evident. The city featured two courthouses, two prisons, a cage, a ducking stool, and stocks in order to keep the local lawbreakers under some sort of control (Dunn 1972:184–85).

Taylor recorded that high living was common in seventeenth-century Jamaica. Although fresh water was in short supply, Taylor reports that Port Royal's people had easy access to rich food and strong drink. While local meat was not up to English standards, the three daily markets supplied plenty of local flesh, including fresh fish, tortoise, pork, and fowl; fruit and salad greens were also in supply. Grocers sold imported sweetmeats, sauces, oils, anchovies, capers, olives, and other such delicacies while pastry cooks vended custards, cheesecakes, and tarts. Taverns and punch houses (which Taylor characterized as brothels) dispensed European wines, brandy, beer, and rum punch. According to his account, businesses were closed between noon and three; during this hottest part of the day Port Royalans ate dinner, drank at the taverns, or napped in their hammocks. In the cool of the evening they could be entertained in taverns, coffeehouses, beer gardens, or music houses (another euphemism for brothels). Nightly, Taylor reports, drunken "wild blades" and "strumpets" were gathered up and caged near the Turtle Market until they sobered up (quoted in Dunn 1972:185). Taylor describes Port Royal as a lively place indeed.

The entire city of Port Royal was wedged onto a spit of sand, flanked on three sides by protective forts, overlooking the entrance to Kingston Harbor. The multistoried brick structures contained diverse occupants, providing a large assortment of shops and storefronts manned by local tradesmen offering a variety of crafts and services (Taylor 1686–88:491–507). It was a bustling town with population estimates that vary between 6,500 and 10,000. It is commonly accepted that Port Royal was the leading urban center in the English New World when struck by disaster on June 7, 1692 (Bridenbaugh and Bridenbaugh 1972:316).

On that day, a few minutes before noon, an earthquake rocked the island of Jamaica. The earthquake and subsequent seiche wave that swelled across the harbor rocked the lime rock bed that formed the foundation of the sand spit. The earthquake caused the sand spit to slump into the harbor; most of the city, nearly thirty-three acres (two-thirds of the town), was quickly submerged. The quake and its aftermath, which included a tsunami thought to have been six feet high, took the lives of nearly four thousand Jamaicans, most of whom resided in Port Royal.

Looting and salvage of underwater wreckage began almost immediately after the quake and continued through the centuries. The citizens of Port Royal attempted to rebuild, but, beset by another earthquake, fire, and a number of hurricanes through the mid-eighteenth century, the town never again regained the population, development, or stature of its early days. Through the remainder of the eighteenth and nineteenth centuries, up until 1905, Port Royal served mainly as a station for the British Royal Navy (Pawson and Buisseret [1975] 2000:124). Today, Port Royal is most often described as a sleepy fishing village. Yet beneath her streets, and just offshore, the remnants of the once thriving seventeenth-century mercantile center, buccaneer town, and virtual capital of the English New World are well preserved in the archaeological record.

Archaeology of the "Sunken City"

An examination of the archaeological record, in conjunction with historic documents like Taylor's 1688 description of the city, as well as countless contemporary documents such as wills, probate inventories, and archived correspondence, can paint a broad picture for understanding Port Royal, its inhabitants, and the earliest settlers of Jamaica before the catastrophic event that laid waste to the "wickedest city on earth" in 1692. My study has examined artifacts recovered from five of Port Royal's archaeological sites, in conjunction with contemporary probate inventories, to piece together a picture of the types of tools available to both the average citizen and the tradesmen who populated Port Royal before the quake.

Between 1981 and 1990 Dr. Donny L. Hamilton directed underwater excavations of a small area of Port Royal while working for Texas A&M University and the Institute of Nautical Archaeology (INA) in conjunction with the Jamaica National Heritage Trust (JNHT). The primary area excavated lies at the intersection of the original Queen and Lime streets (Figure 3.1). A total of five buildings were excavated, as well as a contemporary shipwreck that lay across the corner of one of the buildings. The area excavated by Texas A&M lies just offshore from a modern seawall; the old Naval Hospital, part of the colonial naval base in Port Royal, was utilized as a staging area and temporary conservation facility. Rigid controls were undertaken to map and survey the entire excavation, which was based on a grid system tied into a permanent datum set up on the shoreline. A "hookah" system through which multiple lines were connected to an air compressor was used to supply air to divers who worked in three-hour shifts in visibility that usually was less than three feet. After mapping, photography, X-ray, and drawing, most artifacts were stored wet then removed to Texas A&M's conservation laboratory in College Station at the end of each field season. The artifacts were stabilized, identified, and analyzed before being returned to Jamaica.

The materials from the A&M excavation were supplemented with tools recovered during previous investigations of seventeenth-century Port Royal. The other excavations that supplied tools included in this study were conducted with varying degrees of archaeological control. Robert Marx worked in Port Royal for twenty-seven months between 1965 and 1968. Although Marx endeavored to maintain archaeological control, "the excavations, for a number of reasons, [did] not meet accepted archaeological standards" (Hamilton 1984:15). Of particular note is a deep scar on the floor of the harbor, created when Marx dredged part of the sunken city to collect artifacts. "Marx's Hole" lies just to the south and west of the A&M excavations. Many of the ferrous items recovered by Marx were not conserved after recovery and have not survived. The tools recovered by Marx that could be included in this study should be recognized as part of an incomplete collection with no provenience other than that they were recovered from Marx's Hole and thus were most likely submerged by the 1692 earthquake.

Several other excavations in Port Royal produced ferrous tools. In 1968 Philip Mayes supervised the British Sub Aqua Club in an excavation of Fort Rupert. Two ax heads were recovered from that underwater exploration, with no in situ pro-

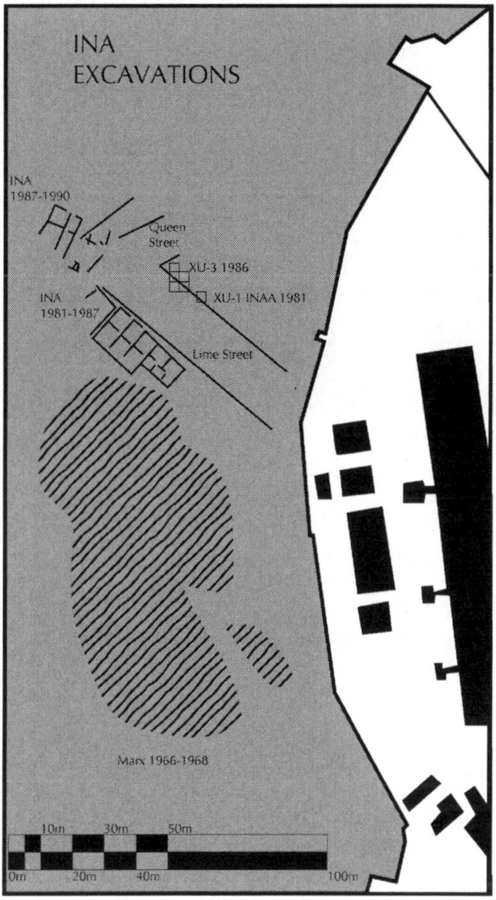

Figure 3.1. Plan view of excavations conducted by the Institute of Nautical Archaeology in Kingston Harbor. Illustration by Mark W. Hauser.

venience. In 1971 Anthony Priddy conducted a terrestrial excavation in the yard beside the present-day St. Peter's Church. Below street level a number of structures dating to the seventeenth century were uncovered and mapped. Using a field-generated site drawing and the recollections of JNHT curator Richard McClure, a site map was constructed and tool locations in situ were reconstructed. Seven tools were recovered and conserved from the St. Peter's excavation and are included in this study. In 1971 and 1972 Priddy supervised the excavation of what is today an empty grassy lot in downtown Port Royal, bordered by New Street, Dove Lane, and Love Lane. Priddy identified a number of levels of occupation and reuse and eventually delineated a 1692 stratum that featured the interior portion of a series of interconnected brick homes and courtyards destroyed in the quake. A rough field map was again overlaid with a site plan to generate provenience for the tools recovered from Priddy's New Street excavation (Figure 3.2).

The tools recovered from these archaeological excavations in Port Royal were studied in conjunction with the contemporary probate inventories recorded from Port Royal Parish. The original inventories, dating from the seventeenth to the twentieth centuries, were housed at the Jamaica Archives in Spanish Town. The inventories were microfilmed and duplicated and returned to Texas A&M University, where they were transcribed. The inventories list all "moveable" possessions of a decedent and often begin by citing the name, parish of residence, and occupation of the deceased. Of the 295 inventory folios in volume 3, 128 that were listed as originating in Port Royal parish were transcribed. The inventories were studied for the type, quantity, and description of any hand tools. Over forty tools were mentioned; these could be further broken down into approximately ninety types, based on either descriptive terms or usage. Table 3.1 outlines the tools mentioned in the probate inventories.

The probate inventories were also examined for the number and types of occupations that were listed. These occupations, in conjunction with Pawson and Buisseret's ([1975] 2000) analysis of occupations mentioned in their transcription and analysis of the probate inventories, appear in Tables 3.2 and 3.3.

Ferrous Tools Recovered from Port Royal

Many of the tools recovered from the various archaeological investigations at Port Royal can be indentified using the typology created from the inventory lists. The tools recovered are discussed below (see Figure 3.3).

Adzes

Adzes are small ax-like tools used to shape wood. Carpenters and coopers commonly use these kinds of tools in their trades. Four adze heads were recovered from Port Royal. Two were common woodworking adzes, while the others may have been used by a cooper, judging by the short length of the remaining wooden handles as well as the shape of the face and blade remains.

Augers

Augers are screw-like tools that are used to place holes into wooden planks and are commonly used by carpenters, coopers, joiners, shipwrights, and other tradesmen who work in wood. Four parts from three augers with gouge or spoon bits used by woodworkers, carpenters, or shipwrights were recovered from Port Royal.

Axes

Twenty-four ax and hatchet heads are included in the study collection of the tools from Port Royal. They include broad axes, felling axes, and a German-style "goose-

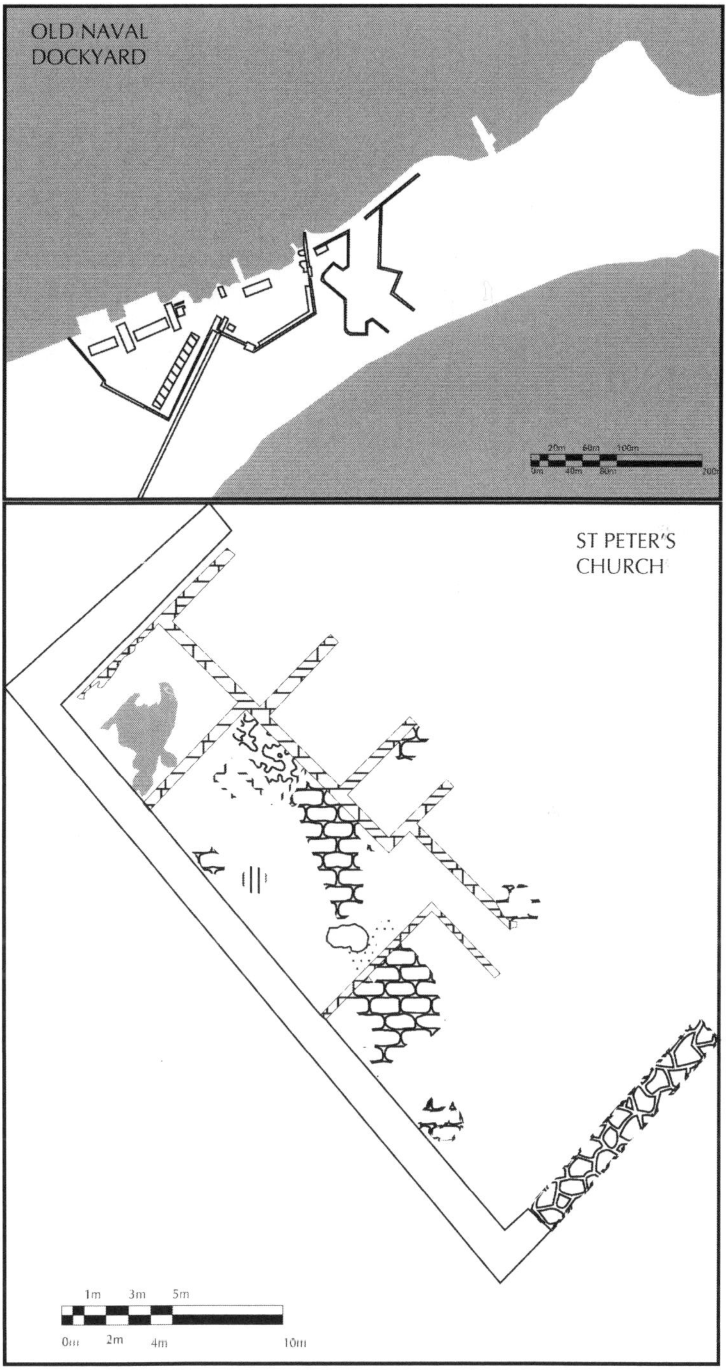

Figure 3.2. Plan view of the Old Naval Dockyard excavated by Phillip Mayes, and plan view of St. Peter's Church excavated by Anthony Priddy. Illustration by Mark W. Hauser.

Table 3.1 Tools Listed in the Port Royal Probate Inventories, 1686–94

Type	Subtypes									
Adzes	carpenter’s	cooper’s								
Anvils	bick	new	great	old	small					
Augers	large	old								
Awls	alls & blades									
Axes	½	broad	carpenter’s	cooper	old cooper	falling	joiner’s	mortising	old rusty	pick
Bills	back bill	indigo								
Bitts	old	shingling								
Borers	bung	sugar								
Calipers										
Carving tools	old									
Chisels	broad	dozen inch	heading	mortising	old					
Compasses										
Crows	iron	cooper’s								
Files	Dutch	half-round	large	old	rasps	small ordinary	smooth	square		
Froes	small									
Gimlets	small	large								
Gouges										
Hammers	large									
Hatchets	half joiners	joiner’s	small							
Hoes	broad	grubbing	narrow							
Howells	cooper’s									

Irons	joiner's	marking	planning	tow			
Knives	butcher	carving	currier	rounding			
Pincers							
Pitch pots							
Planes	carpenter's						
Punches							
Rules	carpenter's						
Saw sets	handsaw						
Saw	crosscut	handsaw	iron handsaw	iron whipsaw	old	steel 3 ft.	steel whipsaw
Screw plates							
Sheep shearers							
Shovels	spades						
Sledges	great						
Slices							
Snip bills							
Stakes	for thimbles	for nails	for staves				
Swages and fullers	nail tools	bold tools					
Tongs							
Vises	cooper's	glasser's	hand	large			
Wedges	old and rusty	splitting					

Source: Franklin 1992:16.

Table 3.2 Trades and Crafts That Utilized Wrought-Iron Hand Tools Represented in Port Royal Inventories through 1694

Trade
Blacksmith (6)
Bricklayer (2)
Butcher (6)
Carpenter, cabinetmaker, joiner (26)
Cooper (13)
Cordwainer (shoemaker) (18)
Glazier (1)
Gunsmith (6)
Mason (4)
Pewterer (4)
Shipwright (4)

Source: Franklin 1992:155; Pawson and Buisseret [1975] 2000:223–31.

Table 3.3 Additional Trades Mentioned in Port Royal Inventories Pre-1694

Architect	Mariner (62)
Baker	Merchant (133)
Barber	Pipemaker
Chandler	Planter*
Chyrurgeon	Porter
Combmaker	Sailmaker
Drugster	Schoolmaster
Fisherman	Swordmaker
Goldsmith	Tailor
Hatmaker	Tanner
Ivoryturner	Tavernkeeper, victualler, vintner (47)
Laborer	Waterman (10)
Limeburner	

Source: Franklin 1992:155; Pawson and Buisseret [1975] 2000:223–31.
*Two planters c. 1692 are listed in Franklin 1992.

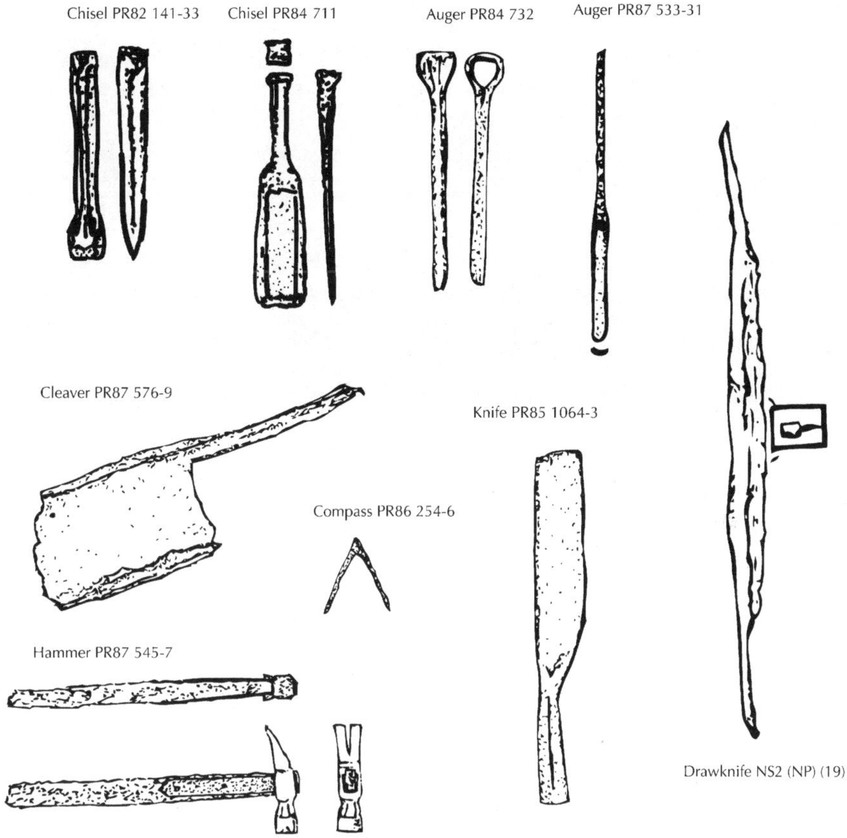

Figure 3.3. Wrought-iron tools recovered from seventeenth-century Port Royal. Artwork based on illustrations by Marianne Franklin.

wing" ax. Two lathing hatchets with stirrups for either side of the missing wooden handle were also recovered from the excavation at St. Peter's and Marx's Hole. These hatchets were used to attach the thin strips of wood to joists or rafters before plaster would be applied. Almost all of the ax heads were wrought iron with no wooden handle remaining. Some were worked around steel bit inserts. Some bore maker's marks, evidence of mass prefabrication, while others were crudely worked and may have been shaped by local blacksmiths.

Blacksmiths and Their Tools in Port Royal

The blacksmith was one of the most important craftsmen in any colonial settlement. Wrought-iron tools, implements, and hardware are staples found in seventeenth-century homes, stores, and shops and on plantations. Many tools were constructed and shipped pre-made to Jamaica and overseas, while others were shaped and repaired in the local smith's shop. While Pawson and Buisseret listed four blacksmiths in Port Royal prior to 1692 ([1975] 2000), the probate inventories in volume 3 (1686–94) list only two, with only one being a definite resident of Port Royal: John Philpott. Philpott was listed as a blacksmith, but he was also obviously a merchant. His inventory lists over a thousand tools in all. There are approximately forty different listings for various types of locks and keys, a variety of hinges, and several sizes and quantities of brads, nails, tacks and bolts, as well as many listings for knives, pistols, needles, scimitars, and saws. Tools mentioned include several different styles and types of chisels, adzes, augers, files, hoes, axes, hammers, and shovels in great quantity. The inventory also lists stock amounts of guns and sword blades and handles, as well as an anvil and a great quantity of scrap iron.

Recovered from the excavations at Port Royal were only four tools used by the blacksmith at work in the forge: a set or sledge with a cutting edge, RM.BS.1 with an oval eye; a flatter or cutting iron, RM.BS.2; a drift or punch for making holes in iron, NS2.A2.1(17); and a swage, PR (NP), which would have fit into an anvil head to shape hot metal. Unfortunately, the swage has no provenience.

Caulking Irons

Port Royal's location on the edge of a deep-water harbor has always made the town an ideal location for naval refit and repair. Several caulking irons have been recovered from the site. A caulking iron is used to drive hemp oakum between wooden plank seams to create a watertight seal. There are several types, shapes, and sizes of caulking irons. A sharp iron is used for the first step of pounding the oakum into the seam. A creasing iron is used to further "drive the oakum home." Specially shaped or bent irons are used for unwieldy butts or corner seams. Scrapers are used to remove excess pitch from a seam (Dodds and Moore 1984:45).

Eight caulking irons and one wider iron with a steel bit insert that may have been used for reaming, or cleaning out the seam before recaulking, were recovered from Port Royal. Most showed signs of extreme wear and use at the blade tips, and may in fact have been used or reused as chisels.

Chisels

Chisels may be used by a cabinetmaker, carpenter, joiner, shipwright, turner, or wheelwright. Specialized chisels are used by bricklayers, file makers, glaziers, slaters, and stonecutters. Most of the eighteen chisels recovered from Port Royal have been identified as having been intended for use by a woodworker; these include framing chisels, firmer chisels, skew, gouge-tipped, dog-leg, and paring chisels, as well as some used as wedges. The handles for these chisels were wither wood inserted into a socket, or the tool was solid metal designed to be moved with a small sledge. The chisels here run the gamut from finely made prefabricated ones to some that were obviously quickly crafted at a simple forge and may have been made by a local blacksmith.

Cleavers

Fresh meat was apparently not difficult to obtain in Port Royal. Taylor mentions that the town housed markets for fresh fish and "fleash," not to mention the easily procured meat from the sea turtles stored in the kraals (Taylor 1686–88:494). The probate inventories list at least one man's profession as butcher. Several inventories mention the ownership of livestock. Presumably, using a cleaver to dress meat would have been a fairly commonplace activity in old Port Royal. Three cleavers have been recovered from the site. Two are large and made completely of wrought iron, while the third is fitted with a tang and ferrule to hold a wooden haft in place.

Files and File Making

The probate inventories mention Dutch, half-round, smooth, and square files, as well as the rasp, and file blanks. A file blank is one not yet marked with chisels and punches to create grooves. Files may be single or double-cut, and may be used to smooth and shape wood or metal. Three files were recovered from Port Royal: a blank, a double-cut flat file, and a rasp.

Hammers

Eleven hammers that have been identified as the basic carpenter's claw hammer were recovered from Port Royal. Five have the remainder of a wooden handle in the eye. Typical of medieval and post-medieval tools prior to the eighteenth century, the best preserved of the hammers has stirrups or iron straps that help secure the head to the handle. Other hammers recovered include a tack hammer, framing hammer, cobbler's hammer, and stonemason's hammer.

Knives

Several sizes, shapes, and types of knives would have been present in seventeenth-century Port Royal. The probate inventories list butcher, carving, currier, and rounding knives. While it is most likely that scissors, shears, fine knives, and swords were made by cutlers in Europe, in America these tools would have been crafted by a blacksmith. No one is listed in the probate inventories as a cutler, though one man was described as a sword maker (John Guepin, vol. 3, fol. 242). The knives listed in the inventories generally appear in small quantities, except for one merchant listing for 144 butcher knives. The knives recovered from Port Royal include a carpenter's drawknife, several tang-fitted blade fragments, and two larger knives similar to machetes.

Pincers

Similar to modern-day pliers, the pincer holds onto an object between two jaws. Two pincers along with a claw hammer were recovered together during the A&M excavation from the front of Room 1 in Building 1 facing Lime Street. The square section on the arm of PR85 945-5 would have been designed to pull leather around a wooden last or foot mold used by a shoemaker. The inventories list eighteen cordwainers or shoemakers in Port Royal prior to the earthquake.

Discussion

While these groups of tools recovered from archaeological sites may represent tool use in the city of Port Royal, another possibility must be considered: salvage. Salvage of the wreckage of Port Royal began almost immediately after the quake. Port Royal was home to a number of professional "wrackers" who made their living salvaging shipwrecks. For a community familiar with the trade, grappling with hooks and buckets, dredging with nets, and free diving for salvage of any goods accessible, recovery of lost items after the earthquake would have been common. Tools, considered to be of great value and still in good condition after a short submersion, must have been among the most highly prized items. Tools recovered from the archaeological investigations, especially the chisels, hammers, axes, sledges, and crowbars, may have been used and then lost during salvage attempts.

It should also be noted that almost every category of tool recovered ran the gamut from the finely crafted imported types of professional tool manufacturers in the Old World to the hastily and crudely crafted tool created to serve a need by the local blacksmith. Neither the tools recovered from the archaeological sites nor the probate inventories alone can be completely diagnostic when discussing the tools and the craftsmen that populated Port Royal before the quake. Yet together, these sources provide the basis for a broader understanding of the scale and magnitude of the types of goods and services found in pre-quake Port Royal, a bustling mercantile trade center pivotal to New World trade operations.

Conclusion

While over one hundred wrought-iron hand tools were recovered from Port Royal, the assemblage yielded only seventeen distinct tool types; in contrast, the seventeenth-century probate inventories examined for this study identified forty basic tool types. The inventories listed thousands of examples of hand-wrought tools. The disparity between the two data sets—the archaeological specimens and the probate inventories—may be explained in several ways. It is very likely that highly valued iron tools were salvaged by survivors of the 1692 earthquake. Furthermore, the small number of tools recovered may be a reflection of the relatively small sample size that resulted from the inevitable limitations of archaeological excavation; artifacts from only eight structures—a small portion of the thirty-three acres submerged by the earthquake—are represented in this study. The high numbers of tools identified by the documentary research also reflect the research methodology, in which the stores of recently deceased merchants were examined to identify the variety of tools available in the late seventeenth century. This does not necessarily reflect the number or kinds of tools owned by individual artisans or workers in the city, and indeed, many of these tools may have been sold off-island as Port Royal was the initial entrepôt for most of the British West Indian colonies in the late seventeenth century.

Another interesting disparity between the archaeologically recovered tools and the listings in the inventories is that the latter reflect a high percentage of agricultural tools. While agriculture was not a significant part of seventeenth-century life in Port Royal itself, plantation agriculture was the central component of the economy of the British Caribbean. The tools that appear in the inventories were likely purchased by planters in Jamaica and other West Indian colonies. In contrast, the majority of tools recovered from the archaeological site were short-handled iron tools most likely used by artisans in Port Royal. The only significant exception to this pattern is the relatively high number of axes recovered, which likely represent domestic activity in the yards located behind the houses of Port Royal. These were likely used for cutting wood or butchering meat for household use.

It is also likely that the tools used in Port Royal were manufactured both locally and in England. Research into the probate records confirms that there were large-scale blacksmith shops operating in Port Royal at the time of the earthquake, while some of the tools were specifically described as having come from London. Variation in the quality of the tools recovered archaeologically suggests that some tools being used in Port Royal were better crafted than others; for example, the finely crafted claw hammer PR87 533-9 was of much better quality than the more crudely fashioned chisel NS13.

Despite the limitations of the data set, the recovery of hand-wrought iron tools from the sunken area of seventeenth-century Port Royal does shed light into the daily activities of those living in "the wickedest city on earth." While not every question about the provenience or use of each of the tools might be answered, the excavations of the sunken city have produced one of the most complete assemblages of iron recovered from a seventeenth-century context. The extraordinary events of 1692—the earthquake and the submerging of a part of the city—created an extraordinary context for the preservation of iron tools that would likely otherwise have been reused or refashioned and might under ordinary circumstances not appear in the archaeological record.

4

Evidence for Port Royal's British Colonial Merchant Class as Reflected in the New Street Tavern Site Assemblage

Maureen J. Brown

Introduction

Port Royal was a major hub for the slave and mercantile trades for the British colonial system in Jamaica and the West Indies. During the late seventeenth century, along with the traditional land-based society, a new "consumerism" and "merchant class" developed and goods became readily accessible, especially to those involved directly in trade. Access was not enough, however, as the new material culture demanded new etiquette and knowledge of use. As Jamaica's primary port town, seventeenth-century Port Royal was booming with taverns where residents and travelers took care of business and consumption needs. Tavern keepers, therefore, had to provide the necessary material to match the perceived needs of the clientele they hoped to attract. Analysis of the 1692–1703 New Street Tavern site assemblage, probate inventories, and historical sources provides direct evidence of rich trade goods in this bustling center and examples of everyday life of the new merchant class.

As the center of Jamaica's mercantile economy, Port Royal was home to a number of these merchants. For our purposes here, a merchant is defined as a wholesaler who traded in foreign markets and resided in the seaport, and whose business and home were located conveniently close to the wharves of the port city. In Jamaica merchants played a key role in the economy, arranging for planters' farm products to move from the countryside to seaports, importing manufactured necessities and luxuries for colonial consumption, and shipping cargoes of raw materials and produce to and from Europe, Africa, the rest of the West Indies (including the Spanish Main), and New England. Merchants had to be flexible and versatile; besides buying and selling goods, they served as financiers by extending credit and transferring funds and acted as insurance underwriters. They often hedged their bets by investing in business or real estate, many owning plantations. A trader could specialize in dry goods (textiles, notions, and certain items of clothing) or wet goods (rum, molasses, coffee, cocoa, etc.). The common reference to a "merchant class" implies that merchants composed a coherent, wealthy group that wielded political and economic clout. But in fact the merchants of Port Royal varied widely in ethnicity, politics, religion, and income. Merchants in colonial cities like Port Royal were able to amass great fortunes and aspired to newly forming class statuses based on the accumulation of wealth.

Breen (1986) has argued that the origins of a class-based Western society were directly related to the acquisition and use of material goods. In his opinion, at the turn of the eighteenth century ordinary people began to find new meaning in material goods. The use of material goods began to shift away from meeting or improving basic physical needs and for the first time many ordinary people began assuming personal habits that were more class-based that culture-bound. Sweeney (1994:6) has noted, "Possessions became tools for actively cultivating a distinctive, genteel style of life that set off 'polite society' from the 'meaner sort.'"

New patterns of personal deportment—of language and of movement—became critical expressions of character and gentility. In places like Port Royal, as well as in England and in other American colonial contexts, manners and education bolstered claims to rising social status based primarily on the possession of wealth. However, it was not the mere possession of expensive things but the widespread prescribed use of them that differentiated new material culture, distinguished by what is referred to as the William and Mary style, from older status symbols. The excessively materialistic values that attached to social status in the new colonies sharpened class differences by making them visible, tangible, and inescapable (C. Carson 1994). Artifacts and the activities in which they were used defined group identities and mediated relations between individuals and the social world they inhabited (C. Carson 1994; Sweeney 1994).

The late seventeenth and early eighteenth centuries were an age when the public arena, as opposed to the private sphere, was important for those wishing to exhibit and keep their newly refined stature. Occasions to eat, drink, play cards, dance, and simply converse offered opportunities for displaying class-based cultural knowledge. Material goods played important roles in most genteel social gatherings, including matched sets of chairs, glasses, plates, rounded tables, and individual eating utensils, and new forms and increased quantities of individual drinking vessels that provided proper containers for such imported beverages as port, sherry, Madeira, rum punch, tea, coffee, and chocolate (Sweeney 1994:8). The combination of fine wines and imported glassware elevated the act of drinking to a social event.

Several archaeological studies of taverns in North American seaports from coastal New England to the Chesapeake have demonstrated that drinking establishments were places where people, generally men, would gather to socialize (e.g., Eckholm and Deetz 1971; Bragdon 1988; King and Miller 1987); as Fred Smith (2008:64) has put it, taverns were a place for "the display of masculine ideals." Such ideals did include the newly developing sense of gentility displayed through the proper use of alcoholic beverages and the accoutrements used to consume them. However, taverns were not only gendered spaces but class-specific places as well; members of different social groups would gather at different kinds of drinking establishments, which functioned somewhat differently depending on their context (Rockman and Rotschild 1984; F. Smith 2008).

Smith (2008:68ff) notes that excavations at several tavern sites in Williamsburg, Virginia, have revealed that specific activities were shared at different kinds of taverns. For example, archaeologists have identified a cockfighting ring at Shield's Tavern, an activity closely associated with gambling. Excavation at the site of the more upscale Charlton's Coffeehouse in Williamsburg produced high-status objects, including Chinese porcelain tea sets. An interesting find, the disarticulated bones of a human hand, thought to come from a physician's anatomy specimen, has been interpreted as evidence that elite activities, in this case anatomy lessons, were shared at the coffeehouse (Levy et al. 2007; F. Smith 2008). High-status individuals, including, perhaps, wealthy merchants, frequented the taverns and coffeehouses to display their new genteel qualities (including the knowledge of proper beverage consumption practices with the proper glassware and ceramics, as well as an interest in science), socialize with their peers, and refine their mannerisms of consumption through the use of both traditional and newfangled material objects.

Taverns in Port Royal

Like their fellows on the North American mainland, the merchants of Port Royal gathered in taverns to socialize and display their developing gentility. The aspirations of Port Royal's merchant class can be interpreted through data collected from the New Street Tavern site (NS.2 site), firsthand accounts by travelers to Port Royal, and late seventeenth- to early eighteenth-century probate inventories of Port Royal merchants. The New Street Tavern site was one of many such establishments located in the town of Port Royal, on the south coast of Jamaica. During the second half of the seventeenth century Port Royal was built on the end of a long sand spit at the mouth of Kingston Harbor. Within a small area of no more than sixty acres, the town grew to be the most affluent commercial center in the British West Indies and perhaps the entire British colonial world. Port Royal developed a reputation as the "wickedest city on earth" and was notorious as a haven for buccaneers and pirates pillaging the Spanish treasure fleets. Port Royal's advantageous location made it a hub of trade and legitimate commerce.

The tavern or victualing house was the most common type of shop in Port Royal,

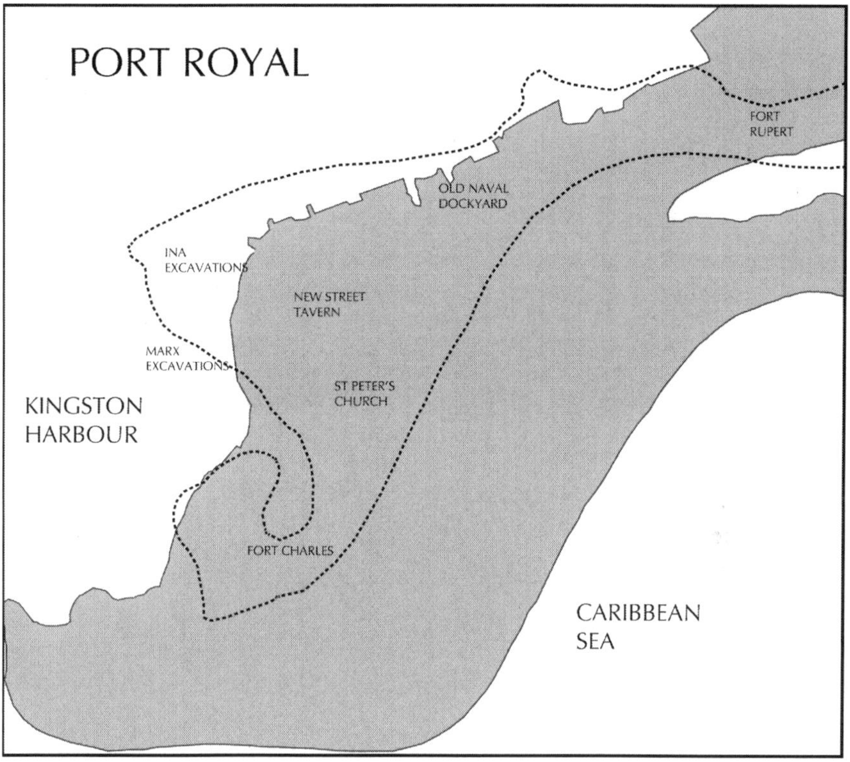

Figure 4.1. Map of Port Royal showing the current coastline (highlighted in gray) and the seventeenth-century coastline.

a fact as true for the fishing community today as it was in the seventeenth century. As early as 1672, Blome (1672:31) noted that the port was "much Inhabited by Merchants, Store-house-keepers, Vintners & Ale-house-keepers, being the only noted place of Trade in the Isle." John Taylor in his account of Port Royal remarked that "here are many Taverns, and abundance of Punch Houses, or rather may be fitly called Brothel Houses" (Taylor 1686–88:262). The tavern was probably the most important social institution, as it was the common meeting ground for all ranks of society. The tavern was the place where people came to drink, gossip, and hear the latest news; it was here that merchants and mariners bargained over cargoes; and it was to here that the courts adjourned. Pawson and Buisseret ([1975] 2000) estimate that there were over forty victualers, vintners, and tavern keepers operating in Port Royal between 1663 and 1688. Describing life in these taverns, John Taylor further wrote: "Now on this port the inhabitants . . . have no other recreation, but by enjoying their friend at the tavern, ore a good glass of wine, a sangaree, or a Joly good bowl of punch; . . . and billiards, cock fighting, stotting at the target, etc. . . .

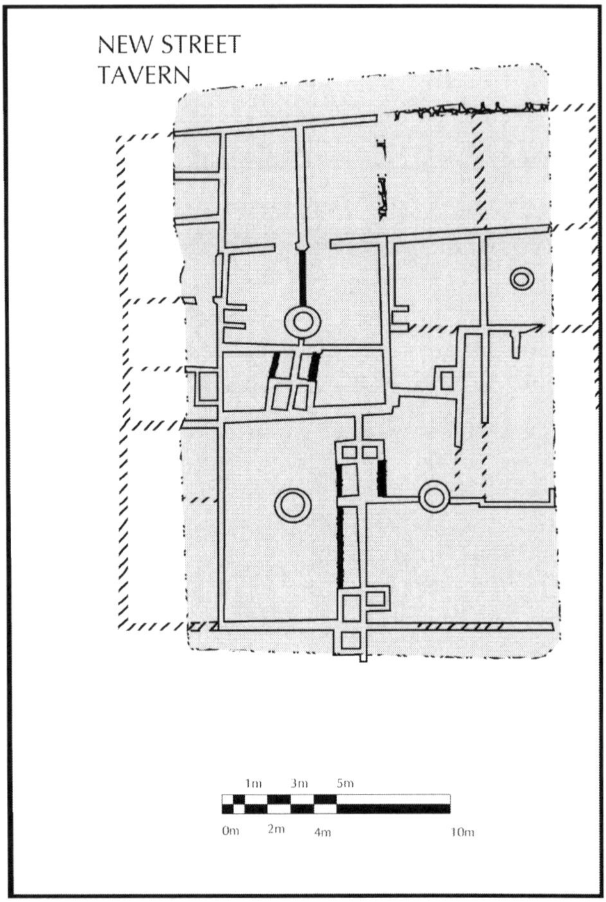

Figure 4.2. Plan view of excavations at New Street Tavern sites excavated by Anthony Priddy.

Also the merchants have commonly at twelve shut up their shops, and other friends they divert themselves either at ye tavern or else on their couches and hammocks, about three a clock they open their shops" (1686–88:262ff).

Amid a volatile climate, English merchants were able to capitalize on opportunities created by conflicts between the Portuguese and Dutch on the African and Latin American coasts. England's naval strength supported her merchant marine and overseas interests throughout the centuries of nearly continuous warfare (D. Johnson 2000:3). Until its 1692 destruction, Port Royal was well placed to develop wealth, as it was the only port of entry for Jamaica. The port was a pivotal station in triangular and direct trades between the New World and the Old World. It was a thriving commercial center for an international community of slave traders. Agents of other nations resided in or near Port Royal, purchasing slaves for the mining and agricultural industries of their colonies and arranging for their transport. English ships and sloops redistributed slaves to English colonies and other islands in the Caribbean as well as the mainland. Alongside the pirates, merchants, and ships of all flags, slavers of many nations weighed anchor at Port Royal and departed rich with holds full of sugar, rum, and molasses.

Sir Hans Sloane, whose collections and recordings of flora and fauna were the foundation of the British Museum, kept one of the best early journals of Jamaica's trade, social life, and customs. Of Jamaica's merchants Sloane observed:

> The Trade of Jamaica is either with Europe or America. That of Europe consists in bringing thither flower, biskets, beef, pork, all manner of clothing for masters and servants, as osnabrigs, blew cloth, liquors of all sorts, etc. Madera wine is also imported in great quantities from the island of that name, by vessels sent from England on that purpose, on all which the merchant is supposed to gain generally 50 per cent profit. The goods sent back again, or exported from the island, are sugars, most part muscavadoes, indico, cotton-wool, ginger, pimento all-spice or Jamaica-pepper, fustickwood, prince-wood, lignum vitae, arnotto, log-wood, and the several commodities they have from the Spaniards of the West Indies (with whom they have a private trade) as sarsparilla, cacao nuts, cochineal, etc. on which they get considerable profit. There is about 20 percent in Exchange between Spanish Money and Gold in Jamaica, and English money paid in England. Their trade among the Spanish privately in America managed chiefly by sloops, is with all those things mentioned to come from Europe, especially clothing, as serges, etc. on which they have either in truck of money 55 per cent gain, one moiety whereof goes to masters and owners of sloops, the other to the merchant adventurer. There are also many Negroes sold this way to the Spaniards, who are either brought lately from Guinea, or bad servants, or mutinous in plantations. They are sold to very good profit; but if they have many cicatrices, or scars on them, the marks of their severe corrections, they are not very profitable.
>
> The commodities the English have in return, besides money, most usually are cacoa, sassaparilla, pearls, emeralds, cochineal, hides, etc. The Trade in Jamaica with the Dutch at Corasol is chiefly for provisions which are wanted very much on that island. The island of Curosol is very small, and very little provision grows on it. The chief advantage the Dutch have of it, is, that tis a place whereto goods are brought to trade with the Spaniards privately on the Continent of America, for which purpose tis very advantageously seated.
>
> There is likewise trade with this island from New England, and New York. It consists usually in an exchange of rum, molossus, sugar, and money, for

> horses, beef, pork, and flower or rusk, tis managed by Brigantines, or small craft, who now and then touch at the Bahama islands, and kill seals, or whales for the train-oil, or sperm ceti.
>
> When the trade of the Assiento for furnishing the Spanish West Indies with Negros was in this island, it was not only very beneficial to the African Company and their factors, but to the Governours of this island, as well as the captains of the frigates who convey'd them to Porto Belo, and on their delivery there had immediately paid them in money agreed on by the head. (1707–25:iv–vi)

In 1692, the disastrous earthquake reduced the town to approximately one-third of its former size (twenty-five acres; eighteen usable acres). All the buildings located to the north as far back as New or Jew Street fell into the water, thus consuming all the waterfront buildings, wharves, storehouses, two forts, and more. One survivor wrote: "On Tuesday, the 7th of June, 1692, betwixt Eleven and Twelve at Noon, I being at a Tavern, we felt the House shake, the Bricks begin to rise in the Floor, and at the same instant heard one in the Street cry. An Earthquake. . . . The Houses from the Jew's Street end to the Breastwork were all shak'd down, save only Eight or Ten that remained from the Balcony upwards above the Water" (letter no. VI, in Sloane 1694; reprinted in Renny 1807:222–23).

The demand for sugar in Europe (partly brought on by the new demand for tea and coffee imports) was insatiable, and the planters in Jamaica increased in power and influence over the latter half of the seventeenth century. Eventually the plantation owners succeeded in quelling the tide of buccaneers that flowed in and out of Port Royal. Although the looting of Spanish treasure fleets became a thing of memory, wealth continued to pour into the port through legitimate commerce, including the trade in African slaves (D. Johnson 2000:4–5). Even as Port Royal was starting to decline, Jamaica's slave trade was on the rise. Although a shell of its former self during the first half of the eighteenth century, Port Royal remained a vital transshipment port, providing slaves for the Caribbean sugar industry. With the trade of the joint stock companies as well as that of smugglers and separate traders (independent merchants who operated under company-granted licenses), the traffic in slaves in Port Royal was a major component of the maritime mercantile community.

The Decline of Port Royal

The decade after the earthquake brought many changes to Port Royal. The British Royal Navy was expanding rapidly and Port Royal was the West Indian hub for His Majesty's ships; Jamaica's export economy was becoming increasingly more valuable to England. In the aftermath of the earthquake, a number of less affluent merchants quit the island for the American mainland. During the same period, trade in African slaves became more profitable to individual merchants, many of whom were Port Royalists. By 1696 it appeared that the town was about to regain its commercial dominance in Jamaica. In researching land transactions through the analysis of Jamaican deed records in Jamaica, Claypole suggested that in the later 1690s Port Royal remained a more expensive and desirable place than Kingston, which saw little growth between 1696 and 1697. In 1698 the Royal African Company was forced to relinquish its monopoly and accept the opening of the trade to private and separate traders, who would pay the company a 10 percent duty. Port Royal was poised to regain its eminence as the leading port in the British West Indies.

However, on January 9, 1703, the inhabitants of Port Royal once again experienced a major catastrophe—this time a disastrous fire. Apparently the twenty-five or so acres of Port Royal that had not slumped into the harbor did not provide nearly enough room for all the merchants who still wished to do business there; the buildings had become very densely packed together, and once the fire started, it spread with devastating effect. It was through this disaster that the New Street Tavern was destroyed. A letter to a gentleman in England written by a merchant who survived the fire remarked that "in three hours time most of the houses were all in flames, and by Ten at night all burnt to the ground . . . nothing but the two Forts. . . . Most parts of Provisions, silks, Linens, Cloaths, Spices and . . . all sorts of merchandizes to an incredible values . . . were totally burnt . . . the fire was so violent swift . . . that few could have time to carry off their cash, much less any goods or household stuff." Apparently "several evil-disposed persons under the pretense of helping the miserable and distressed inhabitants of Port Royal during the fire, did plunder, take and carry away great quantities of all sorts of goods, merchandizes, gold, silver, jewels and plate. . . . A committee was appointed to receive the goods [back] and included Capt. John Lewis, Ezekiel Gomers, and Moses Yesurun Cordoso" (Calendar of State Papers 21/3:522, 1702–3, p. 124, Jamaica Archives).

In great distress from the fire, Port Royal merchants Richard Thompson, Thomas Hudson, Peter Beckford, and Lewis Galdy unsuccessfully requested relief from paying custom duty on wine and cocoa lost in the fire; Galdy's request to import sails from Curaçao to outfit his ship was likewise denied (ibid., 143). Instead, in February 1704, the Council of Trade and Plantations to the Queen equalized the conditions of trade for Port Royal and Kingston (ibid., 1704, 5:27). By 1712, trade was left open and unrestricted. The Royal African Company, which enjoyed protection for the slave trade, suffered from open competition, further depressing the economy of Port Royal. As a spoil of victory in the War of Spanish Succession (Queen Anne's War), the English Crown was awarded the *asiento* (license to trade slaves into the Spanish possessions) at the signing of the Treaty of Utrecht in 1713. The *asiento* was the coveted prize of the international slave trade. Before the Treaty of Utrecht, Spanish colonials bought their slaves primarily from Dutch merchants and, after 1701, from the French. The 1713 contract, which Queen Anne immediately signed over to the South Seas Company, gave the company the sole right to supply slaves to Spain's colonies for a period of thirty years. The company was to supply the Spanish colonies with at least 144,000 slaves under the terms of the 1713 *asiento,* delivering them at a rate of 4,800 per year (D. Johnson 2000:32–33). Because the offices of the South Seas Company were located in Kingston, Port Royal fell further into decline as across the harbor in Kingston, a throng of slave traders supplying both the Spanish and the island's internal market accumulated the wealth that had once flowed into Port Royal. From this point forward it would be Kingston, not Port Royal, that would be the center of British West Indian commerce (D. Johnson 2000:149).

The New Street Assemblage

The New Street Tavern site survived the 1692 earthquake; in fact, when the quake caused the waterfront to slump into the harbor, the tavern site occupied a more visible and prominent place on the street closer to the water. New Street is also occasionally referred to as "Jew Street"; it is two blocks from the location of the Sephardic Jewish synagogue. The New Street block was excavated in the early 1970s by the Jamaica National Trust Commission under the direction of Anthony J. Priddy. Archaeological investigations of the site revealed many different occupation levels and areas dating from 1660 to the twentieth century. I received permission from the Jamaica National Heritage Trust (JNHT) and Priddy to analyze the artifacts from portions of the site that I believed to be the remains of a tavern. I had great assistance from the JNHT archaeologists in Port Royal and Richard McClure, former artifacts officer for JNHT, who assisted Priddy with excavations.

Priddy concluded that there were two houses or buildings with a common dividing wall that faced New Street; this would have been the wall between Houses 3 and 4 as illustrated by Oliver Cox (1984). Cox provides an excellent interpretive illustration of what he thought the New Street structures, yards, and cookhouses would have looked like in 1692. He suggested that most of the buildings were one brick wide and of one or two stories. Next, I consider the range of artifacts recovered from the New Street site.

Ceramics

Beverage consumption (drinking/serving) ceramic forms. As expected, drinking of both alcoholic and non-alcoholic beverages was a primary activity within the New Street Tavern site. Ceramic drinking containers comprised a minimum vessel count of 74 vessels or 27.8 percent of the entire ceramic assemblage. The ceramic forms are typical of the forms found at other tavern sites. A total of six main form categories were recovered; these included individual and communal vessels that served both hot and cool beverages: punch bowls, posset or drinking pots, mugs and tankards, cups or cans, tea bowls/cups, and small jugs. These forms would have contained rum or fruit punch, posset, beer, ale, wine, rum, coffee, chocolate, tea, milk, water, and so forth.

Punch bowls are usually hemispherical vessels with plain rims; monteiths include another variety of deeply scalloped or notched rim. They range in capacity from one pint to several gallons and were used as serving containers into which individual cups or wine glasses were dipped to retrieve punch. A minimum vessel count of twelve English chinoiserie type blue-on-white tin-glazed earthenware partially reconstructed punch bowls were discovered in the tavern site and all were burned (five were solid rimmed and seven were monteiths). Similar monteiths were listed in a 1699 estate inventory of a pottery works at Southwark, London (Britton 1990:67). Monteiths were listed in four different entries as "monteths" under the heading "white and painted perfect ware, and two different sizes, mean middle and small middle, by the dozen and half dozen." They were listed as one of the highest-valued items. One "mean middle monteth" was valued at 20 pence; small ones were valued at 15 pence each. When compared to "5 doz wine cupps att 7 s 6 d," it would have been equivalent to one dozen wine cups at 18 pence. Archaeological investigations at Colonial Williamsburg (Ed Chappell to the author, 1996) have produced no monteiths in seventy years of excavation, bringing credence to the view that they were elements of very genteel dining or drinking scenes.

A minimum vessel count of fourteen mugs or tankards were recovered from the tavern site. Five varieties are represented, including a large burned British brown salt-glazed stoneware tankard, tin-glazed earthenware, German Westerwald type, and Staffordshire mottled refined earthenware.

Sixteen English tin-glazed earthenware drinking cups were recovered from the New Street site. These are small, handled drinking vessels of less than a pint in capacity (Beaudry et al. 1983:29) of various shapes (cans or straight sided or round or bulbous-bodied cups). They were used to consume both alcoholic and nonalcoholic beverages, such as caudle, coffee, and chocolate.

Excavations at the New Street site recovered thirteen English tin-glazed earthenware and one porcelain tea cups or bowls. These were separated from the cup forms because they have no handle and were used to serve and drink tea, coffee, and wine. Just how discriminating the Port Royal users were as to their specific function we will never know. Twelve of these vessels were found in the building area and all show fire damage. They are decorated with a stylized Chinese foliate pattern of fruit and dots and are marked on the interior base. Their style is similar to examples excavated in Williamsburg. Evidence of the tea/wine cups and cans suggests that this tavern may have been a combination tavern and coffee shop. Tea as well as wine and other alcoholic beverages were served in coffee shops during this time

Figure 4.3. Porcelain cups recovered from the "Sunken City" of Port Royal. Courtesy of Donny Hamilton, Texas A&M University.

(Griffiths 1967:18). Although the tin-enamel tea bowls may not have been worth very much money at 18 pence per dozen, the value of their use eclipsed their monetary value. The consumption of tea and the use of tea service items were social acts proclaiming high status (Griffiths 1967; Roth 1961; Sweeney 1994). Charles Booker's 1688 probate inventory in Port Royal for a probable coffeehouse valued tea at one pound per pound, a substantial sum when compared to seven cases of brandy valued at 5 pounds, 5 shillings, fifty pounds of pewter at 2 pounds, and thirteen leather chairs at 4 pounds.

Fifteen small jugs represent 20.3 percent of the ceramic beverage forms from the New Street site. Jugs were handled vessels of bulbous form with a cylindrical neck rising from a pronounced shoulder with or without a gutter (Beaudry et al. 1983:23). These were used as individual drinking vessels or small serving vessels. They may have contained alcoholic or non-alcoholic beverages (e.g., beer or milk).

Beverage storage vessels. This type of vessel includes bottle forms, represented here only by stoneware vessels including three light reddish-brown Bellarmine bottles and one cobalt Westerwald vessel, generally dating from 1650 to 1700. Interestingly, a similar Bellarmine to the one found at the New Street site was recovered from the 1692 underwater earthquake level from a supposed tavern by the Institute of Nautical Archaeology (INA) team.

Food consumption and storage ceramic vessel forms. This group, which includes plates, dishes, porringers, bowls, and jars, comprised 96 vessels and 36.1 percent of the ceramic container assemblage. This is not surprising since Port Royal taverns catered to temporary residents and travelers who would need a place to eat, drink, and possibly sleep. Nine major food consumption vessel types were recovered from the site. Flatware forms used for both solid and liquid foods included plates, platters, and dishes, lobed dishes or "cracknels," and saucers (or condiment dishes). Hollowware included various bowl forms (e.g., porringers, small bowls, and large bowls). Lids and salt cellars were also recovered.

The largest subgroup within this group consisted of plates (n = 23), defined as eating vessels 7 to 10 inches in diameter either with or without a foot ring. Plates recovered from the site included both shallow and deep (i.e., soup) forms (Beaudry et al. 1983:26). Tin-glazed earthenware included four plain white, fifteen blue-on-white, three with two shades of blue and black trekking, and one decorated polychrome. The most diagnostic plates included one octagonally shaped rim form. It is tin-glazed decorated with tassels alternating with five-petaled flowers and has been identified as the William and Mary style pattern, probably made in Bristol or Brislington (Wilcoxen 1992). Phillip Mayes's excavations of Port Royal recovered similar vessels (Mayes 1972:97–98); similar plates have also been recovered at St. Mary's City in Maryland and in London. Eleven tin-glazed earthenware plates were decorated with the same pattern and were located in the building area. Several chargers (n = 3) measuring greater than ten inches in diameter and primarily used for serving food were also recovered.

Lobed dishes or cracknalls were also identified in the assemblage. These are deep, circular, fluted tin-glazed earthenware dishes that were used for serving or display; they may have also been used as fruit dishes. Eighty-one sherds representing a minimum of six vessels were excavated from the building area and all were damaged by fire. One is a small, plain, fluted dish approximately six inches in diameter. Two blue-on-white vessels were decorated with the common William and Mary pattern like the octagonal plate. The form as illustrated is about twelve inches in diameter and has a flat base and twelve fluted sides. Three cracknalls were plain white and highly decorated.

Porringers (n = 19) are small bowls that were usually shallow in relation to the diameter and have at least one and sometimes two handles or lugs. They were used for eating porridge, pottage (stew), or soup (Beaudry et al. 1983:25). Straight-sided porringers were also sometimes used as a bleeding dish for bloodletting. Among the porringers recovered from the site was one vessel from the Saintonge region of western France near the port cities of Rochefort and La Rochelle. It has a white slip under a green copper glaze and features a reddish-colored paste. One blue-on-white chinoiserie tin-glazed and seventeen plain, white, English tin-glazed earthenware porringers were also recovered.

Other forms recovered from this group include several types of bowls. Eleven English tin-enamel small bowls were recovered, as were two blue-on-white English tin-enamel and seven plain large bowls or basins, most likely used for serving, dining, washing, or shaving (Beaudry et al. 1983:26).

At least eighteen plain, white, English tin-glazed salt cellars were represented in the assemblage. All exhibit fire damage. Salt cellars are pedestaled vessels with a receptacle to place and serve salt. Several varieties of standing salts were produced and were recovered from the excavated remains of the tavern site. The building area yielded sixteen salt vessels while two were found in the cookhouse/kitchen. Three varieties of standing salts were recovered, including one small, one medium, and one large early "curle" salts (also called ram's horn). Curle salts have spool-shaped pedestaled bodies, a circular rim and base, and a recess in the top for the salt. A distinguishing feature of this form includes three vertical ram's horn finial supports (or curled knobs) attached to the rim, over which a napkin could be placed to keep the salt from absorbing moisture. Salt was also a symbol of social status and, as a seasoning and preservative for food, was in high demand. Salt is listed in two separate Jamaican probate inventories for 1687 and 1689: Dorothy Richardson of Port Royal had half a barrel of salt valued at 13 shillings (Probate Inventories [PI], Jamaica Archives, St. Jago de la Vega, 3:54), and Sir Henry Morgan's inventory listed "a parcel of salt" valued at one pound and 10 shillings (PI, 3:259).

Food condiment/spice/apothecary storage. These types of vessels were represented in the assemblage by two jars, probably Hispanic, and sixty large galley pots. The galley pots are represented by large blue-on-white squat Abarrello-type English tin-glazed earthenware pots excavated from the site. Forty-eight of these were recovered from the cookhouse/kitchen and twelve from the building area. Because most of these were located in the kitchen, it is believed that they were used to store spices and/or condiments (jams, dried fruit, mustards, allspice, etc.) and not medicine.

Health and hygiene. Four main ceramic vessel forms were used for health and/or hygiene, which included activities associated with storing medicines, ointments, and cosmetics, bathing, and personal toiletries. These included small ointment/apothecary/galley pots (which included seventeen plain) and ten chamber pots. One is possibly Hispanic origin or Borderware, one is a highly burned Westerwald chamber pot, and the rest are plain English tin-enamel ware.

Glass. Fine glasswares were expensive items and are probably one of the best indicators of status within the realm of glass artifacts. The tavern site (building and kitchen areas) contained 141 drinking glassware sherds and included a minimum vessel count of 50 recognizable wine glasses, represented by stems, among a total minimum vessel count of 484 drinking glasses identified by Pat McClenaghan (1988:86) from the Port Royal collection. The majority (72 percent) were excavated from the building area. A total of 121 sherds or 85.8 percent of the wine glass assemblage were burned or melted. A minimum of 41 of these sherds were diagnostic stems. Three main varieties and a total of six subvarieties were identified. All of the stem varieties were handblown and produced in England during the last quarter of the seventeenth century when England was emerging as a leading glass producer. Fifteen Ravenscroft (1675–1700) short, hollow-blown inverted baluster stems were identified, and twenty-two knopped (1695–1725) solid inverted baluster with knop stems and nine solid inverted baluster with basal knop stems (1695–1725) were recovered. The quantity and variety of stemware lends support to the hypothesis that the site existed as a tavern/coffeehouse that catered to clientele of a higher social class.

A total of 2,555 wine bottle glass sherds were recovered, 1,874 from the building and 681 in the cookhouse/kitchen. Many of these (1,029, or 40.1 percent) were burned or melted. Diagnostic necks or lips represent a minimum of 104 bottles.

Pipes. Two types of clay smoking tobacco pipes were recovered from the New Street Tavern. These included imported white tobacco pipes from England and Holland and locally manufactured red-clay tobacco pipes. The red-clay pipes were analyzed by Heidtke (1992). Both red- and white-clay pipes were also catalogued by Richard McClure of the Jamaica National Historical Trust; McClure made the pipes available to me for use in this study.

The tavern site contained semi-whole kaolin pipes, marked and unmarked bowls with stems, and bowl and stem fragments. Counts from the building and the kitchen totaled 2,148 fragments. The minimum count for both areas was 211 pipes. This figure includes the total number of unmarked bowls with stems (119) and the total number of marked bowls (92). The site contained 2,052 measurable pipe stems. These included 202 bowls with stems and 1,850 fragments; over 52 percent measured 5/64 of an inch. Stems with a bore diameter of 6/64 of an inch represented the second highest at 39.8 percent. Applying Binford's (1962) and Hanson's (1969) formula, the combined date of the occupation is 1721.3 (Binford) and 1713.3 (Hanson). It should be kept in mind that Noël Hume (1970:301) argues that a thirty-year tolerance should be applied to pipe stem dating.

The red-clay tobacco pipes represent only a small percentage of the overall artifact assemblage. A total of eighteen red-clay pipe fragments were recovered from both the kitchen and building area. The entire red-clay pipe assemblage at Port Royal was analyzed by Heidtke (1992). He proposed that these pipes were locally manufactured and postulated that the source of clay was the Liguanea Plain region that is now part of Kingston.

Summary

The combined artifact assemblage for the New Street site suggests that the tavern was occupied sometime after the 1692 earthquake through the 1703 fire. The ceramic forms, especially the decorated tin-glazed earthenware styles, date well within the range of the suggested period. The Chinese squatting motif, the William and Mary pattern, the dotted tea cups, and the banded large galley pots were all popular in the late seventeenth century. The total assemblage had an average date of 1702, while the wine bottles dated to circa 1704.5. The white-clay tobacco pipes dated within the suggested tolerance of plus or minus thirty years from circa 1709 to 1724. Comparisons between the New Street Tavern site and other colonial tavern sites suggest that New Street certainly fits criteria as suggested by Bragdon (1988).

The combined evidence based on vessel form suggests that this site served as a meeting place and was probably a coffeehouse.

Analysis of Material Recovered from the New Street Tavern

The New Street Tavern assemblage was analyzed using minimum vessel counts, vessel form, and vessel function (Table 4.1). These forms, historical documents, and comparative sources were used to predict function of vessel use, contents, and activities in relationship to the archaeological context. When all the artifacts are combined it is possible to visualize the activities associated with the tavern and the behavior of the tavern occupants and clientele. No longer do ceramics represent the largest portion of vessels because they have been subdivided into several functions. Thus the results suggest that Port Royal tavern-goers smoked, drank, stored their drink, dined, flavored their food with condiments, and accommodated some standards of personal hygiene.

The New Street Tavern site artifact assemblage also provides direct evidence to suggest that this tavern catered to a clientele that had considerable social standing. Both old and new status symbols were found among the tavern remains. These were reflected in an abundance of desirable goods, the presence of new fashionable decorated wares and vessel forms, individual drinking and eating vessels, and forms that would have contained expensive consumables.

The tin-glazed earthenware assemblage alone reflects the status and social class of the occupants and the intended clients of the establishment. Decorated tin-glazed earthenwares were considered finer wares and were used primarily for drinking/serving, dining/serving, and display. In contrast, the less expensive English slipwares and other coarse earthenwares, such as locally produced yabbas, were less valued. Because the tin-glazed earthenwares were found in such large quantities, comprising over 95 percent of the ceramic assemblage, the New Street Tavern most likely catered to people who defined themselves through their discerning tastes. The tin-glazed earthenware contained fashionable decorative styles and elaborate forms, attesting to the quality of wares being purchased by the owners of the establishment and being used by its patrons. The most traditional status symbols recovered from the site were probably the standing "curle" salt cellars. These included eighteen tin-glazed earthenware vessels of three different sizes. Additionally, the monteiths were decorated in the fashionable chinoiserie style.

More than any other artifact, probably the most recognized new social status items were associated with the preparation, serving, or drinking of tea. Tea was imported from China and was an expensive commodity. In England, it was introduced during the middle of the seventeenth century at the same time that coffee consumption promoted the development of London's coffeehouses (Griffiths 1967:18). It was not until the late 1720s that tea drinking in the North American

Table 4.1 Diagnostic Artifact Sherd Counts from New Street Tavern

	Building		Kitchen		Total Sherd Count	
Artifact Type	n	%	n	%	n	%
Ceramics	2,126	41	541	24.5	2,667	36.1
Wine glasses	113	2.2	28	1.3	141	1.9
Glass bottles	1,874	36.2	681	30.9	2,555	34.6
White-clay pipes	1,053	20.3	952	43.1	2,005	27.2
Red-clay pipes	14	0.3	4	0.2	18	0.2

home, with all its associated paraphernalia of new containers and utensils, was established as the preeminent genteel ritual (Sweeney 1994:8). Until the mid-1700s few outside of the colonial elite could afford to join the select company of frequent tea drinkers (Sweeney 1994:10). The tea cups/bowls recovered from the New Street Tavern site strongly support the premise that the tavern catered to a genteel clientele. This evidence also suggests the possibility that the site was a specialized tavern or coffeehouse. Among the fourteen total tea bowls/cups excavated from New Street, there were twelve matching blue-on-white tin-glazed earthenware vessels decorated with a Chinese symbol in the center of the interior side of the bowl. Additionally, on the exterior of the Nevers-style tin-glazed earthenware cup/can form there is a white-on-blue hand-painted "teapot" design. It is unclear what the significance of this motif was to the users, but it does show that tea drinking was meaningful enough to be symbolized as a decoration on a drinking vessel.

Tableware in matching sets signified each diner's provisional membership at the dinner table (C. Carson 1994). Besides the bowls/cups, other matching sets recovered from the site included eleven tin-glazed earthenware plates. These were all recovered from the building area. They were decorated with a blue-on-white Chinese-style foliate pattern with a meandering border.

New changes in social status were also reflected in individual drinking vessels, such as the tin-glazed earthenware and stoneware mug/tankard, cup, and tea bowl/cup forms, and the wine glass stemware. There were thirty-four individual ceramic drinking vessels and at least fifty wine glasses. Individual drinking vessels (in contrast to communal vessels) represented 66 percent of the total number of drinking vessels; the remaining 34 percent included communal punch bowls, posset pots, and small jugs. The presence of a large number of individual wine glasses suggests that elite manners characterized by increased sensitivity to hygiene and to the individual were taking root among the elite of Port Royal; the imported glass stemware from England demonstrated that even after the earthquake, taverns in Port Royal imported expensive luxury goods (Sweeney 1994:8). Five different varieties were recovered from the site. They represent the creative change in inverted baluster stemware forms that were popular during this short period. Furthermore, the presence of large number of glass wine bottles may also be indicative of a higher social status site. These were used to both store and serve alcohol. Wine bottles were easily broken and more expensive to replace in the initial cost than other storage containers such as barrels.

Finally, the contents of these vessels should be taken into account when looking at the status of the clientele. This could be known by considering the prescribed use of specific kinds of vessels revealed in historical documents. Contents may have been desirable, expensive, or only accessible to certain groups of individuals. In addition to tea, these expensive commodities included wine, salt, coffee, and chocolate. Not everyone had access to these new products, expressed in the wealth to procure them and the codes of behavior defining the rules of their consumption. Historical documents reveal that during the late seventeenth and early eighteenth centuries, Port Royal was a "taste-maker and fashionable center" (C. Carson 1994). Contemporary travel accounts, histories, probate inventories, and letters from merchants and naval officers all corroborate the view that Port Royalists aspired to elite status. Places like the New Street Tavern were gathering spots for the merchants and other residents of Port Royal who sought new social status and cultural knowledge, and expressed that ambition through the public consumption of elite commodities in the taverns of "the wickedest city on earth."

Conclusion

As was the case in North American urban seaports, the wealthy merchant class of Port Royal was responsible for setting new trends, including consumption trends. Successful merchants included both temporary and permanent residents of the city. Merchants from Great Britain, New England, other Caribbean islands, and Spanish America came to live and work in Port Royal. Port Royal had its own set of wealthy merchants, however. By 1690–1700, these merchants included Jamaican-born creoles, English newcomers, and a minority of Irish, French, Spanish, and Portuguese Sephardic Jews.

These Port Royalists would have gone to a tavern/coffeehouse to conduct their business and socialize with individuals of similar tastes, values, and habits. While at the tavern wealthy merchants would have expected to be served with the latest fashionable wares of dishes and glass forms that they themselves were responsible for introducing and that they desired and used themselves. Likewise, the presence of a wealthy merchant class in the seaport would have created incentives for a tavern keeper or owner to stock up on the latest fashions to be able to attract and keep the merchant class clientele. Thus, if the archaeological assemblage from a tavern site suggests that it was catering to a higher social class during the late seventeenth to early eighteenth centuries in bustling seaports, those customers would have been the class of wealthy merchants, sea captains, and probably naval officers.

The analysis of the New Street Tavern archaeological assemblages suggests that the site represented one of the taverns/coffeehouses catering to the local elite. The data support the premise that tavern assemblages can provide evidence for the social class of the clientele—the main users of the tavern. The site assemblages, through archaeological analysis of the vessel form/function and identification of use of vessel contents and perceived status symbols from historical documents, provided evidence for a specific social class—the wealthy merchant or new middle to upper-middle class. In the later 1690s, a wealthy merchant class chose to go to the tavern located on New Street, at that time one of the main streets in the tiny seaport of Port Royal. This particular tavern was, like the rest of Port Royal, consumed by a devastating fire in 1703. Remains reflecting usage were left behind and covered by additional construction after the fire. The excavated artifacts, when analyzed, reflected use and activities of the occupants and clientele.

C. Carson (1994:616) suggests that "the first signs of the consumer revolution appeared almost simultaneously among the freest-wheeling participants in the British and American economy in the later half of the seventeenth century." These participants were the merchant class. Therefore, the more we know, especially about taverns from important seaports during the late seventeenth and early eighteenth centuries, the more we can learn about these first trendsetters that took the lead on introducing a new age of consumerism.

II

THE ARCHAEOLOGY OF THE PLANTATION SYSTEM

5

Reflections on Seville

Rediscovering the African Jamaican Settlements at Seville Plantation, St. Ann's Bay

Douglas V. Armstrong

> Just before the morning break a student called me over to identify an object that she had just excavated. I knelt down to examine it and felt a shiver of anxiety upon recognizing the object and its function. The object, a wrist shackle, was used to restrict and control a person. Recovered from a trash deposit on the boundary of the village . . . it was a salient reminder of a history which survived just beneath the surface at Seville—a history that must not be forgotten.
>
> —Seville African Jamaican Project field notes, June 5, 1991

Introduction

Archaeological and historical investigations at Seville Plantation have produced a broad body of data that can be used to examine the conditions of slavery and enslavement in Jamaica. It is hoped that archaeological studies like the Seville project will encourage introspective exploration of Jamaica's past by illuminating both the complexity of social interaction and the contexts of dynamic creativity embedded in Jamaica's cultural landscape. Archaeological research is an important tool for uncovering the heritage retained within Jamaica's plantation sites. Since this essay is reflective in nature and designed to summarize what has been and can be learned at Seville, I will begin by setting the stage of my 1987 return to Jamaica, when I began the exploration of the former British colonial sugar estate that is now Seville National Historic Park.

In May 1987 I turned off Jamaica's North Coast Road, just west of the town of St. Ann's Bay, and slowly proceeded up the palm tree–lined lane that serves as an entrance to Seville Plantation. The estate, which takes its name from Sevilla la Nueva, the sixteenth-century Spanish settlement located within its boundaries, was a large sugar estate founded soon after the British took Jamaica from the Spanish in 1655 (see Woodward, this volume). The plantation comprised some 2,500 acres consolidated in 1670 by Richard Hemming. Sugar was produced as a cash crop by an average of 275 enslaved laborers from its founding through the abolition of slavery in 1838. For several years following emancipation, Seville continued as a sugar plantation utilizing wage-labor tenants; in the later nineteenth century production shifted first to bananas and finally to copra, derived from coconut palms. The population of the laborers' villages decreased dramatically with emancipation; however, a small group of tenants continued to live on the estate until the mid-1880s.

As I made my way up the road in 1987 I was taken back in time and filled with questions. Extending from the sea all the way up the fertile strip of coastal alluvium were fields in which sugar cane had once been grown. Both the sugar cane and the laborers who produced it were gone from the cultural landscape of the 1980s; however, their former presence was vivid in my mind. I was curious about what we would learn about the enslaved laborers who once worked these fields. As I drove inland the landscape around me transitioned to foothills framed by mountains. At this point I encountered the estate's sugar-processing works. The sugar works include the ruins of water and cattle mills, a boiling house, and a complex of related processing and storage buildings. Although these structures were overgrown with brush and their roofs had collapsed, they still projected a dominant presence on the landscape. These ruined buildings served as a reminder of the long hot hours of crushing and boiling sugar cane endured by men and women brought from Africa as enslaved labor to produce the lucrative and addictive commodity of sugar (see Mintz 1985). To the right I could see the less obvious but nonetheless curious layout of a series of barbecues, or flat slabs of mortar that were used during the days of slavery to dry pimento berries (allspice, *Pimenta dioica*), the fruit of the richly aromatic endemic bay laurel tree that grows throughout the lower hilly sections of the plantation. More recently, these features rotated between pimento drying and the drying of copra when coconut palms replaced sugar as the estate's primary crop in the late nineteenth century. Copra production remained a significant feature of the estate's landscape until the 1980s.

The combination of sugar and pimento works projects elements of the plantation's social and economic complexity. The estate overseer's house lies within this complex of works and is built upon an earlier cattle mill. This overlap of historical features highlights transitions through time in the industrial growth and managerial structure of the estate. The cattle mill had been replaced by a waterwheel located on the Church River, a year-round source of power made even more reliable by the construction of a dam and a short aqueduct. From the earliest days of the estate's operation in the 1670s, the crushing of cane via a cattle mill represented a form of industrial production; the shift to water power reflects an intensification of industrial production. The transformation of the old cattle mill to a new manager's house reflects a shift in the scale of management to the point of production, as well as a greater social and spatial distance that developed between the planter and the laborers of the estate in the late eighteenth century. The question I pondered concerned how the shifts in industrial production and management strategies were reflected in the conditions and lifeways of the enslaved.

As one moves past the works, the road turns and cuts a diagonal path up the hill. Farther up the hill, and set within a context of a formal lawn and garden, is the planter's residence, known in Jamaica as a Great House. The Great House is associated with stables, a kitchen, and a bake oven; from its hilltop vantage point the Great House looks out over the cane fields, the bay, and the sea beyond. From the seventeenth through the nineteenth centuries, this house would have stood out as a significant structure to anyone coming into St. Ann's Bay by sea; the building was used as a directional vector by mariners entering the bay, as evidenced by a map of the St. Ann's Bay region made in 1721, curated at the National Library of Jamaica. The Great House was built to project the wealth and social prominence of the planter; just as it had been in the past, the Great House complex remains a dominant feature on the historical landscape, even as its role has shifted from a locus of authority and power to its current one as a museum in which the story of the plantation is told.

The managerial houses of the planter, overseer, and timekeeper have endured and provide clues as to the temporal and geographic scales of the sugar estate landscape. The survival of these buildings and their continued prominence in the landscape sharply contrast with the virtual absence in 1987 of any structural remains invoking the presence of the people of African descent who had worked on the estate. Moreover, the embedded implications of power and authority were dug into the landscape in the form of a trench fortification at the front edge of the Great House grounds, immediately above the steep slope up from the plain below. This trench was described as a "rifling lawn . . . with a battery of eighteen small guns *en barbette*" by naturalist Hans Sloane in a discussion of his visit to the estate in 1688 (Sloane 1707–25; Armstrong and Kelly 2000:378). Finally, the prominence of the planters was memorialized by an array of formal gardens and the placement of a planter cemetery on the eastern edge of the formal lawn. Virtually all of the major structural elements of the seventeenth- to twentieth-century English sugar estate founded by the Hemming family were visible during my 1987 visit. The overall landscape retained the general pastoral character and the spatial outlines of the former agricultural industrial complex but without the contrasting context of the underlying economic and social conditions that made this Jamaican sugar estate and hundreds like it so economically profitable and socially oppressive. Notably absent from the visual landscape were the houses of the hundreds of laborers of African descent who had been enslaved on this large estate from its founding in the 1670s through 1838 and who remained on the estate during the post-emancipation era. My challenge was to locate the settlements associated with the enslaved labors of Seville Plantation, define the boundaries of their living areas, and excavate their houses and yards in order to give these sites and the people who had once lived in them a presence in the landscape. In May 1987 I engaged this challenge, knowing that the ruins of these sites were there to be found although they were missing from the visual and interpretive landscape of the late twentieth century.

The 1987 trip was not my first visit to Seville. Over the previous seven years I had made several visits to the site, walked the hillsides, and located ruins that confirmed the location of settlements denoted by small black rectangles on maps drawn in 1721 and 1791. As the archaeological study of the African Jamaican settlements at Seville began I wondered: How much of these ruins still survived? Would I recover individual houses and yards as I had at Drax Hall (Armstrong 1990)? The maps indicated a change in the location of the laborer settlement, and I was excited about the prospect of examining two temporally and spatially distinct settlements; but why were there two villages? In 1981 I had walked through the site with an elderly man, Carpi Rose, who had been born in the more recent settlement. He said that the more recent settlement (the one indicated on the 1791 map) was the only one he knew. As we stood at the site that he said was probably his grandmother's house, he wondered if we would actually find any remains from the house and then mused that it would be nice if we found a favorite toy he had lost in the yard as a child. On the first day of the 1987 survey I wondered: What would I learn about their lives that could be interpreted in publications and in the presentation of interpretive materials at the National Historic Park at Seville? To what extent could I get at the details of life in each of the early laborer communities? Would the project yield specific details concerning the internal dynamics of cultural transformation and community building, power relations, social relations, ethnicity, and identity? Would I find Carpi Rose's toy or at least a record that would project the specifics of the active lives of those who lived in each household and collectively each settlement? I also asked myself if the lives of the laborers at Seville Estate could be projected back into the landscape in a way that signified their presence and the conditions under which they lived.

Archaeology at the African Jamaican Settlements at Seville Plantation

In exploring the archaeological ruins at Seville we were looking for ways by which the laborer community defined and transformed itself given the restrictions imposed by slavery and a constraining economic mode of production. The project aimed to use the data from the settlement to look at life in Seville's laboring community from the inside out, focusing on the materials used by individuals and grouped in spatially distinct households and communities. The studies that would follow explored the origins of African Jamaican society (Armstrong 1992, 1998, 1999), differential contexts of enslaved and free laborers (Armstrong and Kelly

2000; Armstrong and Hauser 2004), and the comparison of these contexts with data derived from houses associated with several levels of plantation management, including planters, overseers, and even mid-level estate timekeepers (Armstrong 1998, 1999, 2005). Publications emerging from this study examined a landscape dominated by sugar production and the restrictive controls of slavery, but they also portrayed a dynamic cultural landscape. Archaeological analysis at Seville revealed evidence of social interaction through the comparison of household and community-level data, and even the very personal and reflective data represented by the contextual remains of individual burials discovered within discrete houseyard areas (Armstrong 1998; Armstrong and Fleischman 2003). As the study evolved the unique combination of data gathered at Seville Plantation allowed for the illumination of a much wider array of social contexts than initially imagined, including a detailed examination of the archaeological remains associated with an East Indian laborer household (Armstrong and Hauser 2004). The Seville project provided, and continues to provide, an excellent data set for the exploration of cultural diversity.

Seville Plantation had been one of my initial targets for archaeological exploration in 1980. I had combed the archives and found a wealth of maps and archival records for Seville and several other Jamaican plantations including the nearby Drax Hall Estate (see Higman 1988; Armstrong 1990). Moreover, the Jamaica National Heritage Trust (JNHT) was interested in having Seville studied. However, in 1980 the plantation house was occupied and the property was not accessible for excavations, so I turned my attention to Drax Hall Plantation (Armstrong 1991b, 1991c, 1990, 1985, 1983a, 1983b, 1981). Prior to the 1980 survey a village was known to have existed in an area known as Seville Commons, located west of the planter's house. However, early maps of the estate found at the National Library of Jamaica indicated the presence of another village up the hill and behind the planter residence. The initial survey in 1980 confirmed the presence of seventeenth- and early eighteenth-century deposits consistent with household activities, but the existence of intact structural remains was not confirmed until a detailed archaeological survey of the estate was completed during my 1987 trip.

In 1987, our initial problem was to formally define and excavate the laborer villages at Seville so that information on the African Jamaican population could be incorporated into public interpretation at the heritage park. In addition, our research goals included an exploration of the processes of cultural transformation and creativity within the community. The survey and testing conducted in 1987 confirmed the presence of two distinct settlements. An early African Jamaican settlement, located behind (south and uphill of) the planter's residence, was occupied from at least 1670 (and perhaps as early as the Spanish occupation) to the early 1780s (Armstrong 1998, 2005), when it was apparently destroyed by storms. When enslaved laborer houses were reconstructed they were built in a new area closer to the cane fields located west of the planter's residence. The new village was located in an area still referred to as Seville Commons. This area was occupied from the 1780s until about 1890. However, as early as 1842, a significant portion of the population left the estate, many taking up residence within a free settlement known as The Priory on parcels given to the formerly enslaved in an area located along the island's main coastal road adjacent to the west side of Seville Estate beginning in 1842–43. This survey and testing were followed by six seasons (1988–93) of excavations focusing on the enslaved and later free laborer contexts of the estate (Armstrong 2005, 2000, 1999, 1998, 1991a, 1991b, 1991c; Armstrong and Kelly 2000; Kelly and Armstrong 1991; Armstrong and Fleischman 2003, 1993; Armstrong and Hauser 2004, 2003; Armstrong and Galle 2007). These studies incorporated excavations of several managerial contexts including the planter's residence, the estate manager's house, and a middle manager's (bookkeeper's) house. After the completion of excavations we found that in addition to these contexts, our study had included a mid-nineteenth-century East Indian laborer's household (Armstrong and Hauser 2003, 2004).

African Jamaican Transformation and Creativity in the Face of Slavery

The archaeological studies at Seville used the rich comparative data from house sites associated with laborers and managers to demonstrate the depth of transformative processes at work within the living contexts of all sectors of the plantation population (Armstrong 1991a, 1991b, 1991c, 1992, 1998, 1999; Armstrong and Kelly 2000; Armstrong and Hauser 2004). While the study focused on the recovery of data from spatially distinct houses and villages occupied by enslaved laborers from Africa, it was the broader comparative analysis of both enslaved and free laborers, several different managerial contexts including data from the planter's residence, and the identification and distinct differences in material assemblages found at the East Indian laborer's residence on the property that really allowed for a definitive statement on the processes of cultural interaction and change.

The model of transformative change used in the Seville Plantation study can help explain the diverse array of cultural expressions found throughout the Caribbean region (Armstrong 1992, 1999; Armstrong and Kelly 2000). Laborers at Seville, and throughout the Caribbean, were confronted by harsh living conditions and oppression, yet they not only endured but even under the restrictions of slavery modified the world around them and created new communities and societies. The archaeological evidence shows that while their range of residence options and mobility were restricted by the confines of and legal and economic sanctions associated with slavery, they did in fact take control of fundamental aspects of their daily lives and created their own social systems. These systems involved the reorganization of space associated with individual house sites, burial plots, and community.

They also involved small-scale economic activities including provisioning and the production and sale of goods in local markets.

The model of transformation, as used to explain the archaeological findings at Seville, demonstrates the "utility of a theoretical approach that views people as active agents of change through transformation processes—even under conditions of slavery and indenture" (Armstrong 1990:5–7, 1998:396). In contexts like Seville transformative processes depend on both the creativity of people gained from past experience, including what they or their ancestors learned in Africa, and their application of such knowledge to new contexts. The material record allows us to recreate a scene of social interaction that projects the creative transformations of residents. In the yard associated with one house (House Area 1.16) we found evidence of an array of activities in the yard, including a hearth marked by three rounded stones and ash deposits. We also found cooking pot fragments that derive from African Jamaican pottery production centers in the Liguanea Plain (see Hauser 1997, 2008) and a mix of slipware mugs, delft bowls and ointment jars, and salt-glazed stoneware plates imported from Europe. All of these items were used by the people who lived in the house and perhaps neighbors who joined them in their yard. But how did these objects get there and what do they mean? Further complexity was revealed in other materials we found, including ground cowry shells, glass beads, silver coins, and gaming pieces (reworked ceramics of local African Jamaican–made pottery as well as delftware pieces imported from Europe). These objects reflect complex social interactions that relate to expressions of personal adornment and even monetary exchange. The mosaic of these remains simultaneously reveals the continuity of West African practices and the commingling of African, European, and Jamaican objects in a new context—a houseyard in Jamaica. Moreover, while not overlooking the constraints associated with the power structures of slavery and external controls on the range of options open to these people, the material record of the things left or lost in the yard is indicative of active, creative processes of social interaction.

The collective deposition of these objects, the presence of features like the hearth, and the social interaction implied by the intersection of these features and artifacts within a defined houseyard living space project the actions of individuals living simultaneously in a household and within a community engaged in processes of reformation and reorganization. These processes produced an ethnogenesis marked by the transformative power of material culture, as objects from a range of sources were adapted to serve local needs and social dynamics (Armstrong and Kelly 2000:372). The result was the creation of a new way of life by the people of Seville Estate. It is a remarkable expression of human resilience that despite the oppressions of slavery, the overwhelming preponderance of data tell a story of creative transformation. The creative processes documented in the archaeological record took place in a settlement in which people were held in chattel bondage. Not only were their options restricted but the material record at the site even included the wrist shackle. My thoughts upon the discovery of that shackle serve as a reminder of the limiting parameters of slavery. The processes of transformation that have been used to characterize change and community formation at Seville relate to additive and creative engagement within each household and more broadly within the community. These changes do not supplant one's heritage but intertwine with it. The material record at Seville reveals local decision making and choices in housing design, yard layout, and material use. The result was a landscape and cultural assemblage that drew on a combination of influences including African heritage and local interaction.

Transitions within the Early African Jamaican Settlement

The subsurface preservation of the houses from the earlier settlement is remarkable; floors are intact and postholes are clearly defined through soil discoloration. Activity areas in the yards are clearly indicated by refuse disposal patterns, features like hearths, and the placement of burials adjacent to houses. The houses measure 4 x 6 meters and are each divided into two rooms. The rows of houses face a central path and are tightly spaced with only 2.5–5 meters separating them. The house platforms are constructed of unmodified limestone cobbles with crushed marl (limestone powder) used as filler to even the floor. Postholes are rather evenly spaced and combine with the stone flooring to mark both exterior walls and internal partitions. The larger exterior postholes indicate a post and frame construction supporting wattle-and-daub walls (a woven lattice covered with mud). Smaller postholes indicate interior partitions bisecting each house. All of the doorways face the central path, with no breaks or wear patterns indicative of passageways on any other wall. While the doors opened to the street, much of the living space utilized by the slaves was in the yard behind the house and represents an outdoor rather than an indoor living pattern. Most of the household activities including cooking, gardening, and social gatherings took place behind the house, in the houseyard compound. These activities were out of view from the planter's Great House. It can be argued that this housing arrangement allowed the planter to maintain a sense of order and control, even if it was a false order, with the houses actually serving as a façade that screened the slaves and allowed them a degree of autonomy.

Reformation of Household and Community Space in the Later African Jamaican Settlement

Nearly a century after the founding of the plantation the slave settlement was moved to a new location. The context of this movement is significant in a number of ways. First, the move appears to have occurred as an event rather than a gradual shift. The old village was damaged by a hurricane and a new settlement built to re-

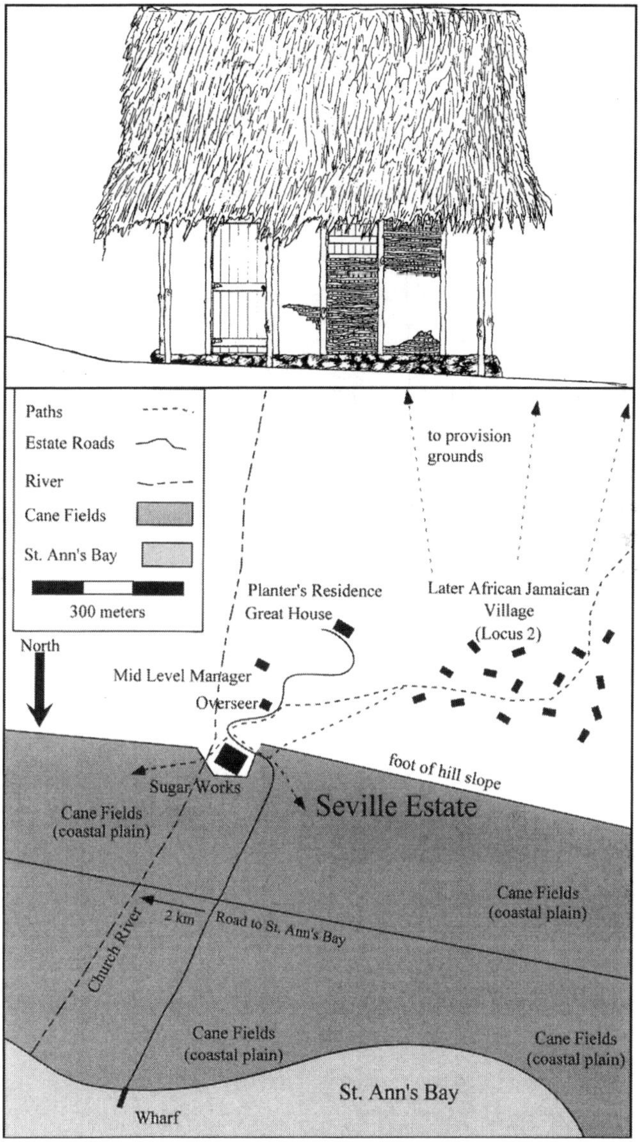

Figure 5.1. *Top:* Hypothetical reconstruction of a house from the early African Jamaican village based on archaeological findings at Locus 1, House Area 16. *Below:* Plan of Seville Plantation, 1780–1838 and beyond. The shift from the linear arrangement of the earlier village to the dispersed cluster of the later village circumvents planter control through unsupervised access between fields, village, and provision grounds.

place it. The new village represented a clean start (perhaps literally given the quantities of refuse and artifacts recovered from the fringes of the earlier houseyard areas). Second, after a century living as slaves the community had an opportunity to define spatial boundaries within the village on their own terms. This was a period of apparent turmoil for the planters, as not only did buildings on the estate require considerable renovation but two generations of planters died in rapid succession and control of the estate was contested in the courts. The new village is seen as an expression of the community that had evolved within the African Jamaican settlement. While the planter controlled decisions concerning the area occupied by the new settlement, there is no indication that the planned community organized in the previous century defined the layout of this newer settlement.

Finally, the new houses exhibit well-defined and expanded houseyard compound boundaries, but they also show considerable variation in the specifics of house design, construction, and alignment. These variations may reflect the internal social organization operative within the community, for instance, differential access to building supplies and clustered groupings of houses, which may reflect social relations.

The slave houses in the later village are loosely clustered in an area northwest of the early village and due west of the planter's Great House. The slaves could travel to and from the fields without directly passing the planter's residence, but the manager's house still retained a pivotal position between the slaves and the works and fields. Initially occupied in the 1780s, houses in this locus were inhabited until the late 1880s and early 1890s. In contrast to the earlier settlement, houses in this locus were repeatedly abandoned and new ones built on new sites, hence we are able to date specific houses to relatively narrow periods of occupation.

Unlike the similarity in form found in the early settlement, each of the houses in the later settlement is oriented on a different axis and expresses a different set of building practices. In terms of boundaries, each houseyard occupies an area at least eight times the size of the yards of the earlier village and the distance between houses averages 20 meters. Actual house size, however, is quite similar, ranging from 4 x 6 meters to 5 x 7 meters.

Building construction ranges from virtually identical to the earlier houses with limestone flooring, wattle-and-daub walls, and thatched roofs to framed wattle-and-daub houses with wood floors and perhaps even a shingled roof (among the remains associated with this house is a commemorative "emancipation" plate dated 1838). Other building forms include combinations of stone foundations and framing. Doorways tend to be oriented toward the prevailing wind and the ocean. However, houses bounding an area that is still referred to by people in the area as "the commons" face this open grassy area.

Yard areas exhibit all of the elements found in those of the earlier village including hearths and cooking areas immediately behind the house. The two major differences appear to be of scale and distance. First, clear yard areas, low artifact density areas, expand out 7–12 meters from the house rather than the average of 5–6 meters in the earlier village; second, most of the houseyards do not run directly from one to another. Instead there are marginal areas with refuse and presumably vegetation. The only houses with abutting yards are those found on the boundary of the commons. But even these indicate marginal, debris-filled zones between them.

The houses of the later village are at a greater distance from the planter's and manager's residences and appear to be loosely organized around a common area. The shift in the location of the village brought it closer to the nearest provision grounds (located southwest of the village). Significantly, the commons and the village cluster about a road or path that leads to the provision grounds. This path is indicated on the 1791 map and remains the primary route traversed by Jamaicans traveling to and from current houses and farms located southwest of the archaeological ruins and the markets of St. Ann's Bay.

Spatial Transformations: A Landscape of Power and Resistance

The evidence of creative transformation in the reorganization of space is seen in changes to the layout and organization of household space and the wholesale restructuring of houses and yards at Seville once the village moved in the 1780s. The initial layout of the laborer village appears to have been designed to maximize planter surveillance and control—among other things, from the planter's house managers could look up the row of orderly houses and see the doorways of all of the laborers' houses. However, the laborers engaged in a different use of their residences, and the distribution of features and materials indicates that much of the daily activities took place outside and behind the rows of houses in interconnected yards. Not only was this pattern of spatial use more consistent with traditional houseyard practices in Africa, but it was cooler than being trapped inside a steamy house and allowed for greater social interaction between households and a more direct point of access to the fields farther up the hill, which became the primary provision grounds for the residents of the village. When the village was moved in the 1780s, the move may well have been under orders from the planters and certainly could not have been carried out without their approval, yet the move allowed a wholesale change in village layout. In place of the controlled lineation, the village was rebuilt in a series of household clusters, with eight times the yard area per house and with clusters of houses sharing common yard frontages in which cooking and social activities took place.

Through archaeological study we documented the increase in yard size, the alignment of doorways facing one another, and the presence of features such as hearths, all of which support the importance of the yard in terms of social interaction and discourse. The fact that the area is still called Seville Commons is indicative of the notion of common space and interaction within the village. Individuals and families may have built their own distinct houses and held these structures as personal property, but the area as a whole was viewed as a place held in common by the community, even though the lands were within the legal boundaries of the planter's residence and held in legal title by the planter. The importance of ownership of land is seen again in the departure of a significant portion of the Seville laborer population when given the option to leave and take up free parcels of land at The Priory immediately following emancipation. While many left Seville following emancipation, the issue of internally defined controls and decision making within the laborer village can also be seen in the decision of some to stay on the estate and maintain traditional homes, yards, and familial relationships through the nineteenth century (see Armstrong and Kelly 2000:379–91).

The evidence for engagement in the local production, purchase, and sale of goods and the incorporation of items acquired by choice within the parameters of their economic means can be seen in the overall assemblages of artifacts found within each household. These reflect choice in the purchase and use of specific items by individuals and households. The materials that we recovered represent the portion of the goods that were lost or broken and that could survive deposition in the ground in a tropical environment. In many ways the basic economic model of the Jamaica plantation encouraged a degree of independence in the production of foods and the acquisition of goods, as this made "owning" slaves less expensive for planters. Hence, with the exception of imported provisions like codfish, cloth, and other items which in time the planters were mandated to distribute to the enslaved, much of what was used in the daily life of the Seville laborers was acquired through social and economic transactions within the village. Food, tools, and various craft items were grown or made by the laborers or acquired by them at markets, which were legally sanctioned as they were perceived by the planters to benefit them. These markets were a source of goods and services that the managers of estates would not have to supply in order to sustain their labor force (Hauser 2008).

Spatial Transformations: A Landscape of Change

The shifts demonstrated in the layout and location of laborer settlements represent only one facet of the complex social relationships expressed in the layout of Seville Plantation. Archaeology has helped us locate and date sites that can be analytically projected onto the landscape. The result is a mosaic of interaction that defines both power relationships and more subtle impacts of social interaction that crosscut racial, ethnic, economic, temporal, and social boundaries.

Certainly, the layout of Seville Plantation was designed to maximize sugar production and to assist with management and control of the labor force. The cane fields were the primary source of economic wealth and were unencumbered by industrial works and residences. The landscape of the north coast of St. Ann's Parish has a narrow alluvial plain that becomes steep and hilly rather abruptly. The plantation works were strategically placed at the intersection of the plain, the hills, and the Church River. Positioning mills and factory at this point placed these important elements of the estate's landscape so as to minimize the distance between the cane fields and the works without encroaching on the fertile plain. Moreover, placement along the river allowed for easy transport of cane from fields on either side of the river and the capture of water power in the water mill. Managerial houses were located immediately across from the works and ensured control and surveillance of the factories. While changes were made in the specifics of mills and factory, including the abandonment of an early cattle mill and later the replacement of sugar with copra production, the primacy of this location for processing the produce of the estate did not change. The hill then rises steeply and one finds another paired relationship between the planter's residence and laborer housing. Initially, the British-period planter residence was a sprawling rectangular compound, which to the north had a sweeping view of the bay, the cane fields, and the works, as well as a direct line of sight to the slave village. The planter's house was comfortably removed from the heat, fire, and stench of the works but close enough to survey and control activities in the village. By contrast, the village was located in a position that did not provide a view of the cane fields and works but which, from at least the formal perspective of the doorways and path through the village, was in clear sight of the Great House.

I have already proposed that the laborers transformed their space and used the yards behind the houses, an action that reflects a degree of resistance to the expressed organizational authority of the planter. Moreover, when the village was moved the enslaved reorganized their space to accommodate more yard space and realigned their doorways to face one another. However, the move also changed the organizational arrangement of the estate (Armstrong and Kelly 2000). With this move to the west side of the estate, parallel to the planter's residence, the laborers no longer had to pass the planter's household as they headed to work in the cane fields to the north and east. The move occurred during a time in which the planter's residence had shifted from a primary home for a resident planter to more of an occasionally occupied country house for the planter family. As the manager's house by the works became the critical managerial quarters of the estate, the workers still passed by a place of authority when heading to the works. In fact, it is quite possible, based on the combination of dated archaeological sites and structures shown on maps, that the rebuilding of structures on the plantation after the 1780s hurricane damage included the construction of the overseer's house atop the older cattle mill. The overall spatial data suggest a bilateral shift in the relationship between planter and manager with greater importance placed on the role of overseer and more flexibility in the mobility and living spaces of the enslaved. During this time, the ownership of the plantation shifted back and forth between a local planter and indirect management by attorneys and overseers in trust for a series of underaged estate owners.

The plantation house retained its position of prominence and authority, but it was rebuilt several times. As evidenced by an extant keystone and a drawing of the house on the 1721 map, the massive two-story Georgian structure had replaced the original hacienda-style compound by 1723, reflecting a mid-eighteenth-century pattern of construction modeled after British country houses and the most prominent estate houses of Barbados (such as St. Nicholas Abby and Drax Hall). The Georgian country house at Seville may have emulated the Great House at nearby Drax Hall and reflected an architectural style common among Jamaican estates in the mid- to late eighteenth century (Armstrong 1990; Higman 1988:98–100). This type of construction projects the owner's access to significant wealth and capital. This house dates to a time when the plantation owner resided on the island. However, its design was not particularly well suited to the environment of Jamaica in at least two ways. First, even with a large window, this design forced the occupants to live indoors. Second, the building was designed to project an imposing edifice on the landscape and the wealth and prominence of those who owned and lived in it. This massive building with thick stone walls was no match for the periodic cyclonic storms that hit the island; by the early 1780s it, like many of the less permanent structures on the estate, including the laborer houses, was damaged by a hurricane. The roof and the top floor of the house were toppled. When reconstructed, the new house reflected a greater knowledge of life in the Caribbean and in some ways was more like that which had stood on the site in the seventeenth and early eighteenth centuries. The organization of space in the newly designed house was in fact similar to spatial designs expressed in the enslaved laborer village for more than a century previous. The new house was a one-story structure; while the upper floor was not rebuilt, the space on the ground floor was more than doubled in size. Most of the new space was expressed in an expansive veranda that extended across the full length of the front of the house and wrapped around its side. Additional porch-like rooms were added to the back of the house, tying the exterior kitchen and servant quarters together. The only remaining evidence of the two-story structure is a disjunction in the walls and impressions in the walls where floor joists once provided anchors for the second floor. The first floor ceiling is about 1.2 meters taller than its predecessor; the top of the old stone walls was capped off by wattle and daub on the interior walls. If one crawls up into the attic, one can see remnants of the old second story including an inset window now filled with wattle and daub.

These changes to the Great House reflect processes of transformation as significant as those seen in the laborer villages. In this case the planters modified their lifeways to conform to both the tropical environment and Jamaica's cultural setting. The use of wattle and daub in the new walls is consistent with construction techniques used in the village at the time and is indicative of the role that African Jamaican craftsmen played in modifying the structure. These changes shifted what must have been a rather uncomfortable pattern of indoor living to a creolized lifeway; with the new house design, a significant portion of the living space, including much of the non-sleeping quarters, was experienced outdoors, as it was in the African Jamaican village. Thus, even as the landscape of power and authority was retained it was also transformed. It was into this restructured house that Lady Maria Nugent made her way in March 1802 (P. Wright 1966:81) when she visited Seville with her husband, the lieutenant governor of Jamaica. Lady Nugent's published diary details facts about the planter's residence, which, while distinguished in space and representing a place of authority, was not all that separate from the lives of many of the enslaved laborers of the estate. For example, upon returning early to the Seville Great House from an evening of entertainment at Drax Hall, Mrs. Nugent surprised the house servants, who would otherwise have avoided being present in certain parts of the house during waking hours. She wrote, "I could not help laughing, as we entered the hall at Seville, to see a dozen black heads popped up, for the negroes in the Creole houses sleep always on the floors, in the passages, and galleries" (P. Wright 1966:81; Armstrong 1990:200). Nugent's comments are revealing about more than the enveloping power and authority of the planter class. She observed that the majority of those who resided within the planter's household were not the planter's family as indicated in most formal records but were the enslaved house servants who lived much of their lives in the Great House while maintaining places of residence and position in the laborer village.

Degrees of Freedom

Emancipation changed much in terms of the relationships and economic structures of the plantation, but those changes are seen only indirectly in the archaeological record. Post-emancipation changes in the laborer quarters took place over an extended period of time rather than immediately upon emancipation. There is little evidence for structural or spatial change at the Great House or the works following emancipation; these landscape features remained the primary economic focus for the estate until sugar production came to an end in the late nineteenth century.

Emancipation did have a direct impact on the laborers, expressed both in the legal sanctions of their new freedoms and the planters' recognition of their need for a stable labor force; social conditions began to change even before emancipation. As early as the late 1780s, the ability of the enslaved to redefine their living areas is evident in the spatial layout and organization of houseyards and villages when the settlement moved to Seville Commons. With emancipation the plantation management initiated measures to improve living conditions on the estate (Green 1976:207–8). These measures may partially explain the construction of wood frame houses in the settlement at about this time. Still, the most striking changes in the landscape relate to the choice that many of the formerly enslaved made to move away from the estate. The archaeological record defines a decrease in the number of households dating from the 1840s and later. We know that many left the estate and took up parcels of free land offered by a missionary society at The Priory. The Priory settlement was established in 1843 along the main road on the western boundary of Seville (Intitute of Jamaica 1843). Lands were given in title to male heads of households and many of those who took up residence were formerly enslaved at Seville. Those who remained on the estate were primarily elderly men and women and women caring for children. The number of people living in the African Jamaican laborer settlement at Seville gradually decreased throughout the later nineteenth century until it was completely abandoned in the 1890s.

The issue of the transition from slavery to freedom is currently in focus as scholars reexamine the implications of the two hundredth anniversary of laws outlawing the slave trade along with related legal actions and rebellions that led to emancipation. As part of the commemoration of the bicentennial of the cessation of the African slave trade by the British and American governments, I presented papers at both the World Archaeological Congress (WAC) in Jamaica (June 2007) and the Theoretical Archaeology Group (TAG) conference in York (December 2007) that explored archaeological perspectives on the transition away from slavery, which is best considered a continuum between slavery and freedom I call "Degrees of Freedom." This concept encompasses differential access to basic rights, including ownership of self (personhood, oneself) and ownership of property (goods, materials, and land, but not people), and the relationship of these attributes of freedom to the ability to "control one's labor during the era of slavery and its aftermath in the Caribbean" (Armstrong 2010).

The "Degrees of Freedom" concept encompasses the philosophical tenets of freedom, including the right to life, liberty, and property as defined in Locke's second treatise on government, and uses these tenets as relative measures of personal freedom from the seventeenth century to today (Locke [1690] 2007; Mill [1869] 1999; United Nations General Assembly 1948). With respect to Jamaica, I have previously argued that "in spite of slavery, in time, and through the resilience of human cultural processes, people bound within chattel slavery took a degree of control. They negotiated and transformed their lives creating new social constructs and social relations within the diverse cultural landscape of the Caribbean region. Examples of this are abundant in the enslaved laborer quarters at Seville plantation and Drax Hall plantation" (Armstrong 2010). However, the transition from slavery to freedom was gradual and in practical terms often did not coincide with the legal declaration of emancipation. All too often in Jamaica the transition from formal chattel slavery to legal emancipation left the population in a situation of de facto bondage enforced by formal rules of attachment to wage labor and laws binding the former slaves to land they did not own. This has been referred to by Mary Turner as "wage slavery" (1995).

For many formerly enslaved Jamaicans, emancipation did not mean freedom. They remained tied to the estates. If they left an estate they lost the legal basis to retain their homes and provision grounds, yet the wages offered were low and designed to keep them on the estate. At Drax Hall we found that many emancipated workers initially stayed but did not have access to provisions like codfish that had previously been provided by the estate. In the immediate post-emancipation era their diet shifted to include a wide array of small shellfish species gathered from the rocky shoreline of the estate (Armstrong 1990). These people were truly trapped in the post-emancipation cycle of "wage slavery." In contrast, those who resided at Seville Plantation had options including landownership within The Priory free settlement. The people at Seville had viable choices via the combination of a more enlightened managerial strategy aimed at improving conditions on the plantation, which was documented by Parliament (Green 1976:207–9), and access to land and tangible real property. The Priory thus provided a safety valve mechanism for the expression of freedoms for the formerly enslaved of Seville Plantation.

Those who took up parcels and gained title to land at The Priory could negotiate the conditions of their labor at Seville and on neighboring estates or in the growing town of St. Ann's Bay. They could also set out on their own and establish trades and businesses. All of these options reflect an ability to choose, rooted in property ownership; as landowners, the residents of The Priory could choose how and for whom they would work. While the underlying logic shaping the improvements and low rents at Seville in the post-emancipation era is not specified in the report to Parliament, it may well be that this enlightened strategy was influenced by the knowledge that the estate management was competing for the work of laborers both on the estate and in the fields. While the number of free villages and settlements established at the time of emancipation is very small compared to the overall population of the island, one cannot underestimate the significance of free settlements like The Priory, Sturge Town, and Steer Town, where individuals and groups were deeded land. These settings allowed for a greater degree of freedom for the newly emancipated who took up these parcels and perhaps even for those in the vicinity who chose to remain on the estates that had held them in bondage (Armstrong 2010).

Expressions of Differential Ethnic Identity among Laborers

Despite the development of free settlements and the incorporation of liberal terms of employment at places like Seville, many of the formerly enslaved decided to abandon plantation agriculture altogether. The movement of laborers away from the estate in the 1840s caused a labor shortage that was dealt with in part by importing contract wage laborers from India (M. Thomas 1974:101–2). At Seville, an East Indian laborer household was uncovered within the area of the old African settlement. The East Indian household projected a distinctly different layout than the African Jamaican houses. It was built overlaying the earlier ruins of a house in the early African Jamaican settlement but at right angles to that earlier house. It was nearly twice the size of any of the enslaved laborer houses and was constructed of different materials, including a pink mortar floor and a separate room for cooking. Unlike the hearths in the yards of African Jamaican households, the East Indian household's kitchen was attached to the house but in a separate room with a brick floor (Armstrong and Hauser 2004:16). The orientation, alignment, and organization of space within this household conformed to the practices of architecture and design seen in areas of South Asia and appear to reflect the internal organization of space expressed in Vastu design associated with South Asian Hindu vernacular architecture (Armstrong and Hauser 2004:16–17). Moreover, the material assemblage at this household, while consistent with the proportions of functional and cost-based groupings of artifacts of the African laborers (enslaved and later free) at the estate, showed a distinctively different assemblage of artifacts associated with personal activities, including higher proportions of items associated with clothing and adornment and less use of health- and hygiene-related items (e.g., pharmaceutical bottles, combs, toothbrushes) than were found in any of the other laborer or management contexts at Seville (Armstrong and Hauser 2004:15). The evidence suggests that these newly arrived laborers practiced a distinct medical system focused on diet and herbal remedies. Showing less reliance on allopathic practices and patent medicines, the assemblage associated with this mid- to late nineteenth-century household reflects a different archaeological signature than expressed in either the African Jamaican laborer households or managerial households at Seville (Armstrong and Hauser 2004:15).

The presence of the East Indian household relates to changes in labor and labor relations at the plantation following emancipation. The archaeological sites at Seville provide an excellent data set for comparing laborer and managerial contexts as well as similarities and differences in the living conditions and lifeways of two ethnically distinct groups of laborers from Africa and South Asia.

The study of ethnicity and preferences related to one's ethnic background has been particularly difficult to pursue archaeologically, as most sites primarily project the economic difference between labor and management. In a setting of wealthy planters and impoverished slave laborers, the archaeological record of the enslaved laborer villages is largely the residue of economic limitation and restricted access to goods. We can see and measure the differences in material use between plantation managers and the estate laborers at Seville. The planters had access to an array of expensive items; we recovered expensive wine glasses and a range of relatively expensive ceramics. Economic difference is further evidenced through the use and discard patterns of bottle glass, which was particularly visible in middens containing large quantities of whole bottles reflecting use and immediate discard off the manager's porch. However, the serendipitous recovery of an East Indian laborer household at Seville provides a unique opportunity to explore the lives of those who came as indentures from India to Jamaica to fill the labor void that occurred following emancipation. The presence of this household of East Indian laborers also made possible an analytical contrast between parallel laborer contexts emerging from discrete and distinct ethnic contexts. Thus Seville provided not only the first archaeological data from an East Indian household context but the presence of distinct laborer contexts representing African and Indian laborers in Jamaica. This allows us to demonstrate that much of what we see in the archaeological record relates to not only economic settings but also the ethnic identity of the people.

The archaeological record of the two groups showed commonalities related to the fact that both were laborers that did not have access to anywhere near the range of worldly goods available to the estate planters and managers. Moreover, when one looks at the material assemblage as a whole, one can see objects that project similarity in condition and setting among African and East Indian laborers. All laborer contexts project higher ratios of goods and wares associated with food production and consumption than their managerial counterparts. Among managers, there are simply more wares and a greater access to items like furniture hardware including hinges and locks, manufactured goods used in house construction, and in the surplus of goods that allowed the managers to use and discard and the laborers to use and reuse (presumably including the use of goods discarded by the managers). Yet, the patterns of material use found in the African Jamaican households and settlement are far different than those found in the East Indian Jamaican household at Seville.

Expressions of Identity of the Living and Commemoration of the Dead

Burials were found in association with houseyard compounds in the early settlement at Seville (Armstrong and Fleischman 2003; Armstrong 2000). The burials, while only four in number, represent an important aspect of the material life of the enslaved recovered from Seville Plantation. Moreover, the analysis and reburial of these remains resulted in a means of recognizing the important presence of the African Jamaican communities at Seville (Armstrong 2000). The Seville burials were all found in association with houseyards in the early village and appear to date from the early and mid-eighteenth century. They were purposely placed within actively occupied houseyard compounds as a means of honoring and commemorating the dead.

The analysis of burial practices and the human remains provides significant information on social relations within the enslaved settlement: "each individual was interred within a separate house-yard and with a unique set of artifacts that yield information about their unique identities and positions within the Seville community" (Armstrong and Fleischman 2003). The placement of the burials within active houseyards is reminiscent of house and yard burial practices reported by Merrick Posnansky in his research in interior Ghana at the West African trading center at Begho and by Christopher DeCorse in his study of the coastal African community of Elmina in Ghana (Posnansky 1983; DeCorse 1992, 2001). African Caribbean burials have been identified in a variety of cemetery contexts. The most extensive study of such burial practices has been reported by Jerome Handler, Frederick Lange, and Robert Corruccini in a series of publications related to the Newton Plantation cemetery in Barbados (Handler and Lange 1978; Corruccini et al. 1982; see also burial studies in Montserrat in Watters 1987). The Seville burials were the first documented burials within houseyard contexts in the Caribbean, but given West African burial practices, it had been expected that further studies would reveal additional house and yard burials throughout the region. More recently, the practice of burials has been confirmed for free blacks living in houseyard compounds within the East End Community of St. John, formerly part of the Danish West Indies (Armstrong 2003).

The Seville burials are important in that they demonstrate a strong bond between the living and the dead. In this case, a space located within an active household's yard was used, thus linking that individual's life with those who continued to reside at the house and use the yard. Burials reflect a set of behaviors by which the living honor and commemorate the dead. At Seville each of the four individuals was buried in a hole dug into the limestone bedrock; all were buried in wooden caskets on or near an east-west axis with heads at the west end. Three males were buried in deep graves while a single female was buried in a more shallow grave that barely broke into the limestone bedrock. The study of these burials provides significant detail on harsh living conditions. All projected bioanthropological hallmarks consistent with persons of African descent (Armstrong and Fleischman 2003:50). Pathologies present that may have contributed to the deaths of these individuals included acute anemia for the young female (who died in her late teens or early twenties) and osteomyelitis affecting the tibia of the oldest individual (who died in his mid-forties), and the presence of hyperextension of the hallux, or scribe's toe, may be an indication of the occupation of another individual as a cart driver whose toe bones were altered by continuous pressure used to apply brakes to stop the cart.

Each individual was buried with a distinctive set of grave goods that reflect recognition of the life, skills, and preferences of those who died by those who buried them. One was buried with a knife and an unused white-clay pipe; another was buried with a lock. The young female was buried with a pecked glassware bottle stopper. The oldest male had a refined brass and iron carpenter's compass or spacer (Armstrong and Fleischman 2003:49). These objects project the skills and social roles of these individuals during their lifetimes and the acknowledgment by the living in their community of those roles. The individual with the carpenter's spacer probably was a carpenter in life. The tool itself was one of the most expensive items found at the site, with a calibrated brass plate fixed to a well-fitted wrought-iron hinge, creating a compass tool used for measuring in woodworking. Having found evidence of an enslaved carpenter, we went through the inventory of slaves on the estate and found five carpenters listed between the years 1753 and 1759. We then found that three of those listed in 1753 were no longer listed in 1759 (John, James, and Thompson). It is quite possible that this site was used to bury one of these individuals in a houseyard burial context. Hence, through the study of these burials we are able to examine not only conditions affecting these individuals in life but also the specific skills and knowledge they possessed and the expressions of respect and commemoration that those living in the settlement extended to them through burial practices.

The Seville burials were exhumed as part of the exploration of their living contexts and as a means of protecting them from possible destruction based on their location outside the boundaries of the JNHT historic park. Once analysis was completed, they were returned to Jamaica and reburied in a new burial plot located on the lawn of the plantation's Great House (Armstrong 2000). This new marked burial ground is located adjacent to the burials of the plantation owners and was designed to bring attention to the African laborers' contribution to the history of Jamaica and to provide them with a place of honor in the visual landscape of the estate (Armstrong 2000).

The burials, while representing a very small segment of the Seville laborer population in comparison with the totality of findings from archaeological contexts, provide some of the clearest evidence of intensive social interaction associated with community formation within the laborer contexts at the site and, together with the broader array of data, are indicative of the creative aspects of cultural transformation and human cultural bonds that were present in the everyday lives of those who lived at the estate.

Summary and Prospects for the Future

The archaeological examination of the diversity of living contexts at Seville projects both the complexity of the plantation's living environment and the creativity of those who lived at the estate. The data provide strong and definitive evidence of the limitations and harsh conditions imposed on a plantation organized with enslaved labor. The power of elite planters is sharply contrasted with the conditions of the enslaved. This is seen in everything from the broadest layout of the plantation's cultural landscape, with the planter residing in an expansive Great House residence and the enslaved living in a circumscribed group of small houses, built in such a way as to maximize control and surveillance. Yet, even as those structures were created and power relations expressed in ways that decisively controlled much of the daily life of the enslaved, we also find that those who were held as chattel slaves worked in and around the enveloping structures of social and economic division to rework their living spaces. They used the very walls of their well-organized rows of houses to create a barrier to block direct surveillance, and they modified their living areas to engage in activities in their yard that included everything from the daily practice of cooking foods to the modification of ceramics to create gaming pieces used in daily social interaction within a yard space unseen by the planter. Moreover, they not only lived their lives in these yards but commemorated their dead in their own way within these areas of active living.

The Seville study shows how those in the African Jamaican settlement created their own community through processes of transformation. When their village was devastated by destructive hurricanes in the 1780s, a new village was built that even more clearly expressed the importance of both exterior space to the African Jamaican houseyard area as well as the relationships among households. In this new configuration houses were built around a common yard space in a village area still called Seville Commons.

The presence of an East Indian laborer household provided the first archaeological evidence of a residential site associated with a new group of laborers who were brought in after emancipation. It also gave us a clearer view of the areas in which the material record of the enslaved and free laborers on the estate acted in relation to their economic position and impoverished condition as well as on the basis of clear and distinct choices influenced by their heritage and ethnic backgrounds.

The planter's residence at the estate shows modifications in its layout, which also reflect cultural transformations. When the residence was reconstructed after the storms of the 1780s, the planters abandoned its impractical massive two-story windward design that had expressed both their power and authority and their links to the Georgian world of eighteenth-century England. The new house was a single-story building whose core was the old stone structure but expanded with sprawling external porches, allowing the planter's household to take advantage of the cooling coastal breeze rather than locking the household behind sweltering walls. This vernacular shift not only incorporated external living areas but also used wattle-and-daub construction as found in the African settlement. However, even as planter and enslaved living areas became more similar in overall design, the social distance between planter and laborer may have grown. The planter no longer engaged in direct surveillance but delegated that to a managerial class. The enslaved now bypassed the planter's house on their way to work and instead encountered the manager's house along the way.

With emancipation the format of interaction shifted once again. Many of the newly freed moved away from the estate despite efforts to enhance living conditions at Seville that were singled out as having been more progressive than generally practiced for the island in the post-emancipation era (Green 1976). Those who had lived at Seville had the option of retaining their familial houses and provision grounds on the estate or leaving the estate and moving to The Priory, a free settlement created on land by the main road on the west side of the estate. Many chose this option or simply left the area entirely. The archaeological record documents this movement from the estate as well as the continuation of a few households into the last decades of the nineteenth century.

At its most basic level the archaeological study of Seville Plantation shows that there is much more to the estate than simply the massive cut stone buildings that characterize the surviving structures of the estate—the planter's residence, the mills, the works, and the overseer's house. The less permanent housing of the majority population of the estate, the enslaved and later free laborers on the property, were rediscovered using the tools of archaeology and have now been reintroduced into the plantation landscape both in terms of small-scale reconstructions that provide examples of what houses and yards looked like and the things that people used as part of their daily life and as part of the broader interpretation of the estate and the social conditions that were part of the plantation economy. We never found the toy lost by Carpi Rose, but through excavations we did explore his grandmother's house and add its existence and dimensions to the record of the estate. Moreover, the exploration of Seville provides clarity with respect to the complexity of the estate. It provides evidence of the harsh conditions of slavery and the creative forces of transformation linked to community formation, ethnogenesis, and social interaction.

Looking to the future, I hope to see an integration of data from the diverse social contexts of Seville that extends beyond the temporal and political boundaries of the British colonial setting to include comparisons of these findings with those representing lifeways from the prehistoric sites on the property, including the indigenous village known as Maima and the array of Spanish-era sites that are found throughout the property. Is there evidence at Seville and the St. Ann's Bay vicinity relating to Columbus's yearlong stay in Jamaica? Most recently, Robyn Woodward has completed extensive studies of the Spanish-period occupation. How were agricultural, milling, and labor management practices organized by the Spanish, how did the use of the landscape differ, and how did the Spanish use of this part of the island impact the creation of plantations such as the British-period sugar estate at Seville Plantation?

The inclusion of data from two of the houseyard areas from the early laborer settlements in the Digital Archaeological Archive of Comparative Slavery (DAACS) is an important step toward the integration of data from this site into our knowledge of life in plantation contexts in the Caribbean (Armstrong and Galle 2007). This database allows us to compare data from sites throughout the Americas by utilizing a uniform structure of analysis and detailed documentation in a format that is accessible to the public via the Internet. Houseyard Areas 1.15 and 1.16 were selected for inclusion in this database because of the clarity of spatial layout and sample size represented. The entire house and yard were excavated for each of these houseyard complexes and each had clear representation of house structures, yard features like hearths, and an associated burial (Armstrong 1998; Armstrong and Fleischman 2003; Armstrong and Galle 2007).

Seville National Historic Park in Jamaica projects one of the longest and diverse histories in the Americas. The archaeological record at this site extends well back into prehistoric times and includes an overlay of historic sites representing diverse groups and social settings. It is my hope that in the near future efforts will be renewed to see the creation of a heritage park that integrates the rich history into an interpretive center that engages both international visitors and the local population—from schoolchildren to local businesses. Seville has been on the list of sites eligible for World Heritage designation, and two attempts have been made to create a management plan for the site. I hope that in the near future efforts along these lines will be renewed and that an economically viable, environmentally responsible, and publicly engaged plan will be put into action not only to gain formal World Heritage site designation for the complex of archaeological and cultural resources that rest within the boundaries of this property but to put forward Jamaica's rich history in this remarkable setting for future generations of Jamaicans and visitors to see and experience.

Acknowledgments

The Seville Plantation study was made possible by funds from National Geographic, the Wenner-Gren Foundation, Syracuse University, and the JNHT. The JNHT and Jamaica's Land Evaluation Office provided a range of services from housing to transportation. Several colleagues assisted in the study including Elizabeth Reitz (University of Georgia), who contributed analyses of faunal remains, and Mark Fleischman (Syracuse University), who studied the human skeletal remains. Several of the key field assistants on this project have gone on to excel in their archaeological endeavors, including James Delle, Suzanne England, Kenneth Kelly, Mark Pedelty, and Matthew Reeves. The project was assisted by hundreds of students from Syracuse University and several students from the University of the West Indies, Mona. Jamaican archaeologists Ywone Edwards and Dorrick Gray assisted with logistics, excavation, and analysis, and E. Kofi Agorsah, then at the University of the West Indies, provided a wide range of support and encouragement for the project.

In many ways the project has continued. Some of the data from the early village have recently been incorporated into the DAACS archive (Armstrong and Galle 2007), the local earthenware have been analyzed in detail by Mark Hauser (2001, 2006) and with the data incorporated into his newest book (2008). Moreover, a reconstruction of an enslaved laborer house, based on findings from the 1988–93 excavations at Seville Plantation, continues to mark and commemorate the presence and context of the African Jamaican experience within the Seville Plantation landscape.

6

Maritime Connections in a Plantation Economy

Archaeological Investigations of a Colonial Sloop in St. Ann's Bay, Jamaica

Gregory D. Cook
Amy Rubenstein-Gottschamer

Introduction

The crucial role of shipping in maritime economies cannot be overstated, particularly in the case of island nations like Jamaica. If the birth of the modern era began, as many scholars maintain, with the maritime expansion of Europe into other world areas, then maritime economic connections clearly present a critical element of study (Braudel 1984). Jamaica serves as an appropriate venue for such a maritime study for several reasons. The island became known to Europeans during Christopher Columbus's second and fourth voyages and thus played a role in the first and most dramatic example of Europeans expanding the "geographic size of the known world," ushering in the modern era at the close of the fifteenth century (Wallerstein 1974:38). Later populated by Spanish and British colonists as well as enslaved Africans, the island continued to rely heavily on global maritime connections through its history. Colonial maritime studies benefit from historic sources preserved in Jamaica, as well as from nautical archaeological fieldwork that has been conducted on the island (Clifford 1993; Cook 1997; Hamilton 2006; Parrent, Neville, and Neyland 1991; Parrent and Parrent 1993). While this work is still in its infancy, the excavations at Port Royal, the search for Columbus's caravels, and the study of the Readers Point Sloop all serve as examples of nautical archaeological research in Jamaica. This chapter focuses on the latter topic, the discovery of an eighteenth-century sloop off of Readers Point in St. Ann's Bay, Jamaica, as a case study in how nautical archaeology can contribute to a greater understanding of Jamaica's maritime past.

The Discovery

Archaeologists from the Institute of Nautical Archaeology (INA) at Texas A&M University and the Jamaican National Heritage Trust (JNHT) discovered the remains of a late eighteenth-century merchant sloop in St. Ann's Bay, Jamaica, in 1991. The remains are located approximately thirty feet (ten meters) from shore near a projection of land labeled "Readers Point" on historic maps (Figure 6.1). Readers Point was once part of the Seville Estate, a major colonial sugar plantation during the seventeenth and eighteenth centuries.

The shipwreck was located using sub-bottom sonar during the Columbus Caravels Archaeological Project (CCAP), directed by Dr. James Parrent of INA (Parrent and Parrent 1993). The project's goal was to survey the bay for the remains of two caravels abandoned by Columbus in 1504 during his last voyage to the New World. Although CCAP archaeologists were unsuccessful in locating Columbus's ships, they discovered six eighteenth-century wreck sites near the center of the bay.

Test excavations conducted on the Readers Point site in 1991 exposed a layer of ballast covering intact hull remains. These remains lay under 3 feet (0.9 meters) of water, with an additional 3–6 feet (0.9–1.8 meters) of sediment covering the wreck. Archaeologists excavated a 6-foot-square (1.8-meter square) test unit down to hull remains near the site's easternmost extent. The test unit exposed portions of the vessel's radial cant frames in the bow and allowed the recovery of numerous artifacts including pipe stems and ceramics. (NB: Frames on a wooden sailing vessel make up the skeletal structure of the ship. Frames near the forward end, or bow, of the Readers Point vessel angle obliquely toward the front of the ship; these oblique, or "cant," frames appear to be a common method of framing the ends of vessels in the eighteenth century.) Artifacts and hull construction both suggested that the vessel dated to the late eighteenth century rather than the early 1500s; therefore, archaeologists reburied the site after recording the exposed hull structure.

Excavation

In 1994 archaeologists from INA, the JNHT, and the Program for Maritime History and Nautical Archaeology at East Carolina University conducted a complete underwater excavation of the site. Project personnel consisted of eight permanent crew members, who were assisted by volunteers throughout the four-month excavation. Divers excavated the overburden covering the wreck, then removed the stone ballast while carefully recording the positions of artifacts found within the ballast. This exposed the entire wreck for intensive hull recording. By the end of the excavation divers recovered over six hundred artifacts, recorded the hull structure, and disassembled portions of the wreck.

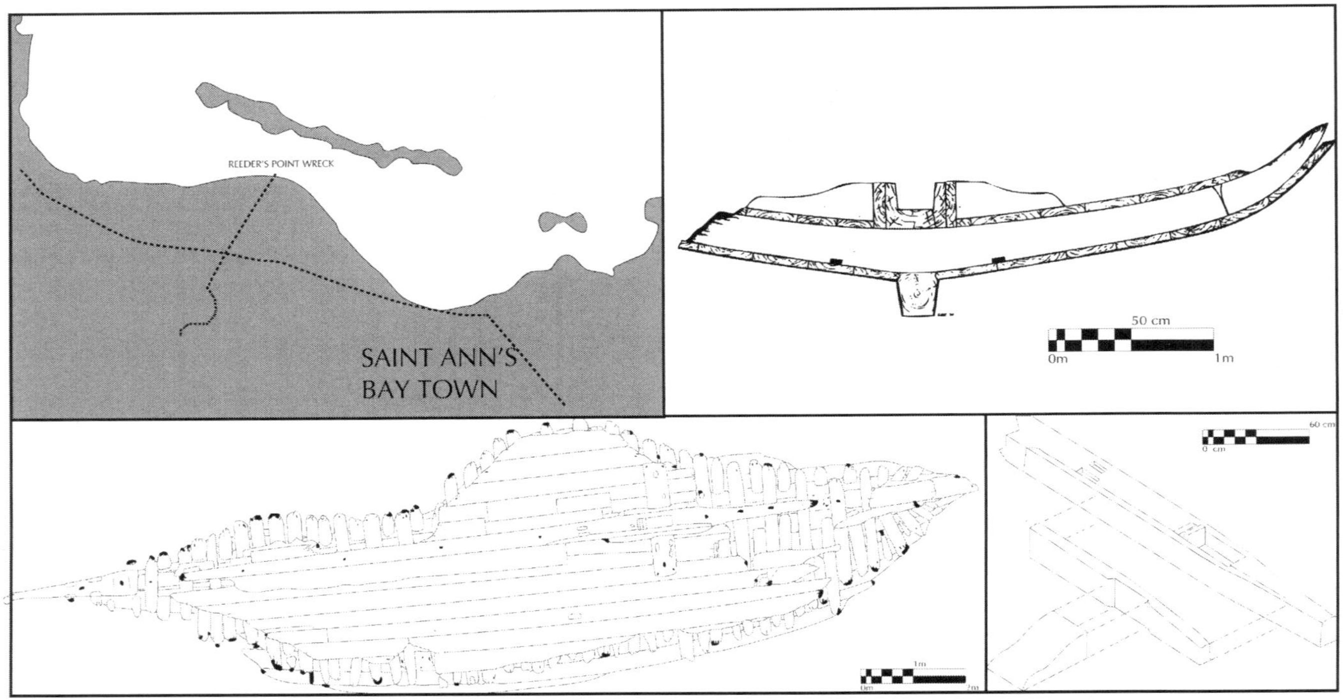

Figure 6.1. Readers Point Sloop. *Clockwise from upper left:* location of wreck in St. Ann's Bay; cross-section of the hull; reconstructed repair on the sloop; shipwreck site plan.

The shipwreck remains are preserved to a length of 56 feet, 6 inches (17.22 meters) and a maximum beam of 14 feet, 4 inches (4.34 meters). The starboard half of the wreck is better preserved than the port side, likely due to the starboard side's proximity to the shoreline and the exposure of the port side to prevailing longshore currents in the bay (see Figure 6.1). The wood used to form the ship's timbers is predominantly white oak and the keel is hard maple, suggesting northeastern American colonial construction (Newsom 1997). The vessel's single mast step survived intact, indicating that the ship carried a sloop rig.

It appears that the sloop was a derelict at the time of its sinking. Artifacts were relatively sparse, and nearly all items were broken and found in the ballast or bilges. No trace of the upper works or deck structure survived, and the pumps and mast had been removed. Signs of wear, heavy use, and numerous repairs suggest a long trading career for the vessel. The date range of the artifacts clusters around 1775, with a terminus post quem of 1765. Charred outer hull planking along the edge of preserved hull timbers suggests the vessel was burned, and a jagged hole in the outer hull planking on the starboard side near the stern could also have caused the vessel to sink.

Artifacts

The Readers Point wreck artifact assemblage includes six primary artifact categories. Listed in order of frequency, they are ceramics, metal (including iron concretions), glass, wood (not including hull timbers), leather, and bone. Only diagnostic artifacts providing dates or other information pertaining to the hull analysis are described below. The scatter of artifacts suggests that a considerable degree of disturbance occurred on the site, limiting conclusions made from artifact provenience. The artifact conservation and analysis from the Readers Point Sloop was carried out by Amy Rubenstein-Gottschamer.

Ceramics

Archaeologists recovered nearly four hundred ceramic sherds from the Readers Point Sloop, spanning nine different categories including creamware, stoneware, earthenware, agate, Astbury, delftware, Jackfield, slipware, and porcelain. The highest percentage of sherds are identified as creamware, subclassified into six types including cloudedware (1740–75), diamond pattern (1760–1800), feather edged (1765–90), dot pattern (no comparable material is available), royal pattern (1766–1820), and undecorated body sherds (A. Brown 1982:16; Noël Hume 1970:123–24; South 1977:211; Towner 1978:84). Creamware vessel shapes represented in the assemblage were primarily plates, along with bowls and a few pieces tentatively identified as mugs (Rubenstein-Gottschamer 1995:37–41).

Stoneware sherds make up the next highest percentage of ceramics recovered from the site, with a total of sixty-three sherds distributed across the stern quarter of the vessel. Stoneware types include Fulham Brown salt-glazed (1690–1775), white salt-glazed (1725–75), and white slipped-brown glazed (1690–1775). The assemblage includes unidentifiable body sherds, mugs, and plates (A. Brown 1982:5, 10; South 1977:210; Rubenstein-Gottschamer 1995:42–44). Agate sherds, composed mainly of mug fragments, were found in the starboard stern area of the vessel, as well as Astbury bowl fragments, both of which date to the early to mid-eighteenth century (South 1977:211; Rubenstein-Gottschamer 1995:25, 26).

Divers recovered twenty-one pieces of delftware jugs and mugs from the starboard stern quarter, as well as nine fragments tentatively identified as Jackfield pitcher sherds (1740–80). The latter have a slightly anomalous black glaze and may in fact be a variation of the classic Jackfield stoneware (Godden 1966:xiv; Rubenstein-Gottschamer 1995:32–37; South 1977:211).

Archaeologists recovered nine sherds identified as slipware, as evidenced by their liquid clay decoration. Slipware dates to 1670–1795, and the nine specimens from the Readers Point Sloop were located in a tight grouping in the vessel's stern. These sherds appear to be pitcher fragments, perhaps belonging to a single vessel. The bow section of the sloop contained two unidentifiable body sherds of English porcelain, dating to 1745–95 (Rubenstein-Gottschamer 1995:41; South 1977:210).

Pipes

Crew members found forty-nine pipe stems, and their provenience spreads throughout the vessel remains. Measurements of the stem bores indicated that the sample can be divided into four basic diameters: 4/64, 5/64, 6/64, and 7/76 inches. While admittedly a small sample, the Harrington method of dating pipe stems indicates that over 90 percent of the pipe assemblage clusters around 1750, with a terminus post quem of 1710 and a terminus ante quem of 1800 (Harrington 1954; Rubenstein-Gottschamer 1995:38). Applying the same sample of stems to Binford's method of pipe dating produces a date of 1751.5 for the collection (Binford 1962; Rubenstein-Gottschamer 1995:3).

Five pipe bowls were located on the wreck. Rubenstein-Gottschamer determined the date ranges for the bowl samples based on form and the presence of maker's marks. Dates spans for the bowls are 1690–1750, 1700–1770, 1720–1820, and 1730–90 (Noël Hume 1970:303; Rubenstein-Gottschamer 1995:40).

Glass

Among the varieties of glass fragments recovered by divers, the majority is classified as dark green glass, commonly associated with bottles in form. The provenience of these artifacts spans the entire site. Included in this category are seven necks, five bases, two lips, and one complete bottle. Two of the neck fragments were sufficiently complete to provide dates of 1795 and 1783, both +/– 22.4 years. Three bases gave dates of 1756, 1804, and 1801, with an error factor of +/− 33 years. The single complete bottle dated to 1794 +/− 15 years (Jones and Sullivan 1989:151, 156; Rubenstein-Gottschamer 1995:46, 47).

A unique leaded glass vessel tentatively identified as a sweetmeat dish or bowl was unearthed just aft of the mast step near the outboard edge of the port side. The vessel exhibits a pattern-molded recurring diamond motif. The style of this vessel is classified as a "double-ogee bowl," which dates throughout the eighteenth century (Thorpe 1927:14; Rubenstein-Gottschamer 1995:48).

Leather

The anaerobic conditions of the site proved excellent for the preservation of organic materials. Archaeologists excavated six leather fragments, three of which were identified as shoe fragments. These artifacts came from the middle of the vessel on the starboard side of the wreck and included a boot upper, a heel, and a sole fragment. The heel exhibited wear patterns, suggesting that it had been worn extensively before being discarded (Rubenstein-Gottschamer 1995:50, 51).

Metals

Examples of cuprous artifacts recovered during the project include three cast buckle fragments and a cast button (Figure 6.2). Two of the buckles were located amidships, and divers found the third buckle fragment and the button in the vessel's stern. The buckles exhibit floral designs and are comparable to other eighteenth-century examples based on form (Rubenstein-Gottschamer 1995:52).

Iron artifacts exhibited the concretion typically present on these objects in a saltwater environment. Excavation team members used a pneumatic air scribe to break into concretions, after which the project conservator cleaned the inside of the molds and cast them with epoxy. Concretions still containing iron were conserved by electrolytic reduction in the project field laboratory. Archaeologists recovered eight barrel strap concretions spread widely across the middle of the vessel. One example recorded in situ measured 1 foot, 9 inches (53.5 centimeters) in diameter. Divers found three plain iron buttons located in the port bow, amidships, and port stern. With no markings present, their date ranges span nearly the entire eighteenth century (Rubenstein-Gottschamer 1995:54).

The Readers Point artifact assemblage contains sixty iron fasteners, including nails, spikes, and bolts. Divers retrieved these artifacts from throughout the entire vessel. Most of the fasteners were recovered as hollow concretions, which the project conservator cast in the field laboratory. Nails and spikes were hand-wrought, and the bolts were cast. The collection includes one nail and five spikes that exhibit a "rose head" configuration.

Among the more interesting iron artifacts recovered from the site include a triangular pressing iron and the mold of a socketed woodworking chisel. The iron is

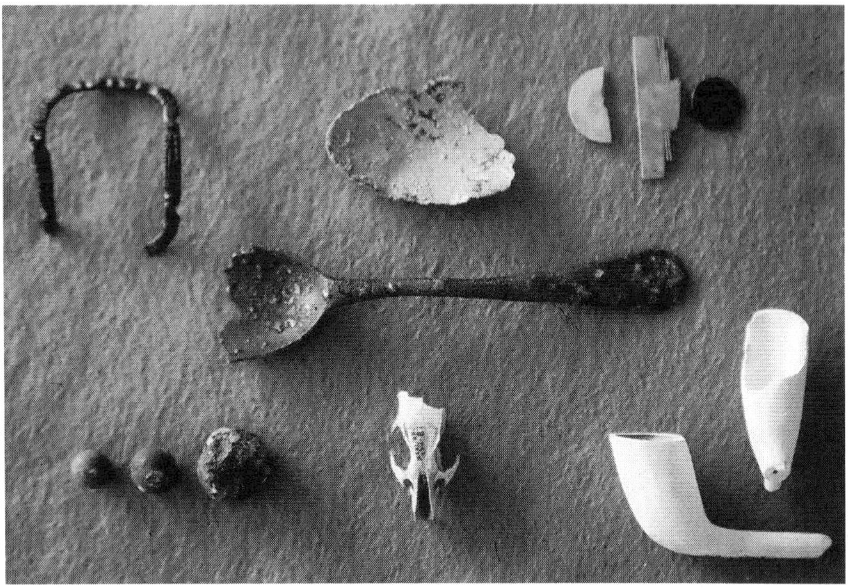

Figure 6.2. Small finds recovered from the Readers Point Sloop. *Clockwise:* buckle, spoon, button, comb, coin, tobacco pipe, rodent skull, lead shot.

not considered particularly diagnostic, though similar irons are dated to the middle of the eighteenth century (Neumann and Kravic 1975:168). The socketed shaft of the chisel may suggest a specialized use associated with ship carpentry (Horsley 1978:120; Rubenstein-Gottschamer 1995:56, 59).

Divers found several pieces of lead shot in the bow, midships, and stern portions of the vessel. Though most examples exhibited considerable erosion, two pieces are identified as .51 and .59 caliber shot. The smaller caliber shot corresponds well with a .51 caliber American firearm dating to 1775–90. The larger shot fits a .59 caliber American fowling piece dating to 1755–59. Contemporary English muskets of this period typically fired larger caliber shot than these examples (Neumann 1967:66, 96, 144–46; Rubenstein-Gottschamer 1995:59).

Pewter artifacts in the assemblage included fragments of three spoons (Figure 6.2). Each of these pieces was recovered in the stern of the wreck. They are not particularly diagnostic, unfortunately, and can only be dated post-1700 (Rubenstein-Gottschamer 1995:60, 61).

Wood

The starboard stern section of the vessel contained four wood sheaves made of lignum vitae. Sheaves served as the wheel inside of wooden blocks that served as critical components in the vessel's rigging. These artifacts showed no evidence of use, and their compact provenience may indicate that they were being stored as spare parts. The largest of these measured 1 inch (2.56 centimeters) thick and 6½ inches (16.5 centimeters) in diameter (Rubenstein-Gottschamer 1995:62).

Archaeologists excavated a carpenter's smoothing plane from the middle of the vessel, adjacent to the starboard side of the keelson. The tool measures 6¾ inches by 2⅜ inches by 2⅛ inches (17 x 6 x 5.5 centimeters). The plane's body consists of a simple block, without handles. The concretion of the iron blade is still present inside the block, held in place with two small wooden wedges (Rubenstein-Gottschamer 1995:64, 65).

Botanical Remains

Archaeologists retrieved fifty-three botanical samples associated with the wreck, representing fourteen different species. This assortment includes nut shells, gourd rinds, pits, seeds, and various fruit parts. The botanical assemblage from the Readers Point vessel was sent to Dr. Lea Newsom, then curator/assistant professor at the Center for Archaeological Investigations at Southern Illinois University, Carbondale. Dr. Newsom is an expert in the field of botanical identification and has extensive experience with material from shipwreck sites.

Many of the Readers Point botanical samples have been identified as drift fruit and are probably intrusive. Those likely to be associated with the working life of the ship include three organic samples that fit into the neotropical cultivar category, including a single calabash (*Cresentia cujete*) and two samples of guanábana or soursop (*Annona muricata*). These tropical American trees are associated with neotropical home gardens. The gourd-like calabash is used for a variety of purposes, one of the most common being a handy bowl or cup. The soursop is still very popular in Jamaica as a sweet, refreshing fruit. The calabash rind and soursop seeds retrieved from the Readers Point Sloop came from relatively deep and secure contexts within the ballast, are very well preserved, and are likely associated with the vessel (Newsom 1997).

Five well-known Old World plant cultivars were included in organics retrieved from the Readers Point Sloop, including watermelon (*Citrillus lanatus*), almond (*Prunus amygdalus*), peach (*Prunus persica*), plum (*Prunus domestica*), and hazelnut (*Coryleus avellana*). Like the neotropical cultivars mentioned above, the specimens showed exceptional preservation and are likely associated with the shipwreck. These species grow in temperate climates and are not associated with tropical Caribbean environments (Newsom 1997).

Faunal Remains

Divers recovered a total of 170 faunal samples associated with the Readers Point Sloop, including bones from mammals (78.2 percent), fish (14.1 percent), birds (7.1 percent), and reptiles (0.6 percent). These samples were sent to Dr. Philip Armitage for identification and analysis with comparative skeletal material. Dr. Armitage is a respected expert in the field of faunal analysis and has extensive experience with shipwreck assemblages in particular. These samples were identified to species and part of skeleton (Armitage 1995). As in the retrieval of botanical samples, the field crew considered only bones found well within the ballast pile, or within intact hull remains, to be associated with the shipwreck.

Most of the bones retrieved from the Readers Point Sloop appear to be related to victualing, with salted beef and salted pork forming the largest percentage of meat eaten onboard the ship. Beef bones make up 42 percent of the total faunal collection from the wreck. A distinctive multiple-chopping pattern exists on nearly 20 percent of the beef bones, suggesting soup/broth preparation on a significant number of bones after cooking/eating the rations of salted beef. The pork assemblage comprises 26 percent of the total bone assemblage. Within the collection of pork bones, the presence of a large number (41.5 percent) of pork rib and loin cuts indicates that the lowest grade of packaged salted pork was used for victualing (Armitage 1995). Other mammal bones associated with victualing include small samples of sheep and rabbit. Rabbits were typically carried onboard vessels in the eighteenth century to provide fresh victuals, despite superstitions that they brought bad luck to ships (Armitage 1995).

Chicken bones (*Gallus gallus*) comprise 7.1 percent of the total faunal assemblage. Vessels of all types commonly carried chickens live in coops for fresh provisions, and this is the likely source of the specimens found on the Readers Point Sloop. A single humerus identified as *Gopherus polyphemus,* or gopher tortoise, suggests that land tortoises also contributed to the sloop's victuals. The habitat of *Gopherus polyphemus* is restricted to the southeastern and Gulf seaboards of North America, including what is today southwestern South Carolina, southern Georgia, Florida, Alabama, Mississippi, Louisiana, and southeastern Texas. Due to the restrictive range of the species, it is likely that the Readers Point Sloop sailed to ports in these areas and that its crew exploited local sources of meat on their voyages (Armitage 1995).

Several mammal bones were recovered that are unassociated with victualing purposes. A canine metatarsal indicates the presence of a dog onboard the sloop. Divers also recovered the cranium of a brown, or Norway, rat (*Rattus norvegicus*). The presence of vermin is not surprising considering the general tendency for rats to infest the holds of ships. However, until the early eighteenth century the black rat (*Rattus rattus*) was the only commensal species in Europe. In the early 1700s the brown rat was introduced and quickly became the dominant species due to its larger size and more aggressive demeanor. The magnitude of shipping conducted in the late eighteenth century provided ample opportunity for the spread of the brown rat to West Indian ports. The presence of the brown rat on the Readers Point Sloop provides more evidence, albeit from a rather surprising source, that the vessel must date after the early to mid-eighteenth century (Armitage 1995).

During the 1991 CCAP excavation, archaeologists found a single human lumbar vertebrae between the first and second floors aft of the bow. In 1994, excavations in the bow produced a second phalange, or finger bone, also identified as human. These are puzzling additions to the Readers Point faunal assemblage and may indicate that a human body was stored in the bow during the ship's working life or after it had become a derelict (Armitage 1995).

All of the fish remains located on the wreck belong to species abundant throughout the Caribbean and thus might be intrusive. Species identified include blacktip shark, green moray eel, and nassau grouper. Surprisingly, there is a conspicuous absence of species commonly used for victualing, such as cod and herring, on the Readers Point site (Armitage 1995).

Hull Structure

The sloop's remains extend 56 feet, 6 inches (17.22 meters) in length and 14 feet, 3½ inches (4.34 meters) maximum beam (see Figure 6.1), and is oriented east-northeast, sitting evenly on its keel. In general her timbers exhibit exceptional preservation, with the starboard side surviving to a greater extent than the port side. The sloop appears to have been constructed with a high degree of skill, as indicated by the well-finished frames and the symmetry of the hull components. Individual hull components are described below, following the approximate sequence of construction (see Table 6.1).

The backbone of the vessel, or keel, is made of hard maple (*Acer* sp.), and extends 42 feet, 5 inches (12.9 meters) from the stern of the vessel to its forwardmost extent, but it originally would have been larger than this, as neither end is preserved intact (Tainter 1995). Archaeologists broke through the outer hull planking in three locations to examine the keel, noting no evidence of scarfs, thus it is possible that the keel was fashioned from a single maple timber. In an effort to afford more protection to the keel, sacrificial planking of white oak (*Quercus* sp.) has been tacked onto the port and starboard sides of the timber. A layer of pitch and hair exists between the keel and sacrificial planking that would have served not only to help secure the planking to the keel but also to prohibit shipworms from boring into the backbone of the ship (Lavery 1987:59).

The forwardmost extent of the keel ends under the fifth floor aft of the bow; in this context "floors" refer to the bottom-most frames that attach directly to the keel, and futtocks are the frames that continue the curve of the vessel outboard of the floors (Steffy 1994:271). Archaeologists excavated a hole under the port side of the hull in an effort to examine the keel/stem scarf. Surprisingly, the keel ends abruptly at this location. The timber appears to have been sawed off, and extensive excavation did not reveal the stem or any other timber continuing forward from the end of the keel. A timber identified as a tropical hardwood lies against the port side of the keel in this location (Tainter 1995). This may represent a repair or brace

Table 6.1 Measurements and Scantlings of the Readers Point Sloop

Overall length	56'6" (17.22 m)
Maximum beam	14'3" (4.34 m)
Keel	42'5" (12.9 m) in length 9⅝" (24.5 cm) sided 10⅞" (27.5 cm) molded
Keelson	36'11" (11.25 m) in length 11" (28 cm) sided 9½" (24.5 cm) molded 1'½" (32 cm) sided and 11½" (29 cm) molded at mast step
Stern knee	7'11" (2.43 m) long 1'4" (41.3 cm) sided 1'2" (35.5 cm) molded
Frames	22" (56 cm) center-to-center spacing
Floors (average)	9½" (24 cm) sided, 10" (25.5 cm) molded, 1'¼" (31 cm) space
First futtocks	8½" (21 cm) sided, 8½" (21 cm) molded
Second futtocks	6½" (16.5 cm) sided, 6" (15.3 cm) molded
Mast step mortise	1'6" (44.5 cm) long, 8" (20.5 cm) wide, 6" (15.3 cm) deep
Outer hull planking	2" (5 cm) thick, 1'2" (36 cm) wide avg.
Ceiling planking	2" (5 cm) thick, 10" (25.5 cm) wide avg.

between the keel and the stem (the timber that curves up from the keel to form the bow of the vessel), possibly strengthening the scarf, which would have joined these timbers. The complete absence of a stem is a surprise, but it suggests that timber salvaging was conducted on the hull.

Although no evidence of the stem is preserved, portions of timbers that would have provided additional support to the bow did survive, notably the apron and stemson, each made of white oak (Tainter 1995). The apron is the largest preserved bow timber and would have been attached to the stem with two iron throughbolts. The port and starboard sides of the apron are beveled to facilitate planking as it runs forward.

A substantial curved timber lies in the stern of the vessel and would have supported the juncture between the aft end of the keel and the sternpost, where the rudder would be fitted. This "stern knee" is made from a single white oak timber and is fastened to the top face of the keel with two iron throughbolts (Tainter 1995). Measuring over 7 feet (2.43 meters) long, it also served to secure several frames near the aft end of the vessel, which is indicated by a series of notches cut out of the timber. At its aft extent the stern knee begins its upward curve, preserved for a vertical distance of 2 feet (61 centimeters). The timber is heavily eroded here, and no original faces are preserved. Wood grain follows the curve from the horizontal stern timber to its vertical arm, indicating that it is a grown timber rather than a vertical piece scarfed into the deadwood timber. Neither the keel nor any sign of a sternpost survives aft of the stern knee. However a small area dredged underneath the stern knee allowed divers to feel the eroded end of the keel approximately 1 foot, 6 inches (46 centimeters) forward of stern knee's vertical arm.

Framing System

The framing on the vessel is completely of white oak (Tainter 1995). Twenty-three floors are preserved, and notches in the stern knee indicate placements for at least two more. Each floor is fixed to the keel with a single iron drift bolt measuring 1 inch (2.56 centimeters) in diameter. Holes cut into the bottoms of floors, commonly known as "limber holes," would allow water to collect near the pump well for removal; these measure 1¼ inches (3.2 centimeters) high and 3 inches (7.5 centimeters) wide.

The hull contains a total of seventy-seven first and second futtocks; these frames extend from the floors to define the curvature of the hull as it rises toward the deck and rail of the vessel. The futtocks are fastened via wooden dowels, or "treenails," to the outer hull planking, and frames are joined to each other with horizontal treenails at nine locations (at floors #2, 4, 6, 9, 12, 15, 18, 21, and 23). The mold frames served as guides to the shipwright, essentially defining the entire hull shape with nine frame locations. These frames were the first to be erected on the keel, along with the floors for the other framing positions. The first strakes of outer hull planking could then be added. When the sides of the vessel had been built up sufficiently, the shipwright treenailed the first futtocks into place between the mold frames. After this, the planking of the hull continued until second futtocks could be positioned. The shipwright continued this process until the completion of the hull up to the sheer line, or the top of the sloop's sides. Near the bow and stern, where hull curvature is greatest, these mold frames are located at every second floor, but spacing increases to every third floor toward midships, where the hull curvature is not as dramatic. Forward of midships, floors are joined to the futtocks situated aft of them, and aft of midships floors are joined to the futtocks forward of them. As the framing system extends outboard, the first and second futtocks are also treenailed together at these locations.

The oblique or "cant" frames in the bow extend radially from the centerline of the hull (see Figure 6.1). These frames are fastened to the outer hull planking with treenails and are not joined to any other frames. Originally twelve cant frames would have supported the sloop's bow, but only nine of these frames survive in the bow construction. Seven of these timbers end close to the apron, but they do not actually butt up against it. The other two cant frames are shaped so that they wedge between the larger bow frames. The inboard ends of these timbers end in points, so that they extend as close to the centerline of the bow as possible.

Keelson

The keelson is made of a single piece of white oak (Tainter 1995) and extends 36 feet, 11 inches (11.25 meters) from its eroded stern end at floor #22 to the eroded forward end just aft of the second floor from the bow. The keelson is very rounded in cross section, which is likely due to erosion, and is attached intermittently to frames with iron throughbolts. To maintain a level plane, the keelson is notched to fit over eight floors, which is another indication of relatively skillful construction techniques.

A hole or mortise cut into the upper surface of the keelson is located at 18 feet (5 meters) from the bow, which corresponds to approximately a third of the vessel's length. The foot or heel of the sloop's mast would have been fitted into this mortise to secure it to the hull. Approximately 2 feet, 9⅝ inches (85 centimeters) aft of the mast step mortise, two smaller mortises are located in the top face of the keelson. These may be pillar or stanchion locations providing support for the sloop's deck. The location of these mortises may also indicate the forward extent of the vessel's main hatch, providing access into the main hold.

Hull Planking

The outer hull of the Readers Point Sloop consists of white oak planks fastened to the floors and futtocks with treenails (Tainter 1995). A protective layer of sacrificial planking overlies the outer hull planking. By the eighteenth century, shipwrights typically added a thin layer of planking to the outside of the ship's hull, often including a layer of animal hair and pitch applied between the two planking layers. This sacrificial planking added to the life of a vessel by taking the brunt of the wear and tear the ship was subjected to during its life. As the sacrificial planking became damaged and worn, it could be easily removed and replaced with additional planking without any serious damage to the primary hull planking. For ships in tropical waters, the layer of sacrificial planking proved a valuable addition to guard against shipworm (teredo) damage (Lavery 1987:59). Shipworms infested the sacrificial planking but could not penetrate the layer of pitch and hair covering the main hull planking. The sacrificial planking on the Readers Point Sloop is composed of ¼-inch (0.5-centimeter) planking of hard pine tacked onto the outside of the hull, with a layer of pitch mixed with animal hair between the planking layers.

The sloop's interior or "ceiling" planking is nearly identical to the outer hull planks. They are attached to frames predominantly with treenails, the general pattern being two treenails per plank at every second frame position. Removable limber boards sat alongside the keelson and would have allowed access to space between the frames for maintenance or cleaning. At several locations on the wreck unfastened southern yellow pine planks lie on top of the oak limber boards, presumably to strengthen weak areas in the limber planks.

Repairs

Numerous repairs on the vessel serve as mute testimony to the long working life of the Readers Point Sloop. Most of the ceiling planking on the vessel is made of white oak. However, eight planks of southern yellow pine were used to reinforce the ceiling at various locations throughout the wreck (Tainter 1995). A lead patch covered a weak spot on an outer hull plank in the stern, just forward of the eroded stern knee. The patch was applied to the outside, with a heavy layer of pitch and hair against the hull plank, then held into place with small copper tacks. A small timber made from a tropical hardwood is fastened next to the keel at its forwardmost extent (Tainter 1995). This timber is described above and may indicate a repair along the keel/stem scarf before the stem was removed by sawing through the keel at this location.

The most striking damage evident on the hull remains occurred at the mast step mortise (see Figure 6.1). A crack runs along the keelson and through the mortise itself for a distance of 9 feet, 7 inches (3 meters). Two iron spikes are driven horizontally into the starboard side of the keelson aft of the mortise to close the break. In addition, two additional longitudinal timbers are attached to the keelson at the mortise with horizontal iron spikes, apparently to support the repair. The port sister keelson is made of white oak and the starboard timber is made of hickory (*Carya* sp.) (Tainter 1995). These are further strengthened with the addition of two large rectangular "buttress" timbers, butting into rebates cut into the sister keelsons and fixed to the floors underneath them with vertical iron spikes. Both of the buttresses are made of white oak (Tainter 1995).

The starboard sister keelson overlaps the forwardmost horizontal spike, closing the break in the keelson. This suggests that the sister keelsons and buttress timbers were added after the break in the keelson and are therefore repairs rather than elements of the original mast step structure. Archaeologists disassembled the mast step and removed it to the shore for detailed recording. Crew members examined the top (inboard) faces of the underlying frames for any indications of fastener holes other than those associated with the buttress timbers, finding no evidence of any other timbers having been attached at the mast step before these repairs. It appears that prior to the keelson break, the mast step simply consisted of a mortise cut into the top (inboard) face of the expanded keelson. The split in the keelson necessitated the addition of strengthening timbers for repairs.

Archival Research

An exhaustive search of the available historical resources in the National Library of Jamaica in Kingston and the Jamaican Archives in Spanish Town failed to provide a concrete identity, name, or origin for the Readers Point Sloop. Unfortunately, there is not enough information available to positively identify the ship in either the archaeological or the historical record. This is not altogether unexpected as there are typically fewer contemporary documents pertaining to merchant craft. Also, because the vessel was a derelict, only a small collection of diagnostic artifacts remained in situ, which limited conclusions. However, data gleaned from archival research did prove useful in adding to our general knowledge of eighteenth-century shipping in Jamaica.

One of the most valuable archival resources was the *Royal Gazette,* a weekly Jamaican publication that carried general news for the island as well as particular information concerning shipping in Jamaica. The *Gazette*'s "Marine Intelligence" section lists the name and type of each vessel entering or leaving Kingston Harbor, the date, the master, and the vessel's origin or destination. Using data from the *Gazette,* we compiled a database containing information on sloops sailing to and from Jamaica in the later eighteenth century. This is not meant to be a definitive study of the total volume of maritime commerce conducted by sloops in Jamaica at this time. Whole weeks or entire years of the *Gazette* were unavailable within the time span targeted for the Readers Point Sloop. Also, illicit trade was so widespread during the late eighteenth century that any port records from this period must be viewed with caution. Finally, the degree of shipping information provided in the *Gazette* varied over time. Certain issues held marine intelligence as a priority, while others hardly mentioned shipping at all. Regardless, the *Gazette* provides a valuable contemporary resource for the origins and destinations of small merchant craft trading in Jamaica during this period.

All available editions of the *Gazette* pertaining to the later eighteenth century were reviewed on microfilm in the National Library of Jamaica in Kingston. The 1792 *Gazette* proved an exceptional year in terms of completeness as well as the amount of shipping information included throughout the year. Although artifact analysis suggests a slightly earlier date for the sinking of the Readers Point vessel, the 1792 *Gazette* provides a nearly contemporary resource.

The *Gazette* lists 190 vessels classified as sloops entering and leaving Kingston Harbor in 1792. The data indicate that 75 percent of the sloops entering Kingston harbor throughout the year had departed from another Jamaican port. The next most popular origin of sloops entering Kingston harbor was North America (notably Charleston), followed by other ports in the Caribbean. Only five sloops during the entire year were listed as arriving from Europe. The vast majority of sloops departing from Kingston headed to other ports in Jamaica. It is interesting to note that while North America was the second most popular origin for ships entering Kingston, most of these vessels then left Kingston for other ports within the Caribbean. This suggests a circuitous trade route, taking advantage of the various markets and ports, rather than a more direct, two-way route. Though small, this sample indicates that the majority of maritime commerce conducted with sloops involved localized, coastal trading within the Caribbean and North America.

Various contemporary sources corroborate the evidence found in the *Gazette.* Captain Frayer Hall gave an account of a typical West Indian trading voyage in 1731. His description of trading among the Caribbean islands in a sloop shows some of the complexities involved in the West Indian trade.

> I have lived in and traded for twenty Years past to the West Indies, and the northern Colonies. I was first there, at our Islands, in 1709, afterwards at Jamaica in 1712, and in 1714 I was Master of a Sloop, and carried a Load of Provisions and Lumber from Philadelphia to Barbadoes. There were more Vessels with Provisions and Lumber, which made the Prices of these Commodities very low at Barbadoes, so I went from thence down to Martinico, where I sold some Flour, and understanding there was a good Market, or great Demand, for Mules there, I went to Curasso, and took in forty-eight Mules at thirty Pieces of Eight a-piece, I bought them of the Governor; these were as many as I could carry, and I carried them to Martinico, I was nineteen Days in my Passage, and lost but two[.] When I came to Martinico, I was forced to get the People to petition for Liberty to sell the Mules, and I gave the Governor a hundred Livres for every Mule; I sold the whole Cargo at six hundred livres a Head, and sold the Mules in Health for seven hundred, any that could stand on their Legs would sell for four hundred; I got near four times as much as my first Expence. I went from Martinico to Barbadoes, and took in Flour, and went down to Curasso again; and in that time there were other Vessels arrived there, two from Nevis, and two French Sloops, but I could not make anything like the same profit; I went a third time, but could make but little of it then by my Mules. Great Quantities of Rum were made near Fort-Royal, and Fort St. Pierre [in Martinique], at that Time, I bought several Hogsheads of Rum and Sugar in Martinico the last voyage, and carried to Curacao. (Pitman [1917] 1945:205)

Discussion

The Readers Point vessel exhibits a relatively highly finished appearance in its construction. Frames are smooth and square, and the shipwrights obviously took care in positioning the nine mold frames on the sloop. Even the mast step repair shows careful workmanship and planning. The sloop's construction implies that the vessel was built by experienced shipwrights who perhaps specialized in West Indian traders.

Wood analysis suggests that the vessel's origin lies in the northeastern American colonies, probably New England. Extensive use of white oak for frames, the outer hull, and ceiling planking, as well as a maple keel, are indicative of construction in this area. Repairs made from species including southern yellow pine and tropical hardwoods suggest contact with southern American colonies and West Indian ports, probably through trading voyages.

The shape of the Readers Point Sloop is also indicative of New England–built vessels, which tended toward full-drafted designs. Cross sections of the hull show a fuller, more capacious cargo hold than other designs with sharper hulls or greater "deadrise." Flatter floors amidships increase cargo capacity at the expense of speed. This also tends to give a vessel shallower draft, allowing the sloop to easily navigate coastal waters and small bays common throughout the Caribbean and along the North American coast. The sloop was shallow drafted and handy enough to manage coastal trade, providing an important link between plantations and other ports.

Colonial shipwrights generally built sloops in two sizes reflecting specialized trades. Smaller vessels of twenty to forty tons plied the coastal trade, while larger sloops of fifty tons and larger were better suited for the Caribbean/North America trade (Goldenberg 1976). This information corresponds with contemporary historic data indicating that small, coastal vessels conducted the bulk of the local trade in Jamaica and larger sloops such as the Readers Point vessel sailed for longer distances to other islands or North American ports.

The Readers Point Sloop was a sizable vessel, with an estimated one-hundred-ton displacement. The vessel is lightly built. Primary timbers such as the apron and stern deadwood are attached to underlying timbers with only two iron throughbolts. In many vessels, these structures are composed of substantial stacks of timbers throughbolted heavily to the keel. The War of 1812 sloop *Boscawen* exhibits this type of construction (Crisman 1985). On the Readers Point vessel, however, a single grown timber acts as the stern deadwood as well as the stern knee. Radial cant frames in the bow of the sloop are attached to outer hull planking without butting up against the apron or stemson. The mast step construction is perhaps the most surprising. A mortise cut into the top face of the keelson left only 2 inches (5 centimeters) of wood on either side to support the mast foot. There is no evidence of supporting timbers before the break in the keelson necessitated adding sister keelsons and buttress timbers as repairs. These timbers, however, are heavily fastened. Perhaps the shipwright making the repairs realized the error of the builder.

The home port for the Readers Point Sloop is unknown, but its relationship with the Seville Plantation suggests the possibility that it was Jamaican-owned. A lucrative market existed in the West Indies during the eighteenth century for New England–built sloops. The combination of a shallow draft, handy sailing capabilities, low cost, and adaptability created a high demand for American sloops in the Caribbean.

The number of repairs evident throughout the hull remains suggests a long trading career before the sloop finally came to rest on the silty bottom of St. Ann's Bay. Further evidence that the owners stripped the vessel of cargo and useful items lies in the relatively few number of artifacts associated with the vessel. The Readers Point artifact assemblage primarily consists of broken and discarded items found in the ballast pile. The location of the ship in association with five other derelicts off Readers Point suggests that this was a disposal area or ship graveyard for eighteenth-century vessels.

Despite the limited numbers of objects associated with the Readers Point Sloop, a sufficient number of diagnostic artifacts helps establish a late eighteenth-century date for the vessel. These include ceramics, kaolin clay pipes, and glass containers. Artifacts making up the Readers Point assemblage are relatively common on eighteenth-century sites, suggestive of a typical working ship of the period. Analysis of artifact date ranges cluster around 1775, and it is likely that the vessel was abandoned after this date.

Organic remains such as plant and bone specimens indicate that salted beef and pork formed a large portion of the meat eaten on the ship. The sloop's crew also consumed mutton, rabbit, and chickens in lesser amounts. Meals onboard the sloop were supplemented with nuts and fruits from both tropical and temperate locales. The ship's crew likely utilized local food sources in the Caribbean and North America during trading voyages. Most notably, the identification of a gopher tortoise in the Readers Point assemblage suggests that the vessel sailed to the southeastern coast of North America.

Conclusion

The Readers Point vessel was probably a merchant ship that traded among the Caribbean islands and North American colonies. Faunal remains suggest the vessel had ventured to the southeast coast of the present United States and repairs were made with both tropical and North American wood species. The excavation of the site provides an opportunity to examine one of the small merchant sloops that were so vital to the growing colonial economy of Jamaica. Designed and built in the Americas for the colonial trade, sloops fulfilled a variety of roles, making them a valuable commodity as well as a practical method of transporting cargoes. The utility of these vessels contributed to their popularity, placing them in high demand in North America and the West Indian colonies throughout the eighteenth century. At the same time, the vessels' builders began to adapt hull shapes and designs for particular trades, reflecting a growing sophistication in the evolution of colonial sloops.

Over two hundred years ago, the owners of a merchant sloop abandoned her in a small bay on the north coast of Jamaica. The ship had served a long life, and it was probably no longer economically feasible to continue operating the vessel in the merchant trade. Stripped of running gear, rigging, mast, and cargo, the derelict was likely burned to the waterline or left floating until she eventually sank in the waters of St. Ann's Bay. Though considered worthless by her owners, the shipwreck's discovery by archaeologists brings a valuable example of Jamaica's maritime heritage to light.

Acknowledgments

The undertaking of any archaeological project is an immense venture, and one cannot hope to succeed without the help of many people and organizations. We owe a great debt to the crewmembers of the Readers Point shipwreck excavation team, who paid their own way to Jamaica and worked tirelessly for the benefit of the project. We are also grateful for the honor of calling each of them a friend.

Amy Rubenstein-Gottschamer kept us on track as codirector of the excavation and project conservator and displayed an amazing ability to create a functional conservation lab despite meager funds and difficult field conditions. Dorrick Gray never lost his enthusiasm for the project, breaking away from his responsibilities with the JNHT whenever possible to help excavate on the site. Clive Chapman played a vital role as the project divemaster and continually took on other jobs including photographer, artist, draftsman, and mechanic. We hope we are fortunate enough to work with him again in the future. We are indebted to David Ames, Darren Hurst, and Chris Sabick. Though we had never met before the excavation, they found their way to St. Ann's Bay in various mysterious ways. By the end of the project they were proficient in all aspects of the excavation and played a large part in our success. It is never difficult to entice Norine Carroll to hop on a plane bound for Jamaica. We benefited from her abilities as an archaeologist, and her presence lifted our spirits.

We cannot sufficiently thank the numerous volunteers who assisted us. Karl Gottschamer, Mike Krivor, Mike Lenardi, Daria Merwin, Tom Shannon, Juan Vera, and Richard Wills all contributed to the success of the excavation. We were fortunate to have a wonderful Jamaican staff as well, including Elsaida "Dottie" Harrison, Olivia "Kay" Sharpe, and Lincoln McKenzie.

Other individuals played key roles outside of the fieldwork, including Philip Armitage, Maureen Brown, Charles Chan, William Charlton III, Kevin Crisman, Marianne Franklin, Karen Fuller, Peter Gail, Michael Haley, Jerome Hall, Donny Hamilton, Fred Hocker, Becky Holloway, Phil Janca, John William Morris III, Lea Newsom, James Parrent, Wayne Smith, Frank Tainter, and Chip Vincent.

Project funding came from several sources. We are grateful to the Institute for International Education for their award of a Fulbright Fellowship, the INA for the Marion M. Cook Fellowship, and a gracious donation by INA board member Frederick Mayer.

Finally, numerous institutions supported our work, including the INA, the JNHT, the Discovery Bay Marine Laboratory, the South Carolina Institute of Anthropology and Archaeology's Bermuda Sloop Project, Paradise Scuba, Taff Office Equipment, and Seascape Dive Resort.

7

The Habitus of Jamaican Plantation Landscapes

James A. Delle

Introduction

Historical archaeology, a field that grew to maturity largely as an auxiliary science to museum-based interpretations of the recent past, has often failed to address questions of anthropological significance. This has not been for wont of trying; since the early 1970s historical archaeologists have attempted with varying levels of success to use anthropological theory to derive interpretations from historical materials. While the reasons for the general failure of historical archaeology to be anthropological are many, one underlying cause is a consistent tension between the nature of evidence used to generate conclusions (both artifacts and historical documents) and prevailing anthropological theories that shape the framework of interpretation.

For several decades, many historical archaeologists adhered to the processual agenda that emerged from the "New Archaeology" of the 1960s. This resulted in myriad studies that tried to correlate artifact patterns with patterns of behavior with an overarching goal of discovering, or expressing, evolutionary generalizations. As was the case with much of the "New Archaeology," the quest for patterns was in fact a search for normative rules of human behavior expressed in the ways that artifacts were deposited. That this quest was largely ahistorical was perhaps best conveyed by Stanley South in his famous monograph on artifact patterning in historical archaeology (South 1977).

A second theoretical framework used widely by historical archaeologists, particularly those somewhat disenchanted by the adaptationalist approach of the processualists, was structuralism, best expressed in the seminal work of James Deetz (1977). Influenced by the structuralist approach adopted by the folklorist Henry

Glassie in his study of vernacular architecture (e.g., Glassie 1975), Deetz attempted to correlate changes in stylistic expressions of such disparate artifacts as gravestones, houses, and dinner plates with larger cultural changes in what would become the eastern United States. The structuralists were generally more successful than the processualists in using both historic documents and artifacts to generate interpretations in this case of culture change. The primary critiques of the uses of structuralism in historical archaeology concerned, on one level, the epiphenomenal concept of culture the theory generally relied upon. Critiques on a second level focused on the vectors of culture change assumed by the structuralists, largely based as they were on the outmoded concept of diffusion; while structuralists were able to document change in practice, the forces that created that change were rarely discussed.

In the 1980s a number of historical archaeologists began incorporating various strains of Marxist theory into their interpretations. Perhaps the most widely cited (and widely critiqued; see Wilkie and Bartoy 2000) Marxist study was Mark Leone's consideration of William Paca's garden in Annapolis, Maryland. Leone argued that formal gardens were an expression of class struggle, inasmuch as local elites, like Paca, extended their control over society to control over landscapes. According to Leone's analysis, this was part of the process of ideology, in which context-dependent social relations were made to appear timeless and natural, creating a false consciousness among the subaltern classes so that they might internalize their marginalized role in a stratified society. Other historical archaeologists followed suit (e.g., McGuire 1988), examining how local elites similarly used the material world to reinforce class divisions. Others using a Marxist approach adapted Wallerstein's world systems theory to interpret the inequities resulting from the development of the capitalist world system (e.g., Delle 1989, 1994; Paynter 1982, 1985). The prevailing critique of such studies maintains that Marxists underestimate the roles individuals play in shaping their own lives. Marxists, it is claimed, privilege epiphenomenal forces over the actions of individual human beings.

In reaction to what is perceived as the normative approach of processualist, structuralist, and Marxian archaeologists emerged a set of critiques searching for a unifying paradigm, generally known as post-processualism. In historical archaeology, the post-processual critique has recently been manifested in a body of work generally referred to as "contextual" archaeology. The contextualists (see Hicks and Beaudry 2006; DeCunzo and Ernstein 2006) contend that historical archaeology is best focused at the level of individual experience. As such, many contextual studies focus on single sites to create microhistories or narratives of individual experience.

Some historical archaeologists uncomfortable with the particularism inherent in the contextual approach have been influenced by neo-Darwinian theory. Tim Pauketat (2001) has described the neo-Darwinian movement as both a reaction to the failings of post-processualism and a revision of processualism. One group of neo-Darwinians, characterized by Pauketat as "selectionists," applies the Darwinian concept of selection to artifacts. This approach has gained some adherents in historical archaeology, most notably Fraser Neiman, who has argued that selective pressures induced change in both ceramics and storage pits (e.g., Neiman 1995). Again, this approach can be critiqued for privileging an ambiguous force, in this case selective pressure, over human agency.

Another trend in historical archaeology is the practice of public archaeology. Influenced by the experiences of archaeologists working with indigenous peoples in the New World and Australia as well as African American groups, particularly after the widely publicized project at the African Burial Ground site in New York City, many historical archaeologists have come to realize that their work, no matter what its theoretical underpinnings, should resonate somehow with the non-archaeological community. This endeavor has been expressed by archaeologists working with descendant communities to define and address questions and issues of local importance. It has also led some historical archaeologists back to (part of) our own beginning—to work with local historians and the historical preservation community, not simply to fill museum displays or to answer architectural questions but to help broaden our understanding of the everyday people of history who sometimes are poorly—if ever—represented in the documentary record. This approach to the material past has recently been described as "a new pragmatism" for archaeology (e.g., Preucel 2010).

While public history and historic preservation efforts remain an important part of what historical archaeologists do, many historical archaeologists have been asking broad questions concerning historical processes and phenomena that are very often relevant to our present. In my case, I have been attempting to address historical processes and precedents that have influenced the way the social world is shaped today, a world in which, still, a minority of people in colonial metropolises accumulate power and wealth while the majority of people in the post-colonial world suffer in poverty, with hundreds of millions of people engaged in a daily struggle for survival, whether it be in seeking shelter from violence, gaining access to adequate health care systems, or simply struggling to get food and safe drinking water. These are issues that threaten not only the health and well being of people in impoverished nations but the stability of the entire post-colonial global system.

While I do not deny that it is important to fill gaps in our historical knowledge about the kinds of building materials people used to construct their houses or the food that people ate at specific times and in specific places—I myself have exerted some effort in answering these kinds of questions about quotidian life—the best historical archaeology, in my opinion, addresses large questions from small things, deriving interpretations about historical and social processes from what the late historical archaeologist James Deetz referred to as the "small things forgotten," what we more broadly define as material culture. I have recently been most interested in examining a specific class of material culture, what historical archaeologists refer to as the built environment, which encompasses such things as buildings and landscapes. Specifically, I have been analyzing the landscapes of early nineteenth-century Jamaican coffee plantations to better understand how spatial organization helped shaped social experience on a variety of spatial and conceptual scales.

Habitus as Historical Process

Influenced by the approaches that look to link the individual experiences of people to the social and historical processes that work to shape their lives, I have been examining the roles such spatial constructs played in the construction and negotiation of social complexity in nineteenth-century colonial Jamaica. Much of my work is based on the proposition that certain buildings and landscapes were designed and constructed to express power, not necessarily by display but through action. Spaces are dynamic phenomena whose nature is experienced only when people move through them. This movement through space helps shape daily ritual and mediates our experiences and relationships with the physical and social worlds in which we are embedded, a phenomenon defined by the French sociologist Pierre Bourdieu as "habitus."

A number of archaeologists have used Bourdieu's concept as a theoretical bridge between approaches focused on determinant structures and those based on ahistorical agency. A difficult term to define, habitus is a social process by which behavioral dispositions are formed within individuals as a result of their constant interaction with their social and physical environment. These dispositions in turn structure the way that the individual experiences the world. Bourdieu argued that habitus, though learned, resulted in a largely unconscious understanding of the parameters of behavior possible within given contexts. The structures of a society would help shape habitus, and habitus would create a spectrum of possible action by individuals. Because each individual would experience the world in slightly different ways—even different members of an enslaved community might have a different relationship to an overseer or a planter—individual action was not only possible but likely. While much of the collective habitus might be similar, each individual would develop an idiosyncratic understanding of the world. Actions and behaviors might be constrained by the structures of society defining habitus, but each individual could create new action within the perceived range of the possible. Charles Orser has applied this concept to archaeological analysis of the process of racialization in North America (Orser 2004, 2007).

The habitus of nineteenth-century Jamaican plantation society was defined by a rigidly structured classist and racist worldview; it is impossible to understand the Jamaican experience outside this context (Delle 2008, 2009). Unlike in the majority of plantation societies in the U.S. South, people of African descent have comprised the great majority of the Jamaican population for centuries. It is eminently clear that the social order in which a small minority enslaved and profited from the labor of a vast majority was one that was built through the expression of unequal relations of power. The constant expression of this power may have been nowhere more necessary than in the remote interior coffee plantation settlements of Jamaica, many of which were physically and socially isolated from the main littoral strip of settlement along Jamaica's coasts, and in which it was not uncommon for blacks to outnumber the dominant whites by ratios of two hundred or three hundred to one.

It seems equally clear that the organization of settlements in the interior had to have as a focus both defensive and coercive elements in order to reinforce the racist social order of plantation slavery and to physically protect the material interests and lives of the white planters and overseers who dominated the social order. The designs of many Jamaican coffee plantation landscapes were executed in such a way as to physically embody the structures of inequality. Of course, the planters who owned the estates and the overseers who managed them lived in lavish houses compared to the small houses occupied by the enslaved. However, it was the spatial relationships between the various elements of the physical plant of individual plantations, the layout and organization of villages, and the spatial relations that existed between plantations that are of interest to me when analyzing how power was expressed spatially.

Historical archaeologists often have an advantage over prehistorians in identifying intent. It is not unusual to find documents describing the behaviors that certain buildings are designed to elicit. Perhaps the classic example of this is in the design of Jeremy Bentham's panopticon, a building form designed to maximize the ability of a minority to keep a majority under constant surveillance. Foucault among others has noted that this form was applied equally to prisons, hospitals, schools, and factories (Delle, Leone, and Mullins 1999; Foucault 1979; Nassaney and Abel 2000). The brutal logic of the panopticon lies in the uncertainty of the watched, who never really know whether they are being watched at any certain moment. This spatial logic is meant to "correct" behaviors deemed inappropriate; it is an effective mechanism to shape people's behavior if they believe they are being watched—certainly it is an expression of power by the watcher over the watched. The intended outcome of all of this is to mold the behavior of some to the demands of others (Epperson 2000).

It is, of course, impossible to keep an entire population under constant surveillance in order to continuously correct their behavior. From the perspective of the sociospatial engineers, it would be much easier to create a situation in which people unconsciously self-correct their behavior in certain contexts to create what in Bourdieuian terms we might call a habitus of acquiescence. If all went according to plan, such habituated behavior would occur at nearly a subconscious level—the majority would correct their own behavior to conform to the intentions of those who designed the spaces in question. This, to borrow a phrase used by Julian Thomas (2002), is a geography of power.

Do such geographies of power actually exist? I think in the case of plantation slavery the answer is yes; an explication of my thoughts concerning this follows, but first, I think it is important to contextualize just what "power" is and how this concept really affected the social realities of Jamaican plantation slavery.

Defining Power as It Existed in Jamaica

Historical archaeologists tend to define power dialectically. Following Gramsci, it has been argued, notably by Robert Paynter and Randall McGuire (1991), that power exists simultaneously as "power over"—that is, the power of elites to subjugate and control—and "power to"—the power of the subjugated to resist social control (see also Miller and Tilley 1984). In stratified societies, including capitalist society, it seems self-evident that social hierarchy is built upon the ability of elites to express "power over" or domination; archaeological residues of such expressions of power are easily read in the traditional markers of status inequality and chiefly or state power—namely monumental architecture, differential grave treatments, and so forth. "Power to," otherwise referred to as empowerment or resistance, is much more difficult to ascertain archaeologically, as it often existed only in the nexus of social negotiation and leaves light material traces, if any at all (though see Delle 1998 and Nassaney and Abel 2000 for examples of how such strategies of resistance can be read in the archaeological record).

Historical archaeologists are at something of an advantage when it comes to analyzing the material negotiation of power, for unlike in most prehistoric contexts, historical players often left behind written records of their intentions. In dealing with situations in which the stated intention of elites was to create economic and social hierarchies reinforced by the built environment, historical archaeologists are thus able, when willing, to discuss many levels of the negotiation of power, from the written intentions and plans of designers, architects, and social theorists, to the implementation of these intentions through the physical manipulation of the landscape, to the sometimes surprising ways that buildings and landscapes were interpreted by those they were meant to subjugate. Historical archaeologists have examined such phenomena most closely in two contexts: in the creation of rural and urban industrial societies, particularly in nineteenth-century New England (e.g., Mrozowski, Ziesing, and Beaudry 1996; Nassaney and Abel 2000; Paynter 1981; Shackel 1993), and in the context of plantation slavery in the U.S. Southeast and the

Caribbean (e.g., Delle 1994, 1998; Orser 1988). Elsewhere (e.g., Delle 1998) I have analyzed plantation treatises to reveal the stated intentions of coffee plantation designers.

It may go without saying that in the historical and social context of Caribbean plantation slavery, power was expressed quite overtly in quotidian social relations, though some have occasionally questioned the extent to which coercive power was exercised (Farnsworth 2001). Nevertheless, the nature of power relations is summed up nicely in this quote from Dr. David Collins, the owner of a Caribbean sugar plantation who wrote in 1811: "A slave, being a dependent agent, must necessarily move by the will of another, which is incessantly exerted to control his own; hence the necessity of terror to coerce his obedience" (Collins [1811] 1971). Collins, like many of his published contemporaries, understood the necessity of exerting power over the subjugated to make the plantation system work.

Those familiar with historical plantations know that plantation owners like Collins stood at the apex of their Euro-centered social hierarchy. In the British West Indies, many plantations were owned by absentee proprietors who remained in Great Britain most of the year; some planters never set foot on their Jamaican estates. The day-to-day activities of the plantation would be organized and supervised by a white overseer, who had the right to inflict corporal punishment on the population. In the absence of a resident proprietor, the enslaved population was at the mercy of these sometimes capricious men. For example, one overseer by the name of Thomas Thistlewood gleefully recorded in his diaries the identities of the women he raped, which numbered in the dozens. He also described the more creative punishments he inflicted on the people under his authority—in one particularly disturbing case he had several men hold down one of their fellow slaves while yet another man defecated in his mouth (Hall 1989). I would certainly argue that Thistlewood exercised power over all of the participants in such instances.

The world of the enslaved, while obviously affected by the social realities of forced captivity and coerced labor, was structured with a simultaneous and quite different logic. Social relations beyond the control of the planters were structured by conjugal and other kin and lineage relationships, community pooling of resources, and an independent market economy, controlled and run by women who sold produce in the markets and men who might sell the products of skilled labor (Armstrong 1990; Hall 1959; Hauser 2008; Mintz and Hall [1970] 1991).

When discussing how power was negotiated in such a context, one must first consider that these two social worlds often collided, but nearly as often they converged, as, for example, in the case of Radnor, one of the coffee plantations located in the Negro River Valley, where an extant plantation daybook indicates that the overseer purchased food for the white estate staff from the enslaved with cash (Delle 1998, 2000b). As hinted in such occasional convergences, black and white worlds were quite obviously never completely separate, but certainly never equal. Until the early nineteenth century, the Jamaican socioeconomy was based on a system of chattel slavery, a dehumanizing system in which those in positions of authority maintained the right to buy and sell human beings as property and to extract wealth through the unrewarded products of their labor. The system in Jamaica was far more unstable than its analogue in the U.S. South, as in Jamaica, the enslaved population outnumbered the free whites by a ratio of 30 to 50 to 1 island wide, a ratio much higher on specific plantations in the interior.

Various methods were used to support this system, including instruments of torture such as whips, stocks, collars, treadmills, gibbets, and shackles. The object, of course, was to elicit specific types of behavior among the enslaved, including acquiescence to the system. Public torture and humiliation were exercised not only to inflict pain and death on those who refused to submit willingly to the power of the whites but, as Dr. Collins described, to terrify the onlookers into obedience. As Foucault (1979) has eloquently and famously argued, more subtle forms of disciplinary restraint, notably surveillance, are dependent upon the omnipresent threat of physical violence. Public displays of torture—commonplace in premodern Europe—were prevalent in Jamaican slave society, as men like Collins attempted to use violence against a few to instill fear among the many, hoping to terrorize the general population into acquiescence.

Physical torture has its limits, of course. The capricious use of such power could, and did, inspire revolt among the enslaved, as about once every other generation there was a large-scale slave rebellion, the largest of which included tens of thousands of rebels and informed the final debate over the abolition of slavery in the British colonies. Despite the end of slavery, the white elites in Jamaica—and those with West Indian interests in England—struggled hard to maintain a social hierarchy that placed themselves at the top. In many ways the social inequality created under slavery persisted in the post-emancipation period, as the planters attempted, consciously, to first create and then perpetuate a spatial order that reinforced the structures of inequality. Both prior to and following emancipation, such sociospatial systems of inequality were constructed on several scales, minimally including what we might consider the regional scale, the plantation scale, and the community scale.

Multiscalar Approach to Understanding Plantation Landscapes

I have explored the relationships between space and power on three scales of analysis in Jamaica. Presented here in order of decreasing scale, these include the Negro River Valley Project, which was conducted at a regional scale, the Yallahs Drainage Project, which examines space at the level of the individual plantation, and the

Marshall's Pen Project, which has been focusing on the spatial organization of an enslaved village at the community scale.

Analyzing Power on the Regional Scale

It has long been recognized that the location of sites within a region can be usefully analyzed to say something about how power was exerted through space. The study of settlement patterns and how they relate to social complexity has been a mainstay of prehistoric archaeology in both the Old and New worlds for generations (Adams 1965; Sanders 1956; Sanders, Parsons, and Santley 1979; Willey 1953). In the early 1980s Robert Paynter (1982, 1983) demonstrated how historical archaeologists could use settlement pattern analysis to interpret power dynamics within the capitalist social order. In his examination of spatial inequality in western Massachusetts, Paynter argued that space should be considered as not only a vector of social inequality but an active creator of capitalist hierarchies. Similar studies focused on regional settlement systems (e.g., Delle 1994; Leone 1984; K. Lewis 1984) eventually led to the creation of a virtual subfield of historical archaeology generally known as landscape archaeology (Kelso 1989; Kelso and Most 1990; Yamin and Metheny 1996). While some landscape archaeology focuses on the renovation or restoration of historical landscape features like gardens (e.g., Goodwin et al. 1995; Metheny et al. 1996), other historical archaeologists have argued that some landscapes are created intentionally and experienced variously and actively within class-, race-, and/or gender-based webs of power (Delle, Leone, and Mullins 1999; Kryder-Reid 1994; Leone 1984; Weber 1996). Jamaica's Negro River Valley is one such regional landscape.

The Negro River is a tributary of one of Jamaica's largest interior waterways, the Yallahs River. Originating in three springs located at approximately 5,000 feet above sea level on the southern slope of the Grand Ridge of the Blue Mountains, the Negro River descends 3,500 feet over the course of approximately four miles to its confluence with the Yallahs River. As a highland riverine valley, the Negro River Valley is characterized by very steep terrain. The river itself, like the Yallahs into which it flows, is too steep and shallow to be navigable over any significant distance. Transportation in the valley is thus dependent on terrestrial vehicles; in the past mules were the preferred mode of transportation, while today the upper reaches of the valley are accessible only by four-wheel-drive vehicles.

Historically, there have been a number of coffee plantations located in the Negro River Valley, and some of the famous Blue Mountain coffee originates here (Delle 1998; Beghiat 2008). While the land in the Blue Mountain region, and the Negro River Valley in particular, was patented as early at the 1770s, large-scale coffee production did not get started in the region until the opening decades of the nineteenth century. The Jamaican coffee industry has experienced a classic series of boom-bust cycles: initially profitable during the Napoleonic Wars, the coffee economy suffered from an immediate peacetime depression in the late 1810s, regained somewhat in the 1820s, contracted again in the late 1830s following the abolition of slavery, had a brief resurgence in the 1860s, declined again until the 1980s hipster coffee boom, and is now once again suffering a decline, brought on by overspeculation, the collapse of Asian financial markets (as much as 80 percent of Jamaica's coffee crop is exported to Japan), and through rumored corruption in the agrarian sector of Jamaica's political economy.

Not surprisingly, the history of settlement in the Negro River Valley parallels the booms and busts of the coffee industry. In the early decades of the nineteenth century, coffee was an extremely profitable commodity for British colonials, primarily because the Haitian Revolution had cut off Europe's main supply of coffee. The Jamaican highlands, featuring an ecology not dissimilar from the highlands of nearby Haiti, became a locus of coffee production as colonial agents attempted to fill the European coffee vacuum. The political ecological landscape of the valley was imprinted at this time, as a number of coffee plantations were carved out of the tropical forest; to this day, the administrative divisions and locations of settlements in the valley are based on the location of these original plantations. Interviews with local informants and an analysis of the cartographic history of the valley indicate that during the first boom era, at least fifteen plantations operated in the Negro River Valley, including Brook Lodge, River Head, Windsor Forest, Friendship, Woburn Lawn, Eccleston, Upper New Battle, Lower New Battle, Sherwood Forest, Minto, Epping Farm, Farm Hill, Radnor, Whitfield Hall, and Abbey Green.

One of the richest primary sources for reconstructing the economic history of Jamaica is a series of documents kept by the colonial government recording the amount of produce exported by individual estates, known as the Accounts Produce or Crop Accounts. These records indicate that coffee was exported out of the Negro River Valley as early as the opening decade of the nineteenth century—Sherwood Forest exported coffee in 1801 and Radnor in 1806. It seems that some of the plantations never turned much of a profit; for example, although both Brook Lodge and Eccleston are evident in the cartographic and archaeological records, neither appears in the Accounts Produce (although this may be an artifact of the owners' processing or storing coffee elsewhere, or out and out selling it as a raw product to another estate). By 1837, both Brook Lodge and Eccleston were referred to in the documents as being "appendages" to Sherwood Forest. Reflecting the post-emancipation collapse of plantation production in Jamaica, by the mid-1850s, all of the estates disappear from the documentary record; the Accounts Produce were suspended in 1866 when Jamaica was brought directly under the control of the British government as a crown colony. In these decades, many estates in the Jamaican highlands were subdivided and sold to small farmers—emancipated slaves and their descendants—though the coffee works, Great Houses, and immediately surrounding land were largely kept in white hands (Satchell 1990). In the late nineteenth and early twentieth centuries, Jamaica went through a period of land consolidation. During this time, most of the Negro River Valley estates were acquired and co-opted by a local land baron named Robert Stott, who was reputedly a harsh landlord, holding thousands of acres of land until his death in the late 1950s, apparently making most of his money off of rents. After Stott's death, many of the estates passed again into numerous smaller holdings. Coffee cultivation began again in earnest in the early 1980s, though many of the estate houses and industrial works had fallen into ruin.

As a highland valley that produces an exportable commodity, the Negro River Valley is a contained ecological system connected to the outside world through a complex political economy. During the nineteenth century, this political economy relied on the expression of coercive power—both corporal and economic—to extract the amount and kind of labor power required by coffee planters to produce exportable crops. The various coffee planters, rather than being competitors, operated under a colonial economic system in which they constituted a class—defined by world systems theorists as a "regional elite" (Paynter 1985; Peregrine and Feinman 1996; Wallerstein 1979, 1980, 1989)—that shared many common interests. Among these were an interest in keeping the cost of labor low either by maintaining the structures of slavery or, following its abolition, by keeping post-emancipation wages low, dominating ownership of coffee works, land, and other means of production, and thus controlling the material factors of a social hierarchy in which the white planters maintained control over the costs of export production.

How, though, were these phenomena materially expressed? In valley systems, one manner by which elites can express power is through the strategic placement of buildings on the landscape. It is well-known that in prehistoric urban settings, temples, palaces, and other structures in which power is housed are often raised up on platform mounds or on the top of stepped pyramids. Such placement reinforces the authority of the ruling class by symbolically raising the elites above the natural view of the commoners (Emerson and Pauketat 2002). Such logic has long been in place in capitalist contexts (Delle et al. 1999; Epperson 2000). In the case of the Negro River Valley coffee plantations, the most symbolic structures, those endowed with the most symbolic power, were the Great Houses in which the elites lived. During an archaeological survey of the Negro River Valley conducted in 1998, it became obvious that the placement of Great Houses had little ecological logic; some were placed so close to the edge of precipices that they have since eroded into the river. Although a suitable ecological explanation for locating expensive houses on friable soils delicately balanced in some cases over one hundred feet above the river is not immediately obvious, it would seem that they were placed high in the valley to create a panoptic view for the elite inhabitants, not unlike that created by Jefferson at Monticello (Epperson 2000). However, upon further reflection, the placement of plantation buildings was based on a more subtle spatial logic.

One way to model the logic behind the placement of such seemingly important structures in such precarious locations is by analyzing what has become known as viewshed, that is, modeling what can be seen by the human eye from particular points in the landscape. This type of analysis has gained a number of adherents and has been usefully applied to archaeological studies in the Caribbean. For example, Joshua M. Torres and Reniel Rodriguez Ramos (2008) have used viewshed analysis to model the visual connectivity between individual islands in the Caribbean archipelago. Viewsheds can be relatively easily constructed using desktop GIS applications, like ESRI's ArcView package. To accomplish this, my students and I constructed a three-dimensional model of the Negro River Valley and its immediate environs by digitizing a topographic map of the region. Using the elevation data from this map, we created a three-dimensional model of the landscape, known as a TIN (triangulated irregular network) image. The TIN image has the elevation data embedded into it; thus it is more than a static image of the landscape. ArcView can easily interpolate how much of the landscape can be viewed from any particular point on the TIN, from any distance above the ground. In our models, we calculated the viewshed visible from the center points of the Great House locations, determined through the survey of the valley conducted in 1998; at that time, we were able to locate the sites of seven Great Houses, three still standing and occupied (Abbey Green, Farm Hill, and Sherwood Forest) and four in ruins (Radnor, Eccleston, Upper New Battle, and Lower New Battle). We chose to calculate viewsheds from three meters above the surface of the ground from each of these points, providing a relatively conservative estimate of the entire viewshed visible from each Great House. (NB: The viewsheds from somewhat higher would encompass more of the landscape than could most likely actually be seen; for the purpose of modeling we chose to err on the conservative side.) It should also be noted that the model does not take into account sight lines obscured by tree growth. While it is likely that much of the forest cover would have been cleared to create open fields for planting coffee trees, it is impossible at this point to know just how much land was cleared in the middle of the nineteenth century. Nevertheless, despite these shortcomings, this spatial modeling gives us a good idea of how much of the valley could be seen from the perspectives of the Great Houses.

The most striking result of the viewshed analysis is that each of the Great Houses whose locations could be reconstructed—with the sole exception of Sherwood Forest—was strategically placed so that its view would encompass the location of at least two other Great Houses. From the Eccleston Great House, one could simultaneously see the Great Houses at three other plantations; from Farm Hill three; from Abbey Green four; from Upper New Battle four; from Lower New Battle five; from Eccleston four; and from Radnor four. Although Sherwood fell into the viewshed of only Lower New Battle, it is likely, given the house's orientation to the south, that Sherwood would have fallen into the viewshed of other plantations located down river into the Stony River and Yallahs River valleys, areas not covered by our 1998 survey.

Placing Great Houses in direct view of each other and elevated above the valley floor allowed several things. This placement allowed the whites inhabiting these houses to be in visual, and possibly audible, contact with one another, literally creating a communication network in an area that did not have telegraph lines and to this day exists beyond the terminus of traditional phone lines in Jamaica. From these vantage points, messages could have traveled very quickly from one house to another. Such a system of communication would have been an extremely powerful tool; one elderly informant reported that his grandfather remembered sometime around the turn of the twentieth century that the white inhabitants used to talk to each other from house to house using megaphones to warn each other of local labor unrest (Lewis Richards, personal communication, 1998). Establishing such a network in which messages could be passed up the valley very quickly allowed the planters to exert control over the entire length of the Negro River Valley. Equally important, the local laborers in the valley would have known, as my informant's grandfather apparently did, that the whites would be able to quickly mobilize should there be unrest in the valley; this knowledge could well have been a deterrent to collective action in the valley. Certainly, this political ecology reflected a geography of power on a regional scale.

Power at the Plantation Scale: Plantation Layout

It is possible to interpret similar phenomena at a local site-specific level by examining the layout of plantation buildings and the design of space on individual plantations. Unfortunately, during the survey of the Negro River Valley, we came to learn that in the early twentieth century a flood of biblical proportions (one hundred inches of rain was said to have fallen in a week) washed away many of the plantation buildings, leaving too little trace of where, for example, slave villages were located. However, Clydesdale, a nearby contemporary plantation on the Clyde River—like the Negro River a tributary of the Yallahs—provides an interesting analogue that can shed light on how power was spatially negotiated in the Negro River Valley.

Although the layout of individual Jamaican coffee plantations is somewhat idiosyncratic, the basic structural logic of a plantation layout was based on the relationships between several landscape features. As discussed above in the context of the Negro River Valley survey, most Jamaica plantations feature a Great House, which would be the full- or part-time residence of the plantation owner. The management of the estate would generally fall to the overseer, who resided in a separate building (the overseer's or busha's house). Coffee plantations would, of course, feature coffee fields, in which the coffee trees would grow, and the produce would be picked by plantation workers. Once harvested, the coffee would be processed for export.

This involved several processing stages. The coffee berries would be pulped in a wet process by which the seeds (coffee beans) of the tree would be separated from the thick rind and pulp of the coffee fruit. Once pulped, the coffee would be dried, and a thin membrane known as the parchment would need to be removed in a dry process known as grinding. Once the parchment was removed, the coffee would be sorted by bean size and stored to await shipment. This multistage process required an industrial facility known as the coffee works; the processing clearly also required access to water for the wet pulping process. Attached to the works was a set of drying platforms known as barbecues. Another key landscape feature was the workers' housing. The enslaved community lived in small houses organized into a village. Given that the Jamaican plantation system required the enslaved workers to produce their own food, plantations also contained small farm plots allotted to individuals or households. These were located in what were called provision grounds.

To understand how these landscape features were tied together, I have re-created the built landscapes of several Blue Mountain plantation landscapes (Delle 1998, 1999), including Clydesdale and Sherwood Forest. Supplementing survey data with cartographic information, it is possible to create a composite map that can usefully reconstruct the landscape of Clydesdale. Considering the plantation model as a panopticon, the overseer's house would have served as the central point of surveillance, the analogy to the central guard tower of the true Benthamite panopticon. The Clydesdale overseer's house featured two surveillance positions. The first was the entrance door to the domestic quarters, which would most likely have had a small landing at the top of a wooden stair. From this point, the overseer could monitor the slave village, which was located uphill, within the viewscape of this position. The path from the village to both the coffee fields and the industrial works passed directly by this point. Thus, without leaving the confines of his house, the overseer could survey the domestic quarters of the workers and watch them as they walked from their houses to their work.

The second surveillance point was the veranda of the overseer's house. The coffee works and barbecues were located downhill and within the viewscape of this vantage point. Thus, from the comfort of his veranda, the overseer could supervise the coffee works and any activity occurring on the barbecues. During the times when the overseer wanted to exert the greatest measure of control over the workers, he could practice panoptic surveillance over the population. Equally crucial to this method of social control is the spatiality of the observed. By locating the overseer's house in such a way that the overseer could be surveying the village and works from the veranda or even by gazing out of one of the house's windows, the workers could never be entirely sure whether they were being watched. The purpose behind the construction of this spatiality was the construction of discipline in the enslaved workforce; the logic of the panopticon dictated that the workers would cooperate if they thought that someone might be watching them and that they would be physically punished if their overseers saw them acting in a way not sanctioned by the elites.

Similar spatialities may have been constructed at other plantations. However, a composite map for Sherwood Forest is more conjectural than for Clydesdale, as the location of the village is not recorded in the cartographic record. At Sherwood Forest, the original overseer's house was constructed very similarly to the Clydesdale house. From the side entrance to the house, the overseer had a vantage point from which he could survey the flats below the coffee works. Although these flats were heavily disturbed in the 1970s and 1980s when anthurium beds were constructed, several shovel test pits excavated in 1998 revealed evidence of nineteenth-century occupation, suggestive of slave quarters. If, as the evidence indicates, this was the location of the village, the overseer's house would have served as a surveillance point from which the domestic lives of the workers could be monitored. The veranda of this house provided a vantage point from which the overseer could monitor the barbecues. The surveillance of production may have been even more intense at Sherwood Forest than it was at Clydesdale, given that the mill machinery was located in the same building as the domestic space of the overseer. At Sherwood, the overseer could directly monitor the processing of coffee from his room or veranda; it is possible that he also could have surveyed the domestic lives of the enslaved (Delle 1998).

Power at the Local Scale: Spatialities of Movement

One of the methods by which Europeans attempted to further control the African Jamaican population was by restricting free movement through space—the spatiality of movement. To examine this aspect of the spatiality of coerced labor, we can analyze the freedoms and restrictions of movement experienced by the working population. For this analysis, I will again turn to one of the most complete primary documentary sources for the Blue Mountain plantations, the Radnor Plantation daybook, which recorded the daily activities on the estate during the 1820s.

The interpretation of the spatiality of movement from an estate book, like any similar historical exercise, is by default biased from the perspective of those in power, who, after all, recorded the history. From the perspective of the white estate staff, therefore, recorded movement through space can be interpreted as having occurred in two categories: sanctioned movement and illicit movement. Certain members of the plantation workforce had greater latitude to move through space than others by virtue of the role they played in the plantation workforce. For example, groups of workers were expected to transport the processed coffee crop to the wharves for shipment. The men entrusted with the movement of the coffee from the estate to the waterfront were allowed a sanctioned movement through space. Absconding from the plantation, or running away, was a spatiality of movement that was not sanctioned and can be considered a mode of spatial resistance to the expression of power over movement exerted by the planters.

The documents indicate that several of the members of the Radnor community were allowed sanctioned movement through space. For example, on January 21, 1822, Dunkin, a field worker from the first gang, was reported to be "sick in town, and not returned with the wharf book and bags." Three days later, "Dunkin returned . . . from town." By town, as is still the case in Jamaican vernacular, the Radnor Estate book was referring to Kingston. Dunkin was among those on the plantation who were allowed some free movement between Kingston and Radnor. However, his movement was sanctioned by the estate, as it was related to business, in this case, keeping accounts with the wharves from which Radnor coffee was shipped.

Similarly experiencing sanctioned movement through space, small groups of Radnor workers traveled on business regularly to the outskirts of Kingston. The plantation journal kept tight records on how many people went on these trips, how many pack animals were brought with them, when they left, and when they returned. During each month from March to October 1822, one to three overnight trips were taken by groups of six to twelve people to Hope Estate, near Kingston, with coffee; the comings and goings of these groups were closely recorded. In 1823, the traveling season was somewhat shorter, ending in August rather than October. In April of that year, the Radnor managers began to record the names of the people traveling with the coffee to Hope. At the time, Hope was an estate at the foot of the Blue Mountains on the outskirts of Kingston; it has since been incorporated into the city. As an estate on the outskirts of the entrepôt, Hope was most likely a staging area for Radnor coffee from whence it was transported to the docks for export. It is interesting that this was the ending point of the journeys with the coffee rather than the wharves themselves. Although a matter of speculation, this terminus may have been part of a strategy to prevent the enslaved porters from joining the crews of ships and hence escaping slavery.

The only recorded types of punishment inflicted on the population at Radnor can also be interpreted as spatialities of control. The daily work entry for Wednesday, January 23, 1822, contained the ominous passage: "masons with 5 negroes carrying stones preparing to build stocks room." This work continued through February 8; entries for this work alternately defined the space as a "stocks room" and a "stocks house." It is likely that the stone building that was under construction was a separate structure, within which movement would be harshly restricted by restraining people in stocks or pillories. The only overtly recorded punishment in the plantation journal utilized this facility of spatial control. On Tuesday, May 3, 1825, it was recorded that "Mulatto King was detected stealing coffee; is in the stocks." It is unclear how many people were confined in this space of punishment. What is clear is that such a strategy of radically restricting spatial movement, at least on this one occasion, was used on the plantation as a means of discipline. It is likely that the building was used more than on this one occasion. Its very presence, no doubt, served to intimidate and thus discipline the population via the threat of restricting movement by having one's hands and/or feet confined in the apparatus and being locked in what essentially was a stone dungeon. Limiting access to free movement through space was yet another means by which power was exerted in the Negro River Valley.

The workers whose lives the planters sought to control developed spatialities of movement in dialectical contradiction to these efforts. One way in which this was expressed was through the creation of a spatiality of movement distinct from that created by the planters. It is well known that enslaved Jamaicans had access to farms and gardens located in areas of estates defined as "provision grounds"—places that would rarely if ever be visited by the planters. In these spaces, the enslaved acted in a realm far removed from the technologies of surveillance constructed by the elites. More actively, individuals expressed resistance by moving through space of their own volition in acts defined by the planters as absconding, being absent, or running away. The Radnor Plantation daybook records that between January 1822 and February 1826 at least 25 different people, or 16 percent of the adult population of the estate, absconded from the plantation a total of 33 times, for an average of 19 days. In only one instance did the "absconded" fail to return (or be returned) to the plantation. Through this kind of action the workers in the Negro River Valley created a spatiality of movement, unsanctioned by the elites, in direct resistance to the surveillance of action and limitation of movement imposed by the elites. (For a more detailed discussion of the spatiality of resistance, see Delle 1998:155–67; for a discussion of the relationship between gender and space in this context, see Delle 2000b.)

Community Habitus: The Villagers of Marshall's Pen

In my recent work at Marshall's Pen, which is located in central Jamaica, I have been following up the lines of inquiry I opened in the Blue Mountains by archaeologically analyzing spaces built and inhabited by the enslaved.

Marshall's Pen is a former coffee plantation situated in the foothills of the Santa Cruz Mountains of central Jamaica. It began operations as a coffee estate in 1819, when the plantation managers opened up several hundred previously undeveloped acres of woodland attached to another estate known as Martins Hill. A slave village and coffee works were established at Marshall's Pen several years before an overseer's or Great House was constructed on this new plantation, and it wasn't until the late 1820s that permanent white supervisors took up residence on the plantation, as the day-to-day operations of the estate were managed from Martins Hill, some five miles away. Given that the village was constructed with what surely was a low level of surveillance, the village at Marshall's Pen may be one of the best places to examine how enslaved members of Jamaican society organized and lived in their own spaces.

We began our investigations at Marshall's Pen in 1999 with a pedestrian survey and a series of geophysical remote sensing surveys of the areas around the landform upon which the village was situated, still referred to as Negro House Hill. We conducted magnetometry and soil conductivity surveys in the village, and in a cemetery located just to the south of the village where a number of grave markers were still visible. During that first field season, we conducted a controlled surface collection of the entire village, piece plotting the locations of each artifact recovered. We also mapped existing stone walls and house foundations, creating a digital base map of the site that we could superimpose on the aerial photograph and use to begin preliminary analyses of spatial phenomena in the village. Our final task of 1999 was to conduct preliminary excavations on two features, one a house foundation visible from the surface, the other a large magnetic anomaly we had discovered from the magnetometer survey.

This latter feature turned out to be a large area of burned soil. Thinking at first that we might have a burned house, we assembled a flotation system out of local materials and conducted water flotation on the burned soil in the hope of recovering carbonized botanical materials.

In 2000 we returned to Marshall's Pen with the goal of completely excavating one house to get a fuller understanding of architectural techniques and possible use of space around a house. In 2001, we returned again, with the goal of excavating a cluster of houses, hoping to archaeologically shed light on how space was used within what we believe are house compounds. As was the case with Radnor, documentary evidence suggests that the white estate staff purchased foodstuffs from the people who lived in this village. To examine how the diets of the overseers and slaves may have compared, we excavated what was the overseer's outhouse, using a flotation system to recover botanical remains from the bottom of this privy.

Through the mapping project we have been able to determine that the village was organized into at least eleven different compounds or house areas, each of which was bounded by a stone wall or located on a well-defined terrace. Each compound contained three to five houses, and several of them featured a stone animal pen at the periphery. Excavations in a midden area located in a sinkhole revealed pig bones with cut marks; we thus tentatively concluded that these were pigpens, and the stock—or at least the pen itself—may have been shared by the members of the various compounds (Figure 7.1).

Analysis of the burned feature we discovered with the magnetometer produced early nineteenth-century ceramics, several pieces of iron cutlery, and fragments of iron cooking pots. We also recovered some carbonized beans (*Phaseolus vulgaris*). We have concluded that this was a kitchen area, where the primary midday meal

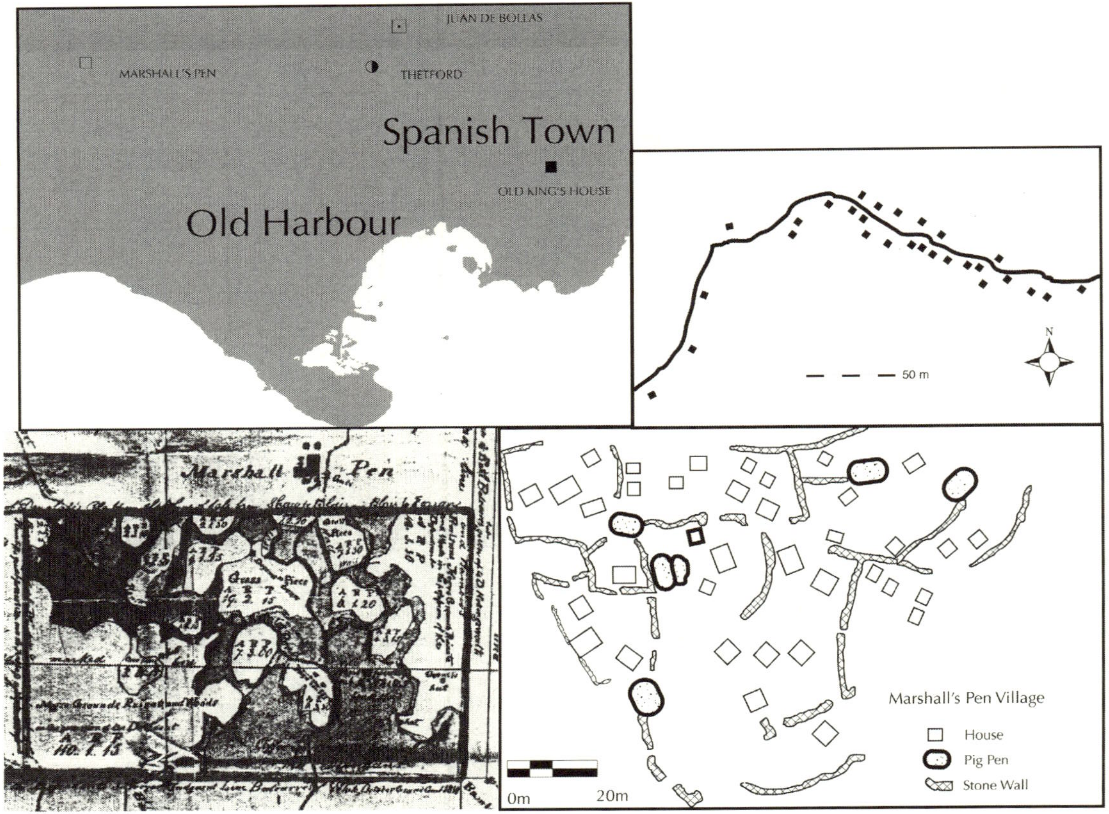

Figure 7.1. Marshall's Pen. *Clockwise from upper left:* location of Marshall's Pen in south-central Jamaica; composite reconstruction of the layout of Balcarres Township (note the settlement pattern that features single rows of houses on either side of main roads); archaeological reconstruction of the first workers' village; nineteenth-century plan of the provision grounds. Sources: Jamaica Survey Department, Crawford Muniments.

would be prepared for the labor gangs and from which it was probably delivered to them in the fields.

Several lines of evidence indicate that there was a considerable shift in village organization between 1812 and 1821. The earlier village, which was constructed in several phases, was built largely without direct supervision by the white estate staff, whose functions included not only supervising the construction of Marshall's Pen but the day-to-day operations of two other estates, including Martins Hill and Shooters Hill Pen. Two early maps of the estate indicate the location of the two villages and give a rough approximation of the shapes of the villages. The earlier village consisted of a clustered series of houses ranging up a hill, while the second village was more rationally organized in two rows of houses lining either side of a central road. As part of our archaeological investigations, the earlier village was mapped, as the ruins of the village, including house platforms, retaining walls, and animal pens, are still visible from the surface. The second village was transformed after emancipation into a settlement still known as Balcarres Township; we could not conduct a similar survey there. However, the layout of the modern township, which can be reconstructed from government survey maps and aerial photographs, does give a sense of how the township—and quite likely the antecedent village—was organized.

The results of our archaeological survey indicate that the earlier village was organized as a series of eleven multihouse compounds, each bounded by a stone fence or a series of retaining walls. The houses tend to surround a central yard space, and several are flanked by stone pigpens. European observers had difficulty understanding the spatial logic of villages organized this way. The missionary James Phillippo, for example, described slave villages as unsightly; to his eyes the houses "were thrown together without any pretense to order or arrangement" ([1843] 1969:216). What he may well have been witnessing was a settlement organization very similar to the clustered house compound pattern we recorded at Marshall's Pen and similar village plans noted elsewhere in Jamaica by Barry Higman (1998) and Doug Armstrong and Kenneth Kelly (2000). The cartographic data also indicate that several houses were dispersed among the provision grounds and coffee fields of Marshall's Pen. This arrangement would have allowed people the opportunity to live nearer to their fields. Alternatively, these may represent smaller houses that were occupied periodically by people who lived in the villages but maintained smaller shelters near their provision grounds, using them for shelter during sudden storms or as a private retreat. This settlement pattern can still be observed among Jamaican farmers today, who may reside in a village or other settlement but maintain a small house on lands they cultivate, which sometimes can be several miles away from their main home.

The rationalization of slave housing and villages was a topic some planters thought deeply about. In the years following the 1807 abolition of the slave trade, a number of treatises were published to provide advice on how best to keep the existing enslaved population alive. This was of particular concern to the planters following the abolition of the slave trade, as the enslaved Jamaican population had not previously been able to maintain itself through natural increase. Such advice on what was termed "amelioration" of the conditions of slavery can be read as a system of modernization, or the imposition of the ideas of modernity onto the enslaved population. To this end, one reformer, Dr. David Collins, suggested that the organization of houses and villages attached to estates needed to be rethought. In his estimation "houses should be placed more apart than they are now; an interval of thirty feet being the least that ought to be allowed. . . . They should be arranged in equidistant lines . . . to admit a more direct communication between them" ([1811] 1971:118–19). Such advice seems to have informed the construction of the second village at Marshall's Pen and thus, by extension, the settlement organization of Balcarres Township. The linear, equidistant arrangement of houses, reflecting the symmetry and order of modernity's imagined social structure, is visible both in the historic map of the pre-emancipation village and in the modern settlement pattern of Balcarres Township. It should come as no surprise that the population was evicted from the older village, organized as it was into house compounds with shared access to yard, garden, and animal pen space, and moved to the more "rational" settlement that would become Balcarres Township. By thus removing people from the spaces they had designed and occupied, including the provision grounds, the plantation managers created a condition by which the villagers would be required to work for wages in order to pay rent on their houses in Balcarres Township.

Conclusion

Archaeologists have modeled the relationships between social power and space in a variety of contexts and on a variety of scales, from the kingdoms of Mesoamerica to the complex chiefdoms of the American Bottom and Pacific islands, to the rise of empires in the Andes and throughout the Old World. Most agree that the negotiation of power can be interpreted at multiple scales. Regionally one can examine these processes through the analysis of settlement patterns and locally through the examination of site structure. In the Negro River Valley, it seems clear that the historic settlement pattern was based on locating Great Houses predicated on a logic of political ecology: while coffee works were located within ready access to water, the location of Great Houses conforms to a geography of power, as does the placement of structures within the plantation building complex.

One social locus of the expression of power was through the negotiation of class (Delle 1999). By locating the most monumental structures—Great Houses—in such a way as to visually control the valley, the planter elites were accomplishing several things. First, they were reinforcing their class solidarity by ensuring that they would be in constant visual and auditory contact with each other. Second, they were able to literally command a view of the valley. As one local informant described this landscape to me, "the whites would be able to keep an eye out, and warn each other, in case there was war" (Richards, personal communication, 1998). The war the whites would be concerned about was not invasion but uprising, a common form of resistance to the white-dominated social order, exemplified by a large uprising in 1865 in the nearby town of Morant Bay (Heuman 1994). By commanding a view of the valley and keeping each other within view and earshot, the whites would minimize the chance that they could be taken by surprise, at least from the valley, while reinforcing their solidarity among each other and their superordinate status above first the enslaved laborers and later the small tenant farmers living and working around the valley. In the end, the placement of Great Houses within the Negro River Valley visually reinforced the social hierarchy that the elites hoped to defend. Keeping workers on the plantation under surveillance by placing overseers houses in panoptic locations between villages and works reinforced the class hierarchy and was a further expression of power, as was the control of movement through spaces on and between plantations (Delle 1998; Holt 1992).

Despite the attempts at sociospatial control, the enslaved workers created a world of their own and lived much of their lives outside the gaze of the white planters. Whether in their houseyards within the village or working on the farm plots in the provision grounds, the African Jamaican population created a habitus of their own, apart from but, at least through the present day, simultaneously intertwined in the spatial logic of the plantation.

Acknowledgments

I would like to express my heartfelt gratitude to all who have helped with this research over the years, especially the late Arthur and Robert Sutton, Ann Sutton, the Earl of Crawford, Ainsley Henriques, Dorrick Gray, Roderick Ebanks, the staffs of the National Library of Scotland, the British Library, the Colonial Records Office, the National Library of Jamaica, and the Jamaica Archives, and the many students and colleagues who have made this work possible. This research was funded by grants from the Wenner-Gren Foundation for Anthropological Research, the American Council of Learned Societies, Franklin and Marshall College, and Kutztown University.

8

Excavating the Roots of Resistance

The Significance of Maroons in Jamaican Archaeology

Candice Goucher
Kofi Agorsah

Introduction

Since it was established at the University of the West Indies in 1990, the Maroon Heritage Research Project (MHRP) has conducted archaeological surveys, mapping, and excavation of Maroon and Maroon-related sites across the island of Jamaica and other parts of the circum-Caribbean region, including Suriname. Earlier phases of the project were conducted on Jamaican Maroon sites, including Nanny Town, Old Accompong Town, Seaman's Valley, Gun Barrel, and Reeder's Pen. This research contributed to a better understanding of the complexity of the Maroon past, including interactions between Maroons and dominant Atlantic cultural groups, as well as freedom-fighting partnerships Maroons forged with indigenous peoples and enslaved Africans. These studies have also explored Maroon survival strategies and their guerrilla lifestyle, using archaeological evidence for the first time, to examine the flexibility of Maroon sociospatial relationships as well as the formative process and subsequent transformations of their settlements and culture. As with any long-term investigation, many questions remain unanswered. However, cultural data on settlement locations and patterns, spatial behavior, mortuary practices, technological strategies, artifact patterns, and soil chemical analysis and dating have shed light on land use, spatial relationships, group dynamics, and other aspects of the Maroon experience. Our objective has been to employ archaeological evidence, supported by ethnographic and archival data, to identify the range of Maroon cultural responses and adaptations and thus to create a more nuanced understanding of the ecological, social, and economic conditions experienced by Maroons during the colonial era.

Maroon archaeology has revealed that a complex set of interactions emerged from the oppressive context of plantation slavery. Furthermore, the material evidence of Maroon resistance to the plantation complex in the Americas challenges the historiographical assumptions that relegate the achievements of small-scale societies to a secondary place in New World history. Rather than a marginal aberration, the Maroon experience was a central, defining feature of the post-1500 Atlantic world. Archaeology provides evidence previously unavailable for the reconstruction of the history of the pioneer freedom fighters, whose past weaves through five centuries of history and culture in the Americas. The combined use of ethnographic, archival, and archaeological evidence in studying past societies has been found to be valuable to both anthropological and historical research (Gould 1980; Posnansky 1984; Agorsah 1985; Singleton 1985). Introducing archeological evidence to the study of Maroons also helps make the large volume of written documentation and ethnographic data more complete and meaningful. The focus on resistance goes beyond the common approach to the study of small-scale societies as victims of slavery in the Americas. As an important single constant strand in resistance history, the Maroon evidence also provides temporal and cultural links between the experiences of the Maroons in Jamaica and other New World societies (Figure 8.1).

The story of the Maroons—enslaved Africans and their descendants—who fled from bondage and fought a long series of wars to maintain their freedom goes back to the very earliest days of European settlement and slavery in the New World (Thompson 2006). Documentary evidence from early sixteenth-century Hispaniola mentions the first known African slave to escape his captors and flee into the interior. Others later joined him to form the first documented Maroon society on an island off the coast of Hispaniola. In the succeeding centuries, hundreds more runaway communities would emerge throughout the New World. Many of the slaves escaped from the mines and plantations of the European colonizers and fought to maintain their freedom. Although small in size and in their operations, Maroon communities were among the first Americans, in the wake of 1492, to resist colonial domination, striving for independence and defining the experience of freedom. They forged new cultures and identities and developed solidarity out of diversity through processes that only later took place on a much larger and more visible scale. Colonial Maroon societies ranged in size from small groups of a few people to powerful groups often referred to as bands, although some numbered up to a thousand or more. Maroonage was a common phenomenon in all parts of the western hemisphere where slavery was practiced. Wherever large expanses of inaccessible and uninhabited terrain permitted, as in the rough and rugged mountains of Jamaica and the Dominican Republic, or the equatorial forest and marshlands of Suriname, or the marshlands of Oklahoma, Virginia, or Texas in North America, these communities proliferated (Figure 8.1). For example, in the British North American colonies, and later the United States, where unoccupied yet habitable spaces were not as plentiful, more than fifty Maroon settlements are known to have come into being between 1672 and 1864 (Bilby and N'Diaye 1992). It was in

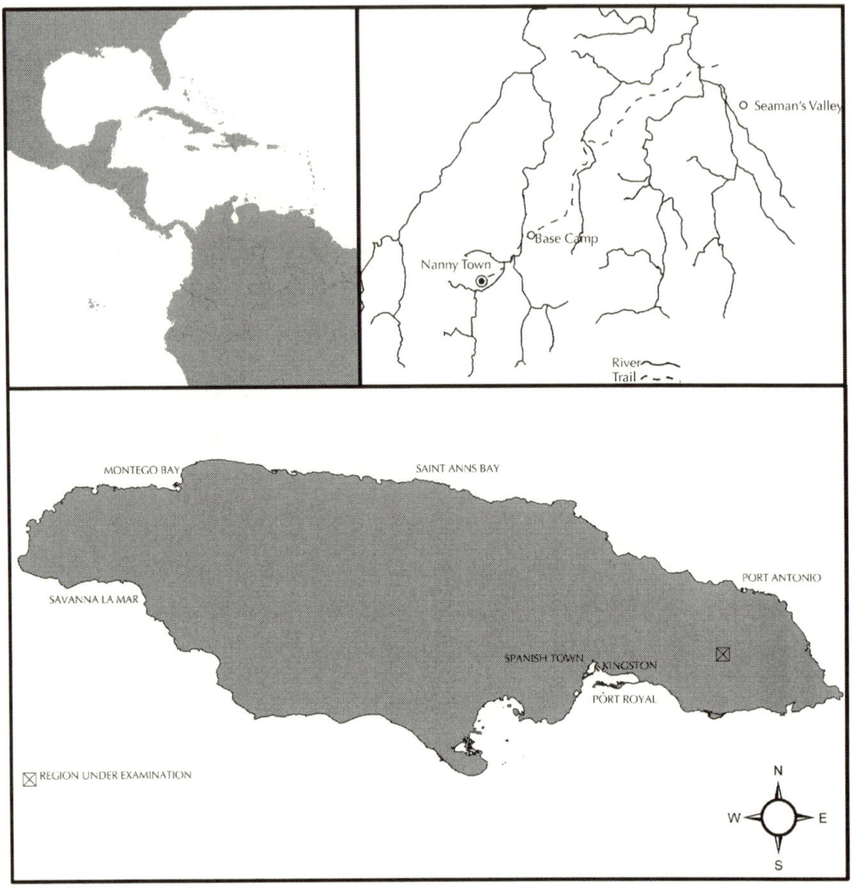

Figure 8.1. Maroon settlements. *Clockwise from upper left:* map of Maroon settlements in the Americas; location of Nanny Town Project Survey Area in Jamaica; location of Nanny Town.

these inaccessible areas that the Maroons found security, forging new cultures and setting the pace for freedom from slavery.

Following the abolition of slavery, many Maroon groups were assimilated into the larger societies that surrounded them. Like other small-scale historical communities so absorbed by larger societies, Maroons are sometimes scarcely remembered as ancestral freedom fighters. This neglect is compounded by the fact that much of the documentary evidence about the Maroons comes down from the very colonial people against whom they fought and whose intention it was to create divisive relationships among peoples of African and indigenous descent. Archaeological evidence has filled in some significant gaps in our knowledge of Maroonage while providing more tangible material to broaden our understanding of the complexity of colonial societies more generally. An important collective contribution of Maroon studies has been the provision of explanations for cultural successes, adaptations in family lifestyles, subsistence, technology, on-the-ground political organization, settlement pattern, and spatial behavior and how these in turn contributed to Maroon survival outside the boundaries of the surrounding society. Many lines of evidence can be adduced to support the assertion that the Maroon experience is emblematic of broader processes that shaped the heritage of the western hemisphere. Not only were Maroons in the forefront of resistance to slavery, they were pioneers in exploring and adapting to the more remote, unsettled spaces in both American continents and the Caribbean. In the French colony of Saint-Domingue, for example, Maroons helped launch the Haitian Revolution, which gave birth to one of the first independent republics in the Americas in 1804. In Jamaica, they were among the first to establish communities in the remote Blue Mountains and Cockpit regions. Although there is a large body of scholarly writing about Maroons based solely on archival and oral history, relatively little is known about the processes of the formation of these persistent societies of freedom fighters.

Maroon Archaeology in a New World Context

Early archaeological studies in the circum-Caribbean paid no attention to Maroon sites. These studies focused on surface collections, subsurface recovery of artifacts and structures, the study of architectural details and physical layouts of structures and sites, and historical documents. Such studies mainly concerned the pre-Columbian past and thus neglected Maroon heritage despite the fact that the Maroons were a major link between indigenous Amerindian groups and later European and African peoples. Consequently, a gap has long existed in the heritage of the Caribbean and indeed the wider New World. It is against this background that the program on Maroon archaeology was initiated following the establishment of a teaching and research program in archaeology at the University of the West Indies (UWI) in Jamaica in October 1987. The research project was initially dubbed the UWI Mona Archaeological Research Project (UMARP) and later MHRP (Agorsah 1991a, 1991b, 1992a). In addition to several reports, an edited volume with contributions from various symposium participants, including Maroon chiefs, was published in 1994, and numerous articles have explored in depth the strands of research summarized in the following sections.

Nanny Town

A crucial site that has revealed much about Jamaica's Maroon heritage is Nanny Town, one of the most important strongholds of the Jamaican Maroons. It is located in the heart of the Blue Mountains on a fairly level but well-protected plateau.

Since 1990 the site has been the focus of a series of reconnaissance investigations as well as a full-scale excavation; several reports have emerged from this (Agorsah 1992b, 1994). Excavations at the site yielded over four thousand artifacts including local earthenware, local and imported smoking pipe stems and bowls, grinding stones, wine and pharmaceutical bottles, fragments of gun barrels, musket balls of various sizes, coins, fragments of lead, iron knives, beads, brass buttons, nails, and glass. Some of the artifacts, particularly those from the lowest of the three levels, appear to be prehistoric and are therefore considered to be associated with the indigenous Taino. Terracotta figurines and Spanish coins found in association confirm that Taino inhabited parts of Jamaica when the British took over the island in 1655, indicating that some indigenous people, thought by some to have long since been exterminated, survived into the seventeenth century. That stratigraphic level appears to predate the Maroon presence in the area and is represented by a mixture of local ceramics, shells, and stone artifacts.

The recoveries of the indigenous artifacts suggest a possible Maroon interface with the indigenous people of Jamaica. Those finds also challenge the myth that all the Amerindians in Jamaica had been exterminated before the arrival of the British. The Spanish coin finds strengthen the speculation that native runaways had found their way into the hills before the Spaniards, who tried to enslave them, left the island; it also suggests that African fugitives may have joined an existing refugee community in the interior mountains. This further supports the hypothesis that the Maroons and Taino coexisted. Such a situation would be comparable to the relationship forged between the African runaways and the Seminole in Florida, an alliance that was confirmed by the oral history of the Black Seminoles.

The excavations also produced evidence of a distinctly Maroon occupation of the site; artifacts included grinding stones and a considerable quantity of charcoal, gun flints, fragments of gun barrels, musket balls, iron nails, a red-clay and several kaolin smoking pipe bowls and stems, and green and clear glass bottle fragments. This occupation phase probably dates between 1655 and 1734. The third phase of occupation was represented by a stone fortification and an engraved stone. The archaeological evidence from Nanny Town made it possible to link the Maroons to the remnant Amerindian population in clear stratigraphic relationship, although the nature and process of the evolution of the settlement remain unclear (Agorsah 1994). These archaeological data along with evidence from the significant site of Guanaboa Vale in the hilly Juan de Bolas region of central Jamaica have helped document the appearance of African-indigenous interactions through the seventeenth century, thus substantiating colonial records and suggesting the foundation of geographical and other local knowledge that must have been transmitted among the earliest generations of Maroons.

Finally, the location of Nanny Town is even today remote and difficult to access; this has prohibited unwanted access to Maroon settlements. This was a strategic choice that no doubt furthered the chances for survival. The archaeologist Paul Healy (1980) has observed similarly difficult terrains selected by Maroons in the Rivas Region of Nicaragua. Healy further notes the resultant challenges for the archaeologist, "[from] the almost complete absence of building in stone, the scattered settlement pattern and the disappearance of perishable structures and materials in consequence of the general humidity of the climate" (1980:3–4). Jamaican Maroons acknowledge the significance of their ancestors' choice of rugged locations as necessary to the success of their struggle to remain an independent people and survive in resistance to the expanding European plantation complex. Thus, Maroon archaeology of these remote and nearly inaccessible sites has itself been a struggle to find even the most meager clues to the elusive Maroon past.

Old Accompong Town

The Maroons in Jamaica inhabited two regions: the Windward Maroons lived in the eastern mountains around Nanny Town, while the Leeward Maroons lived in the central karst-dominated region known as the Cockpit country. The site of Old Accompong Town with its tropical karst and unique vegetation of the Cockpit country is a place where the Maroons set an unprecedented example by using guerilla tactics to successfully fight the British military to a stalemate in a protracted military struggle known as the First Maroon War (1731–39). The main archaeological sites in the neighborhood of Accompong (Agorsah 1990) include the site of Kindah (a place-name interpreted to mean "We are a family"), said to have been the camp where Maroon military wing leaders met to coordinate tactics against the British forces. In addition, Kodjo's (or Cudjoe's) Burial Ground, thought to be the grave site of the great Maroon leader, is located in a fairly level ground about half a kilometer down a rugged slope northeast of Kindah. Other sites around Accompong include Big Ground Grass site, an open area to the east of Kodjo's Burial Ground, and the Peace Cave site, also called Ambush, which sits at the eastern edge of the Accompong Maroon lands. The cave was used as a hideout by the Maroons because it overlooked their opponent's military camp and the colonial plantations to the east. The final battles of the First Maroon War took place in the valley below on a site now known as Petty River Bottom.

During excavations in the Accompong district, three main stratigraphic levels of Old Accompong Town were identified. However, only one clear cultural level was observed and it consisted mainly of eighteenth- and nineteenth-century material including local earthenware, a glass bead (probably imported), a copper bracelet, fragments of green glass bottles, and a few musket balls. Three cowrie shells (*Cyprae moneta*) with a West African provenience were also recovered. Doug Armstrong (1991b) has also reported recovering similar West African cowrie shells from excavations at the site of Seville. Because indigenous shell currencies were also persistent in other parts of the Americas during the early centuries of European interaction, their appearance in later Maroon contexts suggests the similar importance of independent economic systems of trade, exchange, and monetary circulation in Jamaica.

Seaman's Valley

The Seaman's Valley site (see Figure 8.1) is one of the few known sites in Jamaica in which the Maroons came into open combat with the British military. The colonial military force was the largest ever sent against the Maroons, yet it suffered total annihilation. The eighteenth-century site was not only a battle site but also, and perhaps more importantly, a Maroon contact zone. Visible features at the site consist of the ruins of a plantation waterwheel, a mill housing full of debris, weeds, house foundations, clusters of roofing slates, and widely scattered local and imported ceramics, metal scrap, and other artifacts and traces of house walls.

The main archaeological finds consisted of a wide variety of items and in very varied quantities: imported ceramics including stone jars, pearlware, and roofing tiles; bricks; glass, including fragments of wine, alcoholic, and pharmaceutical bottles; metal scraps and implements; fragments of a gun barrel; musket balls of various sizes and weights; nails; scrap lead; and fragments of such other metal objects as a knife, a spearhead, door hinges, a cast iron (three-legged) pot, buckles, and horseshoes. Also recovered were kaolin (white-clay) smoking pipe bowls and stems, glass and stone beads, and metal buttons. Generally the range and type of finds are not too different from those found at Nanny Town and appear to support the speculation that the Maroons possibly had a strong link with the site in pre-treaty years, raiding it from time to time, or had intelligence or supply agencies there. Seaman's Valley evidence indicates that although not a Maroon stronghold, it supported the survival of Nanny Town as a stronghold. The technological basis of Maroon material culture will be further discussed below.

Linking Maroon and Enslaved African Communities

The Maroon experience was predicated on a collective struggle to live apart from the world the Europeans made. Entwined in the struggle to remain socially, politically, and economically independent is the concept of survival. Not necessarily a search for remnant "Africanisms," work linking Maroons to the enslaved African population of Jamaica can address what practices—including the production of material goods—did emerge from African precedents to shape Jamaica's colonial experience. After all, the Atlantic colonial era provided opportunities for forging links not only between continents and peoples but between their technologies as well. As part of the dramatic and complex cultural transformations of the era, Caribbean technology in particular reflected significant contributions of the world beyond Europe. While the assumption of the inevitable replacement of African industry by European technology has long held sway, closer examination of Caribbean evidence for technological innovation, patterns of demand, organization of production, and imports suggests an alternative narrative. The historical archaeology of other sites of material interaction has made it possible to examine the variety of evidence for the African contributions to the metallurgical industry on the island of Jamaica. The struggle to remain in control of the production of iron—a powerful object in many West African contexts—can thus be seen, like Maroonage, to be part and parcel of a wider historical process of survival and resistance.

Reeder's Pen

Jamaica's oldest and largest iron and brass foundry was Reeder's Foundry, located on the western edge of the town of Morant Bay in the parish of St. Thomas. Founded in 1772 by the Devon coppersmith John Reeder, the foundry relied on African metallurgical expertise, which drew from a rich iron-making tradition (Goucher, Herbert, and Saltman 1986). According to Reeder, the 276 laborers, including enslaved Africans, Maroons, and free Africans who operated the foundry, were "perfect in every branch of the iron manufacture, as far as it relates to casting and turning of wrought Iron." With a knowledgeable, though enslaved, African labor force at his disposal, Reeder applied for permission from the Jamaica Assembly (the island's legislature) to erect charcoal-fueled iron-smelting furnaces. The foundry operations were short-lived and ended abruptly. Ten years after its founding, the governor ordered that it be dismantled, fearing that it could fall into enemy hands if the island were invaded by French and Spanish forces.

Excavations of Reeder's Pen, including the foundry site, confirmed the large-scale works that supplied the Royal Navy and local plantations with much sought-after iron tools, weapons, machinery, and repair work. The extensive factory site's structural foundations were partially mapped and a test pit was excavated by the authors with students from the University of the West Indies and Portland State University. Large quantities of slag, iron and copper-alloy objects, pottery, glass, and clay pipes were uncovered and dated by association to the seventeenth to twentieth centuries. Tentative identification of the hearth and forge features inside the foundry building matches the known descriptions of similar operations in England. Possible identification of the water-powered mill and canal system proposed by Reeder suggests the rechanneling of the Morant River waterways in subsequent decades.

Ironworking, and the use of iron objects, was not restricted to planter-owned foundries; many enslaved Africans worked on plantations as blacksmiths, a skilled craft that survived among African Jamaicans into the twentieth century, though few blacksmiths now remain. In the 1990s, we had the opportunity to interview one of Jamaica's last blacksmiths, a man who operated a small forge at Ginger Ridge, a site of Maroon occupation between Linstead and Chapelton; his smithy operated much as it might have in earlier times. The historical linguistics of Jamaican blacksmithing reveal the ties to resistance and survival linking skilled artisans to the Maroons. For example, blacksmiths referred to anvils as the "mother" of their forges, a term entirely consistent with the West African conceptual links between gender and technology (Goucher and Herbert 1996). Although no blacksmiths survive in the area around Reeder's Foundry, their vocabulary does. Local informants were able to provide the African (Twi) word for a ceremonial cutlass excavated at the foundry site and remembered in the context of Kumina ceremonies in Jamaica, a form of African spiritual revivalism. As in West Africa, changing stone to metal and bending iron through heat treating at the forge were thought to harness both technical and spiritual forces. Iron knives were used in the most sacred of rituals, including blood oaths and in the signing of Maroon peace treaties. While some iron weapons and guns were obtained by theft and raiding, historians have often discounted the technology required to refashion and repair the items obtained. Further, metallurgical skills have also been described as integral to slave rebellions. For example, around 1791, cutlasses were reportedly being manufactured in Maroon communities and lead shot was secretly cast (Geggus 1987:287n62). Finally, not only were Jamaican Maroons armed with guns, but every man, woman, and child reportedly carried an iron hoe. Despite the fact that enslaved Africans arrived in shackles, the historical archaeology of Maroons has demonstrated that iron technology was at the heart of resistance, empowerment, and survival.

Maroon Archaeology beyond Jamaica

Maroon archaeology has been based on the conviction that for any given period of time, place, or people, it should be possible to archaeologically observe and explain the relationship between human behavior and the material evidence resulting from that behavior. The spatially patterned remains of the Maroons of colonial Jamaica should be considered as potentially informative about the spatial structure and the way the otherwise hidden society organized itself. In particular, the social structure of a group generates behavior patterns that in turn redefine the social structure. Early on, the Maroon project sought evidence to explain Maroon survival in terms of social adaptations, including family networks and relationships, settlement patterns and adaptive spatial behavior, and related phenomena. Although the excavations in Jamaica helped reconstruct some aspects of Maroon cultural behavior and confirmed the partnership of enslaved Africans and Amerindians in freedom fighting, questions concerning sociospatial relationships and formative and transformative processes of Maroon settlements and culture remained unanswered. These are important issues, which may be addressed by the Maroon experience in Suriname, where the sites are larger with more visible surface and habitation features. In moving the MHRP beyond Jamaica to Suriname, we have been able to address many questions left unanswered in Jamaica, including questions concerning transformations in ecological, political, and economic conditions experienced by Maroons during the colonial era. In doing so, the project has demonstrated that the Maroon experience was an essential part of the search for freedom in the New World. This objective has presented its own challenges. In expanding our goals and research focus to transcend the common approach to the study of small-scale societies as victims, we have sought to identify contributions Maroons made to the development of New World heritage. As this project unveils scientific archeological evidence, the large volume of ethnographic and historical data available on the Maroon experience (e.g., Price 1983, 1992; Robinson 1992; Bilby 1984; Bilby and N'Diaye 1992; van Velzen and van Wetering 1988; Hoogbergen 1991) will become more complete and meaningful.

While the excavations at the Jamaican sites broke new ground in Maroon heritage studies, the lack of evidence from houses and structural features limited our analysis of spatial data crucial to understanding spatial flexibility as a Maroon adaptation. Questions about the internal physical plan and organization of Maroon settlements and their spatial relationships, mortuary practices, and inferences about foodways remain undetermined. While the Maroon sites in Jamaica did not permit the acquisition of material to address these and other related issues, comparative sites in Suriname appear, from preliminary reconnaissance, to have the potential for evidence that could be used to address some of these unanswered questions, wholly or at least partially, and they have suggested new directions for future research. Availability of extensive ethnographic material on Maroons of Suriname (Price 1983, 1992; Hoogbergen 1995; Bilby 1984, 1995; Harris 1994) should make this goal more attainable over time.

Maroon sites in Suriname provide comparative data on settlement development using evidence from the sites of Kumako, Tuido, Bakakum, and Sentea (Figure 8.2), which span the earliest, middle, and later periods of Maroon history in the region in that order. Evidence of physical and locational changes in house features indicates adaptation to the settlement space available to them and adjustments in their social relationships over time. Subsequent phases of the project in Suriname also have provided the additional opportunity of obtaining transformation data about Maroon societies that would provide evidence of longer sequence and continuous occupation or habitation of the same area. Without the archaeological portrait, histories of such small-scale societies, which give a place texture and dimension, are often elusive and fragile, as the Jamaica data suggest.

Maroon Sites in Suriname

The Maroon areas of Suriname are located south of the coastal plain, primarily in the tropical forest region in northeastern South America. The Maroon groups include the Saramaka, Ndjuka (Djuka), Matuwari (Matawai), Paramaka, Kwinti, and

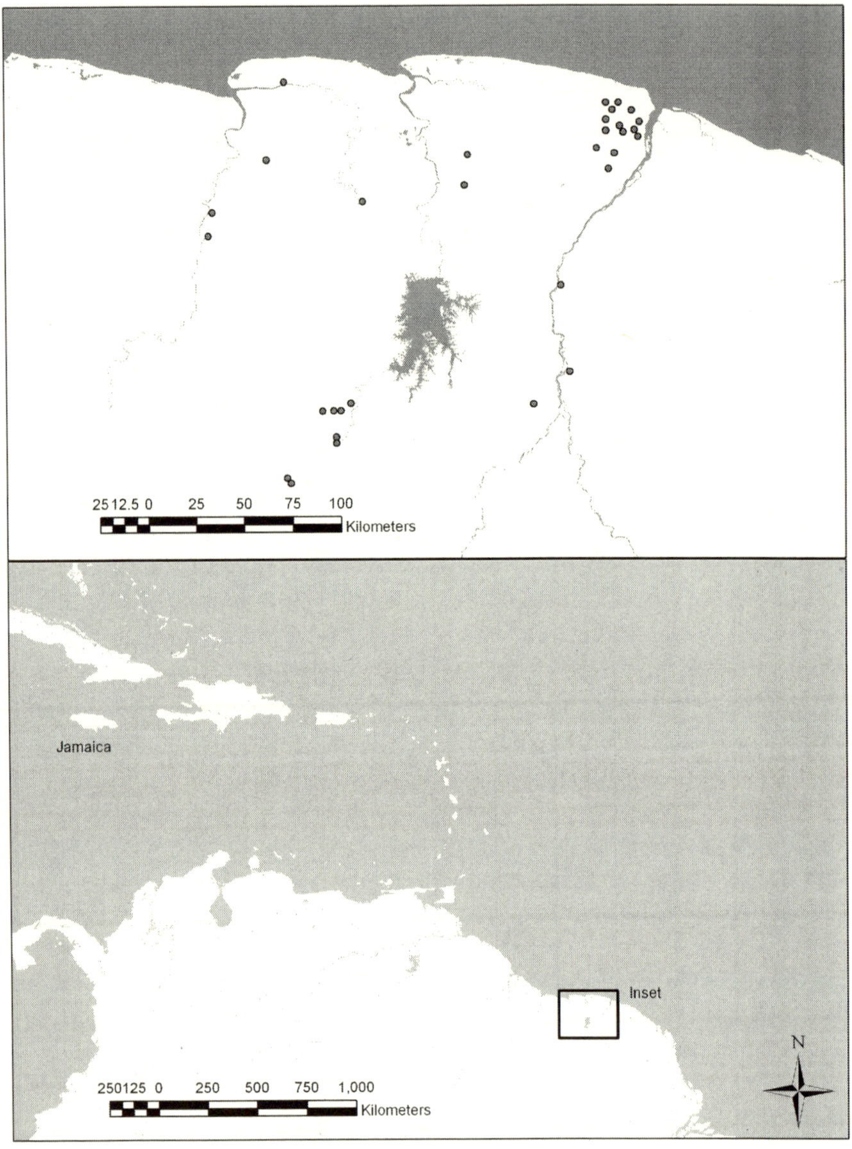

Figure 8.2. Location of sites in Kumako Survey Area, Suriname.

Aluku (Boni). More than thirty Maroon archaeological sites have been identified in the basins of the major rivers, particularly the Suriname and Saramacca rivers (Hoogbergen 1991). In the late 1990s, research expeditions sponsored by Portland State University and supported by the Suriname National Museum and Maroon chiefs completed reconnaissance surveys of the basin of the Suriname River, recording forty-one Maroon settlements. It was observed that while many sites were being destroyed and modern Maroon settlements being displaced by operations of timber and gold mining companies through concessions granted by the Surinamese government, many more continued to be inundated by the construction of hydroelectric dams.

Based on their known distribution, Maroon archaeological sites were stratified into zones defined by cultural context, drainage pattern, and other geographical considerations; each served as a survey zone and formed the basis for the data collection. Survey of two areas was conducted by small crews assigned to relocate known or identify new Maroon sites and determine the geographical limits (boundaries) of those sites based on the distribution of artifacts and surface features. Archaeological data were supplemented with ethnographic information and descriptions obtained from local informants. Ecological studies involved recording data on the topography, soils, drainage patterns, site modification, vegetation, or plant resources and included recording local place-names. Samples were collected and soil chemical analysis was employed to help differentiate, define, and delimit activity areas and site boundaries. Supported by the National Geographic Society, two additional expeditions were undertaken in 1997 and 1998 to further explore the sites using oral traditions, place-names, and other ethnographic information. Two sites were studied in some detail: the Saramakan site of Kumako and the Matawai site of Tuido (see Figure 8.2).

Kumako and Tuido

Site identification has benefited from investigation of the place-names remembered by local communities. According to the Surinamese anthropologist Hermes Libretto (personal communication, 1999), there are many modern Maroon place-names that help identify the strategic nature of those locations, such as Kumako ("Kuma hill"), Tuido ("a very distant location," presumably far away from the white man), Bakakum ("behind the hills"), Dangogo ("bottom of the falls"), and Baka-afetihila ("white man likes conflict"). There are others that reveal control by specific leaders or groups, including Dosu kiiki ("Dosu's creek"), Kofi kiiki ("Kofi's creek"), Negroe Will ("Negro village"), Kofijompo ("Kofi jumped/escaped"), Kwakugron ("Kwakuís ground" or "land"), Congo Kiiki ("Congo creek"), Daume ("Dahomey"), and Kwamikondre ("Kwamiís village" or "town"). Many of these names directly or indirectly suggest a specific West or Central African origin for the inhabitants of the settlements. The formation of alliances may have occurred more spontaneously in the wake of the "divide and rule" tactics used by colonial authorities to enslave others. As Rebecca Bateman suggests, "Blacks and Indians sometimes found themselves allied in a mutual fight against Euro-American domination; at other times, the 'divide and rule' policies of whites pitted the two groups against each other" (1990:1). They formed hamlets of small hideout villages after running away. In Suriname these were referred to as kibrikondres or "hidden villages," which may be the equivalent of the large-scale mocambos of the Maroons in Brazil. The quilombos in Brazil refer to smaller settlements or hideouts. These would constitute the midway hideouts expected to be located along their escape trails.

Kumako was one of the earliest Saramakan Maroon sites in Suriname. The site is located on a ridge at a considerable distance from the coastal plantation area and at a strategically chosen spot between the Eba Top Ridge and the headwaters of the Kleine Saramaka that protected it. Trees such as lokisi and dwumu abound at the site, confirming Maroon traditional belief in the cultural, medicinal, and spiritual importance of these trees. Evidence of floors, but none for house structures, indicates the possible use of hammocks, as was the practice among the natives of the forest. Artifacts including ceramics and musket balls indicate military activity. The site is one of the largest open areas in the thick forest with several large and tall trees to the west of Tutubuka and south of the stream that flows into the Akogandi Creek, which curves around the northern limits of the ridge. Approximately 3.4 acres, the site appears to be securely located within the loop of the Akogandi and Paaba creeks that surround one half of its circumference. Several mounds were identified and appear to be limited to the drier parts of the site. Test pits and surface study yielded several earthenware vessels, some of which were very poorly fired, and several pieces of quartz and quartzite. A large rock at the center of the site and a few raised small mounds, possibly burials, have also been observed and excavated but yielded very little material. Some of the Kumako ceramics meet descriptions of those of known native people in the area. The site may offer evidence of transition from the native traditions to those of the later African escapees, who occupied the site three hundred years ago. Radiocarbon dates obtained for the Saramaka Maroon site of Kumako (Agorsah 2007), while confusing at first sight, have since been interpreted as evidence suggesting interface between the native cultures and those of the Maroons. Any conclusions must await cooperation between archaeologists dealing with those two eras of studies (prehistoric and historical) in Suriname.

The dates include:

(Beta 197585) 1860+/−60 BP and 1800+/−60 BP (Cal AD 80–390; 1870–1560)
(Beta 197584) 1640+/−60 BP and 1630+/−60 BP (Cal. AD 260–560; 1690–1320).

It is clear that the above dates are prehistoric and predate the Maroons. It appears that we are probably working at a Maroon site that was later located over a prehistoric site. These dates will be reexamined in the context of later development of the new trends of the research. Two other dates from the same site in the more recent levels are:

(Beta 197586) 280+/−50 BP and 270+/−50 BP (Cal. AD 1490–1680; 1770–1800)
(Beta 197587) 420+/−40 BP and 420+/−40 BP (Cal. AD 1420–1520; 1590–1620)

Interpretation of these dates must await further work and more dates. However, the dates indicate the possibility of future identification of the interface between the two cultures. At this time, the relevance of these dates for the evidence remains unclear. Results of earlier research on the indigenous people of Suriname provide an excellent foundation for speculating about the evolution of the culture of the indigenous people of Suriname. However, cooperation or interaction with the later African escapees in a cultural interface that has so far been ignored in Suriname Maroon studies remains to be examined.

Tuido, a Matawai settlement located on the Pikin Tukumutu Creek, a branch of the Saramacca River, is described in oral traditions as a very large Maroon village consisting of many clan groups with several separate entry points. Tuido (see Figure 8.2) is located in a bend of the Tukumutu Creek near its confluence with the Tupi Creek. It is a much later site, possibly dating to the end of the nineteenth century. Located much farther inland, with prohibitive distance and access, the site has clearly defined floors as well as mounds with hearth areas that appear to divide the site into group living areas. The site depicts a location on which several groups would have converged. Owing to its later foundation, Tuido also reveals clear floors with cooking clay hearths, lots of imported European artifacts such as green glass bottles, stoneware, and a wide variety of local ceramics. Different mound areas with hearths probably also represented group areas or quarters according to family or clan relationships. The Tuido site, according to oral traditions, lasted until the early twentieth century. Thus, while Kumako could be chronologically placed at the early part of the Maroon trail, Tuido would be placed toward the furthest part of the trail. Evidence of spatial and artifact patterning and changes from the earlier (Kumako site) to the later (Tuido) and further observed patterning in modern settlements, such as Tutubuka, should help provide evidence of a continuum of settlement and cultural development that could explain the formation and transformation of Maroon heritage and culture. Although still a theory, it can be claimed that recent Maroon ceramic vessel types could have constituted an aspect of the Maroon cultural paraphernalia established while in the process of transformation into the more stable river culture.

The initial survey was based on the four areas into which the site was logistically divided. The site was observed as consisting of sections marked by mound clusters.

Each cluster of mounds is also marked by copses of large trees with open land areas between the sections. The mounds are thought to represent collapsed huts. Other surface features included clay hearths, stone circles, approximately seventy large and small pieces of black to dark brown earthenware including large flat pieces and rim and body fragments, and imported stoneware. Excavation of these sites will provide data on settlement development from the earliest (Kumako) through Tuido to the latest (Bakakum and Sentea) sites.

As indicated at the outset of the Maroon Heritage Research Project in Suriname, determining the locational and spatial transformations continues to constitute the main challenge. Identifying social relationships using comparative analysis of spatial regularities and artifact patterns at the project's modern and archaeological sites heightens the challenge. Ultimately, it should be possible to reconstruct transformational relationships between the observed patterns and the functional adaptation and related cultural responses of the Maroons of Suriname through time. Material remains at the sites will eventually help define the category to which each site belongs in the chronological scheme. We should not be led into thinking that the present settlements of the Maroons along the rivers are located on the original sites. This is one of the reasons why there is an ongoing argument over the fact that we do not yet know all that we need to know about the formation of Maroon heritage. It also suggests the significant contribution Maroon archaeology will make in the interpretation of evidence and reconstruction of the past.

Local Community Support

The successes of the preliminary expeditions were due to the strong support and cooperation received from the Suriname Administration, the National Museum of Suriname, the Directorate on Culture and Education, and the paramount chiefs (Granman) and sub-chiefs (Kapiten) of the entire Saramakan and Matawai Maroons, who actively participated in the 1997 and 1998 National Geographic Society–sponsored trips by joining in the entire survey, mapping and field walks, and test excavations and by placing all their local resources at our disposal. Surinamese student participation was very encouraging. The experiences in both Suriname and Jamaica have proven local community collaboration to be critical to the historical archaeology project. As excavations and research were under way, the involvement of collaborators and consultants in all phases of the project gave further promise to the feasibility of the project goals, while the participation of students, staff, chiefs, and local elders and scholars have helped provide recognition of the historical meanings necessary to preserve the sites in the arena of each country's public history.

Maroons in other parts of the world also reveal some interesting points for comparative study and insight into the Caribbean world. Like Jamaica, the Indian Ocean island of Mauritius was home to a European-dominated plantation economy based on sugar cultivation, enslaved Africans, East Indian indentured laborers, and Maroons. Archaeological work by Amitava Chowdhury (2003a) has demonstrated that Mauritian Maroon sites are typically low-density, short-term occupational sites. A significant shift in geographical locations of Maroon sites through time has been observed, with sites tending to be located on top of inaccessible mountaintops and underground lava tunnels only during the expansion of plantations during French occupation of the island (as opposed to open-air Maroon sites during the earlier Dutch occupation). One of the key differences is the absence of indigenous communities in Mauritius. While in the Caribbean, Maroons had the option of taking refuge in Native American settlements and thus, conceivably, could use Native American adaptive techniques in coping with the new way of life, such an option was not available to Mauritian Maroons. Thus the formation of Maroon culture in Mauritius retained the characteristics of the African European cultural continuum. In contrast, Jamaican Maroons forged one of the first global societies, fueling their resistance through interactions with Afro-Eurasian and American peoples.

Conclusion

Ethnohistorical evidence from the Caribbean appears to suggest that both accommodation and conflict characterized processes of cultural continuity and innovation in Maroon heritage. Archaeological interest and research have paid a disproportionate attention to the contributions of enslaver and enslaved experiences in New World history, thereby marginalizing the historical role of freedom-fighting resistance communities. Owing to the mosaic character of the observed historical pattern of cultural transformation in the Caribbean, the identification of the component features of resistance behavior patterns appears to be elusive given only ethnographic and historical writings. The study of Maroons is even more seriously flawed when archaeological data are absent. These challenges may be expected to be encountered by future Maroon research, since much more work remains. The focus on resistance also goes beyond the common approach to the study of small-scale societies as victims of slavery in the Americas. As an important single constant strand in New World history, the Maroon evidence may eventually provide temporal and cultural links between the experiences of the dominant society and other small-scale communities. While written documentation has characterized Maroon heritage in terms of military conflict, the historical archaeology provides perspectives on the indispensability of accommodation and collaboration with a variety of cultural groups from prehistoric communities to enslaved Africans within the plantation complex. Underpinning Jamaican history is the understanding that the formation and transformation of Maroon cultural identity are as central to the story of indigenous survival and African heritage as they are to the traditions of New World freedom at the heart of the earliest globalization.

Acknowledgments

We would like to acknowledge the generous support of the University of the West Indies, the Jamaica National Heritage Trust, the Wenner-Gren Foundation for Anthropological Research, Earthwatch and Center for Field Research, and the Archaeological Society of Jamaica. We thank the staff at the Devon Record Office, Exeter, for access to the John Reeder Papers (J16). We are grateful for the assistance of Roderick Ebanks in identifying and visiting the Ginger Ridge blacksmithing forge with Candice Goucher.

III

THE ARCHAEOLOGY OF JAMAICAN SOCIETY

9
Of Earth and Clay
Locating Colonial Economies and Local Ceramics

Mark W. Hauser

> Kingston at this time pays one hundred pounds yearly to a police officer, who as a retail shopkeeper himself, will feel the force of what follows. . . . If he should observe that this useful and deserving class of citizens, have their trade interfered by schoals of idle and disorderly slaves who infest our streets and lanes, obstruct the common pathway and keep extensive shops in the piazzas (to the constant annoyance of the foot passengers and the peace of the inhabitants) for the sale of beef, pork, herrings, saltfish, shads, salmon, bread, flour, rice, corn meal, biscuit, and every possible article of edible commerce—even to our horses' grass—how can this hired officer pass by such flagrant breaches of our laws without remembrance to our duty?
>
> The miscreants here described, who live free from rent and taxes, and who frequently recruit their stores with the spoils of the night, can well afford to undersell the honest white traders. Negroes in general, will most assuredly prefer that mode of purchase where tenfold advantages offer, that is, in buying stolen goods from their own colour, rather than give a full and fair price to the merchants of this commodity.
>
> —Simmonds 1987:36

Introduction

Of the scores of market towns located on the island of Jamaica, none is more famous locally and in traditional song than Linstead Market. A space of economic and social exchange, Linstead Market has long thought to have been founded after the abolition of slavery, when the Jamaican Railway was constructed. The assumption that Linstead Market was a nineteenth-century institution follows a line of scholarship suggesting that Jamaica's internal market system was built around the English colonial infrastructure. It has become increasingly clear, however, that places like Linstead Market existed well before the nineteenth-century railroad but outside the sphere of control of the colonizing British. The assumption that the creation of Linstead Market was a reaction to British "internal improvements" emerged from a clearly Anglocentric frame of reference, which has long underestimated the importance of markets to the independent development of African Jamaican society.

As many scholars working in the Caribbean have pointed out, systems of production and oceanic networks of trade disciplined enslaved and freed labor into colonial subjects; it has long been assumed that even if the British could not control every aspect of the lives of the enslaved, they at least surveilled and kept close watch over their activities. Recently, a number of scholars have questioned the depth of British control over Jamaica's enslaved. The picture emerging is a complex one of interrelation and overlapping spheres of interaction in which British pretensions to regimentation and control were regularly contested and challenged by the African descent population of the island.

One significant nexus of contestation was the development of market exchange, controlled in part by people of African descent, located at places like Linstead Market. What I refer to elsewhere as "black markets" existed at the periphery of British control but were central to the experience of the African diaspora in Jamaica. While numerous commodities were produced by the enslaved and sold by them in the many markets that existed in colonial Jamaica, one such class of commodity of particular interest to archaeologists is a form of locally produced low-fired earthenware known in Jamaica as yabbas. In this chapter I examine market activities and trade among enslaved laborers, writ as disorderly acts by colonial officials, and examine the ways in which markets were contested colonial frontiers. Using locally produced ceramics as a point of entry, I suggest that Linstead Market, located on what was known in the eighteenth century as Sixteen Mile Walk, was a space of colonial interaction and confrontation. Archaeological evidence points to an eighteenth-century establishment of Linstead Market as not only a space for pottery to be exchanged across the island but a social space for the exchange of ideas contesting the colonial order, culminating in what has been referred to as the 1765 St. Mary's Revolt, one of the major acts of resistance by enslaved laborers of eighteenth-century Jamaica. In this chapter I also demonstrate how the spaces and actions of local commodity production and exchange in places like Linstead Market were arenas for social negotiation outside the control of the European colonial order.

The role of Linstead Market in the internal economy of post-emancipation Jamaica has been the subject of numerous popular and academic discussions. Indeed, there is ample documentary evidence that points to its existence at least as early as the 1840s. Any arguments regarding its existence in the eighteenth century at this point are speculation based on models of economic necessity, our understanding of the organization of enslaved labor resistance and struggles, and demographic probabilities. At the time the area in which Linstead Market would be based was called Sixteen Mile Walk and was home to numerous plantations. The difficulty in trying to ascertain the organization of such markets in the eighteenth century is that they were inevitably poorly documented with only fragmentary accounts. In this essay I attempt to antedate Linstead Market using multiple sources of evidence including published accounts, unpublished ethnography, and archaeology. Specifically, analysis of production and distribution of yabba, a local Jamaican ceramic, suggests an eighteenth-century establishment of Linstead Market, thus tying this space to one of the significant wars of resistance organized by enslaved laborers in eighteenth-century Jamaica.

The Concept of Plantations and Change in the Everyday

By the eighteenth century the plantation had become the dominant economic institution in Jamaica and was the most evident expression of European strategies of production and control of island landscapes. However, the world into which abducted Africans entered when they arrived in eighteenth-century Jamaica was not entirely alien to them; the economic institutions, regional political powers, and regimes of social organization all had strangely familiar but distant analogues in Africa. While there were factors, merchants, and some fortified presence in West Africa, it is questionable whether Europe ever established the same level of territorial control there that they had established in the Caribbean as early as the eighteenth century. In the Caribbean, where projects of colonization had essentially been completed, technologies of control had reached near totalizing effects by the eighteenth century. The system of chattel slavery became an all-encompassing ideology where laborers became divested of their humanity (Patterson 1973, 1982; Mintz and Price 1992; Burnard 1999, 2004; J. Morgan 2004, 2006). Likewise, regimentation of trade through treaties, legal statutes, and precedent governed all levels of economic interaction, at least in theory.

Michel de Certeau, in *Practice of Everyday Life* (1984), attempted to outline a way in which people navigate the spaces that are sometimes unconscious, sometimes tactical, but always produced out of recombinant practices, rules, and spaces. Structured through strategies that are designed to reproduce themselves through the very things they make, institutions such as cities become important mechanisms for shaping taste and disciplining movement. In a sense, the Jamaican plantation is like a city in that it had become a "concept" in the manner described by de Certeau, where the vantage point produced by the technologies of colonial administration—plats, maps, slave lists, and Accounts Produce—collapsed a series of social, economic, and political relations for the purpose of rational organization and created a "universal and anonymous subject"—the plantation. The plantation was ultimately about control—control over space, time, and social interaction—and from the vantage point of the documents that reveal its location and operation, there was little room to maneuver for the agents that operated within it. Maps fixed the colony and the plantation into a peripheral function of empire where the colony was a source of wealth through commodity production and consumption: Accounts Produce fixed a value to this spatial relationship; plats located slave villages within plantation boundaries in places meant to maximize economic efficiency or produce optics of control; laws proscribed actions and promoted certain kinds of transactions and paths of movement within and between plantations by enslaved laborers; and lists managed diversity of a captive population from a socially, linguistically, politically diverse part of the world.

Yet, in the collapsing of these relations and the conceptualization of the plantation, opacities are produced that provide possibilities of tactical evasion of control and oversight that were not initially anticipated by the mapmaker, surveyor, census taker, owner, or assemblyman. When one examines the economic activities of the enslaved, it appears that the apparatus of control was never all encompassing. Despite the best British efforts to control the African descent communities of the island, many different kinds of spaces, including Maroon communities, provision grounds, and black markets, existed outside British control. The epigraphical passage opening this chapter, written by an anonymous author, is one of several contemporary depictions of British Caribbean market scenes that describe not only British frustration at the existence of spaces outside their control but some of the economic activities that eighteenth-century Afro-Jamaicans practiced. As Sidney Mintz and Richard Price point out, actions like those described in the passage "could have served as a catalyst in the processes by which individuals from diverse societies forged new institutions, and could have provided certain frameworks within which new forms could have developed" (1992:14). The epigraph suggests that while the impact of European capitalism on colonial subjects was encompassing, it was not complete. While there were regimes of economic control, the practice of market participation was somewhat contrary to colonial expectations of totalizing subjection. This leads to the question of how these same colonial subjects actively structured the Atlantic world that was intended to subjugate them.

By the mid-eighteenth century, the internal market system figured centrally in Jamaican economic and social lives. The social importance of the combination of street markets, itinerant sellers, and small-scale trade is one of the reasons why such institutions have figured so prominently in the historiography of the African diaspora. As many have noted, the internal economy was a locus of independent acquisition, marketing, and production among the enslaved (N. Hall 1977, [1980] 1991, [1985] 1991, 1994; Bush 1990; Simmonds 1987, 2004; Tomich 1993; Boa 1993; Gaspar and Hine 1996). This economy also presaged a Caribbean peasantry rooted in the houseyard and market (D. Hall 1959; Mintz [1974] 1992; Craton 1982; Trouillot 1988). In the eighteenth century, few other institutions were as explicitly impacted by the rural and urban freed and enslaved. Everybody in Jamaica was dependent on the internal economy, some to a greater extent than others.

The independent production by enslaved laborers on provision grounds and the exchange of those goods were activities that found constructed spaces on the margins of the planters' figurative and material control (Pulsipher 1986, 1990, 1991, 1994; McKee 1999; Pulsipher and Goodwin 1999). Consequently, the informal markets as a meeting place of goods and ideas of the enslaved can be viewed as a locus of interaction where the enslaved could transgress the social and geographic boundaries imposed by the plantation. Legal codes guarded against engrossing the price of staples, while allowing for the enumeration of market disorder; a 1728 code, for example, stipulated that any "Indian, Mulatto, or Negroe" required a ticket for transportation of goods to the market (Jamaica 1738: 223). Planters attempted to circumscribe market participation through a series of legislative mechanisms (see Mintz and Hall [1970] 1991; Simmonds 1987, 2004; Hauser 2008). Planters were essentially worried about two things: theft and association. The legal code essentially monitored these two threats through a system of tickets and surveillance (Hauser 2008:56).

As Barry Higman has noted in his analysis of documents associated with and artifacts recovered from Montpelier Estate, that community emerged out of a shared sense of locality, kinship, language, values, and reciprocity. More important, the people living at Montpelier were not confined geographically to the boundaries of the estate; rather, their social landscape extended beyond the estate grounds through direct and indirect means (Higman 1996; 1998:297–305). By way of example, Higman cites the Baptist War, the 1831–32 uprising organized by enslaved laborers that consumed the western parishes of Jamaica. He highlights that for the individuals responsible for its conception and execution, the markets provided one locus for planning in which information could be passed and the uprising organized (Higman 1998:262–63).

It is possible that riots, uprisings, and wars in the eighteenth century were also organized through the social circuitry of the internal market system. This question first became apparent to me when I read an excerpt of a letter written in 1765 by Simon Taylor (an attorney for absentee planters who later became a wealthy Jamaican planter) to a friend in London.

> We about a fortnight ago had an Alarm of Rebellion in St. Mary's when Matt. Byndloss and my Overseer were both murdered by a parcel of new Negroes belonging to the Overseer of Whitehall and Ballards Valley. . . . Another of them was taken up in this Town who has impeached all the coromantees on Albion Trinity and the Frontier and their design was to have broke out a Month after Christmas and to have attackt the fort at Port Maria to gett arms and powder and from thence to go to Sixteen mile walk where there were many of their countrymen and that the Negroes of Scots Hall were to have joined them. That it broke out was occasioned by the New Negroes declaring

> that they would wait no [longer]. There is report that there was to have been some disturbances at Westmoreland. (Wood and Lynn 2002:30)

This passage describes an uprising that occurred in an area of Jamaica where St. Mary's Parish, St. Thomas of the Vale Parish, and St. Andrew's Parish met. The places Taylor's letter identifies were affected by the action as well as Port Maria and Sixteen Mile Walk. What is important about Sixteen Mile Walk? Why would the "coromantees" decide to meet there?

The area around Sixteen Mile Walk later came to be known as Linstead Market. While we know Linstead Market was in operation at least as early as emancipation (Robertson 2005:200), the excerpt from Taylor's letter suggests there might have been a market there prior to emancipation although on a less formal basis. It is also interesting to note that one plausible candidate for a source of pottery manufacture continues to be the area around Sixteen Mile Walk. This would potentially enable us to locate in place and time a market feared to have existed but that was ultimately outside of Taylor's knowledge. By the mid-nineteenth century, however, this market becomes "established" when a visiting governor described it as a newly established township (Robertson 2005:200).

Archaeology, with its focus on material culture and the distribution of material goods both within and between excavated communities of past peoples, can provide a tool through which to establish potential sites of social and economic interaction. Indeed, rather than remaining at the level of descriptive analysis of discarded things, archaeologists have attempted to apply explanatory devices to determine the processes through which artifacts find themselves in the kitchens of the elites and the houseyards of laborers. In the case provided here, by looking at one form of material culture, Jamaican yabbas, and determining their sites of use along with potential loci of production, we can begin to perhaps recognize circuits of trade through which commodities, both local and imported, flowed. Given the importance of independent production among enslaved laborers in the provision grounds and houseyards, and their reliance on the system of street markets and higglers, the internal economy of Jamaica has become an important explanatory device to understand the material life of the enslaved.

The Everyday and Material Worlds of Jamaican Houseyards and Kitchens

The plantation could have been viewed as a discrete orderly unit in which its inhabitants, enslaved laborers producing wealth for the owner of the estate and his metropolitan backers, were the ultimate consumers of the products of empire-manufactured goods such as ceramics and glass, processed foods such as salt fish and pork, and so forth. As such they can be seen as reinforcing the spatial relationships of empire and slavery. However, from the vantage point of the individual walking within and between the laborer villages, such goods can constitute idioms of material expression that were refashioned through alteration or assemblage into ways unexpected by those who organized their production. These assemblages can also speak to the more local networks of reciprocity, exchange, and market activity in which both enslaved laborers and planters partook (Hauser, Kelly, and Armstrong 2007).

Beginning with Anthony Aarons and Barry Higman's excavations at Montpelier (1998) and Douglas V. Armstrong's excavations at Drax Hall (1990, 1991), the Jamaican houseyard has been a key unit of analysis in the archaeology of plantations and more specifically the lives of enslaved laborers. As a locus of community formation and social transformation, the houseyard has been a useful unit of observation for archaeologists seeking to understand the material constituents of everyday enslaved life (see Galle, this volume, for a comparative analysis of consumption of enslaved laborers). It has become somewhat of a truism that all plantation colonies varied in terms of regulatory mechanisms, systems of social control, and methods of provisioning for the maintenance of the enslaved. It is also true that no two plantations within these colonies were the same. However, when one looks at the archaeological record, there is one fascinating similarity: the archaeological assemblages in houseyards on Jamaican plantations are all constituted of very similar materials.

In general, assemblages excavated from houseyards tend to consist of a range of European-made, mass-produced goods including, but not restricted to, tableware, glassware/stemware, glass bottles used for storage, items of adornment, such as jewelry, and items associated with personal hygiene (Table 9.1). The ubiquity and quantity of these goods on archaeological sites associated with enslaved labor are such that they often allow us to statistically date with relative certainty the occupation of a site through the material assemblage alone (see South 1977; Galle, this volume). Given the quantity of imported ceramics recovered from these sites, it is possible to conclude that the enslaved had access to a world of material goods that is not always intimated by the documentary record. Early in the archaeology of plantation sites it was assumed that these materials wound up in the contexts of the enslaved through a system of provisioning by planters and curation by the enslaved (Handler and Lange 1978). However, as many scholars in recent years have demonstrated, these goods were purchased by the laborers using money they earned selling provisions (Howson 1995; Reeves 1997) and could potentially reflect the "taste" of the enslaved (see Wilkie and Farnsworth 1999, 2005).

Elsewhere, I have explored the relationship between material culture and the internal economy through an examination of eight previously excavated sites dating to the eighteenth century (see Hauser 2008, map 1). On the whole, these sites represent an occupational history that extends from the seventeenth to the twentieth

Table 9.1 Kinds of Materials Recovered from Domestic Assemblages from Eighteenth-Century Plantation Villages, Administrative Urban Residences, and Naval Laborer Residences

	JW	GL	TP	RC	PC	TG	CC	SL
Seville	X	X	X	X	X	X	X	X
Drax Hall	X	X	X	X	X	X	X	X
Juan de Bolas	X		X	X		X		X
Thetford	X	X	X		X	X	X	
Old King's House	X	X	X	X	X	X	X	X
Old Naval Dockyard	X	X	X	X	X	X	X	X
St. Peter's Church	X	X	X	X	X	X	X	X

Note: JW = jewelry; GL = glassware; TP = tobacco pipe; RC = local ceramic (regional and island-made pottery not identified as yabbas); PC = porcelain (English and Chinese); TG = tin-glazed ceramics (primarily Dutch); CC = cream-colored wares; SL = slipware

century. Materials analyzed include those associated with houseyards of enslaved laborers at Seville (Armstrong and Kelly 2000), Drax Hall (Armstrong 1990:74), and Juan de Bolas (Reeves 1997:50), and from the provision grounds of the laborers who worked at Thetford (Reeves 1997:43), kitchens of the governor's residence at King's House in Spanish Town (Mathewson 1972b:3), urban residences of free and enslaved laborers at St. Peter's Church (M. Brown 1996:23), and the Old Naval Dockyard (Mayes 1972:6).

On plantations, organized to maximize economic efficiency (Armstrong and Kelly 2000), mark difference, and exercise control (Delle 1998, 2001), it can be assumed that the majority of the domestic assemblages recovered from the houseyards of the enslaved are associated with the people who lived there. Assemblages at Drax Hall, Seville, Juan de Bolas, and Thetford highlight the accumulation of material wealth among the enslaved (Table 9.1). At King's House, it is likely that much of the assemblage was created by the refuse of the servants who worked for the governor. The same phenomenon most likely occurred at St. Peter's Church and the Old Naval Dockyard. While the most socially visible individuals in the households in the eighteenth century were white (the governor and his family, soldiers, sailors, and a priest), this does not necessarily translate to archaeological visibility. Servants purchased the wares in which the meals were cooked. In all likelihood, they also discreetly ate from the same wares as the rest of the family. The material in the midden analyzed is the aggregated trash of the whole household: African, creole, and European.

One of the items found in the material assemblage, yabbas, is an excellent means of exploring past economic relationships of the enslaved because of their persistence in the archaeological record, the likelihood of their production by people of African descent, and their use and ultimate deposition by enslaved and free laborers. The yabbas recovered from these sites were primarily used as cooking vessels, which might explain their ubiquity on archaeological deposits dating to the eighteenth century (Hauser 2008). I argue that the ubiquity of this type of ceramic also provides a potential, testable hypothesis for understanding the social circuitry through which commodities were distributed in eighteenth-century Jamaica. Since we have, by the nature of the archaeological contexts from which they have been recovered, an idea of their ultimate site of consumption, and we can locate through a combination of material testing and the documentary record the place where they were made, we can infer the various paths through which they were traded. Using written accounts as well as archaeological evidence, we can potentially link at least one site of production to the area around Sixteen Mile Walk, which might indicate a market center that antedates Linstead Market.

Yabba Manufacture and Distribution

For de Certeau, the strategies created in the administration of the city leave room for tactics on the part of its inhabitants to recombine rules, things, and ways of doing that can bring about change. Indeed, there is an aspect of being hidden in plain sight that enabled enslaved laborers and the things they made and used to exploit opacities in the plantation system. While such opacities were invisible to the technologies of governance, some kinds of material goods reveal their location. At the heart of change is the capacity for things seen as "extra and other" to be inserted into an accepted framework, thus creating a superficial conformity but belying a capacity for change.

In Jamaica the term "yabba" refers to several types of ceramic. Yabbas are local coarse earthenwares produced in Jamaica as early as 1692 and continue to be made today. They can be either glazed or slipped, and they are handmade (as opposed to wheel thrown) and of local manufacture. Indeed, yabba-type pottery can be made into a pot, a Spanish jar, a monkey jar, or a yabba. The form yabba refers to a large restricted-orifice, direct-rim bowl used to cook stews, rice, and fried foods. These ceramics were used by people of African descent, made by people of African descent, and, most important, sold in the internal markets of Jamaica. (See Hauser 2008 and Hauser and DeCorse 2003 for review of studies on this pottery; for descriptions of Jamaican pottery, see Armstrong 1990; Ebanks 2000; Hauser 2001; Higman 1998; Mathewson 1972a, 1972b, 1973; Mayes 1972; Meyers 1999; and Reeves 1997.)

Archaeological excavations of sites occupied in the seventeenth and eighteenth centuries have recovered numerous yabba-type pottery in three types (varieties based on differences in manufacture, surface treatment, and decoration). These include a variety that was coil made, fired in an open pit, and treated with a red slip and polished with a burnishing stone. The second variety was coil made, treated with a lead glaze on the interior, and fired in a kiln. The third variety was formed from a slab, remained untreated, and was fired at a relatively low temperature (Figure 9.1). Our knowledge of pottery production in Jamaica during the eighteenth and nineteenth centuries is dependent on numerous complementary sources. These source include (1) contemporary travel accounts with brief mentions of ceramic manufacture, clays used by potters, or laws intended to either facilitate or proscribe craft production among the enslaved; (2) inference from ceramic sherds recovered from archaeological deposits that date to the eighteenth and nineteenth centuries; and (3) the documentation and scholarship of museologists and anthropologists in the twentieth and twenty-first centuries.

There are some references in published accounts from the eighteenth and nineteenth centuries identifying the presence of the ceramic and discussing its manufacture and use (Sloane 1707–25; Long [1774] 1970; Edwards [1793] 1972; Anonymous 1797). While it is generally understood that such texts, used in isolation, are a flawed resource for the reconstruction of Jamaican society, they have been valuable sources of information to archaeologists in framing questions and isolating potential features (Armstrong 1990, 1991c; Delle 1998, 2009; Reeves 1997). These accounts are incredibly useful in helping identify particular kinds of ceramics we find in archaeological assemblages and in determining the way they were used. This kind of ethnographic analogy is one of the fundamental tools of the archaeologist, and it has been used frequently in building interpretations of African American sites and material culture. In this essay, I also rely on published works and unpublished field notes of various scholars working on ceramics in the African diaspora to build inferences where the archaeological and documentary records are silent.

The final set of analyses I employed were derived from material science and geology and applied to the archaeological ceramics recovered from the abovementioned sites. I used a combination of ceramic petrography, which explores the mineralogical fingerprint of ceramics under a microscope, and Neutron Activation Analysis (NAA), which determines the ceramics' chemical fingerprint. I could not analyze all ten thousand ceramic sherds recorded; I took a small, statistically significant sample of ceramics (n = 185) to determine the potential provenience of their manufacture. These techniques do not give the actual location of manufacture. They provide the archaeologist with the ceramic recipe, the combination of raw materials and choices made by the potter to create the pottery that people ultimately used (Hauser 2006, 2008; Hauser, Descantes, and Glascock 2009). Ceramic recipes, in combination with the geographic references in the documentary record, can potentially help us locate where past potters obtained their clays and made pottery for sale.

Figure 9.1. Yabbas recovered from seventeenth-century underwater contexts in Port Royal, Jamaica. *Clockwise from upper left*: glazed yabba with handle; slipped and burnished pot; untreated yabba with punctated decoration. Yabbas from the Marx Collection, Port Royal, Jamaica. Photographs by Mark W. Hauser.

Extent of Ceramic Distribution

It turns out that there were relatively few locations of ceramic manufacture, indicating an extensive trade network (Figure 9.2). One of the most interesting sets of evidence for the sale of Jamaican ceramics comes from a series of nineteenth-century watercolors, daguerreotypes, and photographs. One photograph depicts a group of sellers on the side of Port Royal Street at the turn of the century. It is apparent from the photograph that several types of pottery are being sold in the markets. The type of pottery on the right-hand side of the photograph is the glazed yabba. These yabbas were very popular and found throughout Kingston houseyards.

Street marketers were responsible for making the crucial link between the producers and the ultimate consumers of this pottery. In 1929 Mary Beckwith wrote, "Earthen bowls, hand-turned and covered with a rude glaze, are always to be had in the Kingston market" (1929:47). In the early twentieth century, it appears that Lebanese and Syrian immigrants began to control the retail commerce in Jamaica (Nicholas 1986:55–56). Indeed, as noted by Jerry and Henia Handler in the oral histories they captured, "If a woman was good at making yabbah she might produce several dozen a day. They were given to people to sell in town, 'mostly Syrian,' who would carry them down and make '100 percent profit.' A small yabbah about five inches high, 8 inches across were sold to the seller at a shilling a dozen. The seller would sell them for 2 pence or threepence a piece" (1970). Because of these accounts we have a clear discussion of the ways that this particular ceramic was sold at least in the twentieth century.

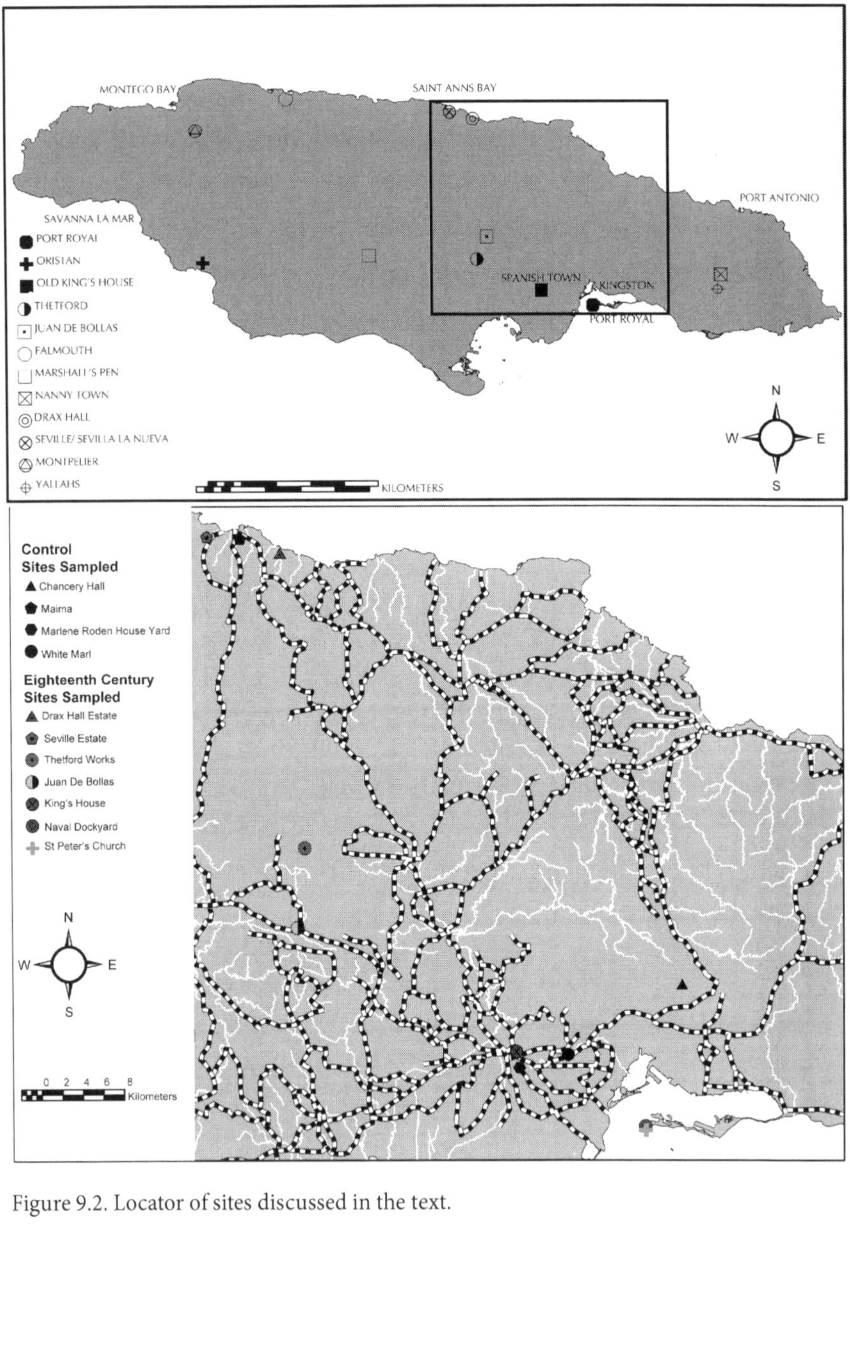

Figure 9.2. Locator of sites discussed in the text.

The pots on the left-hand side of the photo functioned primarily as water-storage vessels. The tall pot illustrated is a form commonly called a Spanish jar. This type of pottery also appears in the 1838 Belisario print titled *Pot Sellers*. These vessels were common items sold in the market. Belisario goes on to describe the hawkers: "The characters represented in the print are apprentices, who sally forth daily with the description of jars above alluded to for sale in a wooden tray, called by them a bowl. In England, a hawker of such things would convey them in a small hand cart. . . . A humourous kind of appeal is made to the public, to include a sale of the jars in some such style—'Who want to cool him heart, who want to cool him heart? must come make me cool um one time' and then pretending to have been called by a customer, smartly replies, 'I comming Mam, no se me da ya?'" (Belisario 1838:n3). These vessels are also common in the archaeological record and, for the most part, it has been assumed that they were imported from the Spanish colonies of Cuba, Puerto Rico, and Hispaniola (Armstrong 1990:147).

Below the Spanish jars in the Port Royal Street photograph are vessels commonly referred to as monkey jars. Monkey jars are slipped or untreated, coarse, low-fired, teapot-shaped vessels. Monkey jars do not appear in the archaeological record until well into the nineteenth century (cf. Heath 1999c:213) and then only as a small component of any assemblage (Armstrong 1990; Reeves 1997; Delle, 2009; Higman 1998; Mayes 1972). To the left of the monkey jars in the Port Royal Street photograph are vessels. I simply identified them as pots as their function is not known. The shape of these vessels could imply multiple functions and the documentary record is ambiguous. In the accounts written by an anonymous author (1797:252) and Hans Sloane (1707–25:xix), there are excerpts that describe earthen vessels used to cook "pepper pot." I believe these pots were primarily used for cooking, water storage, transportation, and drinking (Hauser 2008; Reeves 1997:185–86, 251).

Archaeologists tend to find these pots in contexts associated with their use and ultimate deposition. However, no one has excavated a kiln site, where the ceramics were made. Therefore, in addition to evidence gleaned from the documentary record, we also need to analyze the physio-chemical makeup of the pottery to infer the scale of pottery manufacture and trade. In doing so, my goal was to determine whether the ceramic recipes used to make pottery were similar to or different than those for ceramics recovered from different parts of the island. If they were similar, it would indicate an extensive commodity trade. If they were heterogeneous, a much more limited scope would be implied. I will limit the discussion of the technique and concentrate on the interpretation of the results summarized in Table 9.2. (For discussion of methods, see Hauser 2001, 2006, 2008; Hauser, Descantes, and Glascock 2009; and Descantes and Glascock 2005.)

The question I began my research with—whether archaeological ceramics recovered from the south coast were made using the same recipe as archaeological

Table 9.2 Cross-Tabulation of Sample Membership in Chemical and Petrographic Groups

Chemical Group	Mineral Group*	Drax Hall	Seville	Thetford	Juan de Bolas	King's House	Naval Dockyard	St. Peter	Roden Houseyard	Total
1	2	3	2	-	1	4	2	3	-	15
	3					1				1
	4	1								1
	N/A					1				1
	OUT		1							1
2	2		1					1		2
	3	1	1	3	1	3	3	1	2	15
	4				1	1	1		1	4
	5	1	1		1	1	1			5
Out	NA				1					1
Unassigned	2				1					1
	3				1		1			2

*These groups were derived from the relative abundance of quartz, plagioclase feldspar, and potassium feldspar observed in ceramic samples under a polarizing light microscope using a point counting technique described in Hauser 2008. Underlining indicates groups that we can possibly link to specific locations of manufacture in Jamaica.

ceramics recovered from the north coast—was answered through an analysis of compositional groups and their distribution across the island (see Hauser 2008). For example, samples identified as petrographic groups 2 and 3 were recovered from each of the archaeological sites in the study area (see Table 9.2). Samples identified as chemical groups 1 and 2 were also recovered from each of the historic period sites. The significance of this is that the pottery from the north coast was most likely made by the same potteries as pottery recovered from the south coast. This suggests a network of trade in pottery that spanned these two coasts. In the rest of the essay, I attempt to use the documentary record to determine the actual location of the potteries, the true provenience.

Determining Production Loci

The Liguanea Plain

One known area of manufacture that can be linked to archaeological ceramics was the area immediately surrounding Kingston. Hans Sloane's published description of the island of Jamaica is the earliest to explicitly identify a local ceramic industry in the Liguanea Plain (Sloane 1707–25:xlviii). In this case Sloane is describing the industry that increased the demand for industrial wares required for the processing of sugar. He goes on to describe different ceramics and their uses (xxiv). The forms described are identified in the archaeological record as drip jars, sugar cones, and Spanish jars. Sloane also identifies the location of their manufacture as the Liguanea Plain.

Between 1782 and 1838, owning a pottery could be a profitable business venture in and around Kingston. In his late nineteenth-century history of the island of Jamaica, William Gardner alludes to John Conery, "known for many years as a manufacturer of very good pottery" (1873:328). At about the time Conery was running this pottery, water and cooking utensils appear to be a primary concern for the potteries emerging around Kingston in the eighteenth and nineteenth centuries. According to Belisario, "Water-jars—those in ordinary use are manufactured at Potteries near the City. . . . However we may favor these plebian utensils, it must be observed, they are not presentable at the sideboards" (1838:n3). Here we have two very important pieces of information: first, the identification of a particular form of ceramic, and second, its manufacture in and around the Liguanea Plain.

In the twentieth century, we continue to see evidence of this tradition of pottery manufacture (see Beckwith 1929:47). There is little ethnographic evidence of the production of glazed yabbas in the twentieth century. On January 13, 1970, Henia and Jerome Handler conducted several interviews with Cecil Baugh, a master Jamaican potter: "In this interview, Baugh described how he first became interested in making pottery and how he learned the craft. During this discussion he alluded to both the glazed and slipped Jamaican ceramics. He said that yabba, 'should only be applied to bowls, large or small, of earthenware'" (1970). Several days later Baugh went on to describe potters living along Mountain View Avenue in Kingston (Handler and Handler 1970). These potters are a subject that Baugh would return to in an interview recorded by Pat Cumper in 1975: "At that time, the 1920's, what we call Mountain View Avenue and the called Long Mountain Road, was the home of folk potters of Jamaica: here the young Baugh watched the women who made and fired Yabba bowls. . . . The clay was dug by the potters themselves from any of the numerous places it could be found on the Liguanea Plain, and prepared for use by simple over night soaking" (1975:18). Baugh himself, after moving to Kingston, would begin to learn this pottery tradition from the women who worked there (Cumper 1975:18). All of this evidence points to an industry based in and around the Liguanea Plain that began as early as the 1680s and continued well into the first quarter of the twentieth century. This was not by any means the only industry described in the documentary record.

In the same interview Baugh described how he learned to throw pottery on a wheel on Windward Road, just south of Mountain View Avenue (Cumper 1975:18). The wheel was used by the potters to make monkey jars, Spanish jars, flower pots, and drip jars. Baugh said that both the wheel-thrown and handmade ceramics used clays mined from the same source and were fired in "the same cylindrical kilns using wood cut on the slopes of the Wareika Hills" (Cumper 1975:18).

These lines of documentary evidence give us some solid clues to look for both chemically and mineralogically in the analysis of ceramics. Clays contain quartz, feldspar, and calcite (Hill 1978:68). We are looking for pottery that is relatively uniform chemically and has fairly well-sorted mineral inclusions as a result of the clays being left to soak overnight. Material analysis was very helpful in identifying this ceramic group. Ceramics from chemical group 1 and petrographic group 2 (Table 9.2) were relatively homogeneous. Archaeological ceramics with these recipes have been excavated on the north coast, Lluidas vale, Spanish Town, and the south coast. These samples were glazed yabbas and similar to those Cecil Baugh described as being made on Mountain View Road (Handler and Handler 1970).

Spanish Town

A second locus of ceramic manufacture was in Spanish Town along the Rio Cobre. One of the earliest descriptions of this pottery tradition comes from James Phillippo: "Particles of golden mica have been found in districts near the source of the Rio Cobre, and sometimes, near Spanish Town, it has been incorporated with the potter's clay" ([1843] 1969:72). Quite possibly Edward Long referred to this tradition and this clay: "The first is used in claying muscavado Sugars as well as for a better sort of earthenware, manufactured by the Negroes" ([1774] 1970:3, 851). The clay described by Long is possibly the tradition alluded to by Phillippo in 1843.

Two present-day descriptions exist for yabba production. Roderick Ebanks interviewed and documented pottery manufactured by Ma Lou (Louisa Jones) and showed that potteries responsible for the production of at least one type of Jamaican pottery in the early to mid-twentieth century were concentrated in family compounds and organized around female members of the family (Ebanks 2000:33). Born in 1911, Ma Lou had learned her skill from her mother, and pottery formed a family enterprise. Ma Lou had to become a domestic servant in the 1950s when the economy crashed (Ebanks 2000:31). Beginning in the 1970s, a growing involvement by the middle class in Jamaican arts and heritage revived interest in yabbas, especially those that evoked linkages to African traditions. Ma Lou began making yabbas again to sell at craft markets and cultural expositions in Kingston.

Marlene Roden, Ma Lou's daughter, took up pottery making and continues to sell pottery at 50 Job Lane outside Spanish Town. Moira Vincentelli (2003), Roderick Ebanks (1984), and I have had the opportunity to talk to Roden on several occasions. From my conversations, I know where she obtains her clay, how she prepares it, and how the pottery is thrown. More important, I had ethnographic examples collected from her houseyard with which to compare archaeological examples.

Returning to the combined material analysis, we have strong evidence linking at least one group of ceramics to clays from the area around Spanish Town. The geologist Vernon Hill argues that inclusions within clays from the Rio Cobre will be much finer than those of the Liguanea Plain (1978:69). Samples identified in Table 9.2 as chemical group 2 and petrographic group 3 were recovered from all seven historic period sites sampled. More important, they were also recovered from the houseyard of Roden. Since we know where she acquires her clay, we can link this ceramic recipe to this specific region.

Sixteen Mile Walk

The final area that might have been a site of ceramic production was the area surrounding Linstead Market. The clay recovered from the area around the vale known as Sixteen Mile Walk has long been remarked on for its high quality. An 1869 report on the geology of Jamaica singles out St. Thomas in the Vale as producing a superior clay (Sawkins, Gay, and Wall 1869:32). Probably the most direct evidence comes from Edward Long. In his description of pottery on the island he describes the clay in Sixteen Mile Walk: "In Sixteen-mile-walk, the soil in general is a reddish clay, upon digging into which a small depth are found detached veins of a white clay, resembling that from which tobacco pipes are made; it bears the fire well, and might doubtless answer in manufacture" ([1774] 1970:3, 851). Long refers to this clay as a pipe clay, which is generally described as having a much higher kaolin content.

There is no ethnographic information regarding the production of pottery in Sixteen Mile Walk; we have to work using the abundance of clay in the area around the present market as well as some anomalous findings in the combined mate-

Table 9.3 Cross-Tabulation of Groups Represented from Samples

	St. Peter's Church	Naval Dockyard	King's House	Juan de Bolas	Thetford	Drax Hall	Seville
Group 2	14	16	14	1	2	6	5
Group 3	8	12	12	6	9	1	3
Group 4	2	3	4	1	1	1	1
Group 5	6	2	3	1	1	1	1
NA	1	3	2	2		1	2
Outlier		2	1				1

rial analysis. Hill describes the clays from the Linstead area as containing anatase, quartz, and goethite (1978:69). Some ceramics seen as a variant in the combined analysis fit this description.

Returning to Table 9.2, one trend to notice is that within chemical group 2 there was wide variation in the kinds of mineral inclusions found in the ceramics. Most samples identified as chemical group 2 belong to petrographic group 3 or 5 (Table 9.3). Here, one is seeing the results of ceramics that are made of clays and temper that derive from parent material associated with the Rio Cobre. While we can attach petrographic group 3 to Spanish Town because of the analysis of pottery from Roden's houseyard, we have no idea where petrographic group 5 is from (Table 9.3).

The ceramics from this group contain mineral inclusions that indicate a parent material that has undergone a significant amount of alteration due to weathering. Some minerals, like orthoclase feldspar, react readily to the environment and transform into the clay minerals sericite and illite. In other words, the soils containing these mineral inclusions were exposed to the elements for an extended period of time, changing the chemical makeup of included minerals. In the case of the soils around Linstead, there is an underlying layer of mature clay containing primarily kaolinite and silica. Overlying this layer is a modeled clay that contains kaolinite, quartz, iron, and aluminum oxides (Beaven and Dumbleton 1966:376). Present in the group 5 samples are small laterite inclusions, which are derived from the weathering and accumulation of iron oxide around silica particles.

This potentially links the production of these ceramics with the soils surrounding Linstead Market. It is far from conclusive, however. In order to test this hypothesis one needs to test potential source material using the same set of techniques that were employed in the analysis of the archaeological ceramics. Of course, the existence of a pottery type does not necessitate the existence of a market. It does, however, complement existing lines of evidence. First, the size of Linstead tends not to be temporally ephemeral. There tends to be precedent for a market center in this vicinity. Second, while some potters do take their wares to market, the documentary and ethnographic record indicates a complicated commodity chain in which pots were sold to ultimate consumers through a chain of middlemen.

Conclusion

In this essay I have emphasized that pots did not remain confined to the matrifocal household but became embedded in broader networks of exchange. They were exchanged, purchased, traded, and consumed over wide distances. Here, compositional analysis proved instrumental in showing (if only partially) the extent of these commercial activities. The clay pots moved, but not of themselves. They did so in fields of social relations. And so we are poised to retrieve the humans and the social forces guiding the actions behind the distributions of archaeological collections on the site level, the regional level, and even the oceanic scale. This should encourage us to avoid reifying ceramics as inert containers of identity or economic rationale and instead seek to understand them as strategic elements in human choices and interactions.

The goal of this chapter was to see if an informal market existed in the area near present-day Linstead Market through complementary evidence. If the antedating of Linstead Market, as suggested by this preliminary data, bears out, it demonstrates the foundation of a cultural space constructed through the transactions of enslaved laborers on the metaphorical and material limits of the planter's knowledge. As such the eventual formalization and legalization of the market could be understood as the appropriation of a preexisting institution developed by the enslaved.

Of all the island's provincial markets, Linstead is probably the most well known among modern Jamaicans. The market's foundation has generally been placed with the establishment of the Jamaican Railway, following a line of scholarship that suggests the internal market system was built around English infrastructure. The data presented here suggest a real place for archaeology in the historiography of preemancipation Jamaica and are more than a contribution of new information to answer old questions (Scott 2004). Rather, archaeology can be used to shape and form the intellectual and past cultural landscapes (see M. Johnson 2007).

This analysis opens up for discussion archaeology's role in understanding formations of slavery, markets, and empires. Because these were constitutive elements of the growth of the British imperial regime in both intellectual and economic capital, understanding the unexpected economic activities of the enslaved was central. At the same time they potentially undermined the successful operation of the colony. Such institutions and activities cannot be reduced to dyads of structure versus agency or power versus resistance.

This provides a methodological problem especially related to text-aided archaeology. Analysis must rely on the uneasy realization that oftentimes texts and artifacts of a given location do not necessarily address the same concerns. On the one hand, enumerative texts are useful in establishing a political ecology of slave society, at least from the perspective of the metropolitan administrator or the colonial assemblyman. It does not capture, however, the potential agencies or subjectivities of slavery's subjects. On the other hand, artifacts of everyday life could be and were used and transported in ways unexpected by the producer of the good, the financiers, or its wholesaler. As such the presence of such goods is not direct proof of the shaping of taste or the change of effect, nor is it a mechanism to see idioms of long-term material expression. Rather the opacity between text and artifact is the strength of historical archaeology. By simultaneously looking at colonial frames of order and use and the ways in which materials are used and reused in unexpected ways, new questions emerge that are not directly apparent from the archaeological record or the documentary record alone.

10

Household Market Activities among Early Nineteenth-Century Jamaican Slaves

An Archaeological Case Study from Two Slave Settlements

Matthew Reeves

Introduction

This study endeavors to assess how the household can be used as a unit of analysis for examining the lives of Jamaican slaves during the last four decades of slavery (1800–1838). At their core, archaeological assemblages are used to assess the ability of enslaved households to obtain market goods. These household assemblages were recovered from two slave settlements, one on a coffee plantation (Juan de Bolas) and the other on a sugar estate (Thetford). Both communities are located in the nineteenth-century parish of St. John, now part of the modern-day parish of St. Catherine; both used the market of Old Harbour. The underlying assumption for this study is that households working at plantations of different crop types would have varying labor demands and this difference would impact the amount of time they had for household production. Central to household production was the responsibility Jamaican slaves had for growing their own food and selling excess to obtain their household goods at the island markets. Given these dual but conflicting roles—laborers and household members—it was assumed that the differing labor demands of the two plantations would become manifest in the household archaeological assemblages. Inherent in this case study is deciphering the source and range of goods available at market, comparing household goods, and attempting to explain differences in access to these goods between households.

In carrying out my fieldwork, I excavated trash deposits from nine households at the two plantations. What I observed during these excavations is that these assemblages did vary in their material signatures. Quantifying and qualifying these differences entailed much more than simply letting the artifacts "talk," as the goal was to differentiate complex patterns seen between and among household assemblages. What quickly became apparent was that sometimes the household artifact assemblages differentiated themselves at the household level, other times at the community level, and at times at the regional level.

For example, the presence of low-fired, locally produced earthenware, known as yabbas, can be explained at varying levels of analysis. The vast majority of these wares are produced in the southern part of the island, most particularly the Liguanea Plain outside of Kingston, and the St. Catherine Plain outside of Spanish Town (Hauser 2007). The households examined for this study used markets that were within these production areas and thus had ready access to yabbas. In contrast, excavations carried out at households residing along the Jamaican north coast at Seville Plantation and Drax Hall by Doug Armstrong and Montpelier by Barry Higman yielded fewer yabbas (Armstrong 1990; Higman 1998:222). This difference in access to yabba and its presence among enslaved households can be explained at the regional level with residents on the south coast attending markets that contained a wide array of yabba pots, bowls, and jars. On the north coast, such yabbas were not as available. Thus on the regional level, there were differences in access to yabbas that served as an external constraint for community members seeking to acquire these market wares.

Given these island trade and production patterns, the inhabitants of Juan de Bolas and Thetford were on an equal footing in terms of market access to yabbas since they used the same market of Old Harbour in the St. Catherine Plain. Despite this homogeneity of intraregional access, within the household assemblages recovered at the two plantations, there was a higher number of yabba water jars recovered among Thetford households than at Juan de Bolas. A potential explanation for this difference was found in the proximity between water sources and the two community settlements. At Thetford sugar estate, the settlement and works were located on a ridge to take advantage of breezes for the windmill, thereby removing inhabitants from water sources. In contrast, the settlement and works at Juan de Bolas were located in a gully with a stream to drive the water mill. With the greater distance from Thetford to the gutter drawing water from the Rio Cobre, the community utilized water jars to a much greater extent; the high percentage of gray salt-glazed stoneware and yabba jar vessels may corroborate the need for water storage vessels.

Explaining patterns seen at the level of household artifact assemblage necessitates a deeper understanding of the varying scales of influence and historical context for the communities, including regional and local influences.

In this relatively simple example, analysis at the level of individual household did not provide an adequate context to explain the presence or absence of water jars. While choice concerning the purchase of yabba jars was still being made by individuals at the household level, the accessibility of these jars through regional markets (availability of yabbas) and community needs (distance needed to transport water) tended to dominate household decisions. The decision to purchase yabba jars was heavily influenced at the scalar levels of regional market availability of yabba water jars and community needs for transport and storage of water. For understanding both of these differences, the level of patterning for yabba assemblages needed to be established (inter- or intracommunity differences) in conjunction with the appropriate historic context (need for transport of water and availability of yabbas) for each region and settlement.

With this analysis model in hand, I use household material assemblages from Juan de Bolas and Thetford, in conjunction with the known history of the two plantations, to evaluate how labor demands stressed household domestic production on two levels: the level of the community in general and the level of individual household. The measure of this stress is derived from the amount and diversity of market goods present at the various household assemblages sampled for this study. To carry out these different levels of analysis on household assemblages, I am guided by what William Marquardt refers to as "effective scale" in human actions (1993:107). Marquardt defined effective scale as a measure (both temporal and spatial) through which observed behavior (in this case artifact patterns) can be meaningfully understood. What Marquardt and others assert is that we are more likely to ascertain broader social actions that influenced patterns seen in archaeological assemblages by examining these patterns through a range of spatial and temporal scales (Marquardt 1993:111; R. McGuire 1994; Wilkie and Farnsworth 1999). In this case these scales through which enslaved households' decisions were made can be seen at the level of the household, the community (Juan de Bolas or Thetford), the region (all of the communities using Old Harbour for their market), and even the nation (Jamaica as it is tied into the global economy).

Using different scales (regional, community, and household) to view enslaved Africans' material record allows interpretation of various aspects of the whole realm of their living conditions and social relations. If we view household access to material culture solely at the household level we would be blind to differences operating at the community level, such as the impact that different plantation labor systems had on the community as a whole. If we interpret household assemblage patterns in relation to the community level, we gain insight into how households within the same community may have used different strategies to counteract the stresses being placed on the community as a whole. In the same manner, to view actions solely as operating at community level would cause our analysis to be blind to the forces working at the regional and even global levels. To take into account these complex forces, an effective means of assessing influences and choices at the individual, household, community, regional, and global levels needs to be created.

To use archaeological assemblages to assess household access to market goods, the various factors that influenced these households at the community and regional levels need to be determined. Factors include the regional locale of markets in relation to the two slave settlements, the ethnic basis for each community (creole or African born), the stresses that differing crop production placed on households, and how differential hierarchy within each community influenced daily life. By understanding the myriad scales present in the historical record, these sources of historic context can be drawn from to explain patterning seen in the archaeological record. The first two sections of this essay will establish the context in which the actions of the two enslaved communities were set.

Background on Market Economy

For enslaved Jamaicans, their lives as household members were a contradiction of the political system that legally bound them to their owners (Bakan 1990). During their off time, enslaved Jamaicans participated as both small-scale producers and consumers in an island-wide market system through which excess produce grown in provision grounds could be sold, bartered, and traded for market goods. Given that slaves used provision grounds to provide the majority of their food, they were an important part of any large plantation operation in Jamaica. Proof of the importance of slave provisioning is borne out by the fact that on average, Jamaican coffee plantations used close to 60 percent of the acreage for provisions and at sugar estates a little under 50 percent was reserved for provisions (Higman 1986b:83, 1988).

For the two plantations examined for this study, documentary and oral histories point to active sets of provision grounds during the early nineteenth century. At Juan de Bolas, the provision grounds are noted on an early nineteenth-century survey plat (National Library of Jamaica, Unaccessioned Plats for the Parish of St. Catherine). The grounds are located in steep terrain where the risk of washouts made coffee planting undesirable. While the map does not contain details of the size of the grounds, estimates based on comparable coffee plantations suggest that of the 650 acres at Juan de Bolas, close to 100 were in provision production (Higman 1986b). For Thetford, the provision grounds were likely located within a 670-acre landmass known as Thetford Mountain. Similar to Juan de Bolas, this area is characterized by steep slopes unsuitable for large-scale mono-crop production, in this case sugar cane. The association of this landmass with provision grounds is based on the combined factors of the name ("mountain" often referred to provision grounds for slaves; Higman 1988) and the fact that following emancipation, documentary and oral sources record that former slaves left Thetford sugar estate to live in this area (Craton 1978). Often, newly emancipated slaves settled areas of their former provision grounds (Higman 1988).

An important aspect of provision production is that it took place at the level of the household—which serves as the underlying premise of this household-based archaeological study. Caribbean scholars have noted that household-based provision production tended to encourage household units structured around family (extended and nuclear; for an extended discussion of household structure, see Higman 1991) as control over labor was essential to the success of provision production (Higman 1991; Morrissey 1991; Patterson 1973). The tuber-dominated provision production of slaves was also well adapted to the household unit as there was no need for harnessing large amounts of labor for successful production. This factor is what made household provision production such an attractive alternative over wage labor for former slaves after emancipation in 1838.

Ethnohistorical sources also note the importance of the household in provision production with women often cited as working the grounds and men clearing new areas for crops (M. Lewis 1834:308; Moreton 1790:150; Edwards [1793] 1972). The grounds were usually assigned to household units and often passed down through slave families along with material possessions (Edwards [1793] 1972:125; Dallas 1803). This household basis for provision production also extended to the sale of these goods at Sunday markets.

The crops that Jamaican slaves produced in their provision grounds and gardens not only fed their own households but were the sole supply of fresh produce for the urban class of Jamaicans living in Spanish Town, Old Harbour, and the island's other urban centers (Mintz and Hall [1970] 1991:328). The reliance of urban Jamaicans on this sale of produce was so great that the Jamaican legislature specifically protected the rights of enslaved laborers to sell "provisions, fruits, fresh fish, milk, poultry, and other small stock of all kinds" (Votes of the Assembly of Jamaica, 1735, National Library of Jamaica). It was through the sale of this excess produce that Jamaican slaves became the prime producers and consumers in this informal market economy. Contemporary estimates report that nearly 80 percent of the island's small currency was in the hands of enslaved individuals (Long [1774] 1970).

At the Sunday markets, there were three groups of retailers: the white merchants who sold imported goods (largely Jewish merchants who, unlike Christian merchants, were free to open their shops on Sunday); the free blacks who sold locally produced goods; and the enslaved who sold provisions (Long [1774] 1970:573). As part of the market economy, enslaved Jamaicans were not only producers but also consumers. They either bartered with their produce or bought with cash the items that were available in the marketplace. Based on archaeological excavations at Juan de Bolas and Thetford, these included a wide range of imported items such as ceramics, jewelry, buttons, glassware, and cutlery. Another large segment of this economy was the local artisans who produced alternatives to the imported items, likely at a much lower cost. These artisans include pewter smiths who produced cutlery, potters who made a wide variety of low-fired earthenware yabbas, blacksmiths who manufactured tools, and a wide range of artisans producing and selling such items as baskets, wooden items, and furniture. Available evidence speaks to the imported items being sold at a much higher price than locally produced wares due mainly to the extended trade network in which such goods were enmeshed. Beginning with the sale from the factory, through the redistribution via English merchants and the long transatlantic voyage, and finally to resale through white merchants in Jamaica, these imported goods ran through a series of markups and tariffs. Comparisons of contemporary sources indicate that for an average slave, the purchase of a painted ceramic bowl would require a week's worth of produce sold at market (DeLaBeche 1825; Reeves 1997:172). Given the high cost of imported goods, enslaved residents at Juan de Bolas and Thetford would have considered such purchases very carefully.

An important aspect of this study is the time period under consideration. In the early nineteenth century, English market goods exploded onto the global market. Most notable among these items were low-priced ceramics that arrived from England on a daily basis (Miller, Martin, and Dickinson 1994). Jewish merchants purchased these items with the end customer in mind—the slaves who bought and sold items at Sunday markets (Bickell 1825:66; Long [1774] 1970:573). With a bewildering variety of ceramics being produced, Jewish merchants were in an excellent position to obtain items that could satisfy a wide range of economic scales and choices. The wide-scale availability of English ceramics ensured that almost every enslaved household had some plate, bowl, or cup that originated overseas. What this availability of market goods ensures is that household goods with a wide availability and broad diversity, such as English ceramics, provide excellent indicators for market choice, access, and tradition (Majewski and O'Brien 1987).

With choice in market goods being a central tenet of this study, it is imperative that comparisons between household archaeological assemblages provide a useful means to establish differential market access at the community and household levels. The use of household comparison to assess market access necessitates that two criteria be met. First, all households needed to have access to the same set of markets to ensure comparability of household assemblages. Second, the majority of the household material items being compared from the archaeological record needed to be obtained from these markets. In essence, these two criteria revolve around ensuring that the two communities are set within the same market region that allowed for equal access and choice in market goods. With such criteria being met, the regional scale of analysis can be ruled out as a contributing factor to household choice at market.

I was fortunate to excavate ten house areas from two slave communities that fit these criteria for comparison. The site inhabitants were enslaved African Jamaicans. Six of the households were enslaved on a coffee plantation known as Juan de Bolas and the other four were at Thetford sugar estate. What made the comparison between households at Juan de Bolas and Thetford a viable data set for assessing market access was that the inhabitants of both estates utilized the same market—Old Harbour reached via Guanaboa Vale. Plantation books from Thetford record that Old Harbour was the main market where all plantation goods were bound. Oral history at Juan de Bolas records that prior to widespread use of market trucks

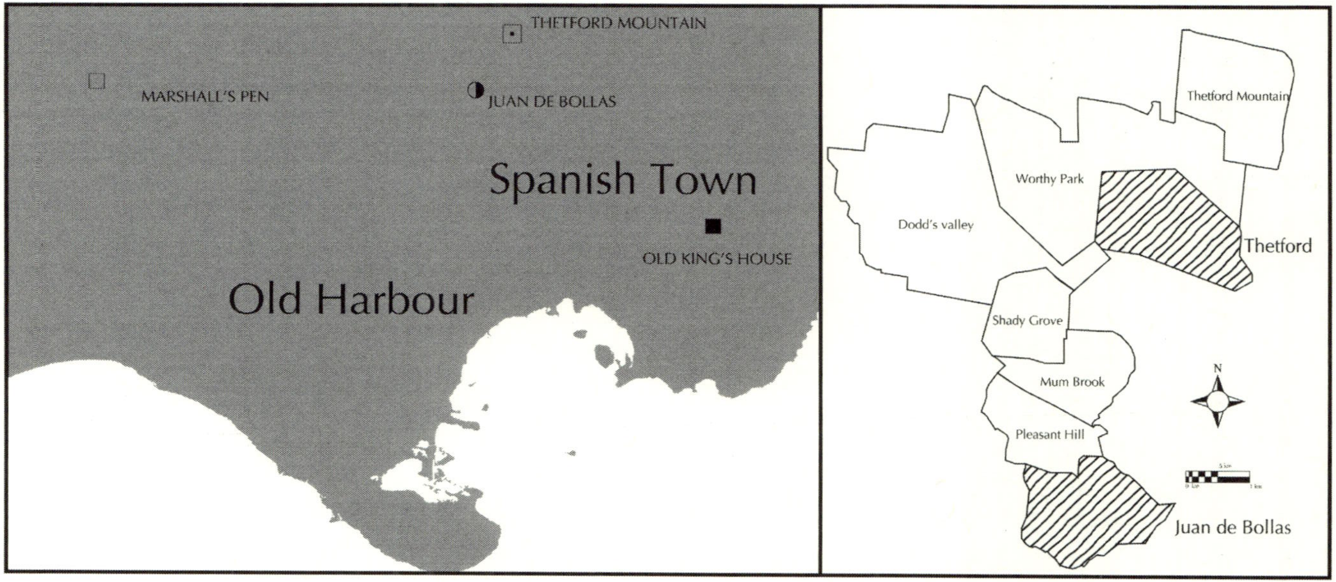

Figure 10.1. Map of south-central Jamaica showing location of Juan de Bolas and Thetford (*left*); map of Juan de Bolas and Thetford area showing estate boundaries and the relationship between the two plantations (*right*).

after the 1960s, countless generations of market ladies had made the ten-mile trek to markets at Old Harbour. Combined with this, the plantations of Juan de Bolas and Thetford were separated by less than three miles by path and were literally within sight of each other. In addition, with the lands of Juan de Bolas and Thetford being nearly contiguous (Mum Brook was the cattle pen for Thetford Estate), undoubtedly the inhabitants of both plantations used the same markets and were enmeshed in economic and social networks with each other (Figure 10.1). By removing regional market variability from influencing differences between settlement assemblages, any differences between households can be ascribed to variability at the level of the community or household. To begin to assess factors that would influence differences on the community level, the background context for each settlement needs to be established.

The Context of the Plantation Slave Settlements

While this study dwells on the lives, actions, and residues of enslaved household members, their lives were profoundly affected by an incredibly oppressive system of chattel slavery. The intensive stress placed on slaves' lives by plantation labor ensured that issues such as market choice, access to small-scale capital, and trading were influenced by the crops being produced, daily work regime, and history of each individual plantation. As a result, any discussion of slave market activities and access to market goods needs to be predicated by a detailed understanding of the labor expected from the enslaved individuals living and working on these plantations.

Juan de Bolas was first worked by enslaved Africans in the 1720s. Up until the 1770s these enslaved workers produced sugar under the eye of their resident owner, Simon Clarke (IRO Deed, Island Record Office, Spanish Town, Jamaica, 87:113). With the death of Clarke in 1770, the plantation operations switched to provision production until the sale of the property to Samuel Queneborough in 1797 (IRO Inventory 60:174; Accounts Produce 9:152; IRO Deed 445:16). At that time the property and slaves of the Clarke family were sold and Queneborough quickly planted the rugged terrain of Juan de Bolas in coffee fields or "pieces" and converted the lands into a profitable coffee plantation (Accounts Produce 49:2). As a recent arrival to the island, Queneborough populated his new coffee plantation through the purchase of nearly two hundred African-born slaves. This African-born population remained a dominant part of the community well into the 1820s with most creole-born individuals being under twenty years of age (Returns of Slaves, Island Record Office, Spanish Town, Jamaica, 1817–32). With Queneborough's death in 1815, close to half of the population at Juan de Bolas was moved to his sugar estate in Guanaboa Vale. The remaining slaves worked at Juan de Bolas up until emancipation with the plantation being managed by a series of overseers

(Accounts Produce 1816–38). During the years following emancipation, Samuel Queneborough's nephew sold off plots to former slaves in an effort to generate income for the dying plantation operation (Accounts Produce 1839–40). In the end, this sale of land divested the Queneborough family from the district but allowed former slaves to become legally invested in their homes at Juan de Bolas.

Thetford sugar estate began operation in the 1720s and remained a sugar estate in the hands of the Fuller family up until emancipation in 1838 (IRO Deed 74:28; Accounts Produce 1773–80, 1799–1838). As a result, for the time period under study the community of Thetford slaves remained relatively stable in terms of family lines remaining in one place throughout the entire history of the plantation's operation. This resulted in the community's ability to trace their families in an unbroken line of enslavement at Thetford for over 110 years. This remarkable longevity of community stability was offset by the brutal tactics acted out on a sugar estate. For slave owners of large estate operations, the ability to reap profits from the land rested on complete disregard for the health, longevity, and family structure of individuals living within households. Prior to the end of the slave trade in 1807, patterns in slave health and population show that it was more profitable to literally work individuals to death and buy new slaves than to provide for an individual's health and allow for family structure to augment the population (Craton 1978). This changed after 1808, with slave owners showing a marked concern for the ability of slaves to reproduce and providing such thinly veiled incentives for reproduction as allowing a mother who had eight healthy children to be exempt from work (Craton 1978; Higman 1976). Given the priority placed on extracting labor from slaves at any cost, any cohesiveness and stability found among the Thetford community from its long-lived history was more a function of 110 years of shared terror and abuses stemming from sugar production than any stability inspired by the Fuller family. In the end, following emancipation, this community stability was disrupted by the Fullers' attempt to impose the twin criteria of wage labor and rent on former homes (Accounts Produce 1839–42). The final result of this imposed rent system was that former slaves left their ancestral home of Thetford in droves, choosing to resettle at Thetford Mountain in their former provision grounds rather than continue on at the plantation.

The outcome of this history in terms of the present-day descendant community and archaeological record is a stark contrast between the two plantation landscapes. When one visits Juan de Bolas Plantation today, one sees a small community that is spread out across the countryside through small landholdings. Essentially all the lands making up Juan de Bolas are settled by small farmers, most of whom are descendants of Queneborough's slaves. During the time of slavery, however, the population was much larger and concentrated into two settlements: Tophouse and Slave Center. Sitting between these two settlements, the ruins of the mill complex are still evident, in addition to the coffee barbecues (where the beans were spread for drying after the bean cherry had been crushed off) and the footprints of the slave hospital and main house. While evidence of the slave settlements is not at all present on the landscape, the oral history within the community descendants of the Bolas plantation has preserved the location of the settlements some 170 years after their abandonment. Discussions with local residents revealed myriad early nineteenth-century lore ranging from the names of overseers (confirmed through Accounts Produce in the Island Record Office) to anecdotes of "slaves at Tophouse walked down to the mill, while those at Slave Center walked up to the mill" (Linton Rhule, personal communication, 1994). From these two settlements, six house areas were identified and sampled for their early nineteenth-century goods. Excavations in the garden patches located in the "bush" adjacent to modern farmers' homes revealed much about the life of these farmers' enslaved ancestors.

In our excavations of the two slave settlements at Juan de Bolas, the household goods coming from the six excavation sites did not provide evidence as to whether the two settlements demarcated different classes of slaves. Given the size of each area, it seemed that the majority of slaves lived in Tophouse. Oral history hinted that Tophouse served as the homes of the main gang of slaves and Slave Center served as the residences for the head people (drivers, carpenters, and house slaves). Whatever the case, it was evident that excavating house areas in both settlements at Juan de Bolas was important to provide a representative profile for the range of households present within the enslaved community.

In contrast, fieldwork and research carried out in the early 1990s revealed that the mill complex and slave settlement at Thetford had been abandoned in the 1840s and then used for pasture up until the mid-1990s. With the descendant community dispersed for over 160 years, locating the slave settlement at Thetford proved to be a more difficult prospect. While its windmill, cattle mills, boiling house, and distillery were extremely overgrown, they (along with the site of the main house) were quite visible on the landscape. The locale for the slave settlement, on the other hand, was as elusive as the oral history at Thetford—with the settlement and plantation being abandoned in the early 1840s, there was no local history to document its position. Extensive subsurface testing, however, revealed the location of dense trash deposits near the works, and excavation units placed in the unplowed context for Thetford's settlement soon yielded much material evidence for daily life within the house areas' buried yard surfaces. Unlike excavations at Juan de Bolas, some of the patterning seen from the archaeology suggested locale within the slave settlement was linked to status. Of the four house areas sampled, the two with the highest amount of material goods were located on a ridge away from the mill complex (House Areas 41 and 42). Those with the lowest amount of material goods (House Areas 43 and 44) were directly below the mill and would have been subject to the heat and malodors of the factory complex.

What inspired me to excavate the household trash deposits from these two separate communities was their potential to produce comparative data on life for slaves between two contrasting labor contexts. I hypothesized that the more intensive labor organization at Thetford (sugar) would have had a much more negative impact on a household's time for provision production, selling goods at market, and, in the end, the amount of items they would be able to purchase at market as compared to the organization at Juan de Bolas (coffee). Archaeological excavations at the slave settlements' house areas revealed the living situation for the enslaved community (as seen through the archaeological assemblages) to be much more complex than this simple assumption. The trick to understanding the complex array of attributes derived from house assemblages was devising an analysis technique that brought order to the chaos of available information.

Devising a Market Goods Typology

In the analysis of the nine household assemblages, I found that there were very noticeable differences among the artifacts recovered from various house areas—in some cases, the household assemblages were dominated by yabbas (most especially House Areas 43 and 44 at Thetford). Among these household assemblages, there was very little in the way of imported goods other than bottle glass and some ceramics. At other house areas, there was a large amount of decorated, imported ceramics and a large number and diversity of other imported wares, such as glassware, and personal items. This indicated that households had different access to the two classes of market goods: imported and locally produced wares. Among the nine household assemblages that I sampled there was a wide range of artifact types, categories, and styles that comprised a rich yet challenging data set for assessing access to market goods.

To facilitate the comparison of these household assemblages, I devised a two-part analysis script. The script, which is basically a "recipe" creating a guideline for the data analysis, consisted first of plotting imported goods against locally produced items and then analyzing specific artifact groups. The first part of this script is based on the breakdown of household material goods by acquisition source: imported goods (such as English refined whiteware) and locally produced goods (such as yabbas and locally cast pewter spoons). While other items found in the assemblages could be grouped into additional categories such as those produced by the household (recycled items such as barrel hoops, lead and copper cuttings) and yet another category of yearly plantation allotments (knives and thimbles), these items were found in small enough quantities as not to serve as a viable means of analyzing household access to goods.

The second part of the analysis involved breaking each of the acquisition source categories into subcategories based on ware type and function. For example, the acquisition source category of imported market goods was broken down into the subcategories of ceramics, utensils, glass tableware, beverage and water vessels, clothing and adornment, and tobacco pipes. Information garnered from this secondary analysis was used to further refine and explain the patterns deciphered from broader acquisition categories of imported versus locally produced market goods. Within and between these various levels of analysis, comparisons among the household assemblages were used to differentiate between the scales of community and household differences. Thus, if comparisons between household assemblages reflected more intercommunity differences (i.e., Juan de Bolas household assemblages clustering in patterns distinct from Thetford households), this would reflect actions and choice at the scale of the community. On the other hand, if household comparisons reflected intracommunity differences (i.e., households not clustering along community lines), this would reflect actions and decisions at the level of the household. As I found in this study, market access appears to have been a complex interplay between these two scales of analysis, all set within an even more bewildering array of regional and global contexts.

Analysis and Comparison of Household Goods

On the first level of analysis, the quantities of locally produced goods were plotted against imported goods. Instead of the house areas from each respective plantation community grouping in two separate clusters, the range of goods from each settlement formed two distinct patterns (Figure 10.2). For the Thetford community, the four house areas are spread across a wide range of imported and locally produced goods. Two house areas cluster as being dominated by locally produced goods and two are in the mid-range of all nine house areas sampled. For the Juan de Bolas households, the striking feature is that all of the house areas cluster in the graph as having a high amount of imported goods. All the households at Juan de Bolas contained over 60 percent imported goods with only a twenty-percentage-point spread between households. We can see from this broad-scale comparison of market goods that the house areas at Thetford tend to demonstrate a wide range of material access while those at Juan de Bolas tend to be more homogeneous.

While this initial stab at patterning of household material goods seems to indicate a wider range of access between households at the Thetford sugar estate, what does it mean in terms of relative cost and diversity of goods present among households? In other words, do the two households at Thetford really rank in the mid-range of all households as represented by Figure 10.2? One clue that this is not the case is the sheer volume and diversity of materials recovered from House Areas 41 and 42 as compared to those at Juan de Bolas. As the graph of imported versus locally produced goods only reflects percentage of imported goods to locally produced goods, it does not accurately represent the quantity and diversity of market goods. To flesh this difference out, we need to proceed to the second level of

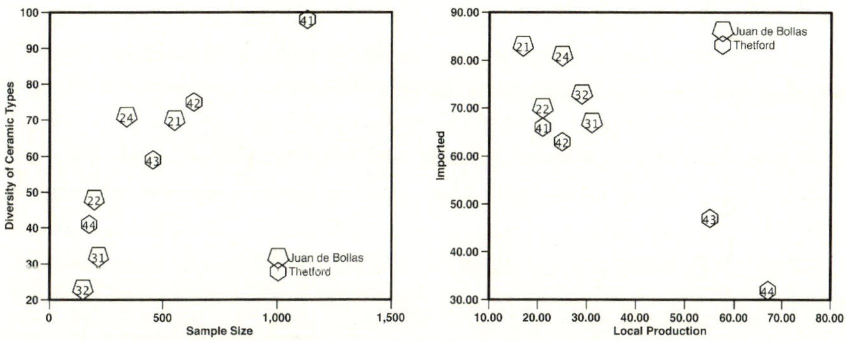

Figure 10.2. Biplot of imported vs. locally produced goods for house areas at Juan de Bolas and Thetford (right); diversity of ceramic types by house area (left).

analysis in which particular artifact groups are examined for quantity and diversity of goods.

Ceramics proved to be one of the strongest indices for access to imported goods. This was due to their presence at all household assemblages and to the ease of identification in terms of decoration and form, features that have made ceramics a useful analytic component for many archaeologists (see Miller, Martin, and Dickinson 1994; Majewski and O'Brien 1987). During the excavation and physical analysis of the assemblages, it was noted that the two households that contained a high amount and large diversity of imported ceramics were House Areas 41 and 42 from Thetford. In contrast, the other two house areas at Thetford (43 and 44) tended to contain very little in the way of imported ceramics. At Juan de Bolas, the house areas tended to demonstrate a middle range of these two extremes. While this observable patterning was similar to what the market-source analysis reflected in terms of the Thetford households having more divergent assemblages, initial observations indicated that the two households at Thetford (41 and 42) contained a much higher access to imported goods than the Juan de Bolas households. What remained was to find a way to demonstrate these observable differences in a quantitative presentation.

A question that stems from these observations is whether decoration technique on imported ceramics (painted, printed, dipped, or plain) reflects the patterns seen in quantity and diversity. Given the extensive research on decorative type by George Miller, it seemed that the CC-index value would serve as a useful inter-household comparative variable. (It is called the CC-index value as common creamware [undecorated table ceramic] serves as the base value against which other decorative types are measured.) Miller devised a scaling of ceramic value based on price-fixing lists of Staffordshire potters. This index ranges from 1 to 4 (1 = undecorated common creamware, 2 = shell-edged and dipped, 3 = painted, and 4 = printed). What this analysis revealed was that all of the households tended to fall within the index value of 2 (representing edge-decorated and dipped wares). Given the wide variation between households' ceramic assemblages, it would seem that other factors would be influencing this relative homogeneity of decorative types. This potentially reflects an intercommunity preference for dipped and edge-decorated vessels at market or the limited availability of other wares (such as hand-painted and transfer-printed vessels).

Insight into the availability of dipped wares comes from comparisons with excavations of house areas at Seville and Montpelier plantations located on the north coast of Jamaica (all data sets are available on the Digital Archaeological Archive of Comparative Slavery [DAACS] database). Two house areas at Seville Plantation contained ceramic assemblages whose refined-white earthenwares were dominated by dipped wares. These two house areas' ceramic assemblages were very close in date to assemblages recovered at Thetford and Juan de Bolas (mid-1810–20s). In contrast, three house areas at Montpelier Plantation contained ceramic assemblages that were dominated by printed wares (transfer prints). The house areas at Montpelier date to between ten and twenty years later than those at Thetford and Juan de Bolas. One house area at Thetford that contained a similar set of transfer-printed wares was a later dating site (1830s) and was not included due to its nonconformance with the occupation time frame of other house areas used in this study.

In contrasting these decorative types with those found at similarly dating slave house areas in Piedmont, Virginia, there are noticeable differences. Among house areas excavated at Monticello and James Madison's Montpelier, the predominant decorative type is hand-painted wares (warm or earth tones [DAACS]). At sites in the Piedmont, there is a relatively low incidence of dipped wares as compared to sites in Jamaica. These larger differences suggest that regional export patterns influenced the decorative types available for enslaved households. Thus, while global export patterns from Staffordshire potters allowed for the availability of ceramics, it was regional import that determined the types available at markets. It is possible that Jewish merchants in Jamaica selected decorative types, such as dipped wares, based on their ability to sell and make profits at Sunday markets. Whether this was influenced by African Jamaican preference for dipped wares or due to the fact that dipped wares were the cheapest decorative ware available on the market is difficult to state. In either case, it seems that choice in ceramic decoration was influenced more by market availability than individual household preference. In addition, the similarity between decorative types recovered at Seville and the house areas of this study suggests that choice in decorative types among imported ceramics reflects island-wide patterns of trade and limitations on the range of imported ceramics coming into the Sunday markets.

Vessel shapes were also examined to determine market access. In dividing the ceramic vessels by functional category, forms were divided into teaware (cups, saucers, and teapots), flatware (plates), and hollowware (bowls). Vessel shape has been shown to be an indicator of status difference between planters and slaves (Otto 1984) and for changes in food traditions through time (Sanford 1994:125; Armstrong 1990:144). Given the similarity in time and class structure for all households sampled in this study, the question remained as to whether differentiation by vessel would manifest itself on the household, community, or regional level. Vessel forms among households tended to show differences between communities rather than individual households. For all the communities, hollowware predominated among all household assemblages. Comparisons between flatware and teaware tended to cluster households by community affiliation. For example, among Thetford's households, teaware predominated over flatware. In contrast, Juan de Bolas households tended to have more flatware than teaware.

Given that vessel form tends to reflect food traditions, a potential explanation for patterning of vessel form might be the differentiation of the creole-born population at Thetford from the African-born population at Juan de Bolas. Many explanations for these differences are possible, ranging from creole-born slaves at Thetford adapting tea culture to their repertoire of culinary habits to flatware among Juan de Bolas slaves representing a combination of West and Central African foodways that use garnishes in addition to one-pot stews (DeCorse 1999; Cooper 1977:89). In this patterning at the community level, vessel form tended to uniformly reflect traditions set at the level of shared community experience rather than differences between households.

The analysis techniques described above for examining the ceramic assemblages did not provide a satisfactory quantitative measure of the diversity noted in visual observations of the household assemblages. In the end, the diversity and richness of the household ceramic assemblages turned out to most accurately measure what was seen in the individual assemblages during excavation and cataloguing. Richness is a function of the diversity of type categories (in this case defined by ceramic form and decoration evident among the reconstructed vessels) and the sample size. As can be seen in Figure 10.2, the diversity of ceramic types tended to increase with sample size (number of vessels).

For ceramic diversity, the top two contenders were House Areas 41 and 42 at Thetford sugar estate, with House Area 41 standing well beyond the range of other house areas. These two household ceramic assemblages tended to be dominated by a wide range of annular-decorated vessels (bowls, cups, and mugs; Figure 10.3). In addition, many of the wares, especially small bowls, tended to have a uniformity of shape and decoration that suggested they were part of a larger set of dishes. The combined diversity and quantity of goods suggests that these households, espe-

Figure 10.3 Imported slipwares recovered from the site.

cially House Area 41, tended to use imported ceramics on a daily basis and only supplement with locally produced calabash and wooden bowls. The remaining house areas at Thetford and Juan de Bolas tended to have higher numbers of bowls to plates and teaware. In addition, their assemblages did not have as high a number of matching vessel forms that were suggestive of sets. Given the lack of diversity and the lesser quantities of ceramics found among these house areas at Juan de Bolas and Thetford, these households likely were more reliant on calabash and wooden bowls and used imported ceramics for either specialized purposes or specific social events.

Glass tableware (tumblers and stemware) tended to reflect a similar pattern to that seen among ceramic vessels. House Area 41 at Thetford had an overwhelmingly high amount of glass tableware (83 sherds), while other house areas at both settlements demonstrated a low amount of glass tableware (0–8 sherds). For House Area 41, the high amount of glass tableware suggests the daily use of glass tumblers and stemware in dining activities. The predominance of these glassware sherds mirrors the high amount of ceramic vessels from House Area 41.

Personal adornment items were one of the most visible means of conveying status, and the presence of these items in household assemblages seems to be closely linked to market access (Galle 1996; White 2005). Among all the house areas sampled, once again, the one that stood out above the rest was House Area 41's assemblage of faceted beads (n = 15), buttons (n = 4), and diverse array of materials from parasol stays to clock hardware. This house area was followed closely by House Area 42's assemblage of beads (n = 6) and buttons (n = 4). The remaining house areas at Thetford and all of the house areas at Juan de Bolas had much lower quantities of beads, buttons, and other display goods. Bead types also tended to reflect a corresponding influence of market access.

Beads recovered from the house areas at Juan de Bolas and Thetford spanned a wide range of colors and forms. One of the main means of differentiating glass beads was whether they were faceted or smooth. Large amounts of faceted beads were limited to Thetford's House Areas 41 and 42—the same two house areas that contained a higher amount of imported goods. Other house areas at Thetford and those at Juan de Bolas contained either a low number of beads or a higher percentage of unfaceted beads. It is difficult to determine whether the absence of faceted beads among other house areas was dependent upon personal choice or market access. Given that the pattern in presence of faceted beads seems to match the patterns seen in other imported items (House Areas 41 and 42 having higher amounts), it is likely that these households had more access to market goods.

Medicinal bottles were another area that allowed differentiation of household assemblages. Once again, House Area 41 at Thetford demonstrated marked access to market goods by containing the highest amount of medicinal bottles (n = 42 fragments) compared to 0–10 fragments for other house areas. This higher amount of aqua-tinted bottle glass suggests access to medicinal supplies was limited to households that also had correspondingly high access to other market goods.

With this analysis in hand, what we are left with is a pattern at Thetford sugar estate that indicates one household had much greater access to goods (House Area 41), another fell in the mid-range (House Area 42), and the remaining two had very restricted access to market goods, predominantly relying on locally produced wares. Among the Juan de Bolas community, this pattern is very different with household assemblages characterized by a more uniform range of access to market goods that tends to fall below House Area 42 but above House Areas 43 and 44. What this seems to demonstrate is that among Thetford households, there is more intracommunity differentiation while the households at Juan de Bolas tend to demonstrate an intercommunity contrast with those of Thetford. In other words, market decisions made by households at Thetford seemed to be constrained by differentiation with the community while at Juan de Bolas there seemed to be more homogeneity among households. What then to make of this patterning? An important context to address with these household assemblages is the impact that labor structure had on the enslaved community.

Labor Organization at Sugar Estates and Coffee Plantations

As one might expect in an enslaved community, the labor demands or impact of structured labor hierarchy imposed on the community has the most potential for explaining the patterns seen among household assemblages. This is chiefly due to the correspondence between the amount of time and resources available to individuals producing marketable goods (provisions) and how much labor and time plantations demanded during the day. The workloads slaves would experience on a coffee plantation and on a sugar estate serve as the baseline for understanding the amount of time that could be allotted by enslaved households for provision production.

The labor organization for coffee and sugar production in nineteenth-century Jamaica differed in the degree of labor demanded from slaves and in the hierarchy the labor regime imposed on the community. Sugar cultivation was the most labor intensive of all crops produced in Jamaica. There were two forms of sugar cultivation during the early nineteenth century: cane planting and ratooning. Cane planting was the more intensive of the two, as a portion of the cane needed to be replanted with each crop season. In ratooning, the base of the cane and root system remained in the ground after harvest and only a few plants had to be replanted (Higman 1976:20). The wetter soils of Thetford required that after only one or two ratooning seasons the cane be replanted or the cane would not yield as high a sugar content (Thetford Plantation Books, Jamaica National Archives [JNA]). The enslaved laborers at Thetford (assisted by jobbing gangs) had the yearly task of cane holing (using hand tools to carve holes into the ground to plant cane), one of the most onerous jobs of the cane cycle.

The growth cycle for cane required fifteen to sixteen months before the cane was ready for harvest. On average, the harvest lasted for six months and each cane field was staggered over this time period for an efficient harvest. To harvest the cane, enslaved laborers cut the cane, stripped it of trash, stacked it into piles, and transported the piles to the works. All of these activities had to take place immediately after the cane fields were burnt. Burning the fields immediately before harvest raised the sugar content within the cane.

At the works, the cane was fed by hand into the rollers driven by Thetford's windmill. The juices flowed down a gutter to the boiling house. The boiling house consisted of a series of boiling cauldrons, making for a very hot and humid environment filled with the acrid odor of burnt sugar. Workers in the boiling house skimmed off the froth from the boiling vats and turned the cocks (valves) to drain one vat to the next. The cauldrons, known as coppers, to which the cane juices were moved became progressively smaller and hotter with the smallest copper being the location where the sugar was "struck." Striking refers to the point where the sugar begins to crystallize. After that it was cooled and poured into hogsheads and placed in the curing house to season and drain excess molasses (Craton and Walvin 1970:110). The remaining molasses was processed with water, yeast, and sugar skimmings and then double distilled through the copper worms immersed in Thetford's massive brick cooling vat of the distillery to make rum.

Cane had to be processed as soon as it was harvested as the sucrose content breaks down very rapidly. As a result, workers rotated night spells in the factory to grind the cane, ladle the vats of bubbling cane juice, and clean up the vats and mill area. Thus, during the six-month harvest at sugar estates, enslaved workers would only get Sundays off for rest and provision production. The remainder of the week was spent working in the fields during the day and serving a night spell in the factory every other night (T. Cooper 1791:2). One contemporary author referred to night work as "frequently abridging" the rest of enslaved laborers during the crop harvest (Anonymous 1823:486). Thetford's boiling house would glow throughout the night and its windmill would moan, its sails flapping in the breeze. As the enslaved laborers resided near the works, the noises and smells of the factory were a constant reminder of their servitude to the demands of cane.

During the other six months of the year, the community would work during the day and have alternating Saturdays off. Outside of the harvest season, work included weeding the cane, holing and planting new fields, and other tasks that usually added up to thirteen hours of work per day (Beckford 1790:67). The demands of growing and processing sugar cane were stressful on the community throughout the year.

Production of coffee, while a laborious process, did not demand the same year-round drudgery and labor from the community as sugar did. On average, the crop period for coffee was around half the time needed for growing sugar. At some coffee plantations, crop production lasted for only six weeks and at others it lasted for three to four months, anywhere from October to March (Higman 1984:183, 1976:23). The process of harvesting coffee involved picking the berry off the tree (which generally grows within the reach of the hand) and loading the berries into bags. These bags were transported to the mill either on enslaved laborers' heads or by mules. Compared to the harvest on sugar estates, such tasks were considerably lighter. Not only was the amount of carrying severely reduced, but work took place in the shade of coffee groves, not in burning cane fields.

Coffee processing involved five basic steps. The outer skin of the coffee "cherry" was crushed off in a process known as chumming. Once the residue of the skins was washed off, the beans were drained and then spread out on barbecues to dry. Barbecues are large level platforms with basins in the middle. Drying on the barbecues took two to three weeks of exposing the beans to the sun. At night, or if rain threatened, the beans were raked into basins in the center of the barbecues and covered with tarpaulins or banana leaves. After the coffee had thoroughly dried, it was ready for storage. The final step before transport was to crush off the remaining shell of the bean and winnow the chaff from the bean. These steps were usually accomplished by means of a water-driven or animal-powered mill.

Coffee did not require the immediate processing after harvest nor the intense processing to transform the raw field product to its market form as sugar cane did. As a result, coffee processing did not require the same speed and intensity of labor or the round-the-clock operation of the factory as did sugar processing. Once dried, coffee could be kept for nearly a year without loss of its market value. With sugar, after a week the sucrose in the cane begins to break down and renders the cane useless for processing.

During the out-of-crop season, the enslaved laborers on the coffee plantation pruned trees, cut grass for fodder, repaired the works, maintained drainage gutters in the coffee "pieces," and weeded the fields—all considerably less intense labor than that found on the sugar estate (Higman 1976:23; Kelly 1838:18). As a result, some smaller coffee plantations with shorter crop seasons would often job their workers out to other plantations when not in crop season (Accounts Produce, JNA; Higman 1986b). Other coffee plantations made up for the down time by having smaller populations and hiring jobbing gangs during the harvest (Hermitage Estate Letter Book in Higman 1986b).

Thus coffee plantations enabled workers to spend more time cultivating plots. In addition, the average coffee plantation in Jamaica had 30–40 percent more land available for provision production. This allowed slaves to have larger provisioning plots and helped in the production of marketable surpluses. Slave communities on coffee plantations had the potential to produce more provisions per household (due to the availability of time and land), thus allowing for more access to market resources.

The impact of living on sugar estates versus coffee plantations on slaves' health can be seen directly in their death rates and birthrates. Among the Juan de Bolas slaves, age at death tended to be twenty years older than that at Thetford, primarily because the younger slaves at the latter plantation were more vulnerable to sickness and the demands of work (Reeves 1997:55–90). As for birthrates, mothers at Juan de Bolas were more likely to successfully bring their children into their teens than were their female counterparts at Thetford (Reeves 1997). The relationship between labor expectations and overall health on sugar and coffee plantations is presented by a contemporary observer in Jamaica: "On two estates situated in the same district and belonging to the same proprietor, the one a coffee plantation, the other a sugar-plantation, the negroes increase in number on the former, while on the other they are stationary. In both they are exempt from night-work and the fatigue of heavy burthens; so that the cause of their difference is, doubtless, to be sought in the nature of their employment, in the lighter labour of the coffee-estate" (Anonymous 1823:488). What is intriguing about this testimony is the similarity it bears to the situation of Queneborough, who owned two estates: Juan de Bolas and a sugar estate (Lloyds and Aylmers) in Guanaboa Vale. Whether Queneborough is the proprietor that the above author refers to is difficult to determine.

The hierarchy imposed on the slave community at the sugar estate included drivers and craftspeople, both roles that afforded high status in comparison with their fellow slaves in the work gangs. Specific tasks were assigned to individual work gangs; for example, the "first gang" was composed of the youngest and most physically fit workers (predominantly female) and was assigned the most onerous tasks of harvesting and planting the cane (DeLaBeche 1825:21). As this work was not task driven, it was the responsibility of the drivers to ensure that the daily work routine successfully accomplished the goals set by the overseers. In supervising these gangs, a driver had the important task of ensuring that the day-to-day labor was maximized (Higman 1976:189). Drivers' authority as supervisors in the field meant they needed sufficient influence over enslaved laborers to inspire respect—a role that ethnohistorical sources suggest carried over into the community. Within the community, drivers often served as a "bench of justice, which sits and decides, privately, and without the knowledge of the whites, on all disputes and complaints of their fellow slaves" (Stewart 1823:262). In most cases, drivers' careers were dependent upon maintaining a balance between the goals set by the overseers and the needs set forth by the enslaved community. For example, it was the driver's or head person's duty to safeguard the community provision grounds. One planter had this to say about reallocating provision grounds into cane fields: "You must particularly take care, by bribery or otherwise, to get the sanction of the head people, or your slaves would probably get discontented, and careless of their own property and of yours" (London 1807:40 in McDonald 1993:19).

While the previous quote alludes to bribery of the driver, a corollary is that the driver was accountable to the community. Without sanction from the community, the driver's power to sway enslaved Africans was as limited as that of the white management. Protecting community needs, especially in regard to provision production, was in the best interest of the drivers as they directly benefited from the communities' success in domestic production. At the same time, a driver's position of influence was dependent upon the smooth functioning of the workday. If either of these were out of balance, their authority would be compromised.

The hierarchy created by the plantocracy had ramifications on household production of provisions as well. A bookkeeper on an estate in St. George reported that one of his jobs "was to see that the driver did not clandestinely send a Negro or two to work his provision grounds" (Kelly 1838:19). This control over surplus labor was not limited to drivers. When a cooper was presented with the option of freedom he stated, "What good would free do me, to leave the house and the ground I have from massa, and lose my negro who works my ground for me?" (Barclay [1828] 1969:263). Thus, to assume that provision grounds served as the great equalizer of social inequity caused by the labor hierarchy would ignore the manner in which this hierarchy carried over to household production.

It is little wonder that in his observations of differences among enslaved workers' homes, Bryan Edwards was able to generalize in regard to specialized slaves and gang workers in the following way: "In general a cottage for one Negro and his wife . . . they have no great matter to boast . . . a small table; two or three low stools; an earthen jar for holding water; a pail; an iron pot; calabashes of different sizes (serving tolerably for plates, dishes and bowls). . . . [T]radesmen and domestics are in general vastly better lodged and provided . . . a few have even good beds, linen sheets, and mosquito nets, and display a shelf or two of plates of Queen's or Staffordshire ware" ([1793] 1972:126, 127).

The structure of the occupational groups on coffee plantations was considerably less rigid and less hierarchical than that found on sugar estates. On most coffee plantations, work was carried out on a task basis rather than a gang system. Enslaved laborers worked on particular tasks rather than on jobs that required constant supervision (Higman 1976:219). On large coffee plantations, there was a tendency to group the population into gangs (Delle 1998:107), but the function of the gang was not the same as in the sugar fields. Gangs in coffee fields still performed their labor on a task basis (Higman 1988:172), and these tasks were considerably less labor intensive than tasks on sugar estates.

With work being assigned on a task basis rather than on a gang basis, the supervision needed from drivers at coffee plantations depended more on effective delegation than on imposing their will to effect labor. In other words, the successful completion of tasks in the field was guaranteed more by the promise of time off once the task was completed than by being imposed by the driver. Hence, the extreme hierarchy needed in the gang-based labor system of sugar estates did not need to be as intensive on the coffee plantations.

The potential outcome of this difference in labor structure and community hierarchy can be seen in the assemblages discussed earlier. At Juan de Bolas, one would expect that with drivers having less need and opportunity for intensive supervision there would be a correspondingly reduced ability to express that authority within the community. With drivers having less opportunity to use labor position to benefit their status within the community, there would be less likelihood for such reduced differentiation to be expressed in material possessions. This lower degree of hierarchy at Juan de Bolas has the potential to explain the minimal differentiation observed among household assemblages. Correspondingly, the greater differentiation among households at Thetford reflects how the hierarchy of labor influenced an individual household's ability to obtain material goods. When one combines this aspect with the somewhat autocratic extension of power from the master's fields to the driver's provision grounds, one can see where occupational hierarchy would have an influence over the marketing power of individual households on a sugar plantation.

Putting this expression of power in terms of level of influence in the daily domestic lives of enslaved households, one can see that at Thetford sugar estate, such power would differentiate itself at the household level. The ability to access another's labor, time, and resources for one's own household benefit would depend on one's position within the hierarchy of the estate. Such intracommunity differentiation provides a plausible explanation for why some house areas contained much larger quantities of material goods.

On the other hand, the coffee plantation at Juan de Bolas did not have as highly a regimented hierarchy as Thetford, given its task-oriented labor structure. By extension, the relative homogeneity of its household assemblages might be a reflection of this labor structure. The direct application of this community hierarchy to patterns seen in the household assemblages seemed, at first, almost too literal. This correspondence, however, gained strength when birth records among enslaved mothers were consulted as another measure of household response to labor structure (Returns of Slaves).

The age at which enslaved mothers at Thetford and Juan de Bolas gave birth proved to be another indicator of differential stress between the two plantations (for similar studies, see Higman 1976 and Geggus 1993). The age among mothers in the field gang tended to be five to ten years later at Thetford than at Juan de Bolas (Reeves 1997:147). Mothers at Thetford gave birth between thirty and thirty-five years of age, while most female slaves at Juan de Bolas gave birth between twenty and thirty years of age. This difference might reflect the fact that women at Thetford were placed in the first gang between the ages of fifteen and twenty-five. They were worked to their maximum capacity, thereby impacting their ability or willingness to reproduce (Bush 1990:132). In contrast, Thetford's female slaves of mulatto background (who were generally assigned to work in the house) followed a very different pattern, as they had their first child between fifteen and twenty-five years of age, thereby reflecting the lower physical stress of this labor role and how it manifested itself in their ability to reproduce. For enslaved mothers at Juan de Bolas, the highest birthrates tended to be among twenty- to thirty-year-old women, suggesting work in the field had a lesser impact on childbirth than at Thetford. This pattern in age range was seen among both Negro and mulatto mothers, thereby suggesting that unlike at Thetford, Juan de Bolas mothers' level of choice/ability to reproduce occurred across the community rather than being relegated to specific households.

The significance of these age groupings for mothers suggests that at Thetford, overall household health and vitality were constrained by labor role. For mothers working in the first gang, having a child at a later age had a definite impact on household production. Because provision production was a household phenomenon, delaying childbirth for five to ten years meant these mothers were not able to rely on their children's labor in the provision grounds and in the household till much later. This would have had a direct impact on household production and market activities. While the age of mothers who were married to drivers and craftsmen could not be determined from the data at hand (only mothers' names were listed in the Returns of Slaves), it is plausible that being married to a driver was advantageous in terms of timing reproduction in these households. Meanwhile, at Juan de Bolas, a mother's age at childbirth tended to be younger, thereby allowing households to take full advantage of children's labor for an extended period of time.

Thus, not surprisingly, a mother's age at first childbirth tended to follow some of the same patterns seen in relative access to market goods among households at Juan de Bolas and Thetford. In this case, stress from the more hierarchical labor structure at Thetford manifested itself such that mothers from various households gave birth at very different age brackets and that household production was hampered or enhanced by labor role. Meanwhile, at Juan de Bolas, the labor structure did not appear to have such a radical impact on differentiating household production and reproduction. These patterns demonstrate that labor structure resulted in drastic household differentiation at Thetford, but no such radical differentiation occurred among households at Juan de Bolas.

Conclusion

With this description of the labor organization, we can see a parallel with the various household assemblages from Juan de Bolas and Thetford plantations and the plantations' labor organization. First, the coffee plantation, with its less hierarchical structure of task labor, appears to have offered fewer incentives in the daily work regime to concentrate power in the hands of an enslaved supervisor group. This in turn likely resulted in the labor structure having less direct impact on one group's ability to have more access to another's labor, both in the fields and during off time. On the sugar estate, the labor hierarchy was designed to take advantage of the ability of one group of slaves to control the labor and activities of another group through the gang system—a labor organization in which the dissemination of assignments carried from the overseer to the driver to the gangs of enslaved workers. Such control could have been extended such that drivers sent others to work their provision grounds. In the end, this control might explain the variation in access to goods seen at Thetford and the relative homogeneity of household assemblages at Juan de Bolas.

What this study offers is much more than a simple revelation that labor structure at a coffee plantation was quite different from that at a sugar estate. Rather, the material examples provide a unique window into how these differences manifest themselves in enslaved individuals' household goods, thereby offering the chance to not only see what form the differences take but also gain insight into what market goods were available to most enslaved community members and what items were more costly and not accessible to the majority. By carefully examining the assemblages described in this chapter, we can see that while a wide range of goods was available to slaves at market, household access was limited by the amount of cash or barter at their disposal. Thus, while all households had some imported goods, the large variety and quantity of decorated English ceramics, personal items (such as faceted beads, buttons, and apparel such as parasols), table glass, and cutlery were available to only a limited few. In contrast, locally produced items, such as low-fired yabba earthenware sold in the markets, were readily available to all. Various levels of influence from the household to the regional determined this range of access to market goods.

Scalar analysis is a technique that allows the various complexities of a community to be plumbed. As a structured yet dialectic approach to analysis, it embraces the concept that behavior, choices, and daily actions are determined at complex myriad levels that draw from traditions and experiences ranging from the individual to the regional. Within this range, while communal, household, and individual experiences influence each other, choice was always made at the individual household level. Thus, while enslaved individuals from Juan de Bolas purchasing items at market made choices on the household and individual levels, patterns discussed in this study demonstrate that their shared commonality of being African-born slaves influenced their choice in market goods. When one examines how this choice is manifested in household possessions, it appears to occur at the level of the community. In the same manner, when slaves from Thetford and Juan de Bolas visited markets in Old Harbour to purchase yabbas, although choice was made at the individual level, it was influenced by regional patterns of yabba production. In this way, choice was influenced by regional scales of influence. On an even more drastic level, choices made by slaves purchasing English ceramics at the Old Harbour market were influenced by regional trade patterns that brought English goods to the island and the manufacturing changes occurring among the Staffordshire potters in England. In this manner, choice was influenced by national and global scales of influence. The multiple examples presented in this study demonstrate how scalar analysis provides a means to pair observable patterns in the archaeological record with meaningful patterns of human behavior and action.

Paring this analysis back to the community study at hand, the comparative analysis of household material remains between two contiguous slave settlements offers the opportunity to explore the many dimensions that affect individual lives and daily decisions. A contextually informed comparison of household goods can provide a means to explore the multidimensionality of households living within a community and the restraints and flexibility provided by regional and even global market forces. While this idea of examining various scales of influence is not new, what I find exciting is how well scalar analysis is adapted to comparative household studies. Its power lies in the ability to match observable phenomena from specific archaeological and historical case studies to larger historical contexts. In this way, specific patterns drawn from the data can be ascribed to meaningful human actions.

In the end, what one can draw from this study ranges from the specific patterns seen in the material assemblages to the broader applicability of scalar analysis to comparative household studies. The most exciting outcome of this study is the ability to use scalar analysis to pair observed patterning in site-specific data to broader spatial and temporal phenomena. One of the most powerful examples of this broader match between site-specific data and social actions is the link between scalar patterning of household behavior observed from the archaeological and historic records for the Juan de Bolas and Thetford communities and the life decisions these households made after emancipation.

Epilogue

In this study, we have seen the link between access to market goods, health of slaves, and the demands of differing plantation crop production. Such actions as the ability of enslaved households to provide for their homes, health of individuals, and the ability to reproduce are the meaningful actions reflected in patterns of data. Nowhere is the real-life cost of chattel slavery more clearly demonstrated than in the post-emancipation era. When options were available for moving from slave labor to wage labor upon emancipation, few chose to stay on at plantations and most struck out on their own for independent crop production. For Thetford, the results can be seen in the wide array of former slaves that settled on their provision grounds on Thetford Mountain following emancipation (only to be forcibly evicted as squatters in the 1880s). Oral history in Lluidas Vale recounts that the only former slaves who remained at Thetford as wage laborers were the drivers and craftspeople. By 1842, the operations at Thetford failed and the head people remaining eventually shifted to Worthy Park, the neighboring sugar estate that continues in operation to this day (Craton 1978). The vast majority of Thetford's freed slaves chose to leave the estate, striking out on their own as small subsistence-level farmers by squatting on lands that formerly were their provision grounds. At Juan de Bolas, however, many former slaves purchased small plots from their former owner and built new homes; the descendants of these settlers continue to own all the land of the former plantation today. In talking with elders at Juan de Bolas, there is no indication that any former Bolas slaves went to work at the plantation's sister sugar estate of Lloyds and Aylmers in Guanaboa Vale as wage laborers. The outcome of this experience is that while today the Juan de Bolas district is populated by independent farmers descended from former slaves, Thetford is devoid of any semblance of the community that once lived and worked on its lands.

In the epilogue to the communal experience at Juan de Bolas and Thetford, we can see how decisions made in the post-emancipation era largely reflect the patterning seen in household production and reproduction under slavery. For the coffee plantation the structure of labor, history of household production under slavery, and availability of land due to the sale of the plantation provided the opportunity for the entire community to stay on the plantation, albeit in a radically different class structure than under slavery. In this regard, household choice at Juan de Bolas occurred at the community level. For households at Thetford, however, one's position within the labor structure of the estate informed decisions in regard to their fate in the post-emancipation era. For drivers, their experiences and social relations with the plantation management under slavery made wage labor a viable alternative, while for field slaves independent provision production was a more likely survival strategy. Thus, for former slaves at Thetford, decisions in regard to their post-emancipation fate differentiated themselves at the level of the household. In a direct way, this pattern of scalar decisions reflects the same patterns observed in the archaeological record of household goods, reproduction strategies of mothers, and likely many other areas not measured through archaeological and historical records. The close match of these various phenomena reflects what a powerful influence the differing types of crop production had on the historic trajectories of the two communities. Scalar analysis has provided a key to unlocking the influence of plantation labor on two communities that can be seen in the geographic and demographic patterns of the region to this day.

Acknowledgments

I would like to thank all involved in my research in the mid-1990s, including my advisor, Douglas Armstrong, the Jamaica National Heritage Trust, friends who spent several months assisting with fieldwork, and the Juan de Bolas community who literally adopted me during my research. Critical in the success of my research was Linton Rhule, my main informant while conducting my research in Jamaica, teacher of all things Jamaican, and a dear friend to this day. Thanks, Pops! Funding for research discussed in this essay was provided by the Fulbright Foundation and the Syracuse University Graduate School.

11

Assessing the Impacts of Time, Agricultural Cycles, and Demography on the Consumer Activities of Enslaved Men and Women in Eighteenth-Century Jamaica and Virginia

Jillian E. Galle

Introduction

The past two decades have witnessed a growing consensus among social and economic historians that the "consumer revolution" was among the most significant developments in the history of the early modern Atlantic world (Breen 1986; Brewer and Porter 1993; C. Campbell 1987; Carson, Hoffman, and Albert 1994; McKendrick, Brewer, and Plumb 1982; Styles and Vickery 2006). The availability and importance of material culture at all scales, from houses to ceramic wares, accelerated throughout the seventeenth, eighteenth, and early nineteenth centuries. During this same period, the Atlantic region was transformed by the influx of people, many of whom were enslaved Africans, who spoke unfamiliar languages and employed different customs. As voluntary and forced migrants came together in new living and working situations, traditional and culturally specific ways of identifying status were no longer easily identified or universally understood. In this new world, the acquisition and use of consumer goods played an essential role in the strategies invented by people to communicate shifting status and social identities (C. Carson 1994, 2003).

By the 1750s, economic changes in the English-speaking Atlantic world made some degree of nonessential consumption viable for almost everyone, including enslaved people. Almost all sought to acquire the new consumables, but each entered the market constrained by their abilities and motivations. Some people purchased only the occasional ribbon or refined ceramic ware while others updated tea sets and clothing styles with regularity (Ashelford 1996; Carr and Walsh 1994;

C. Carson 1994; Martin 1993, 1994; McDonald 1993; Mintz and Hall [1970] 1991; Simmonds 1987; Styles and Vickery 2006; Walsh 1992). Free people of color and enslaved women and men also participated in the market economy, often acquiring more than just a single nonessential item.

From the Caribbean to the Chesapeake region of North America, enslaved workers shopped in stores and markets and traded and bartered with each other, free blacks, and their owners for items that were not part of weekly or yearly rations. Eighteenth-century travelers' accounts and merchants' records demonstrate that the enslaved purchased items such as sugar, alcohol, tools, ceramic wares, cloth, buttons, and buckles (Baumgarten 1988; Beckles 1989; Fox-Genovese 1988; Heath 2004; Martin 1993; McDonald 1993; Penningroth 2003; Schlotterbeck 1991; Simmonds 1987; Walsh 1992). Archaeological evidence from eighteenth-century slave quarter sites in both regions confirms that enslaved people found ways to earn money and that they spent a portion of what they earned acquiring fashionable consumer goods (Armstrong 1990; Galle 2006, 2010; Hauser 2001; Heath 1999b, 2004; Higman 1998; Reeves 1997).

However, few historical or archaeological studies have sought to systematically measure consumption patterns among the enslaved or to understand the factors underlying their consumer activities. One reason may be that enslaved participation in Jamaican and Virginia markets has been studied in isolation, as local or island-specific phenomena. Here I suggest that enslaved individuals who participated in local economies for fashionable imported goods were simultaneously reacting to and shaping the mechanisms that were driving the consumer revolution across the Atlantic. Although played out on the local stage, slave participation in the market economy was an active response to the growing need for efficient and effective communication in rapidly changing environments. In this chapter I use archaeological evidence to argue that the ability of, and incentive for, enslaved individuals to engage in the market economy, especially for the acquisition of nonessential costly goods, represents a series of strategic responses to the larger demographic and economic changes sweeping across the Atlantic world.

Jamaica and Virginia offer important archaeological and historical case studies in the workings of the larger Atlantic economy. In addition to rich visual and textual accounts, both regions have extensive archaeological resources that are especially useful in light of the limitations of written records related to slave participation in local and regional markets. This study brings together archaeological data from thirty-eight sites located on nine plantations in Jamaica and Virginia. As the largest comparative archaeological study of slavery to date, this research reveals regional consumption trends while highlighting individual household consumption strategies. As we'll see, enslaved Jamaicans and Virginians who participated in the market economy consciously chose objects that created and expressed identity. However, their individual choices were also embedded in and influenced by cultural and economic changes affecting both regions in the eighteenth century.

Signaling theory helps elucidate the contextual factors that structured consumer choice and provides a model for understanding artifact patterns as the result of dynamic regional behavioral strategies.

After briefly reviewing the historical literature on enslaved participation in the local economies of Jamaica and Virginia, I use signaling theory to offer expectations about the use and discard of three categories of expensive, imported European artifacts: metal buttons, refined ceramics, and glass tablewares. A fourth category of imported material culture, glass beads, adds complexity to the data set. Glass beads represent a less costly adornment item that may have been purchased at markets and stores or that may have been brought to the New World on the bodies of enslaved Africans during the Middle Passage. Specific historical variables such as plantation type and demography of each region are used to model the discard of these four artifact classes. Statistical methods such as negative binomial regression and principal component analysis are used to argue that gender-based consumption strategies were active in both regions throughout the eighteenth and early nineteenth centuries.

Market Participation in Jamaica and Virginia

Historians of Jamaica and the Caribbean have focused on the central role that enslaved individuals played in building and sustaining island economies during the eighteenth and nineteenth centuries (Beckles 1989, 1995; Bush 1990; Hall 1987; Higman 1995; Mintz and Hall [1970] 1991; McDonald 1993; Simmonds 1987). While it is easy to assume that all enslaved Africans had similar purchasing power in the Sunday markets, archaeological evidence analyzed here suggests that many enslaved Jamaicans only earned enough money to purchase household essentials that they were unable to make or grow. This is likely the result of Jamaica's provisioning system, which advocated the allocation of provision grounds to the enslaved instead of the regular distribution of food rations (Beckles 1989; Higman 1998; McDonald 1993; Reeves 1997). This system put tremendous stress on enslaved individuals and families. Their survival depended on their ability to cultivate gardens after a debilitating day in the cane fields or the sugar factory and put household production at the mercy of unpredictable and often violent island weather. Despite these conditions, many enslaved Jamaicans produced excess ground provisions that could be traded or sold in exchange for perishable goods that they could not produce themselves. Those who were more successful at growing crops in excess of their family's needs began to acquire nonessential household items.

Enslaved Jamaicans also raised livestock, made lace bark, and crafted brooms, furniture, and ceramics for Sunday markets across the island (M. Lewis 1929; Long [1774] 1970; P. Wright 2002). By the early 1700s, Sunday markets were a routine part of life for many enslaved Jamaicans. Contemporary travelers and planters in Jamaica vividly described enslaved people selling fruits and vegetables to higglers or directly at markets. Despite attempts to control and curtail market activities during the last quarter of the eighteenth century, enslaved participation in Jamaica's Sunday markets was legal and critical to the economic success of white merchants and free blacks (McDonald 1993; Mintz and Hall [1970] 1991; Reeves, this volume; Simmonds 1987). Enslaved Africans, as producers, marketers, higglers, and customers, drove local economies and were an essential component of both rural and urban markets (Hauser 2001; McDonald 1993; Reeves 1997; Simmonds 1987).

In Virginia, enslaved participation in the market economy was not only less visible, it was illegal. Laws passed throughout the eighteenth century prohibited whites from trading with, purchasing from, or selling goods to enslaved Africans and African Americans (Berlin 1998:35; Schlotterbeck 1991:171; Walsh 1992). However, as the eighteenth century progressed, slaves in the Chesapeake, especially males, had increasing opportunities to earn cash, which they used in stores and markets throughout the region. Like their counterparts in Jamaica, enslaved people in Virginia grew vegetables and raised poultry that they sold to their owners and in local markets (Berlin and Morgan 1995; Heath 1999b, 2004; Hudson 1994; Martin 1993; Penningroth 2003; Schlotterbeck 1991; Walsh 1995a, 1995b). Many enslaved women and men sold non-foodstuffs such as baskets and brooms while others earned money from tips or additional work (Berlin 1998:34; Heath 2004:23; P. Morgan 1998:361; Nicholls 1990).

Consumables that dulled some of the harshest edges of slavery such as rum, sugar, and molasses were among the most popular items purchased by enslaved Virginians. However, enslaved people also acquired items that have left traces in the archaeological record. Men frequently purchased tools and raw materials to create salable items (Heath 2004:29). Although slaves in central Virginia acquired the tools necessary to process fiber and make cloth, account books from John Hook's store in Franklin County, Virginia, also indicate that good quality textiles made up the largest percentage of enslaved purchases (Martin 1993:309). Men and women purchased fashionable items like buttons, buckles, ribbons, and hats to adorn provisioned clothing or newly purchased fabric (Genovese 1976:557; Heath 1999b, 2004; Martin 1993:309; Schlotterbeck 1991:177). These fashionable choices are confirmed by early twentieth-century former-slave narratives that point to the importance of distinctive, non-provisioned clothing for communication and self-expression (Baumgarten 1988, 1991; Fox-Genovese 1988; Perdue et al. 1976:316; Rawick 1972; White and White 1998).

Signaling Theory

Why did enslaved Africans and African Americans spend valuable time and energy pursuing fashionable European goods? Why did they endure the risks inherent in acquiring and displaying non-provisioned items? How did enslaved people use costly imported material culture to communicate their identity and position to other slaves, free blacks, and whites with whom they interacted on plantations and in cosmopolitan spaces? One useful way to understand the patterns and processes underlying slave consumption is through a theoretical framework known as signaling theory.

Signaling theory is grounded in the idea that material and physical displays function as forms of communication among individuals and social groups (Bliege Bird and Smith 2005; McGuire and Hildebrandt 2005). Displays that involve economic or physical risks can provide a variety of essential and often difficult to observe information about a person, ranging from economic and social standing to more intangible qualities such as psychological character, physical skill and stamina, and possession of esoteric and cultural knowledge. Signaling theory contends that the successful communication of these personal attributes is vital to establishing and maintaining relationships, especially in large groups.

Honest and costly signaling facilitates personal and group relationships by convincing receivers of the signal that social, economic, or political benefits can be gained through interaction with the signaler. A person has incentive to be a successful signaler since he or she also receives benefits, some of which may include increased social status, the establishment of lucrative trading partnerships, and the selection of reliable long-term sexual and domestic partners. Two critical variables control the payoffs to a costly signal: audience size and familiarity. Signals that reach large audiences are generally more valuable than signals aimed at smaller audiences because the benefits for any given signal increase as the signal influences larger numbers of competitors. Costly signaling is also less likely to be directed at groups that contain a large number of kin since signals are less effective when directed at groups composed of allies instead of direct competitors (Neiman 1997).

Although signaling is understood as a phenotypic behavior that serves to enhance a person's long-term fitness, the form of the signal is a direct result of individual choices that are embedded in, and influenced by, the larger cultural system. Signaling is by definition a social activity that requires signalers and receivers whose interactions actively shape the form and intensity of displays (Bliege Bird and Smith 2005; Boone 2000; Neiman 1997). Successful signalers not only choose appropriate signaling media but are able to gauge the response of receivers and modify or change their signal as status values and other signal costs shift. New signals often develop within pre-established guidelines for the signal. In an example from the late eighteenth-century Atlantic world, yellow metal buttons replaced white metal buttons as fashionable clothing accoutrement while plates made from refined ceramic wares such as white salt-glazed stoneware and creamware replaced plates made from wood and pewter (Heath 1999b; Martin 1989, 1994).

As a result, signaling models are particularly useful for archaeologists precisely because systems for gaining prestige through material displays should be archaeologically visible and measurable. As Neiman has recently pointed out, "[S]ignaling models are explicit enough to deliver detailed predictions about the design and distribution of variation relative to historically specific social and environmental contexts" (2005:243).

Here the signaling model begins with the argument that the sacrifices, compromises, and physical risks required for the acquisition of nonessential goods made them ideal costly signals for slaves. Owning and wearing current fashions may have demonstrated an enslaved person's ability to work late into the night cultivating vegetables or making crafts that were then parlayed into money. Items purchased from faraway markets not only represented a slave's purchasing power but also symbolized the mobility granted to a person by his owner. Material displays of mobility may have also been a declaration of an enslaved person's resourceful ability to travel surreptitiously (Upton 1988). The display of European goods not provided by a slave owner was also filled with potential risk, lest the items and the manner in which they were displayed be perceived as a social or economic challenge to whites (Walsh 1992:9). In these ways, expensive European goods represented not only economic cost but also the willingness to risk physical threats for their acquisition and display. Honestly and effectively advertising these abilities was crucial to success when competing for mates and allies, better food, a good garden plot or house site, or even a warm place to sleep within a large crowded quarter. Costly displays of goods became an effective means of communication among enslaved individuals within regions transformed by the ebb and flow of colonial demographics.

Neither European material culture nor signaling strategies were new to recently enslaved Africans. Both Anglo and African elites used a host of European-produced goods to demonstrate their economic, political, and social abilities (DeCorse 2001; Kelly 2001; Walsh 1992). Many enslaved people understood how and what type of goods were used in successful signaling strategies. They understood both the knowledge and benefits that could be gained from conspicuous displays of costly, imported items. They in turn used the information embedded in the display to aid in their own selection of friends, mates, or cooperative household members. In addition, successful signaling may have convinced free merchants and other whites in the community to engage in legal and clandestine business or social relations. By using costly, displayable, non-provisioned items to effectively communicate their abilities and achievements within competitive and unfamiliar situations, slaves found signaling a crucial strategy for establishing advantageous social relationships, choosing mates, solidifying trading partnerships, and mobilizing collective action.

The Signaling Media

This essay looks at the discard patterns of three artifact classes whose acquisition by enslaved people incurred substantial costs and conveyed little practical benefit: metal buttons, refined ceramics, and glass tableware (see Galle 2006 for discard rates of other artifact classes in the Chesapeake). Two of these artifact classes, metal buttons and refined ceramics, are particularly useful for pinpointing gendered consumption activities among slaves. A fourth less-costly imported artifact class, glass beads, adds complexity to the signaling argument.

Although buttons are one of the most common archaeological finds, their analytical importance has only recently been explored (Galle 2006, 2010; Heath 1999b; White 2002). Metal buttons possessed a number of compelling attributes that made them ideal for use in signaling displays throughout the eighteenth century. First, metal buttons, like clothing buckles, were one artifact type introduced during the consumer revolution whose acquisition by slaves incurred substantial costs and conveyed little practical benefit. They were expensive and their cost scaled with decorative treatments such as plating and engraving (Baumgarten 2002; Hinks 1988; White 2002). Unlike wood and bone buttons, metal buttons were not manufactured in enslaved households. Archaeological evidence from slave quarter sites in the Chesapeake indicate that some bone and wood buttons were manufactured by enslaved people, and buttons made from these materials have been excluded from this analysis. Both enslaved Jamaicans and Virginians found ways to acquire fashionable buttons. Archaeologist Barbara Heath's analysis of store accounts indicates that metal buttons ranked among the most popular items purchased by slaves in central Virginia between 1760 and 1790 (Heath 1999b, 2004). In Jamaica, buttons were acquired in Sunday markets (Buckridge 2004).

Fashionable clothing adorned by buttons indicated that the wearer had the skills to acquire clothes not provisioned by their owners. Jackets, waistcoats, vests, and embellished breeches, all clothing items not regularly provisioned to enslaved men, required numerous buttons. High-style eighteenth-century jackets and waistcoats featured buttons not only as decorative fasteners but also as non-functional embellishments sewn opposite false buttonholes (Baumgarten 2002). Jackets and vests with matched sets of buttons or large bright buttons set their wearer apart from the less fashionable. Finally, fashionable buttons are also one of the few artifact classes that can be associated primarily with eighteenth-century male social and economic activities. With the exception of riding habits, buttons were not used on women's clothing until the mid-nineteenth century (White 2002, 2005). Metal buttons were easily displayable items whose form and cost were finely tuned to shifting fashions. They represented, for both free and enslaved men, the perfect way to display their ability to participate in the market economy.

Visible costliness was also an important determinant in the acquisition of ceramic vessels made in "refined wares"—porcelain, thin-bodied stoneware, and refined earthenware. The introduction of refined ceramic wares in the mid-eighteenth century accompanied a host of new social rules related to the consumption of food and drink (B. Carson 1990). Ceramic manufacturers produced novel vessel forms designed for daily dining as well as the new social rituals. Individual place settings that included dinner plates, dished plates, and bowls replaced communal trenchers and mugs. Ceramic tea bowls, saucers, and teapots, and leaded glass tumblers and stemware were used in the consumption of exotic and costly beverages such as punch, tea, and coffee. These forms and wares replaced functional equivalents traditionally made of indestructible wood and pewter or inexpensive coarse earthenware (B. Carson 1990; Martin 1989, 1994; Roth 1988). The shift in popularity to more fragile refined ceramic wares and their constantly changing forms and decorative designs represent an increase in the costs paid by consumers.

Refined imported ceramics dominate Virginia and Jamaica slave quarter assemblages and the diversity of forms and ware types clearly indicates that they were not all provided by slave owners. In Virginia, slaves purchased imported refined ceramics in stores throughout the eighteenth century (Heath 2004). Because of the lack of primary sources that indicate the distribution of imported ceramics, historians suggest that Jamaican slave owners did not provide their workers with ceramic wares (McDonald 1993; Reeves 1997:173–74). The variety and quantity of imported ceramics wares found on Jamaica slave sites also suggest that enslaved people sought specific ware types and forms.

Even though many elite men were active in choosing and purchasing ceramic wares, it is likely that middling, poor, and enslaved women who prepared and served food to both their families and the elites for whom they worked had a direct hand in the selection and purchase of their families' ceramics. Eighteenth-century accounts from Jamaica and Virginia indicate that food preparation was handled primarily by enslaved women (Ebanks 2000; Fox-Genovese 1988; P. Morgan 1998). If enslaved women had some control over the ceramics they used to prepare and serve food, high discard rates of costly ware types and vessel forms may point to a woman's economic strength or position within the plantation. On Jamaica, most marketers and higglers were enslaved women. Their direct involvement in the marketplace must have given them considerable purchasing power and consumer choice (Beckles 1989; Bush 1990:48–50).

Like refined ceramics, elaborate and costly glass tablewares were also introduced into the Atlantic markets in the early 1700s. By the mid-eighteenth century most elite households owned at least a few specialized drinking glasses. Like refined ceramics, glass tablewares were produced in a variety of specialized forms and displayed a range of decorative embellishments that correlated with cost. In addition, glass tablewares were designed to hold and display expensive foods and beverages (Elmville 1951). Tumblers and stemware were used to serve beverages that were made from costly sugar, exotic fruits, and liquors. Jelly glasses showed off sugar-infused desserts, custards, and sweetmeats. When recovered from archaeological contexts, these artifacts represent expensive and fashionable wares as well as the knowledge and financial ability to fill them (B. Carson 1990).

Unlike metal buttons, refined ceramics, and glass tableware, the acquisition of imported glass trade beads did not incur substantial financial costs. Unlike buckles and buttons, glass beads were not essential elements of elite dress. The lack of emphasis placed on beads in fashionable dress is reflected in eighteenth-century newspaper advertisements in which strands of beads and beaded jewelry sets are buried well below sales announcements for more fashionable dry goods that included "all sorts of gold bands, buttons, and loops" (White 2005; Virginia *Gazette* 1769:3, 1771:3).

Glass beads are one artifact category that may have arrived in the English colonies on the bodies of enslaved Africans transported through the Middle Passage. Recent research also suggests that some enslaved Africans may have acquired beads during the Middle Passage. Enslaved women were occasionally given glass beads on British ships as a means of keeping them occupied with jewelry-making activities (Handler 2009:6). The possibility that these beads represent the only material culture brought from Africa by enslaved people, along with ethnographies demonstrating that beads had, and continue to have, important spiritual properties in African societies, has resulted in a fixation on the presence of beads, especially blue beads, on archaeological sites associated with free and enslaved Africans and African Americans (Handler and Lange 1978; Handler 2009; LaRoche 1994; Russell 1997; Thomas and Thomas 2004; Stine, Cabak, and Groover 1996; Wilkie 1994, 1997). Although European goods ranging from ceramics and glassware to guns and metal tools were available to and used by Africans living in Africa during the eighteenth and nineteenth centuries (DeCorse 2001; Stahl 2001; Kelly 2001; Walsh 1992), European glass beads have been isolated by historical archaeologists as the one object on North American sites that they believe can be directly linked to African ethnic identity and spiritual traditions.

As demonstrated by Christopher DeCorse and others, a plethora of bead styles and colors were imported to and produced in Africa (Carey 1991; DeCorse 1989, 2001; Jargstorf 1995; Stahl 2001). These beads, not just blue beads, had a complex set of uses, thereby making direct associations with specific culture groups or practices problematic at best. As DeCorse points out, the abundance of blue glass beads on North American slave sites may relate more directly to their inexpensive cost in the New World and their abundance in Africa than to a shared pan-African belief system (DeCorse 1999:144). Here bead consumption is explored in relationship to other consumer trends, which allows for a more complex interpretation of the potential meaning and use behind the presence of glass beads rather than a simple one-to-one correlation with African spiritual practices.

Signaling Expectations

Signaling theory predicts that individuals should invest more in costly goods when they interact regularly with large numbers of people and when they interact with people who know little about them. Signaling should also intensify when contextual variables help increase a person's resource-holding potential. It is anticipated that two contextual factors, agricultural production cycles and demographics, played a significant role in an enslaved person's ability to consume metal buttons, refined ceramics, glass tablewares, and glass beads in both Jamaica and Virginia.

Agricultural Diversification

In the Chesapeake, agricultural and economic diversification during the second half of the eighteenth century, characterized by a shift from tobacco monoculture to the cultivation of wheat, ushered in a task-based agricultural system that provided enslaved men with greater opportunities to earn money (Isaac 1982; Walsh 1995a, 1995b). Diversification of agricultural production began in the 1730s and progressed steadily throughout the century. The task-based labor system on diversified plantations resulted in excess labor during specific points in the agricultural cycle. Many owners trained males in skilled trades such a blacksmithing, coopering, and carpentry. These skilled men were then leased to individuals, small workshops, and factories during slack periods in the agricultural cycle. Leased men were given assignments that required them to travel and work for extended periods in urban centers like Norfolk, Williamsburg, and Richmond (P. Morgan 1998; Nicholls 1990; Walsh 1995a, 1995b). Some of these assignments provided slaves with petty cash and the ability to rent rooms outside of their place of work. Although skilled jobs separated men from their families and their home plantations, the increased number of skilled occupations in the second half of the eighteenth century gave enslaved men new ways to earn money while often putting them in cosmopolitan settings that offered opportunities for novel social and business alliances.

Unlike Virginia, which began as a tobacco monoculture economy, Jamaica's economy was built on a number of different plantation types. Sugar, coffee, indigo, and livestock plantations all had strikingly different labor regimes. Labor requirements on sugar plantations were exceptionally brutal in comparison to the daily and seasonal work regimens on coffee plantations and cattle pens (Delle 1998; Higman 1976, 1995; J. Roberts 2006). The extreme physical exertion required during the twenty-four-hour sugar production cycle resulted in frequent malnourishment and severe physical debilitation for many slaves laboring on sugar plantations. One result was the strikingly low birthrates on sugar plantations (-12.4 per year) compared to those on coffee plantations (+1.8 per year) (Higman 1976:123). Physical exhaustion combined with frequent crop destruction from yearly hurricanes limited slaves' ability to produce excess food that could be sold at markets. Traveling any distance to market may have been physically impossible for some (Burnard 2004; Bush 1990; D. Hall 1987).

Like agriculturally diversified estates in Virginia, coffee plantations and cattle pens had less brutal seasonal labor demands than sugar plantations. Both coffee and livestock holdings relied on greater numbers of skilled laborers. Like skilled Chesapeake slaves, these men spent a portion of their time working in cities like

Kingston and Spanish Town. Although coffee and cattle plantations offered less treacherous working conditions than sugar plantations, overall Jamaica maintained the highest mortality rates among slaveholding English colonies (Higman 1976).

Diversity in plantation types and agricultural regimes resulted in the development of an enslaved workforce in both Jamaica and Virginia that possessed nonagricultural skills. These individuals frequently had greater flexibility within their assigned tasks and received benefits such as cash bonuses and travel passes. Those who were hired out frequently interacted with larger groups of individuals. Successful signaling among these skilled laborers could have facilitated the exchange of knowledge and gossip, as well as opened doors for collaboration with potential mates, partners, and allies in noneconomic endeavors such as marriages, runaway attempts, rebellions, and the development of social and religious organizations. As a result, we should expect signaling, as evidenced by the discard of costly imported and displayable goods, to be positively correlated with agriculturally diversified plantations that offered greater opportunities for and payoffs to signaling.

Demographics

Opportunities for signaling outside one's home plantation increased in the second half of the eighteenth century in Virginia. Populations grew, urban centers expanded, and towns increased in number. This expansion allowed more people to regularly interact with non-kin in public spaces. Eighteenth-century account books from stores in central Virginia indicate that shopping excursions on Saturday afternoons and Sundays attracted diverse groups of slaves, lending a social nature to store and market visits while also providing new signaling audiences (Heath 2004). The publicly visible act of shopping, in which a slave was required to pay with cash, was an ideal platform for signaling one's ability to earn money. People would have observed the purchase of tools, ceramics, mirrors, and other goods that they might not actually see displayed or used in the signaler's dwelling. In addition to shopping, social gatherings such as attending church were ideal for displaying non-provisioned clothing and adornment items (Foster 1997; Perdue 1976; White and White 1998).

The late seventeenth- and early eighteenth-century growth of Jamaican urban centers such as Port Royal, Spanish Town, and Kingston meant that urban populations in Jamaica did not expand as dramatically through the eighteenth century as they did in Virginia (Robertson 2005). Urban life was critical, however, to a subset of Jamaica's enslaved population. Travelers' accounts from Jamaica describe scenes similar to those in Virginia in which slaves traveled together to market (P. Wright 2002:65). The social and economic activities that occurred during the trip to urban and rural markets were ideal venues for signaling displays.

Differences in the composition of enslaved populations in Jamaica and Virginia may have also impacted slave participation in the market economy. Between 1700 and 1790, roughly 78,000 enslaved Africans were imported into Virginia (P. Morgan 1998). Approximately 49,000 of the 54,000 slaves living in Virginia between 1700 and 1749 were African born and from the Bight of Benin and Angola regions (Kulikoff 1986:320; P. Morgan 1998). Language and cultural similarities shared by the majority of the enslaved population may have helped the rapid creation of a creole language and an African American culture (Kulikoff 1986:321; Walsh 2000). The high number of conspiracies and group runaway attempts throughout the 1720s, 1730s, and 1740s suggests that some African-born slaves may have quickly formed friendships and alliances that emboldened others in such endeavors (Kulikoff 1986:328–30).

By the 1770s, however, the majority of all enslaved people in the Chesapeake were born in North American colonies (C. Carson 2003; P. Morgan 1998; Walsh 2000). In just over thirty years, a community of Chesapeake-born slaves had formed, a process that resulted in a shift from "support networks based on co-resident strangers, quasi-kin, and country men and women to networks rooted primarily in biological kin ties" (Walsh 2000:2). Archaeological and architectural evidence such as the decrease in house size and subfloor pits corroborates this transition from co-residential strangers to cooperative, kin-based households (Neiman 2005, 2008).

The demographic realities of Jamaica were strikingly different with over 900,000 enslaved Africans imported into Jamaica between 1700 and 1808 (Burnard and Morgan 2001; Eltis 2001). Blacks outnumbered whites 8 to 1 as early as 1710, and 26 percent of all blacks in the British Empire lived in Jamaica by the mid-eighteenth century (Burnard and Morgan 2001). Jamaica's high mortality and low fertility rates resulted in virtually no natural increase in the enslaved population throughout the eighteenth century (Higman 1976, 1995). Heterogeneity in the origins of enslaved Africans was a key feature of Jamaican demographics, with slaves coming from all four of the major slave-trading regions in Africa. With one-quarter to one-half of newly arrived Africans dying within the first three years on the island, there was a constant influx of unseasoned African imports (Burnard and Morgan 2001). The consistently high population of African-born slaves from diverse ethnic and language groups, high black-to-white ratios, and consistent resource stress resulted in high racial tensions and numerous rebellions on Jamaica. In the English Caribbean there were at least seven revolts involving fifty or more enslaved people between 1640 and 1713, the frequency of which only increased throughout the eighteenth century; the majority of slave uprisings during this period took place on Jamaica (Dunn 1972:164–65). By contrast, and despite conspiracies and thousands of runaways, Virginia experienced no major violent uprisings until the nineteenth century.

One final demographic aspect that likely influenced consumption among enslaved Jamaicans during the eighteenth century was the growing population of native-born enslaved women and men who were the products of mixed-race unions.

While countless unions between enslaved women and white men were the result of violence and coercion, others resulted in long-term, openly acknowledged relationships. Although it was illegal for whites to marry non-whites, many established long-term relationships with enslaved and free women of color (Brathwaite 1971). Women in these relationships and offspring from these unions were often given positions within the house or as drivers or estate managers (Brathwaite 1971; Burnard 1991, 1999). White men living in Jamaica were also much more likely to financially recognize their enslaved partners and offspring in their wills than were men in the Chesapeake (Burnard 1991, 1999; Reeves 1997; Rothman 2003; P. Wright 2002:234). Prominent positions within the owner's household or within the plantation hierarchy, as well as overt financial support and bequests, would have certainly contributed to an enslaved person's ability to actively participate in local markets.

Throughout the eighteenth century, unrelated slaves in Jamaica and Virginia formed complex and frequently illegal relationships on individual and collective scales. From marriages and clandestine trading relations to group activities such as religious revivals, fraternal organizations, runaway attempts, and rebellions, the enslaved bonded together in dangerous activities that were mutually beneficial to individuals and the group (K. Brown 1996; Finkelman 1989; French 2004; M. P. Johnson 1981; Newman 2003). In addition to aiding economic transactions, successful signaling may have facilitated the exchange of information and gossip and provided the means to assess the likelihood of success in cooperating with someone for non-economic endeavors such as marriages, runaway attempts, rebellions, and the development of social and religious organizations. Early nineteenth-century South Carolina runaway advertisements suggest just how important building non-kin relationships off home plantations may have been (M. P. Johnson 1981). Advertisements placed by slave owners between 1799 and 1830 demonstrate that many of South Carolina's urban runaways were skilled workers that had developed bonds with non-kin. Between 1799 and 1830, two-thirds of runaway groups were composed of two unrelated individuals who may have known each other through their work (M. P. Johnson 1981:421). In Jamaica, rebellions that were headed by skilled laborers were common (Higman 1998).

If signaling through consumption was a behavioral strategy at work in the eighteenth century, consumer goods should be measurable through the archaeological record. In the following signaling model, measures of costly goods represent dependent variables that should scale with the independent variables that drove consumption, such as temporal, demographic, and agricultural changes. Variations in individual signal levels should be measurable based on the type and abundance of the material culture being consumed. Differences in the quantity and quality of the artifacts ought to point to the maintenance of an active and honest costly signaling strategy (Neiman 2005).

In Virginia we should expect signaling to increase through time as urban centers grew dramatically and plantations diversified during the second half of the eighteenth century. Markets, stores, taverns, and public squares provided large audiences filled with potential sexual partners, allies, and competitors, all of which increased the payoffs for signaling. Agricultural diversification resulted in the development of a skilled corps of enslaved workers, many of whom gained more mobility and earned more money as the century progressed. In contrast, we should not expect consumption of costly goods in Jamaica to rise dramatically throughout the eighteenth century. The establishment of large urban centers as well as the existence of many different plantations types by the 1690s suggests that signaling systems may have developed as early as the first few decades of the eighteenth century. However, different plantation types and the demographics of the island should play a factor in signaling strategies through the eighteenth and nineteenth centuries.

While the majority of people of African descent in the greater Chesapeake region had established families with second- and third-generation members, the rates of first-generation enslaved Africans in Jamaica remained high throughout the eighteenth century. We might then expect a range of African social, linguistic, and spiritual traditions to be stronger and more active in Jamaica than on the North American mainland. This difference—established African American households with greater experience and contact with European customs and material culture versus a consistently high African-born population—may well be expressed in differential discard of signaling media in Jamaica and Virginia.

Measuring Signal Variation

Two significant challenges confront archaeologists undertaking regional comparative studies. The first is the availability of standardized artifact data from multiple sites. The second is the development of analytical methods that acknowledge that each assemblage was excavated from sites with different depositional and excavation histories. As a result, most archaeological studies of slavery focus on a single site or only compare sites from a single plantation that were excavated by the same principal investigator using similar methods (Armstrong 1990; Fesler 2004; Heath 1999a; Higman 1998; B. Thomas 1998). Archaeologists who have executed successful comparative research from multiple plantations either focus on a single artifact class (Agbe-Davies 2004; Neiman and King 1999) or limit their comparisons to architectural data that can be gleaned from site maps (Neiman 2008; Samford 2000, 2007). This broadly comparative study is made possible by the availability of fine-grained standardized artifact data generated by the Digital Archaeological Archive of Comparative Slavery (DAACS, www.daacs.org), a Web-based initiative that currently provides quantitative artifact and context data from over thirty excavated slave quarter sites located in the Chesapeake, Carolinas, and Caribbean. All data used in the following analysis are available through the DAACS Web site, with the exception of the data from the Thetford and Juan de Bolas plantations in Jamaica, which were generously provided to me by Matthew Reeves (see Reeves 1997 and this volume for more information about his research).

The data used in the following analysis come from twenty-one slave site occupations in Jamaica and seventeen slave site occupations in Virginia. Both the Jamaica and Virginia sites have distinct occupational phases that most likely represent different households, thereby allowing for the analysis of discrete episodes of consumption and discard within sites. A total of thirty-eight phased assemblages, each representing different household occupations, contribute to this analysis (Tables 11.1 and 11.2).[1]

The Jamaica sites used in this study were excavated from four different plantations, two located along the north coast and two from central Jamaica. Sugar was the cash crop at the New Montpelier, Seville, and Thetford plantations. The Juan de Bolas Plantation sites used in this study date from the coffee production phase of the plantation (see Figure 1.1). Most of the Jamaica sites in this study were occupied slightly later than the majority of the Virginia sites, with most having mean ceramic dates (MCDs) in the early nineteenth century. The Virginia slave sites used in this study are located on five plantations, four of which were agriculturally diversified. These sites were occupied from the late seventeenth through early nineteenth centuries and are scattered across the Coastal Plain and Piedmont regions of Virginia (Figure 11.1).

The Statistical Methods

Three main statistical methods were used to analyze the large quantity of artifact data from these sites and to test the signaling expectations: abundance indexes, generalized linear models (GLMs), and principal components analysis (PCA). This section provides a brief overview of these methods. (More detailed discussion can be found in Galle 2006.)

The abundance index. An abundance index is used to estimate discard rates of the four artifact classes relative to a baseline discard rate, with the assumption that the base discard rate of the denominator class either does not change or, if the base discard rate does change, it does so in a predictable manner. Here the abundance index (AI) is estimated as

$$\text{AI} = (\text{Artifact Type 1})/[(\text{Artifact Type 1}) + (\text{Artifact Type 2})]$$

where Type 1 is the artifact group whose variation in discard we are interested in measuring and Type 2 represents the base discard rate. Unlike relative frequencies, the AI works by using a single artifact class as the Artifact Type 2 denominator value. By reducing the Artifact Type 2 value to a single artifact class, one only has to be concerned with correlated discard rate variation in a single denominator

Table 11.1 Jamaican Assemblages

Plantation	Site Name	Occupation Phase	BLUE MCD	Region	Plantation Type
New Montpelier	House 24		1820	Jamaica	Sugar
New Montpelier	House 26		1790	Jamaica	Sugar
New Montpelier	House 37		1805	Jamaica	Sugar
Seville	House 15	Phase 1	1772	Jamaica	Sugar
Seville	House 15	Phase 2	1788	Jamaica	Sugar
Seville	House 15	Phase 3	1822	Jamaica	Sugar
Seville	House 16	Phase 1	1761	Jamaica	Sugar
Seville	House 16	Phase 2	1772	Jamaica	Sugar
Seville	House 16	Phase 3	1781	Jamaica	Sugar
Seville	House 16	Phase 4	1787	Jamaica	Sugar
Thetford	House 41		1797	Jamaica	Sugar
Thetford	House 42		1797	Jamaica	Sugar
Thetford	House 43		1797	Jamaica	Sugar
Thetford	House 44		1797	Jamaica	Sugar
Thetford	House 45		1823	Jamaica	Sugar
Juan de Bolas	House 11		1803	Jamaica	Coffee
Juan de Bolas	House 21		1798	Jamaica	Coffee
Juan de Bolas	House 22		1805	Jamaica	Coffee
Juan de Bolas	House 24		1812	Jamaica	Coffee
Juan de Bolas	House 31		1797	Jamaica	Coffee
Juan de Bolas	House 32		1799	Jamaica	Coffee

Table 11.2 Virginia Assemblages

Plantation	Site Name	Occupation Phase	BLUE MCD	Region	Plantation Type
Monticello	Elizabeth Hemmings		1799	Virginia	Wheat
Monticello	Building o	Phase 2	1785	Virginia	Tobacco
Monticello	Building o	Phase 3	1791	Virginia	Wheat
Monticello	Building l	Middle Phase	1796	Virginia	Wheat
Monticello	Building s	Phase 1	1798	Virginia	Wheat
Monticello	Building s	Phase 2	1803	Virginia	Wheat
Monticello	Building r	Early Period	1796	Virginia	Wheat
Monticello	Site 7	Phase 3	1788	Virginia	Tobacco
Monticello	Site 8	Phase 3a	1797	Virginia	Tobacco
Monticello	Site 8	Phase 3b	1790	Virginia	Tobacco
Monticello	Site 8	House 1	1778	Virginia	Tobacco
Stratford Hall	ST116		1787	Virginia	Wheat
Poplar Forest	Quarter		1795	Virginia	Wheat
Poplar Forest	North Hill		1796	Virginia	Tobacco
Utopia	Structure 40		1749	Virginia	Wheat
Utopia	Structure 50		1764	Virginia	Wheat

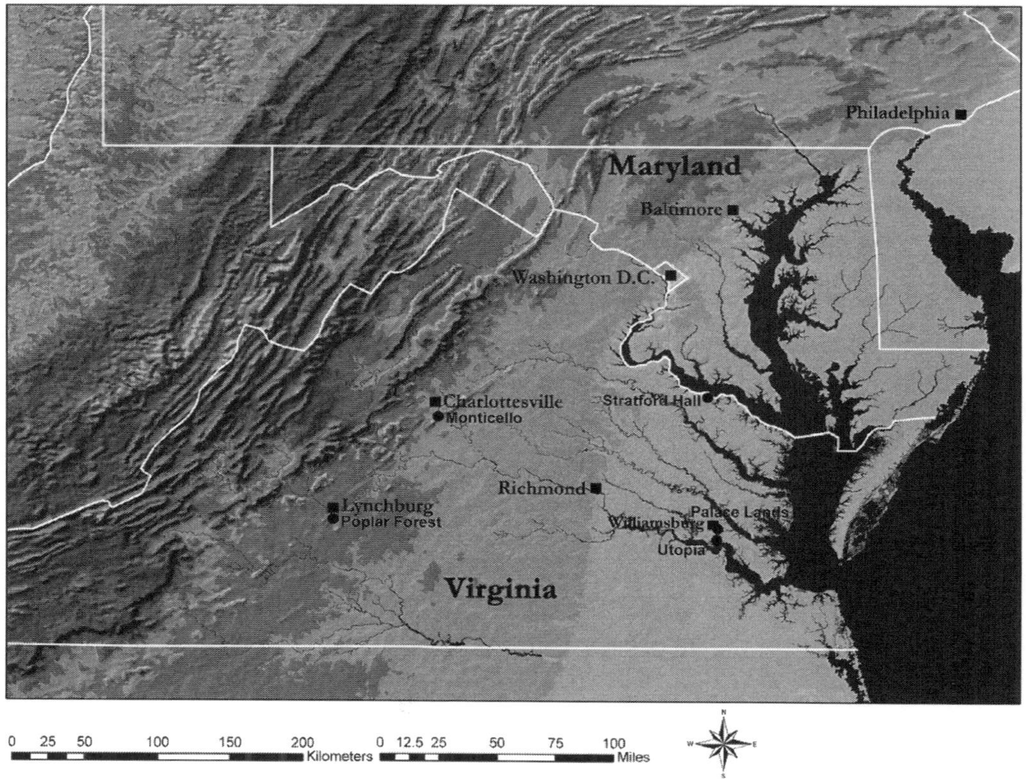

Figure 11.1. Map of Virginia showing plantations contributing sites to this analysis.

class, not in scores of artifact classes. Abundance indexes are therefore less affected by random variation in occupation intensities, durations, and site formation processes than densities since these factors equally affect both the denominator and the numerator artifact classes.

This method for estimating discard rates was derived from large and small mammal measures used in optimal foraging applications (Ugan and Bright 2001). Recently, abundance indexes have been developed for use on historic period sites to estimate artifact discard on late eighteenth-century slave quarter sites at Monticello (Galle and Neiman 2003; Neiman, McFaden, and Wheeler 2000), eighteenth- and nineteenth-century sites in the Chesapeake (Galle 2010), and early to mid-nineteenth-century sites at The Hermitage Plantation in Tennessee (Galle 2004). The challenge in using this abundance index is identifying the appropriate denominator class (Artifact Type 2) that has a discard rate that is either relatively constant across sites or that has a discard rate that varies predictably over time. For this study, wine bottle glass was found to be the most consistently discarded artifact class, and it is used as Artifact Type 2 for each site in this analysis (Galle 2006).[2]

Generalized linear models: negative binomial regression. For each assemblage, the abundance index provides an estimate of variation in the discard of metal buttons, ceramics, beads, and table glass.[3] As we'll see, the differences in the discard of costly goods among sites raise questions about the different historical variables that may have influenced the acquisition and discard of these artifact types. One way to address these questions is to use a statistical method that estimates the overall effect of independent historical and archaeological variables on the abundance of a given artifact class in a given assemblage while holding constant the variation in the other independent variables in the model.

A variety of methods can be used to evaluate the effect that independent historical and contextual variables had on artifact abundance. Since the AI provides reliable proportional abundance measures, generalized linear models (GLMs) offer a powerful statistical method for testing the effects that time and plantation type had on the use and discard of artifacts at sites in Jamaica and Virginia. Generalized linear models are a form of regression that handles non-Gaussian errors and nonlinear relationships. Introduced in the early 1970s, and most fully developed by McCullagh and Nelder (1989), GLMs subsume traditional approaches to multiple regression, analysis of variance, and analysis of covariance while also including relatively new methods such as logistic, Poisson, and negative binomial regression. Two generalized linear models that use the log link function and negative binomial error distribution were used here. One tests the effects of time on consumption (y = AI scores and x = MCD) while the other tests the effects of time and plantation type on consumption (y = AI scores and x_1 = MCD, x_2 = plantation type). The Pearson Goodness-of-Fit statistics for the negative binomial GLMs were all close to 1, indicating that the negative binomial models account for over-dispersion in the artifact samples used in this study.[4]

Consumption and Time

Although the archaeological assemblages of enslaved households in Virginia and Jamaica appear to have very similar types of material culture, the abundance index results and regression models highlight a number of key differences in the consumption patterns in these two regions. First, the abundance indices for metal buttons, refined ceramics, and glass tableware demonstrate that enslaved Virginians discarded much higher quantities of costly imported goods at increasing rates throughout the eighteenth century than did their counterparts in Jamaica (Figures 11.2a–d). The regression estimates and p-values from the negative binomial regression models indicate that the consumption of costly metal buttons, refined ceramics, and glass tableware had a significant positive correlation with time. The temporal effects on consumption in Jamaica are murkier. Although there appears to be a slight increase in the discard of these goods on Jamaica sites through time, there is no statistically significant relationship between time and the discard of costly imported goods by enslaved Jamaicans.

Enslaved men and women clearly responded to the changing social, demographic, and economic environment in Virginia during the second half of the eighteenth century. As Chesapeake demographics shifted—population increased, urban centers grew, and venues for interaction expanded—many enslaved people increased their investment in costly or difficult-to-obtain objects as the social and economic environment became increasingly competitive. The temporal trends meet the expectation that signaling among the enslaved increased as Chesapeake plantations diversified, towns grew, and social and economic opportunities expanded.[5] The discard of costly goods on Jamaica sites did not increase throughout the eighteenth century. As anticipated, the discard of refined ceramics and metal buttons on Jamaican sites remained relatively constant over time since sugar plantations, cattle pens, and urban centers were fully developed in Jamaica by the early eighteenth century. As a result, changes in agricultural regimes or dramatic population growth did not have significant positive effects on the discard of costly imported goods over time in Jamaica.

Consumption and Agriculturally Diversified Plantations

Generalized linear models allow us to test the effects of multiple contextual variables that might be influential in the consumption of these costly goods. Here a negative binomial regression model holds the influence of time constant while testing to see if a plantation type impacts an enslaved household's ability and desire to participate in the market economy (x_1 = MCD, x_2 = plantation type, y = AI).

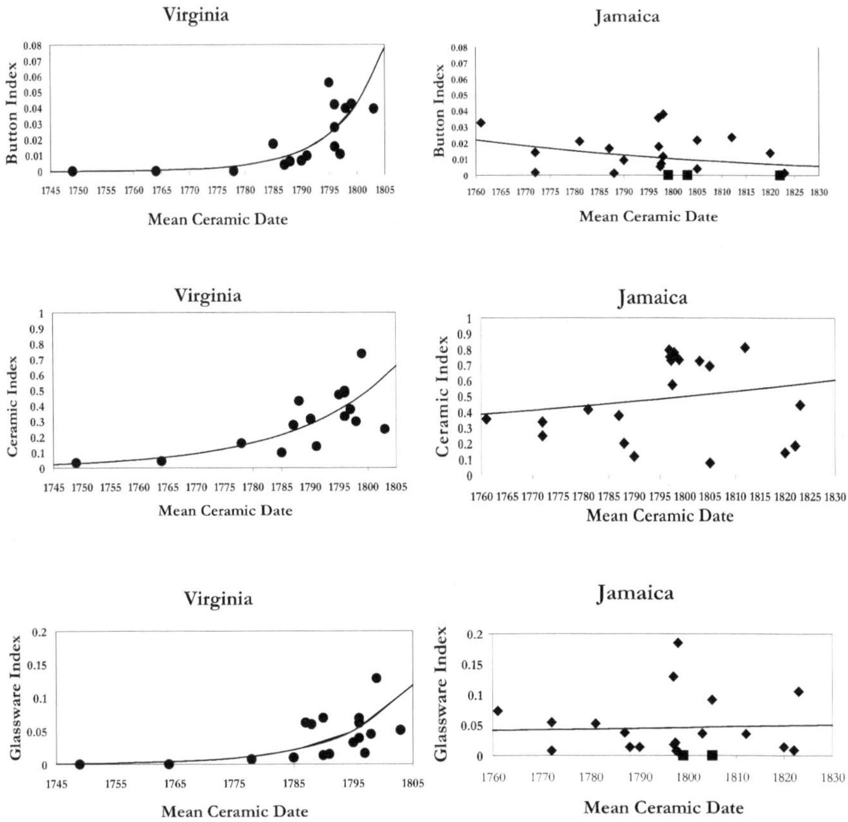

Figure 11.2. Abundance index for metal buttons, refined ceramics, and glass beads plotted against mean ceramic dates: (a) metal buttons from Virginia assemblages (b = .11; p = <.0001); (b) metal buttons from Jamaica assemblages (b = -.01; p = .23); (c) refined ceramics from Virginia assemblages (b = .05; p = <.0001); (d) refined ceramics from Jamaica assemblages (b = .006; p = .5); (e) glass beads from Virginia assemblages (b = .28; p = .03); (f) glass beads from Jamaica assemblages (b = .003; p = .85). Parameter estimates for glasswares from Virginia assemblages are b = .083; p = .0007 and for Jamaica assemblages b = .002; p = .82.

Although time had no impact on the consumption habits of enslaved Jamaicans, plantation type did have a significant positive effect on the use and discard of metal buttons and refined ceramics. Figures 11.3a and 11.3b demonstrate that people living and working at the Juan de Bolas coffee plantation were statistically more likely to have fashionable and imported goods than were people living on sugar plantations. Factors such as distance to urban centers and owner presence were not significant determinants of the use and discard of costly goods, which is not surprising as the Juan de Bolas households were not located closer to cities than were the

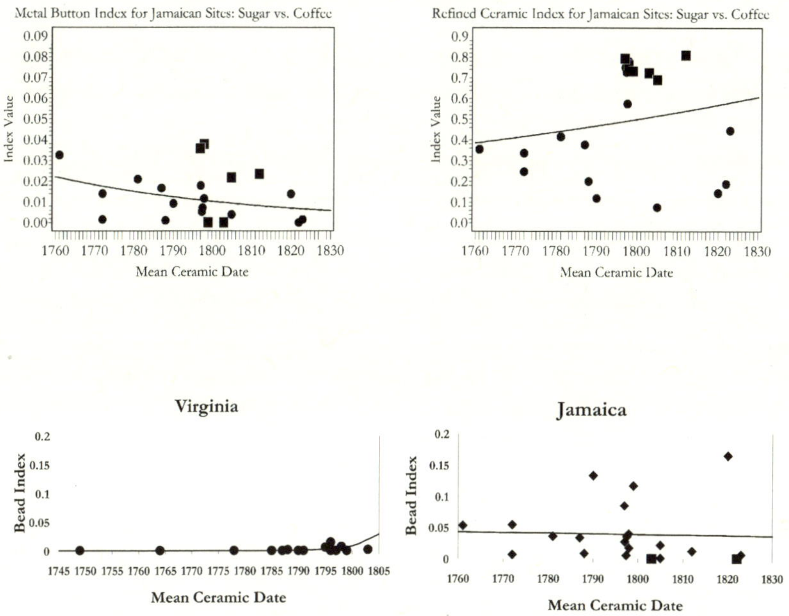

Figure 11.3. Abundance index for metal buttons, refined ceramics, and glass beads from Jamaica assemblages plotted against mean ceramic dates where y = AI, x_1 = MCD, and x_2 = plantation type. Squares represent coffee plantation assemblages, diamonds sugar plantation assemblages: (a) metal buttons from Jamaica assemblages; (b) refined ceramics from Jamaica assemblages; (c) glass beads from Jamaica assemblages. Parameter estimates for this GLM for both Jamaica and Virginia assemblages are provided in Table 11.3.

sugar plantations in this study. These results confirm recent findings by Matthew Reeves (this volume). Although data from additional coffee plantation sites would be ideal, these preliminary conclusions strongly suggest that people enslaved on coffee plantations had greater opportunities and incentives to earn money and engage in local market economies than did their contemporaries on sugar plantations. In this analysis, distance to market was not a factor in slaves' ability to earn and spend money in markets.

Consumption and Demographics

Patterns in the use and discard of glass beads on slave sites in Virginia and Jamaica are particularly remarkable. Glass beads are one category of imported goods that did not incur substantial costs. Whether purchased in the North American and Caribbean colonies, carried on the bodies of enslaved Africans during the Middle Passage, or acquired on that journey, glass beads most likely served a range of uses from individualized fashion displays to expressions of ethnic or spiritual affiliation. Unlike the discard of costly imported artifacts such as buttons, ceramics, and

Table 11.3 Negative Binomial Regression Estimates for Time and Agricultural Diversification (y = AI scores, x_1 = MCD, and x_2 = agricultural diversification)

	Estimate	Wald 95% Confidence Limits LCL	UCL	p
Button Index, Jamaican Sites				
MCD	−.03	−.05	−.003	.028
Diversified	1.3	.38	2.2	.005
Button Index, Virginia Sites				
MCD	.12	.05	.19	.0003
Diversified	−.08	−.85	.66	.8
Refined Ceramic Index, Jamaican Sites				
MCD	−.0008	−.017	.−15	.92
Diversified	.67	.16	1.19	.01
Refined Ceramic Index, Virginia Sites				
MCD	.05	.03	.07	<.0001
Diversified	−.12	−.51	.27	.54
Glassware Index, Jamaican Sites				
MCD	.002	−.02	.02	.82
Diversified	.07	.27	1.4	.88
Glassware Index, Virginia Sites				
MCD	.08	.03	.13	.0007
Diversified	.21	−.48	.91	.54
Glass Bead Index, Jamaican Sites				
MCD	.003	−.02	.03	.84
Diversified	−.03	−1.1	1.1	.95
Glass Bead Index, Virginia Sites				
MCD	.28	.02	.53	.03
Diversified	−.98	−2.80	.89	.3

glassware, here we see that enslaved Jamaicans discarded greater quantities of glass beads than those living in Virginia (Figures 11.2e and 11.2f).

Perhaps even more critical is that the high discard rates of beads on Jamaican sites have no significant positive correlation with residency on a coffee plantation (Table 11.3). In fact, sites with the highest discard of glass trade beads are households from the New Montpelier sugar estate, which the archaeological record indicates is among the most resource-stressed plantations in the sample (Figure 11.3c). As will be discussed in greater detail, New Montpelier had high yearly import rates of newly enslaved Africans between 1790 and 1807.

High discard rates of glass beads may be one of the only archaeological signatures of the high sustained rates of African importation into Jamaica throughout the eighteenth century. It is likely that many individuals arrived with beads around their necks or waists or in their hair. Other enslaved Jamaicans may have purchased beads at local markets for use in personal adornment or rituals, or as inexpensive reminders of the places they were raised. In Jamaica, glass beads may have been an important signal of traditions, customs, lineages, and religious beliefs for the multitudes of newly arrived enslaved Africans.

Consumption and Gendered Choices

Principal component analysis (PCA) is a statistical method that enables us to further interrogate the archaeological record by isolating the specific consumer actions of individual enslaved households within each region. PCA analyzes the residuals from the bivariate temporal regression models (x = MCD and y = AI) and reduces the complexity of the data sets by transforming the Pearson residuals into vectors that can be plotted visually along two or three principal components.[6] In doing so, it isolates and highlights the artifact classes that account for the greatest variation within the sites. When using artifacts that can be generally associated with gendered activities, it is possible to see the influence of male and female consumer behaviors in the archaeological record. The following PCA uses residuals from regression models for two artifact classes associated with gendered consumer behavior: metal buttons that represent male fashionable display and refined ceramics that may represent female dining strategies. The biplots also include residuals from the glass bead regression models.

The PCA correlation matrix and biplot for Jamaican households demonstrate that the discard rates of refined ceramics and metal buttons are positively correlated (Figure 11.4). Jamaican households with above-average consumption of buttons also had above-average access to refined ceramics. Bead consumption is also positively correlated with button consumption, but it is not correlated with the discard of refined ceramics. Among enslaved Virginia households, button and refined ceramic consumption are not correlated. On these sites, individuals or households appear to have focused their consumption efforts on a single class of fashionable goods: metal buttons or refined ceramics. The lack of correlation suggests that many enslaved Virginians used signaling strategies that involved only one type of fashionable object.[7] Jamaican slaves who could afford buttons were also likely to invest resources in the acquisition of costly refined ceramics.

These biplots suggest that there were three different types of consumer behavior at work in both regions, two of which I consider the result of gendered signaling strategies. The first type of consumer behavior comprises enslaved households with residuals that fall in the negative range along principal component 1 (Figures 11.4c and 11.4d). Households in this group consumed far fewer metal buttons and re-

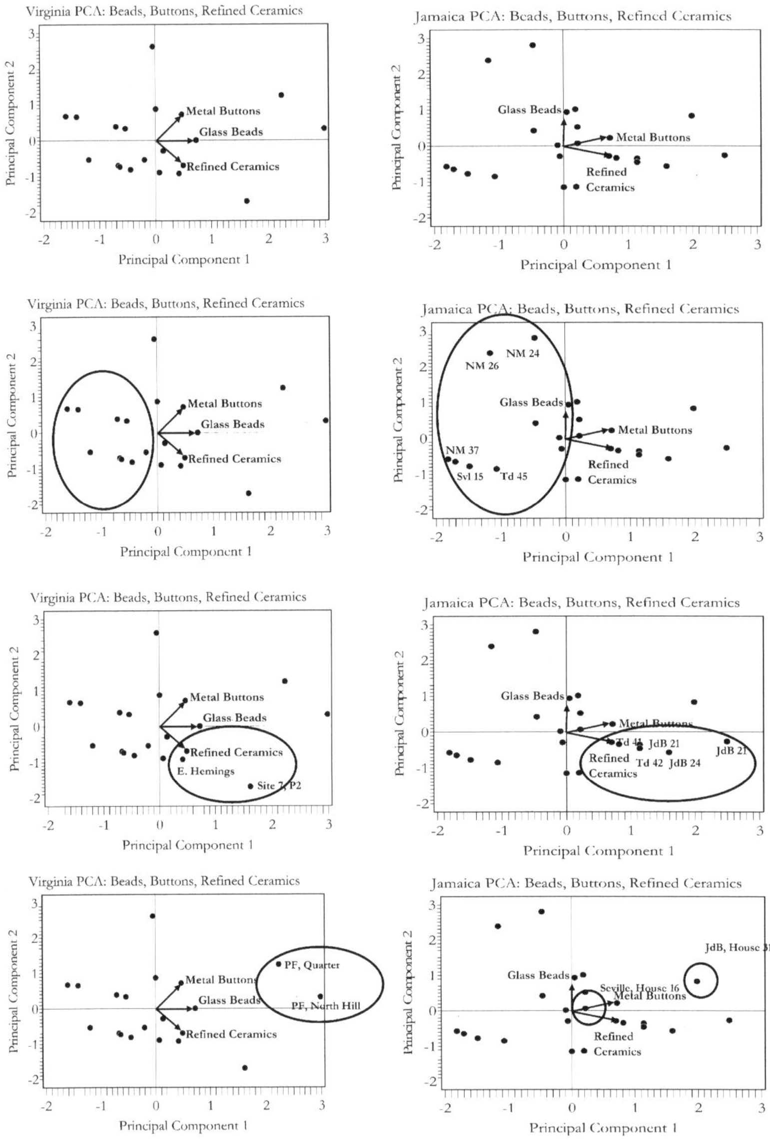

Figure 11.4. Principal component analysis (PCA) using artifact residuals from metal button, refined ceramic, and glass bead GLMs from Virginia and Jamaica assemblages where x = MCD and y = AI: (a and b) PCA for Virginia and Jamaica assemblages without signaling groups indicated; (c and d) group 1 represents low-level signalers characterized by the underconsumption of metal buttons and refined ceramics; (e and f) group 2 represents female and/or successful, cooperative household signaling strategies defined by high refined ceramic consumption; (g and h) group 3 represents male signaling strategies focused on high metal button consumption.

fined ceramics than predicted by the temporal models. In Jamaica, only sites located on sugar plantations, such as House 37 at New Montpelier, Houses 44 and 45 at Thetford Plantation, and House 15 at Seville, fall into this category. Two of the three plantations, Thetford and New Montpelier, were administered by absentee owners who placed overseers and managers in charge of their human chattel (Higman 1998; Reeves 1997). Low-level consumption of expensive and fashionable ceramics and buttons at these sites suggests that if enslaved individuals did participate in the market economy, they may have done so in exchange for perishable goods that left no archaeological trace. Any gains from the sale of excess produce or craft products were mainly applied to the purchase of necessary perishable items that were otherwise unobtainable. A number of regional factors, such as the brutal labor requirements of sugar plantations, high African imports, the scarcity of owner-occupied sites, and black-to-white ratios, may have been significant factors in suppressing the consumption rates of nonessential imported goods among enslaved Africans at these sites.

A few Jamaican households, specifically Houses 14, 24, and 26 at New Montpelier Plantation, discarded more glass beads than expected by the temporal model. At Montpelier, more than 25 new enslaved Africans were brought to the plantation each year between 1790 and 1807 to offset the low fertility and high mortality rates on the plantation (Higman 1998:36). Juan de Bolas, House 32, which falls into the high-signaling group for metal buttons, also had enough glass beads to influence its placement on the biplot (see also Figure 11.3c). Documents indicate that the early nineteenth-century enslaved community at Juan de Bolas was 90 percent African born (Reeves 2000). High importation rates may well account for the large quantities of beads discarded at Juan de Bolas and New Montpelier.

After the abolition of the British slave trade in 1807, the New Montpelier slave population declined steadily until emancipation (Higman 1998:36–37). During this time, slaves from the eastern part of the island were purchased and brought to Montpelier, and many were moved among the three neighboring plantations owned by Charles Seaford: New Montpelier, Old Montpelier, and Shettlewood. High rates of imported African captives prior to 1807, the steady decline in the enslaved population after 1807, and the lower-than-expected levels of ceramic and button consumption indicate that enslaved people at Montpelier were under tremendous stress. These factors may have also been catalysts for the participation of Montpelier slaves in one of the largest rebellions in Jamaica's history. Between December 1831 and January 1832, 20,000 to 50,000 slaves burned large swaths of St. James Parish, with violence spilling into the neighboring parishes (Higman 1998:262). Many slaves from Old and New Montpelier and Shettlewood participated in the rebellion. Enslaved rebels destroyed the plantation works and residences, with the exception of the slave villages, at both Old and New Montpelier plantations. At least eleven enslaved men from Old and New Montpelier and Shettlewood were hanged or whipped for their involvement in the Christmas uprising (Higman 1998:275).

Of the Montpelier and Shettlewood men captured and charged for playing leading roles in the uprising, four were field hands and seven were skilled laborers—one blacksmith, one driver, two head masons, two masons, and one carpenter. Two were African born and all eleven were considered black. Most of these men owned cattle, pigs, poultry, and controlled provision grounds of over 1.5 acres each. Lord Seaford was mystified when he learned the identities of the rebels and wrote that these headmen "had been treated with the greatest indulgence, who were the most intelligent and most civilized, and whose situation has been in all respects the most comfortable" (Higman 1998:274). As leaders of the rebellion living on a resource-stressed plantation, it is likely that their skills, personal resources, and knowledge of the local landscape helped mobilize their fellow slaves to participate in such a large-scale rebellion.

The second consumption group comprises households that consumed refined ceramics in much greater quantities than anticipated by the temporal model, almost to the exclusion of metal buttons (Figures 11.4e and 11.4f). This group may represent kin-based households anchored by women who held positions in the main house or surrounding dependencies. As anticipated, house sites from the Juan de Bolas coffee estate dominate this group for Jamaican assemblages (Figure 11.4f). At the Thetford sugar estate, Houses 41 and 42 contained disproportionately more imported ceramics than other sites on the sugar plantation, and Reeves notes that their location removed from the sugar works and other slave houses may indicate that their occupants held prominent positions within the plantation hierarchy (Reeves 1997:278). In Virginia, the Elizabeth Hemmings site displays high quantities of particularly costly ceramics, such as Chinese porcelain tableware. Located 350 feet south of Mulberry Row and Monticello Mansion, and relatively isolated from other buildings, the site was occupied by Elizabeth Hemmings, the unmarried matriarch of a large extended enslaved family that included Thomas Jefferson's offspring. At the Hemmings household, and among the high ceramic consumers from Thetford and Juan de Bolas, signaling may have taken on intimate forms of costly displays through small group dining and tea rituals.

The third type of consumer behavior seen in the biplots focused on expensive metal buttons. Houses 31 and 32 at Juan de Bolas and House 16 at Seville in Jamaica and the Quarter site and the North Hill site at Poplar Forest in Virginia dominate this group (Figure 11.4). These households discarded fashionable buttons at higher rates than anticipated by the model and may have been occupied by young, mobile, unattached men whose desire for high-quality mates or social allies spurred expenditures on costly and easily displayable fashions. Recent research on stylistic change in metal button decoration suggests that residents at the Poplar Forest Quarter were consciously discarding usable but unfashionable white metal buttons in favor of more costly, fashionable yellow metal buttons (Galle 2010:34; Heath 1999b). Men may have been displaying their knowledge of and ability to maintain current fashions through the discard of usable but unfashionable buttons.

Residents at the Poplar Forest Quarter and North Hill sites consumed more metal buttons than any other household in this study. Although we don't know who lived in these houses, about fifteen unmarried men and nineteen unmarried women between the ages of fifteen and twenty-five lived at Poplar Forest during the early 1790s and 1800s (Heath 2005). In light of this uneven sex ratio, young men at Poplar Forest may have used buttons as part of a signaling system that appealed to women living both on and off the plantation. In 1823, well after the abandonment of the North Hill site, four men between the ages of nineteen and twenty-nine were convicted of attacking an overseer at Poplar Forest (Heath 1999a). These men were sold to New Orleans, but their collective action, like the actions of their counterparts at Montpelier in Jamaica, raises the possibility that signals which communicated independence and a willingness to take physical and emotional risks were crucial means for organizing different types of collective action.

Unrelated slaves in Jamaica and Virginia came together with some regularity to run away and rebel (Finkelman 1989; French 2004; Higman 1998; M. P. Johnson 1981). Costly and highly visible items such as buttons may have communicated a person's ingenuity, ability, and motivation to circumvent an owner's or overseer's direct control, attributes that may have been valued when seeking partners for resistance and rebellion. Men living in these Jamaican and Virginia households may have invested in fashionable male displays that helped smooth economic transactions and created social ties with other slaves or free blacks in the area.

Conclusion

Archaeological studies of slavery often argue that the presence of expensive or unusual, non-provisioned objects are complex expressions of African and African American identity and resistance to the dominant power structure. However, the expression of individual identity through the use of goods would not result in the strikingly consistent patterns of discard seen on sites in Jamaica and Virginia. Identity should instead manifest itself in individual material expressions that are not correlated with plantation type or temporal change. Signaling as a form of communication among the enslaved offers an explanation for the uniform material patterns seen at these sites. Knowledge of how buttons and refined ceramics were used, by whom and in what contexts, points to gendered consumer strategies that left room for individual expression in the styles that were chosen and in how goods were displayed or worn. However, the data suggest that enslaved individuals focused their consumption efforts on specific types of costly goods that would offer the highest payoff to their signaling displays.

Data from thirty-eight assemblages indicate that plantation type, demographics, and time had a significant, positive influence on enslaved individuals' abilities and incentives to participate in the consumer revolution. In Virginia, the shift from tobacco to wheat cultivation and the growth of urban centers provided enslaved people greater opportunities to participate in the market economy. People enslaved on Jamaican coffee plantations, like those enslaved on diversified plantations in Virginia, had greater opportunities to earn money, to travel, and to engage in novel social and business activities. As expected by the signaling model, discard rates of costly goods that played an important role in signaling systems were higher on coffee and wheat plantations where incentives and opportunities for signaling were greater than on sugar or tobacco plantations.

Higher rates of glass bead discard in Jamaica and the lack of correlation between high bead discard and residency on coffee plantations indicate that beads were not consumer goods sought by enslaved people in either Jamaica or Virginia. Together, the archaeological patterns and documentary record strongly suggest that high abundance index scores for glass beads point to sites with first-generation enslaved Africans. The exceptional importation rates of enslaved Africans into Jamaica throughout the eighteenth century may explain the high rates of glass bead discard on Jamaican sites compared to the exceptionally low discard on Virginia sites, which are likely due to the fact that second-, third-, and fourth-generation enslaved African American families were thriving in the Chesapeake by the 1770s. Positive natural increase among the enslaved in Virginia resulted in much lower importation rates, hence fewer glass beads arriving on newly arrived captives.

Large-scale comparative analysis of archaeological data has the power to change our historical understandings of enslaved participation in markets in Jamaica and Virginia. Traditional histories suggest a vibrancy and level of financial investment in Jamaican markets that was not present in the North American colonies, where slave participation in markets was illegal. The archaeological record indicates that while many enslaved Jamaicans acquired nonessential and expensive imported goods, many more living on sugar plantations rarely purchased imported goods, and if they did participate in markets regularly, they mainly acquired perishable consumables such as food and clothing that left little or no trace in the archaeological record. In Virginia, where slave participation in markets was illegal, changing agricultural regimes and demographics offered many slaves, especially men, ample opportunities to purchase and display costly, imported goods at rates similar to those seen in Jamaica. By the late eighteenth century, the discard of costly imported goods on slave sites in Virginia rivaled the discard of those same goods by slaves in Jamaica. In Virginia, however, slaves conducted their purchases illegally, while enslaved Jamaicans did so within a legal, thriving market system created in large part by and for them.

The consumption patterns in these slaveholding societies with different approaches to an enslaved person's role in local markets allow us to begin unraveling the complex historical and contextual mechanisms that drove slave participation in local economies throughout the Atlantic world. It is here that signaling through costly goods becomes most apparent, with slaves in Virginia willing to risk the dangers inherent in market participation to purchase and display buttons and refined ceramics as signaling opportunities throughout the Chesapeake expanded in the late eighteenth century. High rates of discard on sites in Jamaica throughout the eighteenth century indicate that some enslaved individuals in Jamaica, especially those living on coffee plantations, also sought costly, imported goods. Buttons and refined ceramics certainly reflected personal consumer choices but, perhaps more significant, signaled an enslaved person's ability to purchase goods not provided by the owner that were fashionable and not essential to survival in one of the harshest slave-based societies in the Atlantic world.

Acknowledgments

I would like to thank Jim Delle, Mark Hauser, and Doug Armstrong for organizing the 2007 World Archaeological Congress Intersession symposium in Kingston and for all of their hard work in putting this volume together. Fraser Neiman, Jim Delle, Matthew Reeves, and Lorena Walsh all provided insightful comments on versions of this essay. I am grateful to the Thomas Jefferson Foundation for a research leave and to James Horn and the John D. Rockefeller Jr. Library at the Colonial Williamsburg Foundation for fellowship funding that enabled the completion of this research. Finally, I want to express my appreciation to all of my archaeological colleagues in the United States and Jamaica who have generously contributed data to the Digital Archaeological Archive of Comparative Slavery (www.daacs.org). Without their contributions, large-scale comparative archaeological studies of slavery would not be possible.

Notes

1. Following Neiman and Smith (2005), Best Linear Unbiased Estimator Mean Ceramic Dates (referred to here as BLUE MCDs) were used to calculate mean dates for each occupation phase. BLUE MCDs are calculated using:

$$MCD_{BLUE} = \sum m_j p_j \left(\frac{1}{s_j/6} \right)^2$$

where m_j is the manufacturing midpoint of the j'th type, p_j is its relative frequency, and s_j is its manufacturing span. BLUE MCDs give less influence to ceramic types with long manufacturing spans. In doing so, it assumes that type frequencies are Gaussian over time, with standard deviations set to ⅙ the documented span. The BLUE MCDs used in this analysis were calculated using MCD-types posted on the DAACS Web site: http://www.daacs.org/aboutDatabase/MCDTypes.html.

2. Detailed descriptions of these GLMs and methods used in the subsequent principal components analysis are available in Galle 2006, 2010.

3. Kendall's tau correlation coefficients for artifact densities and abundance indexes were calculated for seven artifact classes by time, in this case represented by each site's MCD. The seven artifact classes included buckles, buttons, coins, refined ceramics, coarse ceramics, tobacco pipes, and wine bottle glass. The discard of wine bottle sherds had no correlation with time in Jamaica and Virginia. Discard of the other artifact classes had either strong positive or negative correlations with time, with the exception of coarse ceramic wares, which had only a subtle negative correlation with time. Coarseware discard estimates decreased slightly throughout the eighteenth century but they did so in a predictable manner. Coarseware could have also been used as the denominator class; however, the predictable decrease in discard throughout the eighteenth century would have been reflected in slightly elevated slopes for all artifact classes when index scores are generated using a Coarseware Index relative to abundance scores resulting from the Wine Bottle Index used here. For more information on using abundance indexes on historic-period sites, see Galle 2006.

4. For additional details on these regression models, see Galle 2006. GLMs have two key properties that allow them to handle both linear and nonlinear relationships as well as a number of different variable types and error distributions (Crawley 1993:167–68; Gill 2001). First, GLMs allow researchers to define the error structure contained within the dependent response variables being analyzed. Archaeologists work with a variety of data types, each with its own error distribution. Continuous data, such as sherd thicknesses, rim diameters, and tobacco pipe bore diameters, can be modeled effectively using normal Gaussian distributions. Count data, such as the number of ceramic sherds in a sample, and proportional data, such as an AI score, have non-normal distributions. GLMs allow researchers to specify the error distributions that are appropriate to the data being modeled.

Second, GLMs use link functions to model nonlinear relationships between a set of linear predictors and the predicted or mean value of the dependent variable. Link functions are used to correctly identify the functional form of the relationship between the dependent (X) and independent (Y) variables and different link functions help distinguish one member of the GLM family from another (Crawley 1993; Liao 1994:4). The type of link function used is reliant on the distribution of the dependent data (Liao 1994:5).

Traditional linear regression techniques most frequently used by archaeologists, which include analysis of variance and analysis of covariance (Shennan 1988), require a continuous dependent variable and assume that the error distribution is normal or Gaussian (Liao 1994:1). As noted above, continuous variables with assumed normal distributions include those such as sherd size and sherd thickness. For continuous data, GLMs provide an identity link function that connects the dependent Y variables to the linear predictor (η). With the identity link function, the independent X variables are used to predict the mean of Y, where $\eta = \mu$ where μ = the predicted mean value of Y given a particular X value. The identity link is functionally inappropriate for proportional or count data like those used in this analysis. When the identity link is used with count or proportional data, there is nothing in the model to prevent the results from producing negative counts or proportions that are greater than 1 or less than 0.

Fortunately, GLMs have link functions that allow us to use non-continuous and dichotomous data such as counts and proportions. The logit link is one link function that works well with proportional data. It produces a logistic regression that forces the predictions to fall between 0 and 1. Logistic regression transforms nonlinear relationships into linear ones. It is particularly effective for describing the relationship between dichotomous, or binary, variables and a group of independent "predictor" variables (Menard 2002; Pampel 2000). Unfortunately, the logit link assumes that the data have a binomial error distribution. A binomial error distribution assumes that each artifact within a sample was sampled randomly and independently of other artifacts. This is a problematic assumption to make with archaeological data. Most artifacts are portions of objects, such as pots. It is likely that pots were broken or discarded in a localized area. Contexts with several sherds of creamware, for example, are likely to have many more sherds of creamware, thereby creating a non-independent sample. Non-independent samples are easily remembered as "contagion" samples, where the likelihood of catching the flu is not independent since catching the flu relies on others in the sample having the same bug. Data that are not independently sampled likely contain what is known as extra-binomial variation, which means that the variance (σ2) of the real error distribution is much larger that the assumed binomial error.

GLMs have a log link function and error distributions that can better accommodate assemblage count data. The log link function predicts the log of the artifact count (e.g., the log of the number of refined ceramic sherds). Hence negative predictions are impossible. Poisson error distributions can be applied to count data that refer to knowable cases, such as the number of sherds in a context or the number of flu cases, but that have no information on how many times something did not happen. A binomial model, on the other hand, requires knowing both the number of times an incident occurs and the number of times it did not occur (Crawley 1993:227). Poisson distributions are, however, constrained in that they also assume independence within samples. The assumed Poisson error variance (σ2) is equal to the mean of the dependent variable, which does not allow for much variation in a sample.

The negative binomial error distribution has more forgiving requirements about variation. Unlike the Poisson error distribution, the negative binomial variance can be greater than the mean and it can be as large as necessary to account for lack of independence and the resulting extra-binomial variation within samples.

5. It has been argued that the explosion in the quantity of all classes of material culture on sites dating to the second half of the eighteenth century was the result of the increase in reasonably priced goods. While increasingly inexpensive items no doubt increased consumption and discard rates, the rapid spike in the consumption of costly items such as refined ceramics and buttons moved much faster than the decrease in prices. George Miller's price index, for example, suggests that prices for refined ceramics wares only began to drop substantially by the early nineteenth century (1988, 1990). Based on the temporal regressions, it is clear that slaves living in Virginia were acquiring and discarding costly items at rates that were well ahead of falling consumer prices.

6. This PCA uses the correlation matrix of the residuals from the GLMs. The first principal component should account for the greatest amount of variation, the second principal accounts for the next greatest amount of variation, and so forth. Together, the first and second principal components should account for at least 70 percent of the variation. In the PCA for Virginia sites, principal component 1 (PC1) accounts for 51 percent of the variation and PC2 accounts for 36 percent of the variation, together accounting for 87 percent of the variation in the data set. In the PCA of Jamaica sites, PC1 and PC2 account for 50 percent and 36 percent of the variation, respectively. These percentages meet the thresholds for each principal component as established by the broken stick rule (Legendere and Legendre 1998).

7. PCA transforms the residuals into a visual representation of the relationship between the data. For readers unfamiliar with reading PCA biplots, here is a quick tutorial. When looking at the biplot, select two eigenvectors whose relationship you wish to understand, such as metal buttons and refined ceramics. Starting at the 0/0 point on the biplot, draw a straight line from that point through the metal button data point, the first eigenvector. Draw a second line from the 0/0 point through the refined ceramic eigenvector. If the angle formed by these two lines is less than 90 degrees, this means that the data points are positively correlated. If the angle between the two vectors is greater than or equal to 90 degrees but less than 180 degrees, the data points are not correlated. If the vectors are more than 180 degrees apart, the data are negatively correlated.

12
Identity and Opportunity in Post-Slavery Jamaica

Kenneth G. Kelly
Mark W. Hauser
Douglas V. Armstrong

Introduction

On August 2, 1834, a lead article in the London *Guardian* described the official end of slavery in the British Empire:

> Throughout the British dominions the sun no longer rises on a slave. Yesterday was the day from which the emancipation of all our slave population commences; and we trust the great change by which they are elevated to the rank of freemen will be found to have passed into effect in the manner most accordant with the benevolent spirit in which it was decreed, most consistent with the interests of those for whose benefit it was primarily intended, and most calculated to put an end to the apprehensions under which it was hardly to be expected that the planters could fail to labour as the moment of its consummation approaches. We shall await anxiously the arrivals from the West Indies that will bring advices to a date subsequent to the present time.

Despite the *Guardian*'s prosaic anticipation of a new period of freedom, the legal decrees of 1834 were only a stepping-stone toward freedom and must be considered part of a historical continuum that includes both the 1807 abolition of the slave trade and the 1838 termination of the apprenticeship period that formalized de facto emancipation in 1838. It must also be remembered that the British were but one of the European powers legislating the conditions of labor in the Caribbean, and their endeavor to end slavery must be considered less a punctuated moment and more part of a continuum of abolition. That continuum includes not only legislation like the Abolition Act but also acts of realized or attempted self-emancipation like those experienced in the 1733 St. John Slave Rebellion, the 1794 French Revolution and Haitian War of Independence, abolition of slavery in the French possessions in 1848, and the 1886 transition to emancipation in Cuba.

The binding wholesale abolition of slavery in the British colonies memorialized in the *Guardian* article is as much about the transition in legal status for hundreds of thousands of people in the West Indies as it is an implicit self-congratulation for the British nation and its citizens. The significance of the apparent resolution of the "slavery problem" cannot be doubted, but we must also acknowledge that many aspects of life remained relatively unchanged and that there was a distinct continuity between the social and economic conditions endured by enslaved laborers and wage laborers (Armstrong 2010; Trouillot 1988; Turner 1995). Michael Craton (1985:128) has even argued that the Emancipation Act of 1833 (implemented in 1834) was "a colossal hegemonic trick." In reference to Jamaica, Mary Turner has referred to the transition as simply a shift from "chattel slaves into wage slaves" (1995:33), and Doug Armstrong has discussed a continuum of "degrees of freedom" based on relative access to property in the pre- and post-emancipation eras for each respective colonial domain (2010).

The trials, tribulations, and challenges faced and overcome by enslaved Africans on plantations in the British West Indies have been studied in considerable detail (Delle 1998; Armstrong 1990; Higman 1998; Pulsipher 1994; Farnsworth 2001; Wilkie and Farnsworth 2005). This research has operated under the justifiable argument that the condition of slavery forcefully relegated enslaved Africans to the status of "people without history" and that archaeology was one means by which that history could be recovered. However, in many cases archaeology has not been similarly applied to the post-slavery period, and yet emancipation did not suddenly render workers "with history." In this chapter we examine three related questions.

1. To what extent can we use archaeology to recognize the strategies employed by formerly enslaved laborers and planters in the post-emancipation landscape in Jamaica?
2. What are the implications of these strategies for the post-emancipation lives of former slaves and laborers in Jamaica?
3. Who were these people, and how did they see themselves?

To answer these questions we reexamine archaeological data from Drax Hall and Seville Plantation on Jamaica's north coast (see Armstrong 1990, 2010; Kelly 1989; Kelly and Armstrong 1991; Hauser 2001, 2008). Archaeological data from these estates are contextualized to explore the material consequences of emancipation and how strategies enacted by management to continue to exploit the sugar plantation workers manifest themselves.

Factors and Strategies in the Labor Problem

A key premise of the economic arguments for abolition was the notion that formerly enslaved laborers would easily transition to a new status as wage-earning "free" workers on the plantations. While this may have occurred in some post-slavery West Indian societies where land was circumscribed, larger islands like Jamaica, with lots of apparently available unoccupied land, presented a different situation as many former slaves chose to desert the plantations and establish independent, self-sufficient subsistence "peasant" strategies. In an effort to combat this flight, Jamaican sugar estates generally followed one of two strategies to keep labor attached to the plantation, ultimately identified as the "Push and Pull Hypothesis" for their consequences in relation to labor (Marshall 2003:116). Each strategy revolved around issues of land tenure and property acquisition, particularly the ability to acquire material wealth and to retain a portion of the meager wages offered by the plantation owners (Besson 2002).

The first strategy was a kind of calculated exploitation whereby formerly enslaved people were charged relatively high rents for the houses that used to be "theirs" with the idea that the high rent burden would oblige tenants to continue working on the estate in order to make their payments. Furthermore, the intent was that the rents would have to be paid out of plantation wages, thereby tying former chattel slaves to their respective plantations as wage laborers or de facto wage slaves. This strategy did not account for non-plantation labor and failed to account for the attraction of other sources of income including production of foodstuffs for sale in market gardens, internal production of goods and services for local consumption, and the local commercial and marketing systems. As a result of this lack of foresight, rather than creating a captive labor force, this exploitative management strategy compelled or "pushed" those most able to relocate away from the plantation. In Douglas Hall's words, "The movement of ex-slaves from the estates was not a flight from the horrors of slavery. It was a protest against the inequities of early freedom" (1978:23). Thus, as the strategy backfired, the segment of the population least able to move (the elderly, the infirm, mothers with dependent children, etc.), which was also the least productive, remained behind (Hall 1959:20). It also had the doubly deleterious effect of marginalizing those who could leave the estate who now found themselves on less productive lands in river valleys, on hilltops, and in urban ghettos, often without formal property title or access to "privileges" of *ususfructus* of property as had been traditionally upheld in common law for laborers, even in chattel bondage (see Long [1774] 1970).

Those who left forfeited their rights to property within the estate, which typically included a house and provision gardens. As people abandoned their productive and established provision grounds, this reduced the availability of much of the subsistence produce that made its way into the market economy of the island.

The "pull" hypothesis for laborer movement away from the plantation in post-emancipation Jamaica acknowledges the desire of newly freed people to escape the conditions and environment of their previous enslavement and establish small holdings outside the plantation context. As Woodville Marshall has argued, ex-slaves "possessed a long standing antipathy to the plantation and all of its works and a natural desire to exploit the abundant land outside the plantation for a simple peasant-type existence" (2003:118). While the strategy of tying people to wage labor on the plantation may have been workable on islands such as Barbados, where land was at a premium and the population was highly circumscribed, this strategy failed in Jamaica. Rather, the geography of Jamaica, with its extensive mountains and hills, and with many marginal or failing estates, meant that there were opportunities to eke out a living squatting on abandoned or unoccupied land, or by obtaining land within one of the organized "free villages" set up by missionary and other benevolent societies (Mintz [1974] 1992:159). In an effort to try to negate this pull and stem the flow of labor from the plantations, some planters in Jamaica developed another, less coercive strategy. This strategy involved a more "enlightened" management in which the plantation charged relatively low rents and improved housing in an effort to encourage residents to remain in "their" houses and imposed no requirement as to the source of the rent money (Hall 1959). Through this strategy, it was hoped that the certainty of wage labor and low rents would offset the risk of moving, thereby keeping a resident labor force. This strategy also permitted former slaves to continue to work their established provision grounds, selling the surplus into the local market economy.

The second strategy explored by planters in Jamaica and elsewhere in the Caribbean was to replace the labor leaving the plantation, whether they were "pushed" or "pulled" off the estate, by importing new labor from Africa and South Asia. Unable to attract the necessary volume of "volunteer" wage laborers from "traditional sources" in Africa, Jamaican planters looked to South Asia (M. Thomas 1974:101–2). In 1845 the government reopened immigration from South Asia to the West Indies and the Jamaica Assembly provided funds for the transport of five thousand workers during the 1846 and 1847 seasons, with an initial experimental shipment of two thousand. Thus, East Indian laborers, referred to locally and historically as "Indian coolies" (in reference to a derogatory term for South Asian laborers from the British colonial period in Jamaica), were brought to Jamaica in relatively small numbers beginning almost immediately upon emancipation.

St. Ann's Bay

The pull of mobility and independence was particularly strong in the area around St. Ann's Bay, where the free village of The Priory was established on a former estate immediately west of Seville Estate; the village of New Seville coalesced only a few hundred meters distant from the old slave village on Seville. Abolitionist Baptist and Quaker missionaries created free villages in which the formerly enslaved could live independently of the plantation context. In addition, "from the impetus provided by church sponsorship, other free villages grew without the deliberate patronage of the missionary churches" (Mintz [1974] 1992:161).

The two estates of Drax Hall and Seville, both located in the parish of St. Ann's, provide ideal archaeological contexts for investigating how management strategies designed to cope with the pull of independence impacted the lived experience of the residents. Historical evidence demonstrates that John Pink, owner of Drax Hall, had imposed the more exploitative rental strategy immediately following emancipation. Pink's efforts at labor control backfired and drove the able-bodied laborers off of the estate in such numbers that by the mid-1840s the few tenants remaining were paying dramatically decreased rents; by that time the damage was already done (Armstrong 1990; Hall 1959). In contrast, Seville Estate was acknowledged to be pursuing a more progressive strategy, with the manager, Charles Royes, charging low rents amounting to one day's work per week, and without the stipulation that they be paid from plantation wages. Furthermore, Royes established a sliding wage scale, giving preferential rates to resident employees (Hall 1959:51–52). This suggests that Royes was concerned with the establishment and continuation of good relationships between tenant laborers and management. Indeed, the tenants felt secure enough with the agreements on wages and rents that Royes was able to say that they had "unanimously assented" (Hall 1959:51). Through this arrangement and with the establishment of the nearby free settlement at The Priory, Royes was able to maintain a labor source made up of the previously enslaved population remaining on the plantation, supplemented from the new settlement at The Priory, a short five-minute walk away. The success of this strategy was evident in that Royes was able to retain labor during the unprofitable times immediately following emancipation and made a "ruined" estate profitable again (Hall 1959:88; Green 1976:208).

The importation of East Indian labor into Jamaica took place on a restricted yet important basis as a response to labor shortages caused first by the cessation of the slave trade in 1807 and then emancipation in the 1830s. The labor force required for the production of cash crops had been seriously diminished; consequently, production dropped, which brought on a short resurgence of sugar prices. Managers of plantations, like Seville, that continued to operate following emancipation actively sought ways of holding and attracting laborers. The managers of Seville were singled out as an example of how an estate with a perceived labor shortage should take action to improve living conditions for tenants of the estate (Green 1976:207–8). In contrast to the general trend, they set rents for tenants at a very low rate to encourage the formerly enslaved to stay. Although this was seen as a success for the planters, as we can demonstrate through the archaeological and historical records, the newly freed did leave the estate in large numbers immediately following emancipation; residents left the estate and moved into free lands offered to them at The Priory (IOJ 1843). Archaeological data and a taped interview of Carpi Rose, a community member of St. Ann's Bay, revealed how the third strategy of labor loss mitigation was implemented in this part of Jamaica.

Comparison of Archaeological Contexts

In a classic example of how the push strategy worked, the immediate result at Drax Hall was that the able-bodied workers and their families left the estate to settle at new locations, such as the above-mentioned free village at The Priory, or at Sturge Town in the hills above St. Ann's Bay. Here, formerly enslaved individuals could eke out a living without being compelled to work on sugar plantations. The result of this strategy for Drax Hall is revealed in an archaeologically visible shift of housing toward the main road (perhaps a physical expression of a desire to be linked to the wider world beyond the plantation boundary) and the rapid abandonment of the village with the remaining households being relatively impoverished. This is not unexpected and at Drax Hall was compounded by the elimination of direct managerial surveillance of the village as the plantation managers moved their primary residence to the opposite side of the estate. Coupled with this move, management imposed a "push" strategy, charging relatively high rents and providing few improvements.

The record for Seville Plantation indicates a different path with management employing a combination of strategies including the charging of favorable rents and improvements, allowing the creation of a free settlement on former estate lands at The Priory, and expansion of the labor force via recruitment of indentured laborers from India.

Unlike at Drax Hall, where the slave village remained in the same location for over 150 years, the changing settlement pattern at Seville Estate during the slavery period helps tease out social changes in the years following emancipation. Because of this, it is necessary to outline the settlement changes. Documents, maps, oral history, and associated material culture establish a clear chronology for the Seville Plantation from the establishment of land patents by Richard Hemming in 1670 and the abandonment of the African village site in the late 1880s. Maps and plans of the estate dating to 1721 and 1791 establish the development of the property over the eighteenth century, including the construction sequence for the planter's residence (Great House) and two slave villages (Armstrong and Kelly 2000; Armstrong, this volume).

The 1721 map illustrates the location of the African Jamaican village to the south and east of the planter's residence in the area that we have defined as Locus 1, the early village. Historical documentation and archaeological evidence for Seville sets the range of occupation of Locus 1 from 1670 to its abandonment circa 1780 (the mean ceramic date for this locus is 1753.6).

The 1791 map of Seville defines a new location for the "negroe houses" of the African Jamaican slave settlement as well as a new planter's residence. The historical records do not define a date for the shift in village location, but it must have occurred prior to 1791 and corresponds with major changes in the structure of the planter's residence. The combined historical and archaeological records suggest that a major storm damaged both the planter's residence (which lost its second floor) and the village (which was destroyed) and that both were reconstructed at the same time. The planter's house was modified to its current one-story form and the village was relocated to the area that we have defined as Locus 2 (the later African Jamaican settlement). This location was the residence of enslaved workers and their families for the final half century or more prior to emancipation. Immediately following emancipation many former slaves moved to free holding parcels in a new community called The Priory, and a gradually decreasing number of tenants continued to occupy houses in the later village (Locus 2).

The lands that made up The Priory were part of what had once been the western edge of Seville Plantation. The land was distributed to former slaves by William Smith and his missionary society (Green 1976). According to Carpi Rose, who was born in one of the last houses in the later village between 1885 and 1890, the last houses in this settlement were abandoned circa 1890, or fully fifty years following emancipation (Carpi Rose, personal communication, 1981).

Using an analysis of ceramics, excavated houses of the later village can be subdivided into three temporal contexts (Figure 12.1). The first context includes two houses that were abandoned prior to emancipation; the second context includes six houses that span the period from the move (ca. 1780) to emancipation (1838); and the third chronological context consists of two houses that continued to be occupied as tenant and laborer households following emancipation. Furthermore, an additional post-emancipation house (House Area 14) was present in the area of the old village, and this was part of Kenneth Kelly's original (1989) study. It is in the location of these later houses that clues to post-emancipation life can be gleaned.

In his 1989 study, Kelly compared two houses dating to the post-emancipation period, one each from Drax Hall and Seville Estate, in an attempt to discern whether there were material consequences visible archaeologically that could be attributed to the different strategies of management. The hypothesis under which the study was conducted—that the tenants on Seville Estate would have had greater access to "luxury" goods as a result of access to increased discretionary income and more favorable living conditions than would generally be found on post-emancipation estates typified by Drax Hall—appeared to be borne out by the archaeological data. Kelly's study utilized a suite of then standard techniques such as ceramic scaling

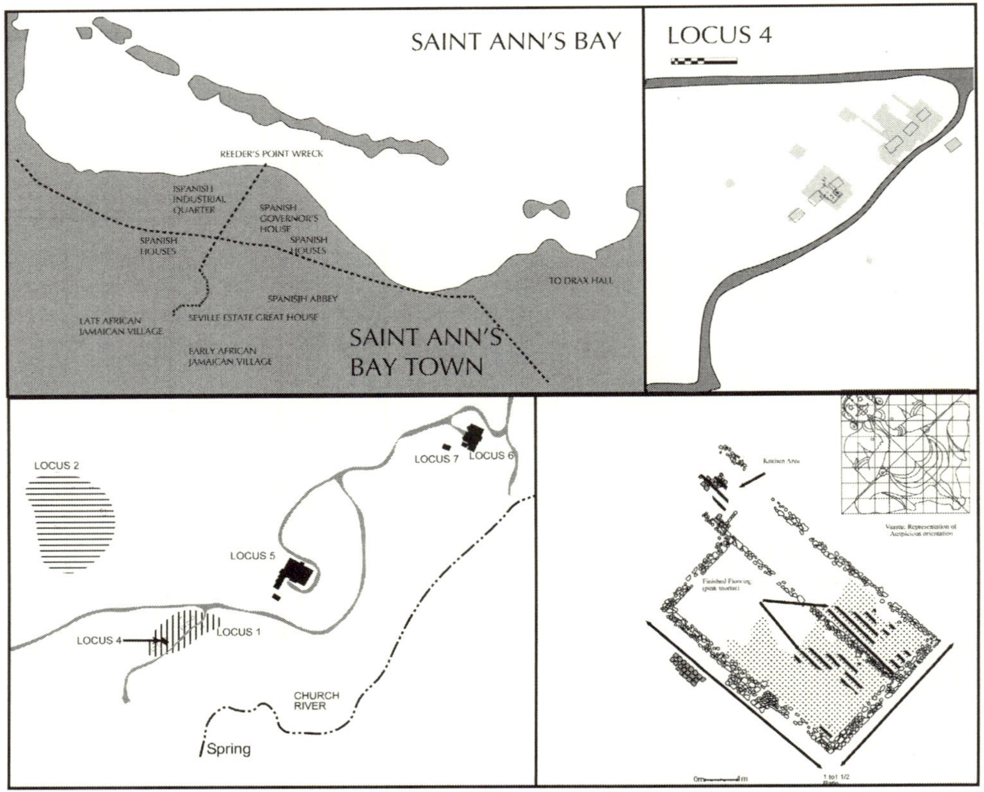

Figure 12.1. Post-emancipation site at Seville. *Clockwise from upper left:* map of English St. Ann's Bay showing location of Seville sites; plan view of the Indian laborer house (Locus 4) at Seville highlighting architectural similarities with a Vastu mandala; plan view of excavations at Seville; location of different estate settlement locations at Seville.

and ceramic indices (G. Miller 1980; Moore 1985) to evaluate a generalized socioeconomic rank or scale that could be used to differentiate the degree of economic comfort of the two houses. Although the results of the study indicated differences between the two houses, with the house at Seville Estate ranking higher on Miller's (1980) and Moore's (1985) indices (see Tables 12.1 and 12.2), it is important to note that although the results of the two analytical indices indicate differences, they are not great, and both indices indicate relative impoverishment for both households.

In addition to the results of the ceramic scaling analyses, the overall artifact assemblage and the architecture of the two houses also indicate significant differences. The overall quantities of artifacts at the two houses are significantly different, with the Seville house yielding 8,012 artifacts, over four times the number (1,777) at Drax Hall Feature 15. The differences in artifact assemblage size are not due to one household being larger, as the two house sites are similar in size (the Drax house is slightly larger than the Seville house). The houses are similar in terms of their appointments as well, with locks on doors, two or three rooms, and adjacent kitchen areas. Yet there the similarities end. Roughly more than two-fifths of the Seville house had a floor that was at one time finished with a coat of cement. This improvement would have required some capital outlay, in contrast to the more inexpensive (or free) flooring alternatives such as wood and marl, materials used to floor the Drax house. In the same vein, iron nails, while composing similar percentages of the architecture-related artifacts, were far more numerous at Seville, numbering 2,752 compared to 606 at Drax. When considering that Drax Feature 15 was a slightly larger house and that Seville House Area (HA) 14 had a cement floor in at least part of the building, this strongly suggests that HA 14 was shingled or board-sided, or both. Lastly, Seville HA 14 also yielded window glass fragments, suggesting glazed windows, whereas no window glass was recovered from the Drax Hall house. These three architectural options—flooring, shingles/siding, and glazed windows—all suggest that more money was spent on the construction and maintenance of the house at Seville. Whether the costs were borne directly by the residents or by the plantation management, the house was more substantial than its Drax Hall counterpart.

When considering household goods, the trends show that the Seville house had significantly greater quantities of material goods than were found at the Drax house. Imported ceramics are nearly six times more frequent at Seville, and aspects of the assemblage beyond the sheer numbers suggested a slightly higher status for the residents of the house. While no porcelains were found at either site, matching transfer-print patterns were noted in at least two instances at Seville. This contrasts with the lack of any pattern duplication among the Drax Hall assemblage, suggesting that the Seville residents were able to purchase either sets of dishes or at least several of the same pattern, while the Drax residents were unable to do so. Imported teaware as an indicator of status also reflects well upon the Seville house.

Table 12.1 Miller's Ceramic Scaling

CC	142 × 1 = 142	836 × 1 = 836
Minimal decoration	166 × 1.225 = 203.35	594 × 1.225 = 727.65
Hand-painted	n/a	n/a
Transfer-print	181 × 1.55 = 280.55	1,080 × 1.55 = 1,674
Total	625.9	3,237.65
Average CC-index value	1.24	1.29

Table 12.2 Moore's Ceramic Scaling

Decorative Class	Drax Hall Feature 15	Seville Estate House Area 14
1 (plain ware)		
N	142	836
%	27.4	32.2
2 (minimal decoration)		
N	166	594
%	32	22.9
3 (hand-painted)		
N	13	85
%	2.5	3.3
4 (transfer-printed)		
N	181	1,080
%	34.9	41.6
	1 × 142 = 142	1 × 836 = 836
	2 × 166 = 332	2 × 594 = 1,188
	3 × 13 = 39	3 × 85 = 255
	4 × 141 = 724	4 × 1,080 = 4,320
Total	1,237	6,599
Average	2.38	2.54

The Drax house yielded teaware at 2.7 percent of the identifiable ceramics, whereas the excavations at the Seville house recovered more than double that at 6.8 percent, indicating that the residents of Seville were conscious of participating in the status-associated tea ceremony or at least in its trappings. More coarse earthenwares were recovered at Drax Hall than at Seville. The bulk of the coarsewares were locally made yabba pots in forms that suggested that they served as lower-cost functional replacements of imported iron cooking pots and ceramic bowls. This is a further confirmation that the residents of the Drax house were under a greater degree of economic stress, requiring the substitution of lower-cost alternatives. Of course, research by Mark Hauser, Leland Ferguson, and others since the original study was completed has demonstrated that there are a host of factors that may govern the use of locally made earthenwares, only some of which are economic.

Glass artifacts, aside from the raw difference in numbers (n = 831 at Seville and n = 100 at Drax), tell the same story as the ceramics. The presence of drinking glassware at Seville and its absence at Drax reinforces the difference in status-conscious consumption seen in teaware. Certainly calabashes and mugs can serve in place of drinking or teaware, but they do not convey the same expression of status-oriented consumption. Additionally, the residents of Seville had the need, desire, and ability to purchase manufactured medicines, as indicated by the presence of pharmaceutical glassware. The remaining group of glass artifacts includes wine and case bottles, of which the Drax house yielded 55 case bottle fragments. In contrast, the Seville Estate house had 513 wine bottle fragments, as well as 35 case bottle pieces. Clearly the occupants of this house had a greater number of bottles, and it is quite likely that they were purchased originally for their contents, probably alcoholic beverages. This indicates yet another outlet for discretionary income at Seville HA 14 that was not being exploited at Drax Hall.

Clothing-related items also show a difference between the two sites. At Seville, 106 buttons were recovered from HA 14, as were 25 beads, whereas at Drax 24 buttons and four beads were recovered. The high frequency of buttons at Seville may be associated with several things, including more cash resources to purchase buttons for personal use or the possibility that tailoring was undertaken on the site, which would be an economic option that would fit within the more "enlightened" management strategy at Seville.

Lest the impression be conveyed that the residents of Seville had an "easy" life, the tools and food remains found at both sites indicate frugality. The tools recovered from Seville and Drax Hall were all broken, fragmentary, and worn out, indicating that every last bit of use was extracted from them prior to discard. Likewise, the food remains from both sites indicate an opportunistic attempt to maximize free resources. In his analysis of the mollusk shells from Drax Hall, Armstrong (1991a) has said that these remains suggest that diversification in species collected following emancipation is indicative of increased nutritional stress after the discontinuation of food supplements, especially protein, at the end of the apprenticeship period (1838). That this diversification occurred at both Drax Hall Feature 15 and Seville Estate HA 14 serves to remind us that food resources that could be obtained for low or no cost remained attractive and that these houses must be seen within the context of continued poverty.

To summarize, the specifics of the artifact assemblages from Drax Hall Feature

15 and Seville Estate HA 14 appeared to uphold the hypothesis that archaeological evidence can help identify variations in material assemblages that are the result of differences in plantation management practices. The differences between the two houses can be explained as resulting from the influences of divergent management strategies upon the individuals who remained resident on the plantations, allowing the residents of Seville Estate a somewhat less trying existence.

In the past decade, work by Armstrong and Hauser (2004) reinvestigated the material culture originating from Seville Estate HA 14. These remains, also referred to as Locus 4 in their 2004 study, were distinctive in size, construction, and associated artifacts when compared to other late-period houses. Particularly notable was the isolation of the house away from the other late-slavery and post-emancipation houses. It was this isolation that led Armstrong and Hauser to designate HA 14 as Locus 4. Relying on an obscure claim in a tape-recorded oral history, along with the historical research of Verene Shepherd (Shepherd 1985, 1986, 1988b, 1993, 1995), Armstrong and Hauser suggest that this structure was very possibly occupied by an East Indian household. Their research uses the data set from this locus to explain the distinctive archaeological characteristics of this structure initially identified by Kelly.

The East Indian Diaspora

Between 1844 and 1917, 36,400 Indians immigrated to Jamaica from East India Company holdings in Bengal and Madras (G. Roberts 1956:128). The population that immigrated to Jamaica represented 8.4 percent of the nearly 500,000 East Indians who migrated to the Caribbean in this era. While the East Indian population represents a small minority within the total population of Jamaica, in the parishes of St. Elizabeth and Clarendon they comprise a significant minority.

Planters in Jamaica attempted to regain control over labor by hiring former slaves and importing labor from Africa and India (M. Thomas 1974:101). Given an inability to attract the necessary numbers of contract wage laborers from Africa, planters looked to India for a labor supply (M. Thomas 1974:101–2). In anticipation of continued labor needs orders were placed for an additional 8,000 East Indian laborers in 1845 (M. Thomas 1974:101; Darling 1845:68). But applications for importation declined rapidly. Planters, apparently reluctant to invest capital to pay importation taxes and apprehensive about new sugar duties, submitted only a little more that 1,200 applications for East Indian laborers in 1846; in November 1846, the assembly acted quickly to halt embarkation from India (Darling 1846; vote of the assembly, 1846–47:27). The continued labor shortage precipitated the Immigration Act of 1858, which reopened the importation of contract labor from India. Large numbers of East Indians were brought to Jamaica in the years between 1860 and 1863. At this time small numbers of laborers were also brought from Africa and China (M. Thomas 1974:189, 190).

Verene Shepherd argues that much of the modern conflict between peoples of Indian and African descent in Jamaica, while predicated on constructs of ethnicity and race, is based on class differences that arose in the post-emancipation period. During this time, planters employed indentured labor as a means to supplement their dwindling labor supply and to keep wages low for former slaves. The planters took advantage of the ensuing antagonism between laborers from India and Africa to retain control over labor (Shepherd 1988b:90). Within this context, East Indian manners of speech were chided by Africans, while Indians espoused racial superiority over Africans. It was not, however, until the postwar depression that this antagonism escalated into violent conflict. This eventually fed into nationalist concerns in the 1940s and 1950s when the task of defining a Jamaican was undertaken (Shepherd 1988b:109). In the end, Indians were considered aliens in the period of nation building in the late 1950s and 1960s.

The Material Analysis of an East Indian Household

All of the laborer contexts at Seville (before and after emancipation) shared a pattern of material use that was dominated by basic subsistence, as indicted by a very high percentage of food-related items in comparison to all loci with managerial contexts (planter, overseer, mid-level manager; see Figure 12.1). However, when one looks more closely at the material record one can find very distinct patterns of material use that reflect differences between the East Indians and their fellow laborers (from Africa) or managers (from Europe). For example, when looking at personal items such as those linked to clothing, adornment, health, and hygiene, the relative proportions of items found are distinctly different. These differences reflect ethnic preferences based on heritage rather than simply economic or class conditions (Figure 12.1). The East Indians at Seville had a broader array of items used to fasten and enhance their clothing, including brass tassels and adornments like beads. While beads were also found in the African contexts, items of personal adornment were nearly absent in the European, managerial contexts. Finally, while the Europeans and Africans had similar proportions of health- and hygiene-related items (pharmaceutical bottles, combs, toothbrushes), very few recognizable items from this category were found for the East Indian context. This suggests distinct strategies of health and hygiene, which would be consistent with Indians using indigenous medical systems such as Ayurveda.

The second set of distinguishing characteristics relates to the layout and construction of the house. One cannot ignore the fact that the East Indian house was built in isolation from the African laborers (Figure 12.1). This is indicative of a recognized difference between laboring groups. In terms of construction, the East Indian house was quite distinctive in layout and design. The basic orientation of the house was 90 degrees different than the houses that had previously been constructed as part of the African village (Figure 12.1). The East Indian house was nearly twice the size of the average African house and had defined internal divisions. While the African houses had flooring of marl or wood, the East Indians used pink-colored mortar in the main living areas and brick in their cooking area. The cooking area was a formal room attached to the house, while Africans cooked over detached yard hearths. Unlike the African kitchen yards where faunal remains are replete in the archaeological record, the East Indian house had a brick floor with no refuse. This is consistent with Indian kitchens in many parts of rural northern India where the kitchen is floored with cow dung (considered a holy and antiseptic substance) and kept scrupulously clean (Wadley 2000).

The layout of the East Indian house loosely conforms to practices of architecture found in areas of South Asia. While the East Indians that came to Jamaica originated from widely divergent areas of South Asia, there are some potential religious themes that crosscut these populations. One of these is the way in which space is organized and employed in the construction of residences. This system, known as Vastu, arises from cosmology derived from Sanskrit texts employed in Hinduism. Vastu employs a mandala (Annanth 1998:82) or a geometric representation of the cosmos (Figure 12.1), in which a god is superimposed over a geometric surface. Through this mandala certain orientations and proportions of the house are preferred (e.g., 1:1¼; 1:1½; 1:1¾; 1:2) (Annanth 1998:130–31). The ground plan of the East Indian house is in the proportion 1:1½, a proportion that would be considered highly auspicious (Figure 12.1). Second, we can locate the kitchen in the northwest corner. According to Vastu, this location is thought to dissipate the power of the wind. The northwest corner is also the home of the gods, and in some populations the kitchen is the home of the household deity. The location of the spring, which supplied the water to the house, was northeast of the structure. This again is consistent with Vastu where Isana is located in the northeast corner of the mandala.

In reassessing this distinctive laborer house site at Seville, this study brings to light the presence of East Indians within the Jamaican plantation context. The data show that as laborers the East Indians shared certain commonalities of economic condition and class structure with their African counterparts. However, these data indicate very distinct preferences and practices derived from cultural traditions that were expressed in this particular household. Clearly, there were divisions among laborers in the post-emancipation era in Jamaica. The East Indians' household was constructed separate and different from those of their African counterparts and reflects distinct patterns of material use and construction. These differences can be tied to preferences related to South Asian and African cultural practices. Given these differences and the reasons for the arrivals of the South Asians within the post-emancipation setting, it is not surprising that these new arrivals were viewed with suspicion and contempt by their African counterparts.

Including the East Indian household into a landscape of post-emancipation St. Ann's Bay complicates our understanding of this period of transition. The contrast between the push and pull consequences of post-emancipation management is enlightening, but Kelly's initial focus on management strategies overlooked another consequence of the post-slavery era—the massive importation of "non-traditional" labor to address the labor shortages arising from the pull of an alternative existence. What Seville shows us is that neither strategy was enacted exclusively. Even at Seville Estate, cited by contemporaries and parliament for its progressive labor management, "enlightened" plantation managers could not keep a sufficient number of laborers on hand and thus imported indentured laborers as a way of maintaining the appearance of freedom in the absence of choice.

Conclusion

The potential of formerly enslaved individuals to successfully make the transition to a form of peasantry has been discussed in important work by Jean Besson, Sidney Mintz, Hall, and others (Besson 2002; Hall 1959; Mintz [1974] 1992; Mintz and Price 1992). John Candler, in reference to the Seville district of St. Ann during the 1840s remarked on the success of market gardening: "[A]lmost all the laborers have provision grounds of almost an acre; . . . [and] if the produce be all sold, will clear to each of these £20 per annum, currency" (Hall 1959:172). In this economic setting, wage work was only required to earn extra money for particular purchases, and "once their consumer goals were satisfied, they retired from estate work until a new demand for income arose" (Green 1976:194). Hence, ironically, prior to emancipation, enslaved laborers had long-established mechanisms of production and both access to and the means to acquire goods. After emancipation conditions changed and there was considerable variation with respect to social and economic conditions based on the "push or pull" strategies of the estate and the ability of individuals to acquire property in the form of lands for both living and provisioning. Former enslaved laborers at Drax Hall and Seville provide a glimpse of the contrast in and implications of these strategies. However, for the island as a whole, former enslaved laborers remained caught in the social and economic web of servitude, repressive wage labor, and an inability to gain access to land and resources (see Armstrong 2010).

Epilogue

Explorations in Jamaican Historical Archaeology

Douglas V. Armstrong

In May 2007, the World Archaeological Congress hosted an intercongressional seminar in Kingston, Jamaica. The meeting revolved around two themes: historical archaeology in Jamaica and archaeological resource protection measures.[1] Jamaica has a long record of engagement in both areas through its heritage preservation legislation and attention paid to the examination of its historical and archaeological legacies. The nation's motto, "Out of Many, One People," expresses a longstanding interest in understanding the diverse heritage of its population, an interest expressed in the deep commitment Jamaicans have to understanding and preserving the rich diversity of the island nation's heritage. For many years, the people of Jamaica and their government have recognized that a significant part of their heritage exists through archaeological remains, and they have been diligent about preserving and interpreting both pre-Columbian and colonial period sites on the island. Each of the authors in this volume has had the privilege of working with the Jamaican people to better understand the complex legacies of those later colonial sites.

The historical landscape of Jamaica, like that of the Caribbean as a whole, integrates global trends with localized cultural expressions. Over the past three decades, examination of local historical archaeology in Jamaica has provided much insight into a wide range of broader colonial processes, reflecting the global landscape of colonial expansion, globalized trade, and the construction of social relations built upon systems of inequality. Various research programs have explored the intersections of contact-period native Caribbean (Taino) people with a variety of European and African migrants, the repressive labor system that used enslaved laborers from Africa and indentured laborers from Asia, the development of local and globalized trade, and the development of local cultures and economies, to name just a few of the topics tackled by historical archaeologists on the island.

However, the historical and archaeological record should not be seen as passive phenomena. The study of the dynamic heritage of Jamaica also considers how the island's people have had the resolve to develop creative solutions to transcend the legacies of colonialism and to create a nation that challenges the systems of inequality it has inherited while simultaneously embracing the diversity of its past. Historical archaeology has played a significant role in the development of Jamaica's deep historical consciousness.

When I arrived in Jamaica in the early 1980s I was impressed by the multilateral resolve to have the story of the people documented and incorporated into daily life. Although the 1980s were marked by political turmoil and economic hardship, all parties agreed on the importance of moving Jamaica's heritage forward. Archaeological reconnaissance of Jamaica's past was a point of common agreement that persisted through economic difficulty and political tension. Despite the vagaries of political change and economic trouble, the Jamaica National Heritage Trust (JNHT) has continued to carry forward a rich tradition of scholarly and scientific research aimed at serving the Jamaican public.[2] This is a tradition of which the Jamaican people are rightly proud.

Jamaican people are deeply aware of the important role their ancestors played in shaping the modern world. Although Jamaica is a small country, the historical archaeology of the island reflects global phenomena that have impacted the entire Caribbean region. While the history of Jamaica has been shaped by broader regional and global interactions, the island has its own unique mosaic of cultural expressions tied to the specifics of its colonial past. Temporal relationships, trading alliances, and local conditions combined to create distinctive sets of material remains and archaeological ruins.[3] As Mark Hauser and I have noted elsewhere for the Caribbean region as a whole, historical archaeology in Jamaica has been pursued from a "wide range of theoretical perspectives and thematic interests, but the composite results highlight the importance of understanding the interconnected nature of social relations from multiple scales of analysis" (Armstrong and Hauser 2009:583).

Historical archaeology has a long and rich history on the island of Jamaica. This volume presents a sampling of the last several decades of historical archaeological work on Jamaica; while representing much of the best recent work, the contributors to this volume owe many debts to the archaeologists that came before them. In this epilogue, I seek to contextualize the contributions presented in this volume through a review of the history of archaeology on Jamaica.

Natural, Native, and Colonial Histories

As early as 1687 the ruins of historic settlements in Jamaica were observed by British naturalist Hans Sloane. Sloane was the author of a historically significant treatise, usually referred to as the *Natural History of Jamaica,* which was published in two volumes appearing in 1707 and 1725. In his *Natural History* Sloane painstakingly documented the flora and fauna of Jamaica and several other Caribbean islands.[4] In addition, Sloane made detailed observations of historic sites in Jamaica, including the ruins of the old Spanish-period Catholic church at Seville la Nueva on Jamaica's north coast. Sloane also provided descriptive detail on an unusual earthwork structure in front of the planter's house at Seville Estate—this unusual trench was cut parallel to the hill in the yard in front of the house. Sloane describes it as designed to defend the estate from possible Spanish attack (1707–25; Armstrong and Kelly 2000). It is interesting that even at this early date, the Spanish period was considered an intriguing unknown even though Sloane's observations were made only half a century after the displacement of the Spanish from Jamaica.

The shift from observation and description to formal excavation of historic sites corresponds with the nineteenth-century emergence of local scientific institutions on the island. A scientific museum, the Natural History Museum of the Jamaica Society, modeled after the British Museum, was founded in 1830. This institution and its collections were later merged with several other scientific organizations to become the Institute of Jamaica (founded in 1879). The Institute of Jamaica sponsored a broad program of scientific inquiry related to "natural history"; its early works included publications documenting archaeological sites dating to both prehistoric and historic contexts (Cundall 1915).

Much of the early interest in archaeology in Jamaica, as for the Caribbean as a whole, was focused on the island's indigenous pre-contact population. However, by the mid-nineteenth century the economic and social condition of the region was in flux; many of the Caribbean's sugar, coffee, cotton, and indigo estates, as well as some of the early military fortifications, fell into disrepair. These ruins and their earlier Spanish counterparts began to be romantically recalled, as exemplified by the descriptive account of Fort James made in 1859 by Jeremiah D. Murphy, a Royal Navy helmet diver who went underwater to examine the ruined military site (Mayes 1972:9).

In the late nineteenth century there were a series of archaeological reports, by both Jamaicans and overseas visitors, on materials recovered from prehistoric sites; much of the data was collected on weekend reconnaissance trips across the island (Blake 1895; Cundall 1895; Duerden 1897; MacCormack 1898; Longley 1914). Descriptive and speculative in nature, many of these initial reports were published with the encouragement of Frank Cundall, the director of the Institute of Jamaica, and appeared in local scientific journals such as the *Journal of the Institute of Jamaica.* The early twentieth century also saw the first of a series of professional archaeologists visit Jamaica as part of an effort to better understand the prehistory of the circum-Caribbean region. As early as 1913, as part of a series of articles on the Caribbean region, Theodore DeBooy published "Certain Kitchen Middens in Jamaica" in *American Anthropologist.* Despite reports by visiting archaeologists like DeBooy, it was Cundall and the Institute of Jamaica that conducted the majority of the early research into prehistoric and historic sites in Jamaica.

The 1879 creation of a local scientific institution, the Institute of Jamaica, reflected two important social trends. First, there was a growing interest in local historical study. Second, by conducting research on local material, Jamaican-born scientists shifted the interpretation of local historic sites away from metropolitan specialists housed in distant, imperial museums and universities. In late nineteenth-century Jamaica, as for much of the region, external economic interests were waning, the sugar and coffee industries had declined following the abolition of slavery, and the large-scale cultural and political infrastructures of colonialism, manifested in such things as forts and plantations, were giving way to new social and economic structures. Many of the old forts, sites that had once been used as land bases for European sea powers, were abandoned. The economic infrastructure for plantation-based agro-industry was in rapid decay, leaving a landscape filled with abandoned buildings that had once been integral components of the island's economic infrastructure. One response made by the local population was to document the monumental effects of the fading colonial regime (Cundall 1900; Cundall and Pietersz 1919). For example, in the early 1900s Governor Sir Sidney Oliver charged Frank Cundall with preparing a "list of historic sites, buildings, and monuments for each parish."[5]

As the methods of archaeology matured in the first half of the twentieth century, prehistorians using the direct historical approach made explicit use of contact sites to define the boundaries of Jamaica's prehistory. They used the archaeological record of Jamaica's contact-period past as a staging ground to frame discussions of deeper, earlier deposits representing otherwise unknown prehistoric ways of life. At the same time both avocational and professional archaeologists in Jamaica began documenting monuments dating to the colonial era, including Charles Cotter in his seminal work on the Spanish site of Seville la Nueva (1946, 1948). Cotter's work to excavate and document the site of the first Spanish capital of Jamaica began in 1937 with the serendipitous discovery of a series of early fifteenth-century structures and related monumental architectural elements including marble carvings associated with the early Spanish settlement (Cotter 1948, 1953, 1964, 1970; Cundall 1915; W. Goodwin 1946; Osborne 1974; Smith et al. 1982; Woodward 1988, 2006a). Cotter's excavations at Seville la Nueva mark the beginning of historical archaeology in Jamaica.

Cotter's work encouraged a flurry of interest in Spanish-era sites that included an effort to find two of Christopher Columbus's ships historically known to have been beached on Jamaica's north coast. Columbus had long been an interest of avocational and professional archaeologists in Jamaica. Like Cotter, William B. Goodwin undertook explorations on an array of reported "Spanish" sites; his work on historic sites began in 1915 and lasted at least until 1938 (W. Goodwin 1940, 1946); Spanish sites were a frequent topic of Frank Cundall's writing. Efforts at addressing early Spanish settlement in the region included investigations by Goodwin, who drew a series of plans of his surveys and excavations in Jamaica and noted an ongoing friendly debate he had with Cundall as to whether various sites should be attributed to the Spanish or English (W. Goodwin 1946:10). Goodwin proposed that many ruins, including sites found at Seville, Annotto Bay, and Drax Hall, were associated with Spanish-era settlements.

In 1946 Goodwin reported on his efforts to locate the Columbus caravels. He had conducted archaeological investigations at several historic sites, including an extensive excavation of Don Christopher Cove at Drax Hall Plantation, in his effort to locate the two ships known to have run aground on Jamaica in 1503. Despite the excavation of 150 test holes and the dredging of Don Christopher Cove with heavy machinery, no evidence of Columbus's ships was recovered (W. Goodwin 1946).[6] Samuel Eliot Morison, the famous biographer of Columbus, was in communication with Cotter and Goodwin and was influenced by the archaeological work they had conducted. Morison, in a sailing expedition sponsored by Harvard University, retraced Columbus's route to nearby St. Ann's Bay (Morison 1942; R. Smith 1987, 1990; Parrent and Parrent 1993). Morison's descriptive account of his expedition was awarded the Pulitzer Prize.[7]

Jamaican interest in historical sites was not limited to the Spanish colonial era. Following World War II, a local organization, the Jamaica Historical Society, garnered support from the British Council to prepare a report, descriptively titled "Buildings of Architectural or Historic Interest in the British West Indies." The resulting volume, published in 1951, included "draft legislation for the preservation of the National Buildings of Jamaica."[8] In 1958, as Jamaicans prepared themselves for independent nationhood (attained in 1962), the Jamaica National Trust Commission was chartered under Law No. 72 of 1958 (referred to as the National Trust Law). This law established the Jamaica National Trust, mandated an annual budget for the trust, and provided for the acquisition of properties to be held by the trust. Many of the properties on the initial list were forts and structures associated with the British colonial era.

Throughout the 1950s, 1960s, and 1970s, monumental historic properties like forts, estate works, and planter residences continued to be documented by historians, sometimes with the assistance of archaeologists. However, the real interest among archaeologists remained with defining the complex prehistory of the Caribbean region, which is characterized by insular variation over time and diversity in the material record among and between affiliated groups and islands. While this great regional diversity is infamously difficult to fathom, the complexity of Caribbean prehistory has set a precedent for understanding the subsequent complexity and variability of the colonial and later historic periods. With even a cursory understanding of the diversity of the region, the complexity of ethnic and social relations, and the distinctive differences in the historical trajectories of each colonial domain and local polity, historical archaeologists rather uniformly found distinctive differences in the material and cultural records from island to island and from colonial domain to colonial domain.

The use of archaeology as a means of understanding the historic past has followed a path rather typical of such investigations throughout the Americas. Archaeology began as a means to understand and interpret the prehistoric contexts of native peoples; archaeology of early historic sites and protohistoric contexts was used as a starting point for the study of more ancient prehistoric peoples (Rouse 1939, 1992; see summary discussion in Keegan 1994). While the focus of early archaeology was on prehistory, scholars viewed interpretation of the ethnohistory of the contact period to be essential to the interpretation of pre-conquest peoples (DeBooy 1919; Rainey 1940; Rouse 1939, 1964, 1986; see overviews in Keegan 1992, 1994, 1996, 2000; Rouse 1992; Wilson 1990; Siegel 2005).

In the postwar era, archaeologists studying Jamaica's prehistory tried to understand the prehistoric indigenous population "in relation to Circum-Caribbean Culture" (Howard 1950). From the 1950s through 1960s a series of studies were carried out to define chronological sequences, define culture history, and explain the culture of the indigenous Taino and their predecessors (Howard 1950, 1956, 1965; Vanderwal 1965, 1967). By the early 1970s, prehistoric archaeologists had encountered and were dealing with the extraordinary cultural complexity of the region; data projected sometimes mind-boggling cultural variation from island to island, belying early efforts made by culture historians and processual archaeologists to normalize and generalize broad cultural traditions for the region (Keegan 1996, 2000). The recognition that the Caribbean's prehistory was characterized by complex cultural variation over a small geographic area provided important insight to interpretations of the later cultural complexity examined by historical archaeologists in Jamaica. Interest in the complexity of Jamaica's archaeological heritage inspired a group of Jamaicans to form the Archaeological Society of Jamaica in 1965. This group began with an avocational interest in prehistoric sites but later, as membership and interest grew, expanded to include historical archaeology as a focus and professional archaeologists as members.[9]

Early themes in Jamaican archaeology, from the nineteenth century through the 1960s, reflected interests in understanding the region's complex prehistory, its early proto-historic period, and the monuments of Spanish and British colonial settlement. In Jamaica, there was a particular fascination with its early Spanish period, the seventeenth-century port town of Port Royal, much of which was destroyed by a strong earthquake in 1692, the ruins of planter Great Houses, and colonial forts. It was only later, with the move toward independence and nation building, that the island's historical archaeological focus shifted away from sites associated with famous or wealthy European colonists to the broader study of historical sites associated with all Jamaicans. In the 1970s and 1980s, attention shifted to the more problematic complexities of the history of the island. With independence came increased scholarly attention to the history of the working class. Historians and archaeologists began to explore the many contributions made to the island's heritage by Africans, East Indians, and Chinese, among others. This shift in focus away from the grand to the everyday coincides with the development of the JNHT as the steward of the island's material heritage. In 1985, the Jamaica National Trust Commission was replaced by the JNHT, whose expanded mandate aimed at preserving and protecting a much wider range of cultural resources in Jamaica than had been envisioned by the original Jamaica National Trust (Jamaica National Heritage Trust Act of 1985). At that time the Archaeological Division of the Institute of Jamaica was moved to the JNHT. The transfer of this division marked a shift in the trust's mandate from caretaker of monuments to active agent in archaeology and preservation efforts across the island. The JNHT remains the steward of Jamaica's rich archaeological resources into the twenty-first century.

One of the first projects undertaken by the newly organized JNHT was the interpretation and preservation of Seville Estate, located near the town of St. Ann's Bay on Jamaica's north coast. The initial protection of the complex of sites at Seville projects the developing interest in protecting sites associated with the island's colonial and prehistoric heritage. The site was initially acquired by the trust to commemorate and preserve the planter's residence and the industrial works of the British-era sugar estate. But more decisively, the site was also acquired to protect the ruins of the early Spanish settlement that was discovered decades earlier by Charles Cotter.

Historical Archaeology Jump-started by the Underwater Revolution

One cannot underestimate the importance of archaeological studies at Port Royal in the development of historical archaeology in Jamaica and in the Caribbean region. While for much of the Americas historical archaeology was a rather ancillary pursuit until the 1970s, in Jamaica historic sites archaeology was jump-started by an early recognition of the potential that SCUBA technology had to the recovery of data from "the sunken city of sin," Port Royal. Beginning with detailed studies in the late 1950s, archaeological studies at Port Royal represent a significant exception to the general trend of that era's focus on prehistory and colonial forts and monumental architecture. The development of SCUBA diving and dramatic changes in the ability to recover material from submerged sites led scholars to begin a series of detailed archaeological investigations of the seventeenth-century ruins of Port Royal. The first wave of these studies began in the late 1950s and lasted through the mid-1970s. Excavators included Edward Link (1960); Robert Marx (1967, 1968a, 1968b, 1968c, 1973, 1979); Philip Mayes (1969–70); and Anthony Priddy (1975). Additional work was conducted in the early 1990s by Donny Hamilton of Texas A&M University and the Institute of Nautical Archaeology (INA). Underwater archaeology allowed access to areas that had been unattainable for archaeologists, and Port Royal provided an excellent venue to utilize this new technology.

Port Royal was well documented as a site that had been catastrophically destroyed and partially submerged by an earthquake in 1692. The first formal report of underwater research at Port Royal was by Marian C. Link in a very visual and popular article published in *National Geographic* (Link 1960). This initial study was followed by a nearly continuous string of archaeological studies from 1960 through the early 1990s carried out under the auspices of the JNHT. The most extensive excavations in terms of pure volume were carried out by Robert Marx (1967, 1968a, 1968b, 1973) using dredging techniques that were by today's standards extremely crude and brutal to the site. Noteworthy among the contributions of more refined studies of the site (on land and in the water) are the work of Philip Mayes (1972; Mayes and Mayes 1972) and teams of scholars from Texas A&M's INA, under the direction of Donny Hamilton.

In addition to presenting a very well-illustrated account of his excavations and the material recovered from Port Royal, Philip Mayes clearly defined locally made coarse earthenware, correctly attributed to potters of African descent who were producing wares for the domestic markets of Jamaica (Mayes 1970, 1972; Mayes and Mayes 1972). His investigation provided a baseline for the study of material culture associated with pottery production, marketing, distribution, and use on the island that has been a significant part of archaeological studies of the African diaspora in Jamaica and the broader Caribbean ever since (see Hauser 2001, 2008).

The studies by Hamilton and his students represent an important shift in methodological and technical expertise with resulting reports providing some of the most refined details in material and spatial analysis for the region (Hamilton 1986, 1988, 2006; Hamilton and Woodward 1984). Reports and publications from the INA studies resulted in details on material use and social interaction in this important eighteenth-century port town (M. Brown 1996; Darrington 1994; H. C. DeWolf 1998; Franklin 1992; Fox 1998; Gotelipe-Miller 1990; Hailey 1994; Heidtke 1992; McClenaghan 1988; C. Smith 1995; Trussel 2004; see also Downing and Harris 1982 for underwater studies of Bermuda, and Leshikar-Denton 1991 for studies of the Cayman Islands). The INA projects have the distinction of resulting not only in a series of detailed reports but also in their wide dissemination via well-maintained Web links such as nautarch.tamu.edu/portroyal/. This Web site is important as it presents both summary and detailed information relating to decades of research that has been made available to all, including those residing within the region.

The findings from Port Royal represent a wealth of information on an important seventeenth-century English colonial settlement; unfortunately, these findings have not been thoroughly incorporated into studies from other regions, particularly North America. As Hamilton points out, the "underwater excavations from Port Royal have resulted in remarkable parallels and even more interesting contrasts with contemporaneous English colonists in North America" (nautarch.tamu.edu/portroyal/PRhist.htm). This observation holds true not only for the Port Royal study but more generally for historical archaeology studies conducted throughout the Caribbean region. Given the Caribbean's historic placement as an intersection for global interaction, archaeological investigations from the Caribbean have shed light on the complexity of cultural interactions and material use over the past five hundred years. It is one goal of this volume to make the historical archaeological community more thoroughly aware of the need to incorporate Caribbean material into comparative studies of the material dimensions of the New World colonial experience.

Plantations and the Study of Slavery and Its Consequences

The initial studies of locally produced earthenware that were completed as part of more broadly defined studies of the colonial period at Port Royal and another excavation at the Old King's House in Spanish Town (Mayes 1970, 1972; Mathewson 1971, 1972a, 1972b, 1973) led to the realization that archaeology could provide significant information on the history of Jamaica's majority African-descent population. Coarse earthenwares recovered from these sites have continued to be studied and their analysis refined by Roderick Ebanks and Mark Hauser (Hauser 2008). Inspired by the insights developed by Mayes and Mathewson in the 1970s, archaeologists soon turned to the heritage of the African-descent community in Jamaica. The cultural landscapes represented by plantations quickly emerged as a significant focal point for Caribbean research. As early as the 1970s, geographer and historian Barry Higman organized excavations at the well-documented ruins at Montpelier Estate (Riordan 1973; Higman 1974, 1975, 1976, 1998).

In 1980, the Institute of Jamaica actively pursued technical assistance in carrying out investigations of African sites in Jamaica. Since archaeological studies had so clearly defined sets of materials made by persons of African descent in the urban contexts of Port Royal and the Old King's House, there was interest in using archaeology to explore issues pertaining to the African diaspora in plantation contexts. The ancestors of the majority of modern Jamaicans were brought to the island as enslaved laborers and lived and worked in plantation settings associated with the production of sugar or coffee. In 1978, Merrick Posnansky visited the island to determine the viability of plantation archaeology projects but had commitments for research in Ghana. Rather than initiate investigations himself, he sent a graduate student to carry out research on the topic; it was through Posnansky's interest in Jamaica that I became involved in the historical archaeological investigation of the African experience in Jamaica (Posnansky 1983). I began my study working with Anthony Aarons (Institute of Jamaica) and Roderick Ebanks (then at the African Caribbean Institute of Jamaica, a division of the Institute of Jamaica). The study began in the archives and took advantage of the extensive collection of maps and plantation documents at the National Library of the Institute of Jamaica. I examined a series of historical maps of the island that identified plantations and the type of processing system used for each estate (Armstrong 1981). As a result of this initial archival survey, a long list of estates was narrowed to seven that had extensive documentary records and were occupied throughout the period of plantation slavery. These seven sites were surveyed to identify the best location for initial archaeological exploration. Enslaved laborer settlement areas were found at all seven sites, but I determined that Drax Hall and Seville Estate retained the most intact and undisturbed residential areas (Armstrong 1983a, 1985, 1990).

My initial survey of Drax Hall was typical of the other sites surveyed. Placements of structures identified on historic maps were plotted on a topographic map and we simply walked right to the site, first finding the ruins of the planter's residence, then moving up the hill to the ruins of houses that had been used by the enslaved laborers beginning in the seventeenth century (Armstrong 1983b).[10] An important element of the Drax study related to our expectations for data recovery. Expectations for material evidence included not only the presence of definitive African Jamaican–produced wares but also the utilization of significant numbers of imported wares made in Europe. The Drax study utilized a model that explored elements of continuity within systems of change, or a model of transformation, rather than cultural replacement. The archaeological investigation of Drax Hall Plantation examined both enslaved laborer and planter/manager living contexts and focused on the bilateral expressions of continuity and change within African and European lifeways recovered from laborer housing and the planter's residence (Armstrong 1990). Material use patterns were shown to reflect aspects of continuity linked to each group's respective heritage as well as in situ, locally defined changes based on social interactions and changing patterns of materials available, through time, within a transforming Jamaican society.

The Drax Hall Plantation study also explored changing patterns in the use of the plantation landscape associated with the location of the housing of both planter and worker during slavery and after emancipation (Armstrong 1991a, 1991b, 1991c: 56). At the time the Drax study was carried out I was in communication with Barry Higman and had an understanding of the materials that had been recovered from the Montpelier site (see Higman 1998). I was particularly impressed by the depth of Higman's historiographic expertise and the potential to integrate archival research into the interpretation of the archaeological record. Hence the Drax Hall study made extensive use of the rich archival record for the island as well as the archaeological materials recovered from the site. This was particularly useful in documenting changing land use over time on the estate and in the detailed study of diet. The Drax Hall dietary study used extensive lists of dietary provisions found in the estate's accounts; I used these records to explain a shift in the faunal assemblage after emancipation, when such provisions were no longer provided by the estate (Armstrong 1990; Reitz 1990). These data provided strong evidence for dietary hardships for the newly "freed" African Jamaican laborers on the estate.

An important element of the Drax Hall Plantation study was a field training school that was carried out in 1983. This field school was funded by the government of Jamaica and brought together twenty-five students and employees of the University of the West Indies (UWI) and the JNHT as well as archaeologists from the University of California at Los Angeles. I co-directed the field program with Kofi Agorsah. It was the first formal field training school organized for Jamaicans and was carried out at a critical time as UWI was in the process of deciding whether to fund an archaeological program. Student participants included individuals who would become leaders in their field, including Verene Shepherd (professor and former chair of the History and Archaeology Department at UWI, Jamaica, former chair of the JNHT board, and current president of the Association of Caribbean Historians), Basil Reid (senior lecturer in archaeology at UWI, Trinidad), and Dorrick Gray (technical director of archaeology, JNHT). Moreover, the project introduced Kofi Agorsah to Jamaica. He returned to Jamaica as the first lecturer in archaeology at UWI in Mona and has remained active in research in Jamaica.[11]

By the late 1980s archaeological explorations of plantation and broader diasporan contexts had increased dramatically in both scale and scope. I followed up the Drax Hall project with excavations at Seville and have continued to publish on Jamaican houseyards (1991b, 1991c, 1992, 1998, 1999; Armstrong and Kelly 2000). While initially focused on two temporally and spatially discrete African Jamaican laborer contexts, the archaeological investigation at Seville was expanded to contrast the finds from laborer contexts with those from three levels of plantation management (1998), shifts in utilization of the plantation landscape (Armstrong and Kelly 2000), houseyard burial practices (Armstrong and Fleischman 2003), and the material expressions of East Indian contract laborers (Armstrong and Hauser 2003, 2004).

Higman's study of Montpelier (1998) provides an excellent example of the integration of archaeological investigation with a rich and detailed understanding of the nuances of the historical record. His study examines life within a Jamaican plantation community from the founding of the estate in 1739 through emancipation (1838) and into the post-emancipation era to the abandonment of the settlement in 1912. Of particular value is the detailed analysis of historical records relating to the laborer community and the reconstruction of the cultural landscape of the village. An example of the strength of combined historiography and archaeology is Higman's ability to use estate inventories to define probable family yard compounds and to tie together kinship groupings of persons living within this compound in the early nineteenth century (Higman 1998:136–38). The study also provides an excellent reconstruction of the cultural landscape of the plantation, its organization, and the internal layout of the laborer village.

With respect to the plantation system and its relationship to landscapes of power and economic control, the starting place for most scholars working on plantation sites in the Caribbean was the series of industrial works and planters' residences that comprise the monumental architecture of this particular society. Probably the most well-documented study of the ways in which European colonialism and capitalism became inscribed on the landscape comes from James Delle's work on Blue Mountain coffee plantations in Jamaica (1998, 1999, 2000a, 2000b, 2001; Delle, Mrozowski, and Paynter 2000). In this study, Delle set out to define the ways in which European ideologies interwoven in emergent capitalism were inscribed on these colonial landscapes. Arguing against approaches in economic history in which economic efficiency was the primary measure of analysis (Higman 1986a, 1986b, 1987, 1988), Delle joins a series of scholars in demonstrating the ways in which European capitalism regimented the daily lives of colonial subjects (1998, 1999, 2000a). Delle highlights the need to not leave the "global" and its concomitant ideologies unexplored. Delle has followed up this work with a multiyear excavation project at Marshall's Pen, a nineteenth-century coffee plantation in central Jamaica (Delle 2008, 2009).

While plantation space did define crucial elements of the diaspora experience, important work has been conducted on communities that have existed outside the agro-industrial context. For the past fifteen years Kofi Agorsah has been researching Maroon communities in Jamaica (Agorsah 1992a, 1993; see also Bonner 1974). These initial studies have been amplified by the creation of a Maroon sites Web page and database (Agorsah 2006). The long-term project combined archaeological testing, oral history, and ethno-archaeology to attempt to delimit and chronicle ephemeral settlements.

Mark Hauser, in his study of eighteenth-century coarse earthenwares (known locally as yabbas) from several sites throughout Jamaica, looked to the ways in which this specific craft industry pointed to a larger world of social relations that pitted informal and formal economic activity against each other. Excavations of Jamaican plantations and urban sites dating to the first half of the eighteenth century and earlier tend to uncover a significant number of locally produced coarse earthenware pots (Armstrong 1990; Hauser 2001, 2006, 2008; Hauser and DeCorse 2003; Mathewson 1972a, 1972b, 1973; Meyers 1999; Reeves 1997; Pasquariello

1995). These low-fired ceramics have long been produced throughout the Caribbean, primarily by women, and have been used for a number of utilitarian purposes (storing food and water, as chamber pots, and cooking stews and pottages). Their production in Jamaica was from a limited number of localities, pointing to a marketing system far more robust than previously imagined.

Studies of the African diaspora in Jamaica have taken on a variety of focal topics that correlate and expand upon plantation studies, earthenware analysis, spatial analyses, and Maroon settlements. These include detailed analyses on burial practice and bioanthropology (Armstrong and Fleischman 2003), metallurgy (Goucher 1990), and remote sensing (Farnsworth 1982). Broader diasporan studies include an examination of an East Indian house site at Seville (Armstrong and Hauser 2004).[12]

New Problems and New Diverse Directions in Research

In the effort to contextualize the studies presented in this volume, this epilogue has presented an outline of the history of historical archaeology in Jamaica and has examined a cross-section of the work that has been accomplished. Jamaica has long been on the forefront of historical archaeological investigations, be it the seventeenth-century observations of naturalist Hans Sloane, the technologically rich reconnaissance techniques of underwater excavations directed by Donny Hamilton, the approach to plantation and material studies put forward by Armstrong, Delle, Higman, Hauser, and Mayes, or the formal recognition of the importance of archaeology and historic site preservation by the JNHT. Jamaica has made the recovery of the rich tapestry of its diverse past a priority and in the process has explored the contributions of many of the components of the "many people" who collectively have formed one Jamaica.

New and expanded archaeological explorations in Jamaica continue to provide new perspectives and detail on Jamaica's rich historic past and the context of social relations from the period of Columbus's arrival to the present. There is now an array of well-qualified Jamaican archaeologists conducting research and carrying out mitigation projects across the island.[13] They along with visiting scholars working in cooperation with the JNHT are continuing to expand our knowledge of Jamaica's past. The JNHT continues in its efforts to protect the integrity of historic properties and to move forward with archaeological initiatives supported by the Archaeology Division of the History Department at the University of the West Indies, Mona, and the Archaeological Society of Jamaica. All of us who have had the opportunity to work in Jamaica owe the JNHT an incredible debt of gratitude for allowing us to study the tapestry of Jamaica's past. In some small way, we hope this volume will serve to pay back the many debts we owe the people of Jamaica.

Notes

1. An Intersession of the World Archaeological Congress Intersessional was hosted by the Archaeological Society of Jamaica and the University of the West Indies, Mona, May 20–27, 2007, http://www.worldarchaeologicalcongress.org/site/confer_inte_jam.php.

2. Information regarding the JNHT may be found at http://www.jnht.com/index.php.

3. A detailed overview of historical archaeology for the Caribbean region may be found in Armstrong and Hauser 2009.

4. Sloane's collection, which included more than eight hundred specimens from Jamaica, is the core of what would ultimately become the initial natural history collection of the British Museum.

5. The initial list was published in the Jamaica *Gazette* in December 1909, http://www.jnht.com/the_trust/messages/messages.php#;.

6. The large-scale dredging operations had a significant environmental impact on this cove, which has yet to completely recover from the excavations.

7. Despite several attempts at reconnaissance, the location of Columbus's two caravels in Jamaica has not been confirmed. However, the author has identified a pair of ballast piles in St. Ann's Bay that have a strong association with contact-period indigenous ceramics. Plans are currently being made to further examine this site.

8. "Buildings of Architectural or Historic Interest in the British West Indies," Colonial Research Studies No. 2, H. M. Stationery Office, 1951, http://www.jnht.com/the_trust/messages/messages.php#;.

9. The Archaeological Society of Jamaica publishes newsletters and periodic monographs. It hosts annual meetings and was the sponsor of the 2007 World Archaeological Congress Intersessional at the University of the West Indies, Mona, Jamaica.

10. Excavation at Seville Plantation was put off until 1987 because in 1981 the main house (former planter's residence) was occupied and the property temporarily unavailable for study.

11. The faculty and staff of the field school also included Christopher DeCorse and Paul Farnsworth (UCLA), Barry Higman, Patrick Bryan, and Neville Hall (UWI, Mona), and Roderick Ebanks and Anthony Aarons (JNHT).

12. For the Caribbean region as a whole, a good overview of the depth and complexity of recent findings can be found in Haviser and MacDonald 2006; Farnsworth 2001; Haviser 1999.

13. Dorrick Gray is currently the acting director of archaeology for the JNHT.

References

Adams, R.

1965 *The Land behind Baghdad: A History of Settlement on the Diyala Plains.* University of Chicago Press, Chicago.

Agbe-Davies, A.

2004 Up in Smoke: Pipe-Making, Smoking, and Bacon's Rebellion. Ph.D. diss., University of Pennsylvania.

Agorsah, E. K.

1985 Archaeological Implications of Traditional House Construction among the Nchumuru of Northern Ghana. *Current Anthropology* 26(1):103–15.

1990 Ethnoarchaeology: The Search for a Self-Corrective Approach to the Study of Past Human Behavior. *African Archaeological Review* 8:189–208.

1991a Evidence and Interpretation in the Archaeology of Jamaica. Paper presented at the Thirteenth International Congress for Caribbean Archaeology, Curaçao, Netherlands Antilles.

1991b Recent Developments in Archaeological Research in Jamaica. Paper presented at the XIV International Association of Caribbean Archaeologists, Barbados.

1992a Archaeology and Maroon Heritage. *Jamaica Journal* 22:2–9.

1992b Jamaica and Caribbean Archaeology. *Jamaica Journal* 6:1–14.

1992c A Report on an Archaeological Expedition to Nanny Town. *Newsletter of the African-Caribbean Institute of Jamaica* 16–20:11–17.

1993 Archaeology and Resistance History in the Caribbean. *African Archaeological Review* 11:175–95.

1994 *Maroon Heritage: Archaeological, Ethnographic and Historical Perspective.* Canoe Press, University of the West Indies, Kingston, Jamaica.

2006 The Other Side of Freedom: The Maroon Trail in Suriname. In *African Re-Genesis: Confronting Social Issues in the Diaspora,* ed. J. B. Haviser and K. C. MacDonald, pp. 191–203. University College London Press, London.

2007 New Trends in Maroon Archaeology in Suriname: Transformation Processes. *Proceedings of the International Association for Caribbean Archaeology* 2:555–66.

Andrews, K. R.
1978 *The Spanish Caribbean: Trade and Plunder, 1530–1630.* Yale University Press, New Haven.

Annanth, S.
1998 *The Penguin Guide to Vaastu: The Classic Indian Science of Architecture and Design.* Viking, London.

Anonymous
1797 Characteristic Traits of the Creolian and African Negroes in Jamaica. In *Columbia Magazine or Monthly Miscellany,* ed. B. W. Higman and D. V. Armstrong. Vols. 1–3. Photocopy located at Syracuse University Archaeological Research Center. Provided by the National Library of the Institute of Jamaica, Kingston.
1823 Condition of the Negroes in Our Colonies. *Quarterly Review* 29(58):475–508.

Armitage, P.
1995 Personal communication. Secondary Collections, Jamaica National Heritage Trust, Kingston.

Armstrong, D. V.
1981 A Preliminary Report on the Drax Hall Slave Settlement. *Archaeology at UCLA* 2:5.
1983a The "Old Village" at Drax Hall Plantation: An Archeological Examination of an Afro-Jamaican Settlement. Ph.D. diss., University of California, Los Angeles.
1983b The Drax Hall Slave Settlement: Site Selection Procedures. Paper presented at the 9th International Congress for the Study of Pre-Columbian Cultures of the Lesser Antilles, Santo Domingo, Dominican Republic.
1985 An Afrojamaican Slave Settlement: Archaeological Investigations at Drax Hall. In *The Archaeology of Slavery and Plantation Life,* ed. T. Singleton, pp. 261–87. Academic Press, New York.
1990 *The Old Village and the Great House: An Archaeological and Historical Examination of Drax Hall Plantation, St. Ann's Bay, Jamaica.* Blacks in the New World. University of Illinois Press, Urbana.
1991a The Afro-Jamaican Community at Drax Hall. *Jamaica Journal* 24(1):3–8.
1991b Recovering an Early 18th Century Afro-Jamaican Community: Archaeology of the Slave Village at Seville, Jamaica. Paper presented at the Thirteenth International Congress for Caribbean Archaeology, Curaçao, Netherlands Antilles.
1991c The Afro-Jamaican House-Yard: An Archaeological and Ethnohistorical Perspective. *Florida Journal of Anthropology* 7:51–63.
1992 African-Jamaican Housing at Seville: A Study of Spatial Transformation. *Archaeology Jamaica* 6:51–63.
1998 Cultural Transformation within Enslaved Labor Communities in the Caribbean. In *Studies in Culture Contact: Interaction, Culture Change, and Archaeology,* ed. J. G. Cusick, pp. 378–401. Southern Illinois University Center for Archaeological Investigations, Carbondale.
1999 Archaeology and Ethnohistory of the Caribbean Plantation. In *"I, Too, Am America": Archaeological Studies of African-American Life,* ed. T. A. Singleton, pp. 299–310. University of Virginia Press, Charlottesville.

2000 Ancestral Burial at Seville. *Archaeology Jamaica* 12:12–13.
2003 *Creole Transformation from Slavery to Freedom: Historical Archaeology of the East End Community, St. John, Virgin Islands.* University Press of Florida, Gainesville.
2005 Seville Plantation, Jamaica: Chronological Refinements in Historical Archaeology. In *Archaeology without Limits,* ed. B. D. Dillon and M. Boxt. Labyrinthos Press, Lancaster, PA.
2006 Archaeology of the African Diaspora in Puerto Rico. Paper presented at La Herencía Afrícana en el Récord Arqueologíco, San Juan, Puerto Rico.
2010 Degrees of Freedom in the Caribbean: Archaeological Explorations of Transitions from Slavery. *Antiquity* 84(323):146–60.

Armstrong, D. V., and M. L. Fleischman
1993 *Analysis of Four Burials from African Jamaican House-Yard Contexts at Seville: Report to the Jamaica National Heritage Trust.* Syracuse University, Syracuse, NY.
2003 House-Yard Burials of Enslaved Laborers in Eighteenth Century Jamaica. *International Journal of Historical Archaeology* 7(1):33–65.

Armstrong, D. V., and J. Galle
2007 Seville Plantation, St. Ann, Jamaica. Syracuse University and the Digital Archive of Comparative Slavery. Thomas Jefferson Foundation.

Armstrong, D. V., and M. W. Hauser
2003 An East Indian Laborer's Household in 19th Century Jamaica. Paper presented at the XIX International Congress for Caribbean Archaeology, Aruba.
2004 An East Indian Laborer's Household in Nineteenth Century Jamaica: A Case for Understanding Cultural Diversity through Space, Chronology and Material Culture Analysis. *Historical Archaeology* 38(2):9–21.
2009 A Sea of Diversity: Historical Archaeology in the Caribbean. In *International Handbook of Historical Archaeology,* ed. T. Majewski and D. Gaimster, 583–609. Springer, New York.

Armstrong, D. V., and K. G. Kelly
2000 Settlement Patterns and the Origins of African Jamaican Society: Seville Plantation, St. Ann's Bay, Jamaica. *Ethnohistory* 7(2):369–97.

Ashelford, J.
1996 *The Art of Dress: Clothes and Society, 1500–1914.* National Trust, Abrams, London.

Bakan, A. B.
1990 *Ideology and Class Conflict in Jamaica: The Politics of Rebellion.* McGill-Queen's University Press, Buffalo, NY.

Baker, T. F. T., ed.
1995 *A History of the County of Middlesex.* Vol. 10. Oxford University Press, Oxford.

Barclay, A.
[1828] *A Practical View of the Present State of Slavery in the West Indies.* Mnemosyne
1969 Publishing, Miami.

Barka, N. F.
1985 The Archaeology of St. Eustatius, Netherlands Antilles: An Interim Report on the 1981–1984 Seasons. Unpublished manuscript, Department of Anthropology, College of William and Mary, Williamsburg, VA.

Bateman, R. B.
1990 Africans and Indians: A Comparative Study of the Black Carib and Black Seminole. *Ethnohistory* 37(1):1–24.

Baumgarten, L.
1988 "Clothes for the People": Slave Clothing in Early Virginia. *Journal of Early Southern Decorative Arts* 14(2):27–70.
1991 Plains, Plaid, and Cotton: Woolens for Slave Clothing. *Ars Textrina* 15:203–21.
2002 *What Clothes Reveal: The Language of Clothing in Colonial and Federal America: The Colonial Williamsburg Collection.* Colonial Williamsburg Foundation in association with Yale University Press, Williamsburg, VA.

Beaudry, M. C., J. Long, H. M. Miller, F. D. Neiman, and G. W. Stone
1983 A Vessel Typology for Early Chesapeake Ceramics: The Potomac Typological System. *Historical Archaeology* 17(1):18–43.

Beaven, P. J., and M. J. Dumbleton
1966 Clay Minerals and Geomorphology in Four Caribbean Islands. *Clay Minerals* 6:371–82.

Beckford, W. D.
1790 *A Descriptive Account of the Island of Jamaica: With Remarks Upon the Cultivation of the Sugar-Cane, Throughout the Different Seasons of the Year, and Chiefly Considered in a Picturesque Point of View; Also, Observations and Reflections Upon What Would Probably Be the Consequences of an Abolition of the Slave-Trade, and of the Emancipation of the Slaves.* Printed for T. and J. Egerton, London.

Beckles, H.
1982 The 200 Years' War: Slave Resistance in the British West Indies: An Overview of the Historiography. *Jamaica Historical Review* 14:1–10.
1989 *Natural Rebels: A Social History of Enslaved Black Women in Barbados.* Rutgers University Press, New Brunswick, NJ.
1991 An Economic Life of Their Own: Slaves as Commodity Producers and Distributors in Barbados. In *The Slaves' Economy: Independent Production by Slaves in the Americas,* ed. I. Berlin and P. D. Morgan. Frank Cass, London.
1999 *Centering Women: Gender Discourses in Caribbean Slave Society.* Ian Randle, Kingston, Jamaica.

Beckles, H., and V. Shepherd
1991 *Caribbean Slave Society and Economy: A Student Reader.* New Press, New York.

Beckwith, M.
1929 *Black Roadways: A Study of Jamaican Folk Life.* University of North Carolina Press, Chapel Hill.

Beghiat, Norma
2008 *The World's Finest: Jamaica's Blue Mountain Coffee.* Ian Randle, Kingston, Jamaica.

Belisario, I. M.
1838 *Sketches of Character, in Illustration of Habits, Occupation, and Costume of the Negroe Population, in the Island of Jamaica Drawn from Nature and in Lithography.* Isaac M. Belisario, Kingston, Jamaica.

Berlin, I.

1998 *Many Thousands Gone: The First Two Centuries of Slavery in North America.* Belknap Press of Harvard University Press, Cambridge, MA.

Berlin, I., and P. D. Morgan

1993 *Cultivation and Culture: Labor and the Shaping of Slave Life in the Americas.* University Press of Virginia, Charlottesville.

1995 *The Slaves' Economy: Independent Production by Slaves in the Americas.* Frank Cass, London.

Besson, J.

2002 *Martha Brae's Two Histories: European Expansion and Caribbean Culture-Building in Jamaica.* University of North Carolina Press, Chapel Hill.

Bickell, R. R.

1825 *West Indies As They Are; or a Real Picture of Slavery: But More Particularly as It Exists in the Island of Jamaica.* J. Hatchard and Son, London.

Bilby, K.

1984 "Two Sister Pikini": A Historical Tradition of Dual Ethnogenesis in Eastern Jamaica. *Caribbean Quarterly* 30(3–4):10–25.

1995 Oral Traditions in Two Maroon Societies: The Windward Maroons of Jamaica and the Aluku of French Guiana and Suriname. In *Born Out of Resistance: On Caribbean Cultural Identity,* ed. W. Hoogbergen, pp. 169–80. ISOR, Utrecht.

Bilby, K., and D. B. N'Diaye

1992 *Creativity and Resistance: Maroon Communities in the Americas.* Smithsonian Institution, Washington, DC.

Binford, L.

1962 A New Method for Calculating Dates from Kaolin Pipe Stem Samples. *Southeastern Archaeological Conference Newsletter* 9:19–21.

Black, C. D. G.

1963 *Spanish Town, the Old Capital.* Sangsters Press, Kingston, Jamaica.

Black, C. V.

1972 *A History of Jamaica.* Sangsters Press, Kingston, Jamaica.

Blackburn, R.

1988 *The Overthrow of Colonial Slavery, 1776–1848.* Verso, New York.

1997 *The Making of New World Slavery: From the Baroque to the Modern, 1492–1800.* Verso, New York.

Blake, L. E.

1895 The Norbrook Kitchen Midden. *Proceedings of the American Antiquarian Society* 9:283.

Bliege Bird, R., and E. A. Smith

2005 Signaling Theory, Strategic Interaction, and Symbolic Capital. *Current Anthropology* 46(2):221–48.

Blome, R.

1672 *A Description of the Island of Jamaica; with the Other Isles and Territories in America, to Which the English Are Related.* T. Melbourn, London.

Boa, S.

1993 Urban Free Black and Coloured Women: Jamaica, 1760–1834. *Jamaica Historical Review* 18:1–6.

Bonner, T.

1974 Blue Mountain Expedition: Exploratory Excavations at Nanny Town by the Scientific Exploration Society. *Jamaica Journal* 8(2–3):46–50.

Boomert, A.

1980 Hertenrits: An Araquinoid Complex in N.W. Suriname (Part I). *Journal of Anthropological Archaeology* 3(2):68–104.

Boone, J. L.

2000 Status Signaling, Social Power, and Lineage Survival. In *Hierarchies in Action: Cui Bono?* ed. M. W. Diehl, pp. 84–110. Center for Archaeological Investigations, Occasional Paper. Vol. 27. Board of Trustees, Southern Illinois University, Carbondale.

Bragdon, K. J.

1988 Occupational Differences Reflected in Material Culture. In *Documentary Archaeology in the New World,* ed. M. C. Beaudry, pp. 83–91. Cambridge University Press, Cambridge.

Brathwaite, K.

1971 *The Development of Creole Society in Jamaica, 1770–1820.* Clarendon Press, Oxford.

1977 *Wars of Respect.* Kingston Publishers, Kingston, Jamaica.

1994 Nanny, Palmares and the Caribbean Maroon Connexion. In *Maroon Heritage: Archaeological, Ethnographic and Historical Perspectives,* ed. E. K. Agorsah, pp. 119–38. Canoe Press, Kingston, Jamaica.

Braudel, F.

1984 *Civilization and Capitalism, 15th–18th Century.* Vol. 3: *The Perspective of the World.* Collins, London.

Breen, T. H.

1986 An Empire of Goods: The Anglicization of Colonial America, 1690–1776. *Journal of British Studies* 26(3):467–99.

Brewer, J., and R. Porter, eds.

1993 *Consumption and the World of Goods.* Routledge, London.

Bridenbaugh, C., and R. Bridenbaugh

1972 *No Peace beyond the Line: The English in the Caribbean, 1624–1690.* Oxford University Press, New York.

Britton, F.

1990 The Pickleherring Potteries. *Post-Medieval Archaeology* 24:61–92.

Brooks, C.

1983 Aspects of the Sugar-Refining Industry from the 16th–19th Century. *Post-Medieval Archaeology* 17:1–14.

Brown, A. R.

1982 *Historic Ceramic Typology with Principal Dates of Manufacture and Descriptive Characteristics for Identification.* Delaware Department of Transportation, Division of Highways, Location and Environmental Studies Office, Wilmington, DE.

Brown, K. M.

1996 *Good Wives, Nasty Wenches, and Anxious Patriarchs: Gender, Race, and Power in Colonial Virginia.* Published for the Institute of Early American History and Culture by the University of North Carolina Press, Chapel Hill.

Brown, M.

1996 An Archaeological Study of Social Class as Reflected in a British Colonial Tavern Site in Port Royal, Jamaica. Master's thesis, University of Texas, San Antonio.

Bryan, P.

2000 Inside Out and Outside In: Factors in the Creation of Contemporary Jamaica. Grace Kennedy Foundation Lecture, Kingston, Jamaica.

Buckridge, S. O.

2004 *The Language of Dress: Resistance and Accommodation in Jamaica, 1760–1890.* University of the West Indies Press, Kingston, Jamaica.

Burnard, T.

1991 Inheritance and Independence: Women's Status in Early Colonial Jamaica. *William and Mary Quarterly* 48(1):93–114.

1999 Theater of Terror: Domestic Violence in Thomas Thistlewood's Jamaica, 1750–1786. In *Over the Threshold: Intimate Violence in Early America, 1640–1865,* ed. C. Daniels and M. Kennedy, pp. 237–53. Routledge, New York.

2001 E Pluribus Plures: African Ethnicities in Seventeenth- and Eighteenth-Century Jamaica. *Jamaican Historical Review* 21:8–22, 56–59.

2002 "The Grand Mart of the Island": The Economic Function of Kingston, Jamaica, in the Mid-Eighteenth Century. In *Jamaica in Slavery and Freedom: History, Heritage and Culture,* ed. K. Monteith and G. Richards, pp. 225–41. University of the West Indies Press, Kingston, Jamaica.

2004 *Mastery, Tyranny, and Desire: Thomas Thistlewood and His Slaves in the Anglo-Jamaican World.* University of North Carolina Press, Chapel Hill.

Burnard, T., and K. Morgan

2001 The Dynamics of the Slave Market and Slave Purchasing Patterns in Jamaica, 1655–1788. *William and Mary Quarterly* 58(1):205.

Burton, R.

1999 *Afro-Creole: Power, Opposition, and Play in the Caribbean.* Cornell University Press, Ithaca.

Bush, B.

1981 White "Ladies," Coloured "Favourites" and Black "Wenches": Some Considerations on Sex, Race and Class Factors in Social Relations in White Creole Society in the British Caribbean. *Slavery and Abolition* 2:246–62.

1990 *Slave Women in Caribbean Society, 1650–1838.* James Curry Press, London.

1996 Hard Labor: Women, Childbirth, and Resistance in British Caribbean Slave Societies. In *More than Chattel: Black Women and Slavery in the Americas,* ed. D. B. Gaspar and D. C. Hine, pp. 193–217. Indiana University Press, Bloomington.

Campbell, C.

1987 *The Romantic Ethic and the Spirit of Modern Consumerism.* Basil Blackwell, Oxford.

Campbell, M.
1990 *Maroons of Jamaica: 1655–1796.* Africa World Press, Trenton, NJ.
Carey, M.
1991 *Beads and Beadwork of West and Central Africa.* Shire Publications, Buckinghamshire.
Carr, L. G., and L. S. Walsh
1994 Changing Lifestyles and Consumer Behavior in the Colonial Chesapeake. In *Of Consuming Interest: The Style of Life in the Eighteenth Century,* ed. C. C. Carson, R. Hoffman, and P. J. Albert, pp. 59–166. University Press of Virginia, Charlottesville.
Carson, B.
1990 *Ambitious Appetites: Dining, Behavior, and Patterns of Consumption in Federal Washington.* American Institute of Architects Press, Washington, DC.
Carson, C.
1994 The Consumer Revolution in Colonial America: Why the Demand? In *Of Consuming Interest: The Style of Life in the Eighteenth Century,* ed. C. C. Carson, R. Hoffman, and P. J. Albert, pp. 483–697. University Press of Virginia, Charlottesville.
2003 Consumption. In *A Companion to Colonial America,* ed. D. Vickers, pp. 334–65. Blackwell, London.
Carson, C. C., R. Hoffman, and P. J. Albert, eds.
1994 *Of Consuming Interest: The Style of Life in the Eighteenth Century.* University Press of Virginia, Charlottesville.
Chappel, E.
1990 Personal communication. Secondary Collections, Jamaica National Heritage Trust, Kingston, Jamaica.
Chaunu, H., and P. Chaunu
1957 *Seville et l'atlantique (1504–1650).* Editions Jean Touzot, Paris.
Chowdhury, A.
2003a *Maroon Slave Archaeological Investigation Project in the Republic of Mauritius.* Project Report, Centre for Contract Research and Consultancy, University of Mauritius. National Heritage Trust Fund Board, Port Louis, Mauritius.
2003b Theoretical Reflections on Maroon Archaeology in Mauritius. *Revi Kiltir Kreol* 3:55–59.
Chowdhury, A., and C. Goucher
2005 Marronage in Mauritius and Its Possible Implications for Caribbean Archaeology. Paper presented at the XXI International Congress of Caribbean Archaeology, St. Augustine, Trinidad.
Clay, C.
1984 *Economic Expansion and Social Change: England, 1500–1700.* Vol. 2. Cambridge University Press, Cambridge.
Claypole, W. A.
1984 The Merchants of Port Royal, 1655 to 1700. Ph.D. diss., University of the West Indies, Mona, Kingston, Jamaica.

Clifford, S. A.
1993 An Analysis of the Port Royal Shipwreck and Its Role in the Maritime History of Seventeenth-Century Port Royal, Jamaica. Master's thesis, Texas A&M University, College Station.

Cobb, C. R.
2005 Archaeology and the "Savage Slot": Displacement and Emplacement in the Premodern World. *American Anthropologist* 107:563–74.

Collins, D. D.
[1811] 1971 *Practical Rules for the Management and Medical Treatment of Negro Slaves, in the Sugar Colonies, by a Professional Planter.* Books for Libraries, Freeport, NY.

Cook, G. D.
1997 The Readers Point Vessel: Hull Analysis of an Eighteenth-Century Merchant Sloop Excavated in St. Ann's Bay, Jamaica. Ph.D. diss., Texas A&M University, College Station.

Cooper, J.
1977 *Anthropologist's Cookbook.* Routledge and Kegan Paul, London.

Cooper, T.
1791 *Facts Illustrative of the Condition of the Negro Slaves in Jamaica.* J. Hatchard and Son, London.

Corruccini, R. S., J. S. Handler, R. J. Mutaw, and F. Lange
1982 Osteology of a Slave Population from Barbados, West Indies. *Journal of Physical Anthropology* 59:443–59.

Cotter, C.
1946 The Aborigines of Jamaica. *Jamaican Historical Review* 1:137–41.
1948 The Discovery of Spanish Carvings at Seville. *Jamaican Historical Review* 1:227–33.
1953 Don Christopher's Cove. *Jamaican Historical Review* 2(1):39–43.
1964 The Jamaica of Columbus. *Jamaica Historical Society Bulletin* 3(16):252–59.
1970 Seville Nueva: The Story of an Excavation. *Jamaica Journal* 4(2):15–22.
n.d. Field Notes of Excavations at Sevilla La Nueva, Jamaica National Heritage Trust.

Cox, O.
1984 *Upgrading and Renewing a Historic City: Port Royal, Jamaica.* British Overseas Development Administration, London.

Craton, M.
1978 *Searching for the Invisible Man: Slaves and Plantation Life in Jamaica.* Harvard University Press, Cambridge, MA.
1982 *Testing the Chains: Resistance to Slavery in the British West Indies.* Cornell University Press, Ithaca.
1985 Emancipation from Below? The Role of the British West Indian Slaves in the Emancipation Movement, 1816–34. In *Out of Slavery: Abolition and After,* ed. J. Hayward, pp. 110–31. Frank Cass, London.

Craton, M., and J. Walvin
1970 *A Jamaican Plantation: The History of Worthy Park, 1670–1970.* University of Toronto Press, Toronto.

Crawley, M. J.
1993 *GLIM for Ecologists*. Blackwell Scientific Publications, Oxford.
Crisman, K.
1985 The Construction of the Boscawen. *Bulletin of the Fort Ticonderoga Museum* 14(6):356–70.
Cumper, P.
1975 Cecil Baugh, Master Potter. *Jamaica Journal* 9(2–3):18–27.
Cundall, F.
1895 Discovery of Aboriginal Indian Remains in the Port Royal Mountains. *Journal of the Institute of Jamaica* 2(1).
1900 *Studies in Jamaican History*. Published for the Institute of Jamaica by S. Low London.
1915 *Historic Jamaica*. West India Committee, London.
Cundall, F., and J. Pietersz
1919 *Jamaica under the Spaniards*. Institute of Jamaica, Kingston.
Dallas, R. C.
1803 *The History of the Maroons*. A. Strahan, London.
Darling, C. H.
1845 *Report of the Agi Oct 28th 1845*. Institute of Jamaica, Kingston.
1846 *Votes of the Honourable House of Assembly of Jamaica St Jago De La Vega*. Institute of Jamaica, Kingston.
Darrington, G.
1994 Analysis and Reconstruction of Impermanent Structures in the 17th and 18th Centuries. Master's thesis, Department of Anthropology Texas A&M University, College Station.
Deagan, K.
1988 The Archaeology of the Spanish Contact Period in the Caribbean. *Journal of World Prehistory* 2(2):187–233.
1995 *Puerto Real: The Archaeology of a Sixteenth-Century Spanish Town in Hispaniola*. Ripley P. Bullen Series; Columbus Quincentenary Series. University Press of Florida, Gainesville.
Deagan, K. A., and J. M. Cruxent
2002a *Columbus's Outpost among the Taìnos: Spain and America at La Isabela, 1493–1498*. Yale University Press, New Haven.
2002b *Archaeology at La Isabela: America's First European Town*. Yale University Press, New Haven.
DeBooy, T.
1913 Certain Kitchen Middens in Jamaica. *American Anthropologist* 15:425–34.
1919 Certain Kitchen-Middens in Jamaica. *Contributions from the Heye Museum* 3:425–34.
deCerteau, M.
1984 *The Practice of Everyday Life*. University of California Press, Berkeley
DeCorse, C. R.
1987 Historical Archaeological Research in Ghana. *Nyame Akuma* 29:27–32.

1989 Beads as Chronological Indicators in West African Archaeology: A Reexamination. *Beads* 1:41–53.

1991 West African Archaeology and the Atlantic Slave Trade. *Slavery and Abolition* 12(2):92–96.

1992 Culture Contact, Continuity and Change on the Gold Coast, 1400–1900 AD. *African Archaeology Review* 10:163–96.

1999 Oceans Apart: Africanists' Perspectives on Diaspora Archaeology. In *"I, Too, Am America": Archaeological Studies of African-American Life,* ed. T. A. Singleton, pp. 132–58. University of Virginia Press, Charlottesville.

2001 *An Archaeology of Elmina: Africans and Europeans on the Gold Coast, 1400–1900.* Smithsonian Institution Press, Washington, DC.

DeCunzo, L., and J. H. Ernstein

2006 Landscapes, Ideology and Experience in Historical Archaeology. In *The Cambridge Companion to Historical Archaeology,* ed. D. Hicks and M. C. Beaudry, pp. 255–72. Cambridge University Press, Cambridge.

Deerr, N.

1949 *The History of Sugar.* Chapman and Hall, London.

Deetz, J.

1977 *In Small Things Forgotten: An Archaeology of Early American Life.* Anchor Press/Doubleday, Garden City, NY.

DeLaBeche, H. T.

1825 *Notes on the Present Condition of Negroes in Jamaica.* T. Caldwell, London.

Delle, J. A.

1989 A Spatial Analysis of Sugar Plantations on St. Eustatius, Netherlands Antilles. Master's thesis, College of William and Mary, Williamsburg, VA..

1994 The Settlement Pattern of Sugar Plantations on St. Eustatius, Netherlands Antilles. In *Spatial Patterning in Archaeology: Selected Studies of Settlement,* ed. D. W. Linebaugh and G. G. Robinson, pp. 33–61. King and Queen's Press, Williamsburg, VA.

1996 An Archaeology of Crisis: The Manipulation of Social Spaces in the Blue Mountain Coffee Plantation Complex, 1790–1865. Ph.D. diss., University of Massachusetts, Amherst.

1998 *An Archaeology of Social Space: Analyzing Coffee Plantations in Jamaica's Blue Mountains.* Contributions to Global Historical Archaeology. Plenum Press, New York.

1999 The Landscapes of Class Negotiation on Coffee Plantations in the Blue Mountains of Jamaica, 1797–1850. *Historical Archaeology* 33(1):136–58.

2000a The Material and Cognitive Dimensions of Creolization in Nineteenth Century Jamaica. *Historical Archaeology* 34(3):56–72.

2000b Gender, Power and Space: Negotiating Social Relations under Slavery on Coffee Plantations in Jamaica, 1790–1834. In *Lines That Divide: Historical Archaeologies of Race, Class and Gender,* ed. J. A. Delle, S. A. Mrozowski, and R. Paynter. University of Tennessee Press, Knoxville.

2001 Race, Missionaries, and the Struggle to Free Jamaica. In *Race and the Archaeology of Identity,* ed. C. E. Orser, pp. 177–95. University of Utah Press, Salt Lake City.

2002 Power and Landscape: Spatial Dynamics in Early Nineteenth-Century Jamaica. In *The Dynamics of Power,* ed. M. O'Donovan, pp. 341–61. Center for Archaeological Investigations, Occasional Paper No. 30. Southern Illinois University, Carbondale.

2008 An Archaeology of Modernity in Colonial Jamaica. *Archaeologies: The Journal of the World Archaeology Congress* 4(1):87–109.

2009 The Governor and the Enslaved: An Archaeology of Colonial Modernity at Marshall's Pen, Jamaica. *International Journal of Historical Archaeology* 12(4):488–512.

Delle, J. A., M. P. Leone, and P. Mullins

1999 Archaeology and the Modern State: European Colonialism. In *Routledge Companion Encyclopedia of Archaeology,* ed. G. Barker, pp. 1107–60. Routledge, London.

Delle, J. A., S. A. Mrozowski, and R. Paynter

2000 *Lines That Divide: Historical Archaeologies of Race, Class, and Gender.* 1st ed. University of Tennessee Press, Knoxville.

Descantes, C., and M. Glascock

2005 *Instrumental Neutron Activation Analysis of Eighteenth Century Pottery from Jamaica.* Research Reactor Center, University of Missouri.

DeWolf, H. C.

1998 Chinese Porcelain and Seventeenth-Century Port Royal, Jamaica. Ph.D. diss., Texas A&M University, College Station.

Dodds, J., and J. Moore

1984 *Building the Wooden Fighting Ship.* Facts on File Publications, New York.

Downing, J., and E. Harris

1982 Excavations at Her Majesty's Dockyard, Bermuda. *Post-Medieval Archaeology* 16:201–16.

Duerden, J. E.

1897 Aboriginal Indian Remains in Jamaica. *Journal of the Institute of Jamaica* 2(4).

Dunn, R. S.

1972 *Sugar and Slaves: The Rise of the Planter Class in the English West Indies, 1624–1713.* Published for the Institute of Early American History and Culture at Williamsburg, VA, by the University of North Carolina Press, Chapel Hill.

Duplessis, R. S.

1997 *Transitions to Capitalism in Early Modern Europe.* New Approaches to European History 10. 10 vols. Cambridge University Press, Cambridge.

Ebanks, R.

1984 Ma Lou: An Afro Jamaican Pottery Tradition. *Jamaica Journal* 17:31–37.

2000 The Archaeology and History of Jamaican Ceramics: 1655–1840. Master's thesis, University of the West Indies, Mona, Kingston, Jamaica.

Eckholm, E., and J. Deetz

1971 Wellfleet Tavern. *Natural History* 80(7):49–56.

Edwards, B.

[1793] *The History, Civil and Commercial, of the British Colonies in the West Indies.*

1972 Research Library of Colonial Americana 1. Arno Press, New York.

Elmville, E. M.

1951 *English Tableglass.* Charles Scribner's Sons, New York.

Eltis, D.
2001 The Volume and Structure of the Transatlantic Slave Trade: A Reassessment. *William and Mary Quarterly* 58(1):17–46.

Emerson, T. E., and T. R. Pauketat
2002 Embodying Power and Resistance at Cahokia. In *The Dynamics of Power,* ed. Maria O'Donovan, pp. 105–25. Southern Illinois University Center for Archaeological Investigations, Carbondale.

Epperson, T. W.
2000 Panoptic Plantations: The Garden Sights of Thomas Jefferson and George Mason. In *Lines That Divide: Historical Archaeologies of Race, Class, and Gender,* ed. J. A. Delle, S. A. Mrozowski, and R. Paynter, pp. 58–77. University of Tennessee Press, Knoxville.

Ewen, C.
1987 From Spaniard to Creole: The Archaeology of Hispanic-American Cultural Formation at Puerto Real, Haiti. Ph.D. diss., University of Florida, Gainesville.

Farnsworth, P.
1982 Geophysical Surveys at Drax Hall, Jamaica. Master's thesis, University of California, Los Angeles.

Farnsworth, P., ed.
2001 *Island Lives: Historical Archaeologies of the Caribbean.* University of Alabama Press, Tuscaloosa.

Fergus, Claudius
2006 African Secret Societies, Their Manifestation and Function in West Atlantic Plantation Colonies. In *Beyond Tradition: Reinterpreting the Caribbean Historical Experience,* ed. Heather Cateau and Rita Pemberton, pp. 22–49. Ian Randle, Kingston, Jamaica.

Ferguson, L.
1992 *Uncommon Ground: Archaeology and Early African America, 1650–1800.* Smithsonian Institution Press, Washington, DC.

Fernández-Armesto, F.
1982 *The Canary Islands after the Conquest: The Making of a Colonial Society in the Early Sixteenth Century.* Clarendon Press, Oxford.
1987 *Before Columbus: Exploration and Colonization from the Mediterranean to the Atlantic, 1229–1492.* University of Pennsylvania Press, Philadelphia.

Fesler, G. R.
2004 From Houses to Homes: An Archaeological Case Study of Household Formation at the Utopia Slave Quarter, ca. 1675–1775. Ph.D. diss., University of Virginia, Charlottesville.

Finkelman, P., ed.
1989 *Rebellions, Resistance, and Runaways within the Slave South.* Garland, New York.

Floyd, T.
1973 *The Columbus Dynasty in the Caribbean, 1492–1526.* University of New Mexico Press, Albuquerque.

Foster, H. B.

1997 *"New Raiments of Self": African American Clothing in the Antebellum South.* Berg, New York.

Foucault, M.

1979 *Discipline and Punish: The Birth of the Prison.* Vintage Books, New York.

Fox, G. I.

1998 The Study of the Kaolin Clay Tobacco Pipe Collection from the Seventeenth Century Archaeological Site of Port Royal, Jamaica. Ph.D. diss., Texas A&M University.

Fox-Genovese, E.

1988 *Within the Plantation Household: Black and White Women in the Old South.* University of North Carolina Press, Chapel Hill.

Fraginals, M. M.

1976 *The Sugarmill: The Socioeconomic Complex of Sugar in Cuba, 1760–1860.* Monthly Review Press, New York.

Franklin, M.

1992 Wrought Iron Hand Tools in Port Royal, Jamaica: A Study Based upon a Collection of the Tools Recovered from the Archaeological Excavations and on Tools Listed in the Probate Inventories of Colonial Port Royal, c. 1692. Master's thesis, Texas A&M University.

French, S.

2004 *The Rebellious Slave: Nat Turner in American Memory.* Houghton Mifflin, New York.

Galle, J.

2004 Designing Women: Measuring Acquisition and Access at the Hermitage Plantation. In *Engendering African American Archaeology: A Southern Perspective,* ed. J. Galle and A. Young, pp. 39–72. University of Tennessee Press, Knoxville.

2006 Strategic Consumption: Archaeological Evidence for Costly Signaling among Enslaved Men and Women in the Eighteenth-Century Chesapeake. Ph.D. diss., University of Virginia, Charlottesville.

2010 Costly Signaling and Gendered Social Strategies among Slaves in the Eighteenth-Century Chesapeake: An Archaeological Perspective. *American Antiquity* 75(1):19–43.

Galle, J., and F. Neiman

2003 Patterns of Tea and Tableware Consumption on Late Eighteenth-Century Slave Quarter Sites. Paper presented at the Society for Historical Archaeology, Providence, RI.

Galloway, J. H.

1977 The Mediterranean Sugar Industry. *Geographical Review* 67:177–94.

1980 *The Sugar Cane Industry: A Historical Geography from Its Origins to 1914.* Cambridge University Press, Cambridge.

1985 Tradition and Innovation in the American Sugar Industry, c. 1500–1800. *Annals of the Association of the American Geographers* 75:334–51.

Gardner, W. J.

1873 *A History of Jamaica.* Stock, London.

Gaspar, D. B., and D. C. Hine, eds.
1996 *More than Chattel: Black Women and Slavery in the Americas.* Indiana University Press, Bloomington.

Geggus, D.
1987 The Enigma of Jamaica in the 1790s: New Light on the Causes of Slave Rebellions. *William and Mary Quarterly* 44(2):274–99.
1993 Sugar and Coffee Cultivation in Saint Domingue and the Shaping of the Slave Labor Force. In *Cultivation and Culture: Labor and the Shaping of Slave Life in the Americas,* ed. I. Berlin and P. Morgan, 73–100. University Press of Virginia, Charlottesville.

Genovese, E. D.
1976 *Roll Jordan Roll: The World the Slaves Made.* Vintage, New York.

Gill, J.
2001 *Generalized Linear Models: A Unified Approach.* Quantitative Applications in the Social Sciences. Sage, London.

Glassie, H.
1975 *Folk Housing in Middle Virginia: A Structural Analysis of Historic Artifacts.* University of Tennessee Press, Knoxville.

Godden, G. A.
1966 *An Illustrated Encyclopedia of British Pottery and Porcelain.* Bonanza Books, New York.

Goldenberg, J.
1976 *Shipbuilding in Colonial America.* University Press of Virginia, Charlottesville.

Goodwin, C. M., K. B. Metheny, J. M. Kratzer, and A. Yentsche
1995 Recovering the Lost Landscapes of the Stockton Gardens at Morven, Princeton, New Jersey. *Historical Archaeology* 29(1):35–61.

Goodwin, C. R., and S. L. Sanders
1998 *Archaeological Survey and Evaluation of Sites at NSGA Sabana Seca, Puerto Rico—Volume 3.* Atlantic Division—Naval Facilities Engineering Command. Report on File at the State Historic Preservation Office. San Juan, Puerto Rico.

Goodwin, W. B.
1940 *The Lure of Gold: Being the Story of the Five Lost Ships of Christopher Columbus.* Meador Publishing Company, Boston.
1946 *Spanish and English Ruins in Jamaica: A Brief History of that Tropical Paradise since the Discovery by Columbus, the Great Navigator, and Settled by his Son, Don Diego Colon in 1509 as Duke of Veragas.* Meader Publishing Company, Boston.

Gotelipe-Miller, S.
1990 Pewter and Pewterers from Port Royal, Jamaica: Flatware before 1692. Master's thesis, Texas A&M University, College Station.

Goucher, C.
1986 *The Blooms of Banjeli: Technology & Gender in West African Ironmaking.* Educational Resources, Watertown, MA.
1990 John Reeder's Foundry: A Study of 18th Century African-Caribbean Technology. *Jamaica Journal* 23:39–43.
1991 African Hammer, European Anvil: West African Iron Technology in the Atlantic

Trade Era. In *Cultural Resource Management: An African Dimension,* ed. B. Andah. WAJA, Ibadan, Nigeria.

1993 African Metallurgy in the New World. *African Archaeological Review* 11:197–215.

1999 African-Caribbean Metal Technology: Forging Cultural Survivals in the Atlantic World. In *African Sites: Archaeology in the Caribbean,* ed. J. B. Haviser. Markus Weiner, Princeton.

2001 The Memory of Iron: African Technologies in the Americas. In *Places of Cultural Memory: African Reflections on the American Landscape.* U.S. Department of the Interior, National Park Service, Washington, DC.

2007 African Metallurgy in Jamaica. In *Archaeology of Atlantic Africa and the African Diaspora,* ed. A. Ogundiran and T. Falola, pp. 277–91. Indiana University Press, Bloomington.

Goucher, C., and E. W. Herbert

1996 The Blooms of Banjeli: Technology and Gender in West African Iron Making. In *The Culture and Technology of African Iron Production,* ed. P. Schmidt, pp. 40–57. University of Florida Press, Gainesville.

Goucher, C., E. W. Herbert, and C. Saltman

1986 *The Blooms of Banjeli: Technology & Gender in West African Ironmaking.* Video. Documentary Educational Resources, Watertown, MA.

Gould, R.

1980 *Living Archaeology.* Cambridge University Press, Cambridge.

Goveia, E. V.

1965 *Slave Society in the British Leeward Islands at the End of the Eighteenth Century.* Caribbean Series 8. Yale University Press, New Haven.

Green, W. A.

1976 *British Slave Emancipation: The Sugar Colonies and the Great Experiment, 1830–1865.* Oxford University Press, Oxford.

Griffiths, P.

1967 *The History of the Tea Industry.* Weidenfeld and Nicholson, London.

Hailey, T. I.

1994 The Analysis of 17th-, 18th- and 19th-Century Ceramics from Port Royal, Jamaica for Lead Release: A Study in Archaeotoxicology. Ph.D. diss., Texas A&M University.

Hall, D.

1959 *Free Jamaica, 1838–1865: An Economic History.* Yale University Press, New Haven.

1978 The Flight from the Estates Reconsidered: The British West Indies, 1838–1842. *Journal of Caribbean History* 10–11:7–24.

1987 Planters, Farmers and Gardeners in Eighteenth-Century Jamaica. Paper presented at the Elsa Goveia Memorial Lecture presented at the University of the West Indies, Mona, Kingston, Jamaica.

1989 *In Miserable Slavery: Thomas Thistlewood in Jamaica.* Macmillan, London.

Hall, N. A. T.

1977 Slave Laws of the Danish Virgin Islands in the Later Eighteenth Century. *Annals of the New York Academy of Sciences* 292(1):174–86.

[1980] 1991 Slaves' Use of Their "Free" Time in the Danish Virgin Islands in the Later Eighteenth and Early Nineteenth Centuries. In *Caribbean Slave Society and Economy: A Student Reader,* ed. V. Shepherd, pp. 335–44. New Press, New York.

[1985] 1991 Maritime Maroons: Grand Marronage from the Danish West Indies. In *Caribbean Slave Society and Economy: A Student Reader,* ed. V. Shepherd, pp. 387–400. New Press, New York.

1994 *Slave Society in the Danish West Indies: St. Thomas, St. John, and St. Croix.* Johns Hopkins Studies in Atlantic History and Culture. Johns Hopkins University Press, Baltimore.

Hamilton, D.

1984 Preliminary Report on the Archaeological Investigations of the Submerged Remains of Port Royal, Jamaica, 1981–82. *International Journal of Nautical Archaeology and Underwater Exploration* 13(1):11–25.

1985 The Sunken City under the Sea. In *Science Year 1986,* pp. 73–81. World Book Encyclopedia, Chicago.

1986 Port Royal Revisited. Paper presented at the Underwater Archaeology Proceedings from the Society for Historical Archaeology, Sacramento, CA.

1988 Underwater Excavations of 17th-Century Building at the Intersection of Lime and Queen Streets. In *Underwater Archaeology: Proceedings from the Society for Historical Archaeology Conference,* ed. C. R. Cummings, pp. 9–12, Reno, NV.

1992 Simon Benning, Pewterer of Port Royal. In *Text-Aided Archaeology,* ed. B. J. Little, pp. 39–53. CRC Press, Boca Raton.

2006 Pirates and Merchants: Port Royal, Jamaica. In *X Marks the Spot: The Archaeology of Piracy,* ed. C. R. Ewen, pp. 13–30. New Perspectives on Maritime History and Nautical Archaeology, G. A. Smith, general editor. University Press of Florida, Gainesville.

Hamilton, D. L., and R. Woodward

1984 A Sunken 17th Century City: Port Royal, Jamaica. *Archaeology* 37(1):38–45.

Handler, J. S.

1963 Pottery Making in Rural Barbados. *Southwestern Journal of Anthropology* 19: 314–34.

2009 *The Unappropriated People: Freedmen in the Slave Society of Barbados.* University of the West Indies Press, Kingston, Jamaica.

Handler, J. S., R. S. Corrucini, and R. J. Mutaw

1982 Tooth Mutilation in the Caribbean: Evidence from a Slave Burial Population in Barbados. *Journal of Human Evolution* 11:297–313.

Handler, J. S., and H. Handler

1970 Field Notes on Ethnographic Research. Folder 8. Courtesy of Jerome Handler.

Handler, J. S., and F. Lange

1978 *Plantation Slavery in Barbados: An Archaeological and Historical Investigation.* Harvard University Press, Cambridge, MA.

Hanson, L. H.

1969 Kaolin Pipestems: Boring in on a Fallacy. *Historic Sites Archaeology* 4:2–15.

Harrington, J. C.
1954 Dating Stem Fragments of Seventeenth and Eighteenth Century Clay Tobacco Pipes. *Quarterly Bulletin of the Archaeological Society of Virginia* 9(1):10–14.

Harris, C. L. G.
1994 The True Traditions of My Ancestors. In *Maroon Heritage: Archaeological, Ethnographic, and Historical Perspectives,* ed. E. K. Agorsah, pp. 36–62. Canoe Press, Kingston, Jamaica.

Hauser, M.
1997 Embedded Identities: Seeking Economic and Social Relations through Compositional Analysis of Low-Fired Earthenwares. Master's thesis, Syracuse University.
2001 Peddling Pots: Determining the Extent of Market Exchange in Eighteenth Century Jamaica through the Analysis of Local Coarse Earthenware. Ph.D. diss., Syracuse University.
2006 Hawking Your Wares: Determining the Scale of Informal Economy through the Distribution of Local Coarse Earthenware in Eighteenth-Century Jamaica. In *African Re-Genesis: Confronting Social Issues in the Diaspora,* ed. J. B. Haviser and K. C. MacDonald, pp. 160–75. University College London Press, New York.
2007 Between Urban and Rural: Organization and Distribution of Local Pottery in Eighteenth Century Jamaica. In *Archaeology of Atlantic Africa and the African Diaspora,* ed. A. Ogundiran and T. Falola, pp. 292–310. Indiana University Press, Bloomington.
2008 *An Archaeology of Black Markets, Local Ceramics and Economies in Eighteenth Century Jamaica.* University Press of Florida, Gainesville.

Hauser, M., and C. R. DeCorse
2003 Low-Fired Earthenwares in the African Diaspora: Problems and Prospects. *International Journal of Historical Archaeology* 7(1):67–98.

Hauser, M. W., C. Descantes, and M. Glascock
2009 Locating Enslaved Craft Production: Chemical Analysis of Eighteenth Century Jamaican Pottery. *Journal of Caribbean Archaeology,* special publication #2, 123–48.

Hauser, M. W., K. G. Kelly, and D. V. Armstrong
2007 What to Do with "Other" Ceramics: Inter-Colonial Trade of French Coarse Earthenware. Paper presented at the XXI International Congress of Caribbean Archaeology, St. Augustine, Trinidad.

Haviser, J., ed.
1999 *African Sites: Archaeology in the Caribbean.* Markus Weiner, Princeton.

Haviser, J. B., and K. C. MacDonald, eds.
2006 *African Re-Genesis: Confronting Social Issues in the Diaspora.* University College London Press, Abingdon.

Healy, P. F.
1980 *Archaeology of the Rivas Region: Nicaragua.* Wilfrid Laurier University Press, Waterloo.

Heath, B. J.
1999a *Hidden Lives: The Archaeology of Slave Life at Thomas Jefferson's Poplar Forest.* University Press of Virginia, Charlottesville.

1999b Buttons, Beads, and Buckles: Contextualizing Adornment within the Bounds of Slavery. In *Historical Archaeology, Identity Formation and the Interpretation of Ethnicity,* ed. M. Franklin and G. Fesler, pp. 47–69. Colonial Williamsburg Research Publications. Dietz Publishers, Richmond, VA.

1999c Yabbas, Monkeys, Jugs, and Jars: A Historical Context for African Caribbean Potterys on St. Eustatius. In *African Sites: Archaeology in the Caribbean,* ed. J. B. Haviser. Markus Weiner, Princeton.

2004 Engendering Choice: Slavery and Consumerism in Central Virginia. In *Engendering African-American Archaeology: A Southern Perspective,* ed. J. Galle and A. Young, pp. 19–38. University of Tennessee Press, Knoxville.

2005 Poplar Forest Slave Database. On file with Barbara J. Heath, Department of Anthropology, University of Tennessee, Knoxville.

Heidtke, K. P.

1992 Jamaica Red Clay Tobacco Pipes. Master's thesis, Texas A&M University.

Heuman, G.

1994 *"The Killing Time": The Morant Bay Rebellion in Jamaica.* University of Tennessee Press, Knoxville.

Hicks, D., and M. C. Beaudry

2006 Introduction: The Place of Historical Archaeology. In *The Cambridge Companion to Historical Archaeology,* ed. D. Hicks and M. C. Beaudry, pp. 1–12. Cambridge University Press, Cambridge.

Higman, B. W.

1974 A Report on Excavations at Montpelier and Roehampton. *Jamaica Journal* 8(1–2): 40–45.

1975 Report on Excavations at New Montpelier, St. James, Jamaica, 22–24 March and 3–18 August, 1975. Master's thesis, University of the West Indies, Mona, Kingston, Jamaica.

1976 *Slave Population and Economy in Jamaica, 1807–1834.* Cambridge University Press, New York.

1984 *Slave Populations of the British Caribbean, 1807–1834.* Johns Hopkins Studies in Atlantic History and Culture. Johns Hopkins University Press, Baltimore.

1986a Plantation Maps as Sources for the Study of West Indian Ethnohistory. In *Ethnohistory: A Researcher's Guide,* ed. D. Weidman, pp. 107–36. Department of Anthropology, College of William and Mary Studies in Third World Societies Publication Number 35, Williamsburg, VA.

1986b Jamaican Coffee Plantations, 1780–1860: A Cartographic Analysis. *Caribbean Geography* 2:73–91.

1987 The Spatial Economy of Jamaican Sugar Plantations: Cartographic Evidence from the 18th and 19th Centuries. *Journal of Historical Geography* 13(1):17–39.

1988 *Jamaica Surveyed: Plantation Maps and Plans of the Eighteenth and Nineteenth Centuries.* University of the West Indies Press, Kingston, Jamaica.

1991 Household Structure and Fertility on Jamaican Slave Plantations: A Nineteenth-Century Example. In *Caribbean Slave Society and Economy: A Student Reader,* ed. H. Beckles and V. Shepherd. New Press, New York.

1995 *Slave Population and Economy in the British Caribbean, 1807–1834.* University of the West Indies Press, Kingston, Jamaica.

1996 Patterns of Exchange within a Plantation Economy: Jamaica at the Time of Emancipation. In *West Indies Accounts: Essays on the History of the British Caribbean and the Atlantic Economy in Honour of Richard Sheridan,* ed. R. A. McDonald. University of the West Indies Press, Kingston, Jamaica.

1998 *Montpelier, Jamaica: A Plantation Community in Slavery and Freedom, 1739–1912.* Press University of the West Indies, Mona, Kingston, Jamaica.

1999 *General History of the Caribbean.* Vol. 6: *Methodology and Historiography of the Caribbean.* Unesco Publishing, London.

Hill, V.

1978 Distribution and Potential—Clays in Jamaica. *Jamaica Journal* 42:64–75.

Hinks, S.

1988 A Structural and Functional Analysis of Eighteenth Century Buttons. Master's thesis, College of William and Mary, Williamsburg, VA.

Hodder, I.

1978 *Spatial Organization of Culture.* Duckworth, London.

Hofman, C. L., M. L. P. Hoogland, and A. L. v. Gijn

2008 *Crossing the Borders: New Methods and Techniques in the Study of Archaeological Materials from the Caribbean.* Caribbean Archaeology and Ethnohistory. University of Alabama Press, Tuscaloosa.

Holt, T.

1992 *The Problem of Freedom: Race, Labor, and Politics in Jamaica and Britain, 1832–1938.* Johns Hopkins University Press, Baltimore.

Hoogbergen, W.

1990 The History of the Suriname Maroons, Resistance and Rebellion in Suriname: Old and New. In *Studies in Third World Societies,* ed. V. H. Sutlive, M. D. Zamora, V. Kerns, and T. Hamada, pp. 65–102. Department of Anthropology, College of William and Mary, Williamsburg, VA.

1995 *Born out of Resistance: On Caribbean Cultural Identity.* ISOR, Utrecht.

Horsley, J. E.

1978 *Tools of the Maritime Trades.* International Marine Publishing Company, Camden.

Howard, R. R.

1950 The Archaeology of Jamaica and Its Position in Relation to Circum-Caribbean Culture. Ph.D. diss., Yale University, New Haven, CT.

1956 The Archaeology of Jamaica: A Preliminary Survey. *American Antiquity* 22(1):45–49.

1965 New Perspectives on Jamaican Archaeology. *American Antiquity* 31(2):250–55.

Howson, J.

1990 Social Relations and Material Culture: A Critique of the Archaeology of Plantation Slavery. *Historical Archaeology* 23:78–91.

1995 Colonial Goods and the Plantation Village: Consumption and the Internal Economy in Montserrat from Slavery to Freedom. Ph.D. diss., New York University.

Hudson, L. E. J.

1994 "All the Cash": Work and Status in the Slave Quarter. In *Working toward Freedom:*

Slave Society and Domestic Economy in the American South, ed. L. Hudson, pp. 77–94. University of Rochester Press, Rochester, NY.

Institute of Jamaica (IOJ)

1721 Map of St. Ann's Bay. Map No. 176. National Library of Jamaica, Institute of Jamaica, Kingston.

1791 Map of Seville Plantation. National Library of Jamaica, Institute of Jamaica, Kingston.

1843 Plan of "The Priory," Parish of Saint Ann, Jamaica. Map for the Reverend J. Smith. Intended for the Purpose of Conveyance for Various Individuals. Map No. 349; N8160. National Library of Jamaica, Institute of Jamaica, Kingston.

Inventory

1753 Seville Estate, Ib/11/3/36, Folios 117a–119b. Jamaica Archives, Spanish Town, Jamaica.

1759 Seville Estate, Ib/11/3/38, Folios 181a–184b. Jamaica Archives, Spanish Town, Jamaica.

Isaac, R.

1982 *The Transformation of Virginia, 1740–1790.* University of North Carolina, Chapel Hill.

Jamaica

1738 Acts of Assembly, passed in the island of Jamaica; from 1681, to 1737, inclusive. London, 1738 [1739]. In Eighteenth Century Collections Online, St. Jago de la Vega.

Jargstorf, S.

1995 *Glass Beads from Europe.* Schiffer Publishing, Atglen, PA.

Johnson, D. A.

2000 Port Royal, Jamaica, and the Slave Trade. Master's thesis, Texas A&M University.

Johnson, M.

2007 *Ideas of Landscape.* Blackwell, London.

Johnson, M. P.

1981 Runaway Slaves and the Slave Communities on South Carolina, 1799 to 1830. *William and Mary Quarterly* 38:418–41.

Jones, O. R., and C. Sullivan

1989 *The Parks Canada Glass Glossary for the Description of Containers, Tableware, Flat Glass, and Closures.* Environment Canada-Parks, Ottawa.

Keegan, W. F.

1992 *The People Who Discovered Columbus: The Prehistory of the Bahamas.* University Press of Florida, Gainesville.

1994 West Indian Archaeology. 1. Overview and Foragers. *Journal of Archaeological Research* 2(2):255–84.

1996 West Indian Archaeology. 2. After Columbus. *Journal of Archaeological Research* 4:265–94.

2000 West Indian Archaeology. 3. Ceramic Age. *Journal of Archaeological Research* 8:135–67.

Keegan, W. F., R. A. Portell, and J. Slapicinsky

2003 Changes in Invertebrate Taxa at Two Pre-Columbian Sites in Southwestern Jamaica, A.D. 800–1500. *Journal of Archaeological Science* 30:1607–17.

Keegan, W. F., A. V. Stokes, and L. A. Newson
1990 *Bibliography of Caribbean Archaeology.* Bullen Research Library 1&2. University Press of Florida, Gainesville.

Keith, R., ed.
1977 *Haciendas and Plantations in Latin American History.* Holmes and Meier, New York.

Kelly, J.
1838 *Jamaica in 1831.* James Wilson, Belfast.

Kelly, K. G.
1989 The Historic Archaeology of Jamaican Tenant-Manager Relations: A Case Study from Drax Hall and Seville Estates, St. Ann's, Jamaica. Master's thesis, College of William and Mary, Williamsburg, VA.
2001 Change and Continuity in Coastal Benin. In *West Africa during the Atlantic Slave Trade: Archaeological Perspectives,* ed. C. R. DeCorse, pp. 81–100. Leicester University Press, London.
2004 Historical Archaeology in the French Caribbean: An Introduction to a Special Volume of the *Journal of Caribbean Archaeology. Journal of Caribbean Archaeology,* special publication #1, pp. 1–10.

Kelly, K. G., and D. V. Armstrong
1991 Archaeological Investigations of a 19th Century Free Laborer House, Seville Estate, St. Ann's Jamaica. Proceedings of the XIII International Congress of Caribbean Archaeology. *Reports of the Archaeological-Anthropological Institute of the Netherlands Antilles* 9:429–35.

Kelso, W. M.
1989 Comments on the 1987 Society for Historical Archaeology Landscape Symposium. *Historical Archaeology* 23(2):48–49.

Kelso, W. M., and R. Most, eds.
1990 *Earth Patterns: Essays in Landscape Archaeology.* University of Virginia Press, Charlottesville.

King, J., and H. Miller
1987 The View from the Midden: An Analysis of Midden Distribution and Composition at the Van Sweringen Site, St. Mary's City, Maryland. *Historical Archaeology* 21(2):37–59.

Klein, W. H. A.
1974 *Antique Bottles of Suriname.* Suriname Museum Foundation, Paramaribo.

Kryder-Reid, E.
1994 "As Is the Gardener, So Is the Garden": The Archaeology of Landscape as Myth. In *The Historical Archaeology of the Chesapeake,* ed. P. Shackel and B. J. Little, pp. 131–48. Smithsonian Institution Press, Washington, DC.

Kulikoff, A.
1986 *Tobacco and Slaves: The Development of Southern Cultures in the Chesapeake, 1680–1800.* Institute of Early American History and Culture, Williamsburg, VA. University of North Carolina, Chapel Hill.

Laborie, P. J.
1789 *The Coffee Planter of Saint Domingo.* Cadell and Davies, London.

LaGro, H. E., and D. H. Haas
1992 Syrup Jars and Sugar Pots: A Preliminary Study of a Class of Medieval Industrial Pottery from Tell Abu Sarbut, Jordan, Pt. II. *Newsletter, Department of Pottery Technology, University of Leiden* 9–10:55–68.

LaRoche, C. J.
1994 Beads from the African Burial Ground, New York City: A Preliminary Assessment. *Beads* 6:3–20.

Lavery, B.
1987 *The Arming and Fitting of English Ships of War, 1600–1815.* Naval Institute Press, Annapolis.

Legendre, P., and L. Legendre
1998 *Numerical Ecology.* 2nd English ed. Elsevier, Amsterdam.

Leone, M.
1984 Interpreting Ideology in Historical Archaeology: The William Paca Garden in Annapolis, Maryland. In *Ideology, Power and Prehistory,* ed. D. Miller and C. Tilley, pp. 25–35. Cambridge University Press, Cambridge.

LeRoux, Y.
1998 *L'habitation Loyola à Rémire, Guyane Française.* Service Régional de l'Archéologie, Cayenne.

Leshikar-Denton, P.
1991 Underwater Investigations of the Eighteenth-Century "Wreck of the Ten Sail." *Fourteenth IACA.* 591–94. Barbados.

Levy, P., M.-C. Garden, N. M. Hayes, L. Fischer, J. Bowen, D. Sawyer, and D. F. Muraca
2007 Life at Richard Charlton's Coffeehouse: A Story of Archaeology, History, and Hot Drinks in Eighteenth-Century Williamsburg, Virginia. Report of the Colonial Williamsburg Foundation, Department of Archaeological Research, Williamsburg, VA.

Lewis, K. L.
1984 *The American Frontier: An Archaeological Study of Settlement Pattern and Process.* Academic Press, New York.

Lewis, M. G.
1834 *Journal of a West India Proprietor, kept during a residence in the island of Jamaica.* London.
1929 *A Journal of a West Indian Proprietor, 1815–17.* Houghton Mifflin, Boston.

Liao, T. F.
1994 *Interpreting Probability Models: Logit, Probit, and Other Generalized Linear Models.* Quantitative Applications in the Social Sciences. Sage Publications, London.

Link, E.
1960 Exploring the Drowned City of Port Royal. *National Geographic* 117(1):151–83.

Locke, J.
[1690] 2007 *The Second Treatise on Civil Government.* World Library Classics.

Long, E.
[1774] 1970 *The History of Jamaica; or, General Survey of the Antient and Modern State of That Island: With Reflections on Its Situations, Settlements, Inhabitants, Climate, Prod-*

ucts, Commerce, Laws, and Government. New intro. by George Metcalf. Ed. Cass Library of West Indian Studies, No. 12. Frank Cass, London.

Longley, G. C.
1914 Kitchen Middens of Jamaica. *American Museum Journal* 14:296–98.

López y Sebastián, L. E.
1986 *Cultural Heritage of Jamaica: Sevilla La Nueva—Archaeology.* Jamaica National Heritage Trust, Kingston.

Luyken, J.
1694 *Het Menselyk Bedryf.* Freiburg.

MacCormack, R. C.
1898 Indian Remains in Vere, Jamaica. *Journal of the Institute of Jamaica* 2(5).

Mair, L. M.
1986 *Women Field Workers in Jamaica during Slavery.* Elsa Goveia Memorial Lecture. Department of History, University of the West Indies, Mona, Kingston, Jamaica.

Majewski, T., and M. J. O'Brien
1987 The Use and Misuse of Nineteenth-Century English and American Ceramics in Archaeological Analysis. In *Advances in Archaeological Method and Theory,* ed. Michael Shiffer, 11:97–209. Academic Press, New York.

Mangan, P. H.
1994 Changes in the Landscape during the Transition from Feudalism to Capitalism: A Case Study of Montblanc, Catalonia, Spain. Ph.D. diss., University of Massachusetts, Amherst.

Mañón, M. J.
1978 Importancia de Los Ingenios Indo-Hispanicos de Las Antillas. *Boletin del Museo del Hombre Dominicano* 10:139–72.

Marquardt, W. H.
1993 Dialectical Archaeology. In *Archaeological Method and Theory,* ed. M. B. Schiffer, pp. 100–129. Vol. 6. University of Arizona Press, Tucson.

Marshall, W. K.
2003 The Post-Slavery Problem Revisited. In *Slavery, Freedom, and Gender: The Dynamics of Caribbean Society,* ed. B. L. Moore, B. W. Higman, C. Campbell, and P. Bryan, pp. 115–32. University of the West Indies Press, Kingston, Jamaica.

Martin, A. S.
1989 The Role of Pewter as Missing Artifact: Consumer Attitudes towards Tablewares in Late 18th-Century Virginia. *Historical Archaeology* 23(2):1–27.
1993 Buying into the World of Goods: Eighteenth-Century Consumerism and the Retail Trade from London to the Virginia Frontier. Ph.D. diss., College of William and Mary, Williamsburg, VA.
1994 "Fashionable Sugar Dishes, Latest Fashion Ware": The Creamware Revolution in the 18th-Century Chesapeake. In *Historical Archaeology of the Chesapeake,* ed. P. Shackel and B. Little, pp. 169–87. Smithsonian Institution Press, Washington, DC.

Marx, R. F.
1967 *Pirate Port: The Story of the Sunken City of Port Royal.* World Publishing, Cleveland, OH.

1968a *Brass and Copper Items Recovered from the Sunken City of Port Royal: May 1, 1966–March 31, 1968.* National Trust Commission, Kingston, Jamaica.

1968b Excavating the Sunken City of Port Royal. *Jamaica Journal* 2(2):12–18.

1968c Discovery of Columbus. *Jamaica Journal* 2(4):13–17.

1973 *Port Royal Rediscovered.* Doubleday, Garden City, NJ.

1979 Port Royal. *Oceans Magazine* 1(5):66–77.

Mathewson, R. D.

1971 CCA Demonstration Project: Restoration of the Prince of Wales Bastion, Brimstone Hill, St. Kitts. *Caribbean Conservation Association Environmental Newsletter* 2(2):34–36.

1972a Jamaican Ceramics: An Introduction to 18th Century Folk Pottery in West African Tradition. *Jamaica Journal* 6:54–56.

1972b History from the Earth: Archaeological Excavations at Old King's House. *Jamaica Journal* 6:3–11.

1973 Archaeological Analysis of Material Culture as a Reflection of Sub-Cultural Differentiation in 18th Century Jamaica. *Jamaica Journal* 7:25–29.

Mathurin, L.

1975 *The Rebel Woman in the British West Indies during Slavery.* African Caribbean Publications, Institute of Jamaica, Kingston.

Mayes, P.

1970 The Port Royal Project. *Caribbean Conservation Association Environmental Newsletter* 1(1):37–38.

1972 *Port Royal,Jamaica: Excavations, 1969–1970.* Jamaica National Trust Commission, Kingston.

Mayes, P., and P. A. Mayes

1972 Port Royal, Jamaica: The Archaeological Problems and Potential. *International Journal of Nautical Archaeology and Underwater Exploration* 1:97–112.

McClenaghan, P. E.

1988 Drinking Glasses from Port Royal, Jamaica, c. 1630–1840: A Study of Styles and Usage. Master's thesis, Texas A&M University, College Station, TX.

McClure, R.

1990 Personal communication. Secondary Collections, Jamaica National Heritage Trust, Kingston.

McCullagh, P., and J. Nelder

1989 *Generalized Linear Models.* Chapman and Hall, London.

McDonald, R. A.

1993 *The Economy and Material Culture of Slaves: Goods and Chattels on the Sugar Plantations of Jamaica and Louisiana.* Louisiana State University Press, Baton Rouge.

McEwan, B.

1995 Spanish Precedents and Domestic Life in Puerto Real: The Archaeology of Two Hispanic Homesites. In *Puerto Real: The Archaeology of a Sixteenth Century Spanish Town in Hispaniola,* ed. K. Deagan, pp. 195–230. University Press of Florida, Gainesville.

McGuire, K., and W. Hildebrandt

2005 Re-thinking Great Basin Foragers: Prestige Hunting and Costly Signaling during the Middle Archaic Period. *American Antiquity* 70(4):695–712.

McGuire, R. H.

1988 Dialogues with the Dead: Ideology and the Cemetery. In *The Recovery of Meaning in Historical Archaeology,* ed. M. P. Leone and P. B. Potter Jr., pp. 435–80. Smithsonian Institution Press, Washington, DC.

1994 *A Marxist Archaeology.* Academic Press, San Diego.

McKee, L.

1999 Food Supply and Plantation Social Order: An Archaeological Perspective. In *"I, Too, Am America": Archaeological Studies of African-American Life,* ed. T. Singleton, pp. 218–39. University Press of Virginia, Charlottesville.

McKendrick, N., J. Brewer, and J. H. Plumb

1982 *The Birth of a Consumer Society: The Commercialization of Eighteenth-Century England.* Indiana University Press, Bloomington.

McNeill, H.

1788 *Observations on the Treatment of Negroes in the Island of Jamaica.* GJ&J Robinson, London.

Menard, S.

2002 *Applied Logistic Regression Analysis, Second Edition.* Quantitative Applications in the Social Sciences, v. 07-106. Sage Publications, London.

Meniketti, M.

1998 The Port St. George Project: An Archaeological Assessment of a Sugar Plantation and Harbor Complex in Nevis, West Indies. Master's thesis, Michigan State University, East Lansing.

Metheny, K. B., J. Kratzer, A. E. Yentsch, and C. M. Goodwin

1996 Method in Landscape Archaeology: Research Strategies in a Historic New Jersey Garden. In *Landscape Archaeology: Reading and Interpreting the American Historical Landscape,* ed. R. Yamin and K. B. Metheny, pp. 6–31. University of Tennessee Press, Knoxville.

Meyers, A. D.

1999 West African Tradition in the Decoration of Colonial Jamaican Folk Pottery. *Journal of Historical Archaeology* 3(4):201–24.

Milanich, J. T., and S. Milbrath, eds.

1989 *First Encounters: Spanish Explorations in the Caribbean and the United States, 1492–1570.* University Press of Florida, Gainesville.

Mill, J. S.

[1869] *On Liberty.* Longman, London.
1999

Miller, D., and C. Tilley

1984 Introduction to *Ideology, Power and Prehistory,* ed. D. Miller and C. Tilley, pp. 1–15. Cambridge University Press, Cambridge.

Miller, G. L.

1980 Classification and Economic Scaling of 19th-Century Ceramics. *Historical Archaeology* 14:1–40.

1988 Classification and Economic Scaling of Nineteenth-Century Ceramics. In *Documentary Archaeology in the New World,* ed. M. C. Beaudry, pp. 172–83. Cambridge University Press, Cambridge.

1990 The "Market Basket" of Ceramics Available in Country Stores from 1780–1880. Paper presented at the Society for Historical Archaeology, Tucson, AZ.

1991 A Revised Set of CC Index Values for Classification and Economic Scaling of English Ceramics from 1787–1880. *Historical Archaeology* 25:1–25.

Miller, G. L., A. S. Martin, and N. S. Dickinson

1994 Changing Consumption Patterns: English Ceramics and the American Market from 1770 to 1840. In *Everyday Life in the Early Republic,* ed. C. E. Hutchins, pp. 219–48. Henry Francis DuPont Winterthur Museum, Winterthur, DE.

Mintz, S.

1971 Toward an Afro-American History. *Cahiers d'histoire mondiale* 13(2):317–32.

[1974] *Caribbean Transformations.* Aldine Publishing, Chicago.
1992

1977 The So-Called World System: Local Initiative and Local Response. *Dialectical Anthropology* 2:253–70.

1978 Caribbean Marketplaces and Caribbean History. *Nova Americana* 1(1):333–44.

1985 *Sweetness and Power: The Place of Sugar in Modern History.* Viking, New York.

Mintz, S., and D. Hall

[1970] The Origins of the Jamaican Internal Marketing System. In *Caribbean Slave*
1991 *Society and Economy: A Student Reader,* ed. V. Shepherd, pp. 319–34. New Press, New York.

Mintz, S. W., and R. Price

1992 *The Birth of African-American Culture: An Anthropological Perspective.* Beacon Press, Boston.

Moore, S. M.

1985 Social and Economic Status on the Coastal Plantation: An Archaeological Perspective. In *The Archaeology of Slavery and Plantation Life,* ed. T. Singleton, pp. 141–60. Academic Press, San Diego.

Moreton, J. B.

1790 *Manners and Customs in the West India Islands.* London.

Morgan, J.

2004 *Laboring Women: Reproduction and Gender in New World Slavery.* University of Pennsylvania Press, Philadelphia.

2006 Accounting for the Women in Slavery: Demography and the Transatlantic Slave Trade. Paper given at the University of Notre Dame, September 14.

Morgan, P. D.

1998 *Slave Counterpoint: Black Culture in the Eighteenth-Century Chesapeake and Lowcountry.* Published for the Omohundro Institute of Early American History and Culture, Williamsburg, VA, by the University of North Carolina Press, Chapel Hill.

Morison, S. E.

1942 *Admiral of the Ocean Sea: A Life of Christopher Columbus.* 2 vols. Little, Brown, Boston.

Morrison, K. D., and M. T. Lycett

1997 Inscriptions as Artifacts: Precolonial South India and the Analysis of Texts. *Journal of Archaeological Method and Theory* 3(3–4):215–37.

Morrissey, M.

1991 Women's Work, Family Formation, and Reproduction among Caribbean Slaves. In *Caribbean Slave Society and Economy: A Student Reader,* ed. H. Beckles and V. Shepherd, pp. 274–86. New Press, New York.

Moxon, J.

1677 *Mechanick Exercises: Or the Doctrine of Handy-Works. Applied to the Art of Smithing, Joinery, Carpentry, Turning and Bricklayery.* London.

Moya Pons, F.

1999 The Establishment of Primary Centres and Primary Plantations. In *General History of the Caribbean.* Vol. 2: *New Societies: The Caribbean in the Long Sixteenth Century,* ed. P. C. Emmer, pp. 62–78. UNESCO Publishing, London.

Mrozowski, S. A., G. H. Ziesing, and M. C. Beaudry

1996 *Living on the Boott: Historical Archaeology at the Boott Mills Boardinghouses, Lowell, Massachusetts.* University of Massachusetts Press, Amherst.

Muehrcke, P. C.

1978 *Map Use: Reading, Analysis and Interpretation.* JP Publications, Madison, WI.

Nassaney, M. S., and M. R. Abel

2000 Urban Spaces, Labor Organization, and Social Control: Lessons from New England's Nineteenth-Century Cutlery Industry. In *Lines That Divide: Historical Archaeologies of Race, Class, and Gender,* ed. J. A. Delle, S. A. Mrozowski, and R. Paynter, pp. 239–75. University of Tennessee Press, Knoxville.

Neiman, F. D.

1995 Stylistic Variation in Evolutionary Perspective: Inferences from Decorative Diversity and Inter-assemblage Distance in Illinois Woodland Ceramic Assemblages. *American Antiquity* 60(1):1–37.

1997 Conspicuous Consumption as Wasteful Advertising: A Darwinian Perspective on Spatial Patterns in Classic Maya Terminal Monument Dates. In *Rediscovering Darwin: Evolutionary Theory and Archaeological Explanation,* ed. C. M. Barton and G. A. Clark, with D. B. Bamforth, pp. 267–90. Archaeological Papers of the American Anthropological Association 7. American Anthropological Association, Arlington, VA.

2005 Comment on Bliege Bird, R., and E. A. Smith, "Signaling Theory, Strategic Interaction, and Symbolic Capital." *Current Anthropology* 46(2):242–43.

2008 The Lost World of Monticello in Evolutionary Perspective. *Journal of Anthropological Research* 64(2):161–93.

Neiman, F. D., and J. A. King

1999 Who Smoked Chesapeake Pipes? Paper presented at the Society for Historical Archaeology, Salt Lake City, UT.

Neiman, F. D., L. McFaden, and D. Wheeler

2000 *Archaeological Investigation of the Elizabeth Hemings Site (44ab438).* Thomas Jefferson Foundation.

Neiman, F. D., and K. Y. Smith

2005 How Can Bayesian Smoothing and Correspondence Analysis Help Decipher the Occupational Histories of Late 18th-Century Slave Quarters at Monticello? Paper presented at the Society for American Archaeology Annual Meeting, Salt Lake City, UT.

Neumann, G. C.

1967 *The History of Weapons of the American Revolution.* Bonanza Publishing, New York.

Neumann, G. C., and F. Kravic

1975 *Collector's Illustrated Encyclopedia of the American Revolution.* Rebel Publishing, Texarkana, TX.

Newman, S. P.

2003 *Embodied History: The Lives of the Poor in Early Philadelphia.* Early American Studies. University of Pennsylvania Press, Philadelphia.

Newsom, L.

1997 Personal communication. Secondary Archaeological Investigations, Southern Illinois University, Carbondale.

Nicholas, D.

1986 The "Syrians" of Jamaica. *Jamaican Historical Review* 15:50–62.

Nicholls, M.

1990 *Aspects of the African American Experience in Eighteenth-Century Williamsburg and Norfolk.* John D. Rockefeller Jr. Library, Colonial Williamsburg Foundation.

Noël Hume, I.

1970 *A Guide to the Artifacts of Colonial America.* Alfred A. Knopf, New York.

1991 *A Guide to Artifacts of Colonial America.* Vintage Books, New York.

Orser, C. E.

1988 The Archaeological Analysis of Plantation Society: Replacing Status and Caste with Economics and Power. *American Antiquity* 53(4):735–51.

1992 *In Search of Zumbi: Preliminary Archaeological Research in Serra Da Barriga, State of Alagoas, Brazil.* Midwestern Archaeological Research Center, Illinois State University, Normal.

2004 *Race and Practice in Archaeological Interpretation.* University of Pennsylvania Press, Philadelphia.

2007 *The Archaeology of Race and Racialization in Historic America.* University Press of Florida, Gainesville.

Osborne, F. J.

1974 Spanish Church, St. Ann's Bay. *Jamaica Journal* 8:33–35.

Otto, J. S.

1984 *Cannon's Point Plantation, 1794–1860: Living Conditions and Status Patterns in the Old South.* Academic Press, Orlando, FL.

Padrón, M. F.

2003 *Spanish Jamaica.* Ian Randle, Kingston, Jamaica.

Paine, T.

[1774] *Common Sense, the Rights of Man.* Signet Classics, New York.
2003

Pampel, F. C.
2000 *Logistic Regression: A Primer.* Quantitative Applications in the Social Sciences, v. 132. Sage Publications, London.

Pares, R.
1956 *Yankees and Creoles: The Trade between North America and the West Indies before the American Revolution.* Harvard University Press, Cambridge, MA.

Parrent, J., J. Neville, and B. Neyland
1991 The Search for Columbus' Last Ships: The 1991 Field Season. INA *Newsletter* 18(4):16–19.

Parrent, J., and M. B. Parrent
1993 The Search Continues for Columbus' Caravels: 1992 Field Report. *INA Quarterly* 20(1):8–14.

Pasquariello, R.
1995 An Analysis of Non-European, Coarse Earthenware from Port Royal, Jamaica. Master's thesis, Syracuse University.

Patterson, O.
1973 *The Sociology of Slavery: An Analysis of the Origins, Development, and Structure of Negro Slave Society in Jamaica.* Fairleigh Dickinson University Press, Rutherford, NJ.
1982 *Slavery and Social Death: A Comparative Study.* Harvard University Press, Cambridge, MA.

Pauketat, T. R.
2001 Practice and History in Archaeology: An Emerging Paradigm. *Anthropological Theory* 1:73–98.

Pawson, M., and D. Buisseret
[1975] 2000 *Port Royal, Jamaica.* 2nd ed. University of the West Indies Press, Kingston, Jamaica.

Paynter, R.
1981 Social Complexity in Peripheries: Problems and Models. In *Archaeological Approaches to the Study of Complexity,* ed. S. E. van der Leeuw, pp. 118–41. A. E. van Giffen Institute, Amsterdam, Netherlands.
1982 *Models of Spatial Inequality.* Academic Press, New York.
1983 Expanding the Scope of Settlement Analysis. In *Archaeological Hammers and Theories,* ed. J. Moore and A. Keene, pp. 233–75. Academic Press, Orlando, FL.
1985 Surplus Flow between Frontiers and Homelands. In *The Archaeology of Frontiers and Boundaries,* ed. S. W. Green and S. M. Perlman, pp. 163–211. Academic Press, Orlando, FL.

Paynter, R. W., and R. H. McGuire
1991 The Archaeology of Inequality: Material Culture, Domination and Resistance. In *The Archaeology of Inequality,* ed. R. H. McGuire and R. W. Paynter, pp. 1–27. Basil Blackwell, Oxford.

Penningroth, D. C.
2003 *The Claims of Kinfolk: African American Property and Community in the Nineteenth-Century South.* John Hope Franklin Series in African American History and Culture. University of North Carolina Press, Chapel Hill.

Perdue, C. L., T. E. Barden, R. K. Phillips, and Virginia Writers' Project

1976 *Weevils in the Wheat: Interviews with Virginia Ex-Slaves.* University Press of Virginia, Charlottesville.

Peregrine, P. N., and G. M. Feinman, eds.

1996 *Pre-Columbian World Systems.* Prehistory Press, Madison, WI.

Phillippo, J. M.

[1843] 1969 *Jamaica: Its Past and Present State.* 1st ed. Reprinted, with a new introduction by Philip Wright. Colonial History Series. Dawsons, London.

Pike, R.

1966 *Enterprise and Adventure: The Genoese in Seville and the Opening of the New World.* Cornell University Press, Ithaca.

Pitman, F.

[1917] 1945 *The Development of the British West Indies, 1700–1763.* Yale University Press, New Haven.

Posnansky, M.

1983 Towards an Archaeology of the Black Diaspora. Paper presented at the Ninth International Congress for the Study of Pre-Columbian Cultures of the Lesser Antilles, Santo Domingo, Dominican Republic.

1984 Toward an Archaeology of the Black Diaspora. *Journal of Black Studies* 15:195–205.

Price, R.

1983 *First Time: The Historical Vision of an Afro-American People.* Johns Hopkins University Press, Baltimore.

1992 *Maroon Societies: Rebel Slave Communities in the Americas.* Johns Hopkins University Press, Baltimore.

Priddy, A.

1975 The 17th and 18th Century Settlement Pattern of Port Royal. *Jamaica Journal* 9(2–3):8–16.

Preucel, R.

2010 The New Pragmatism. Paper delivered at the Theoretical Archaeology Group meeting, Brown University, Providence, RI.

Pulsipher, L.

1986 *Seventeenth Century Montserrat: An Environmental Impact Statement.* Historical Geography Research Series No. 17. Geo Books, Norwich, England.

1990 They Have Saturdays and Sundays to Feed Themselves. *Expedition Magazine* 32(2): 24–33.

1991 Galways Plantation, Montserrat. In *Seeds of Change: Five Hundred Years since Columbus,* ed. H. Viola and C. Margolis, pp. 139–59. Smithsonian Institution Press, Washington, DC.

1994 The Landscapes and Ideational Roles of Caribbean Slave Gardens. In *Archaeology of Garden and Field,* ed. N. Miller and K. Gleason, pp. 202–21. University of Pennsylvania Press, Philadelphia.

Pulsipher, L. M., and C. M. Goodwin

1999 Here Where the Old Time People Be: Reconstructing the Landscapes of the Slavery and Post-Slavery Era on Montserrat, West Indies. In *African Sites: Archaeology in the Caribbean,* ed. J. B. Haviser. Markus Weiner, Princeton.

2001 "Getting the Essence of It": Galways Plantation, Montserrat, West Indies. In *Island Lives: Historical Archaeologies of the Caribbean,* ed. P. Farnsworth. University of Alabama Press, Tuscaloosa.

Rainey, F. G.

1940 *Porto Rican Archaeology.* Scientific Survey of Porto Rico and the Virgin Islands. Vol. 18. Part 1. New York Academy of Sciences, New York.

Ramirez, S. E.

1986 *Provincial Patriarchs: Land Tenure and the Economics of Power.* University of New Mexico Press, Albuquerque.

Ratekin, M.

1954 The Early Sugar Industry in Espanola. *Hispanic American Historical Review* 34(34):1–19.

Rawick, G. P.

1972 *The American Slave: A Composite Autobiography.* 12 vols. Greenwood, Westport, CT.

Reeves, M.

1997 "By Their Own Labor": Enslaved Africans' Survival Strategies on Two Jamaican Plantations. Ph.D. diss., Syracuse University.

2000 "A Profusion of Beads and Trinkets": Enslaved Africans' Access to and Use of Glass Beads in Nineteenth-Century Jamaica. Paper presented at the Annual Meetings of the Society for Historical Archaeology, Quebec City.

Reid, B.

1992 Arawak Archaeology in Jamaica: New Approaches, New Perspectives. *Caribbean Quarterly* 38:17–20.

1994 Tainos Not Arawaks: The Indigenous Peoples of Jamaica and the Greater Antilles. *Caribbean Geography* 5:67–71.

Renny, R.

1807 *An History of Jamaica.* J. Cawthorn, London.

Riordan, R. V.

1973 *Report on Excavations at New Montpelier Estate, St. James, 8–12 January, 1973.* Institute of Jamaica, Kingston.

Roberts, G.

1957 *The Population of Jamaica.* Kraus Reprint Company, Millwood, NY.

Roberts, J.

2006 Working between the Lines: Labor and Agriculture on Two Barbadian Sugar Plantations, 1796–97. *William and Mary Quarterly,* 3rd ser., 63(3):551–86.

Robertson, J.

2005 *Gone Is the Ancient Glory: Spanish Town, Jamaica, 1534–2000.* Ian Randle, Kingston, Jamaica.

Robinson, C.

1992 *Fight for Freedom.* Kingston Publishers, Kingston, Jamaica.

Rockman, D., and N. A. Rotschild

1984 City Tavern, Country Tavern: An Analysis of Four Colonial Sites. *Historical Archaeology* 18(2):112–21.

Romano, R.

1999 The Initial Linkage with America: A General Framework. In *General History of the Caribbean.* Vol. 2: *New Societies: The Caribbean in the Long Sixteenth Century,* ed. P. C. Emmer, pp. 43–61. UNESCO Publishing, London.

Roth, R.

1961 Tea-Drinking in Eighteenth Century America: Its Etiquette and Equipage. *U.S. National Museum Bulletin* 225:61–91.

1988 Tea-Drinking in Eighteenth-Century America: Its Etiquette and Equipage. In *Material Life in America: 1600–1860,* ed. G. B. S. George, pp. 439–61. Northeastern University Press, Boston.

Rothman, J.

2003 *Notorious in the Neighborhood: Sex and Families across the Color Line in Virginia, 1787–1861.* University of North Carolina Press, Chapel Hill.

Rouse, I.

1939 *Prehistory in Haiti: A Study in Method.* Yale University Publications in Anthropology No. 21. Yale University Press, New Haven.

1964 *The Prehistory of Haiti: A Study in Method.* Human Relations Area Files Press, Toronto.

1986 *Migrations in Prehistory.* Yale University Press, New Haven.

1992 *The Tainos: Rise and Decline of the People Who Greeted Columbus.* Yale University Press, New Haven.

Rouse, I., and L. Allaire

1978 Caribbean Chronology. In *Chronologies in the New World,* ed. R. Taylor and C. Meighan, pp. 431–81. Academic Press, New York.

Rubenstein-Gottschamer, A.

1995 Artifact Analysis for the Readers Point Vessel: A Late Eighteenth-Century Merchant Ship from St. Ann's Bay, Jamaica. Master's thesis, East Carolina University, Greenville.

Russell, A. E.

1997 Material Culture and African American Spirituality at the Hermitage. *Historical Archaeology* 31(2):63–80.

Samford, P.

2000 Power Runs in Many Channels: Subfloor Pits and West African–Based Spiritual Traditions in Colonial Virginia. Ph.D. diss., University of North Carolina, Chapel Hill.

2007 *Subfloor Pits and the Archaeology of Slavery in Colonial Virginia.* University of Alabama Press, Tuscaloosa.

Sanders, W. T.

1956 The Central Mexican Symbiotic Region: A Study in Prehistoric Settlement Patterns. In *Prehistoric Settlement Patterns in the New World,* ed. G. R. Willey, pp. 115–27. Viking Fund Publications in Anthropology, New York.

Sanders, W. T., J. R. Parsons, and R. S. Santley

1979 *The Basin of Mexico: Ecological Processes in the Evolution of a Civilization.* Academic Press, New York.

Sanford, D.
1994 The Archaeology of Plantation Slavery in Piedmont, Virginia: Context and Process. In *Historical Archaeology of the Chesapeake,* ed. Paul Shackel and Barbara Little, pp. 115–30. Smithsonian Institution Press, Washington, DC.

Satchell, V.
1990 *From Plots to Plantations: Land Transactions in Jamaica, 1866–1900.* Institute of Social and Economic Research, Kingston, Jamaica.

Sawkins, J., G. P. Gay, and L. B. Wall
1869 *Reports on the Geology of Jamaica; or, Part II. Of the West Indian Survey.* H. M. Stationery Office, Longmans, Green, and Company, London.

Schlotterbeck, J.
1991 The Internal Economy of Slavery in Rural Piedmont, Virginia. In *The Slaves' Economy: Independent Production by Slaves in the Americas,* ed. I. Berlin and P. D. Morgan, pp. 170–81. Frank Cass, London.

Schmidt, P.
1997 *Iron Technology in East Africa: Symbolism, Science, and Archaeology.* Indiana University Press, Bloomington.

Schwartz, S. B.
1985 *Sugar Plantations in the Formation of Brazilian Society: Bahia, 1550–1835.* Cambridge University Press, Cambridge.

Scott, D.
2004 *Conscripts of Modernity: The Tragedy of Colonial Enlightenment.* Duke University Press, Durham.

Shackel, P.
1993 *Personal Discipline and Material Culture: An Archaeology of Annapolis, Maryland, 1695–1870.* University of Tennessee Press, Knoxville.

Shennan, S.
1988 *Quantifying Archaeology.* Edinburgh University Press, Edinburgh.

Shepherd, V.
1985 Transients to Citizens: The Development of a Settled East Indian Community. *Jamaica Journal* 18(3):17–26.
1986 The Dynamics of Afro-Jamaican–East Indian Relations in Jamaica, 1845–1945: A Preliminary Analysis. *Caribbean Quarterly* 32(3):14–26.
1988a Emancipation through Servitude: Aspects of the Condition of Indian Women in Jamaica, 1845–1945. *Bulletin of the Society for the Study of Labour History* 53(3):13–19.
1988b Indians and Blacks in Jamaica in the Nineteenth and Early Twentieth Centuries: A Micro-Study of the Foundation of Race Antagonism. In *After the Crossing: Immigrants and Minorities in Caribbean Creole Society,* ed. Howard Johnson, pp. 95–112. Frank Cass, London.
1993 Indian Females in Jamaica: An Analysis of the Population Censuses, 1861–1943. *Jamaican Historical Review* 18:18–30.
1995 Gender Migration and Settlement: The Indentureship and Post-Indentureship Experience of Indian Females in Jamaica, 1845–1943. In *Engendering History: Carib-*

bean Women in Historical Perspective, ed. V. Shepherd, B. Brereton, and B. Bailey, pp. 233–57. James Currey, London.

Sheridan, R.

1965 The Wealth of Jamaica. *Economic History Review* 18(2):292–311.

1968 The Wealth of Jamaica: A Rejoinder. *Economic History Review* 21(1):46–61.

1973 *Sugar and Slavery: An Economic History of the British West Indies, 1623–1775.* Johns Hopkins University Press, Baltimore.

1976 The Crisis of Slave Subsistence in the British West Indies during and after the American Revolution. *William and Mary Quarterly* 33(4):615–41.

Siegel, P. E., ed.

2005 *Ancient Borinquen: Archaeology and Ethnohistory of Native Puerto Rico.* University of Alabama Press, Tuscaloosa.

Silva, A. F.

1996 Slavery in the Iberian Peninsula at the End of the Middle Age: A Review of the Situation, Sources and Problems Related to the Investigation Activities. In *Slaves with or without Sugar.* Atlantic History Study Centre, Regional Tourist and Culture Office, Funchal, Madeira.

Simmonds, L. E.

1987 Slave Higglering in Jamaica, 1780–1834. *Jamaica Journal* 20:31–38.

2004 The Afro-Jamaican and Internal Marketing Systems: Kingston, 1780–1834. In *Jamaica in Slavery and Freedom: History, Heritage and Culture,* ed. K. Monteith and G. Richards, pp. 274–90. University of the West Indies Press, Kingston, Jamaica.

Singleton, T., ed.

1985 *The Archaeology of Slavery and Plantation Life.* Academic Press, New York.

1991 The Archaeology of Slave Life. In *Before Freedom Came: African-American Life in the Antebellum South,* ed. E. D. Campbell Jr. and K. S. Rice, pp. 188–91. University of Virginia Press, Charlottesville.

Singleton, T. A.

2006 African Diaspora Archaeology in Dialogue. In *Afro-Atlantic Dialogues,* ed. K. A. Yelvington, pp. 249–88. School for American Research, Santa Fe, NM.

Sloane, E.

1964 *A Museum of Early American Tools.* Ballantine Books, New York.

Sloane, H. S.

1707–25 *A Voyage to the Islands Madera, Barbados, Nieves, S. Christophers and Jamaica, with the Natural History of the Herbs and Trees, Four-Footed Beasts, Fishes, Birds, Insects, Reptiles, &C. Of the Last of Those Islands; to Which Is Prefix'd an Introduction, Wherein Is an Account of the Inhabitants, Air, Waters, Diseases, Trade, &C. Of That Place, with Some Relations Concerning the Neighbouring Continent, and Islands of America. Illustrated with Figures of the Things Described, Which Have Not Been Heretofore Engraved; in Large Copper-Plates as Big as the Life.* Printed by B.M. for the author, London.

Smith, C. W.

1995 Analysis of the Weight Assemblage of Port Royal, Jamaica. Ph.D. diss., Texas A&M University, College Station.

Smith, F.
2008 *The Archaeology of Alcohol and Drinking*. University Press of Florida, Gainesville.

Smith, R.
1987 The Search for the Lost Caravels. *American Archaeology* 6:109–14.
1990 Ships of Discovery in the Caribbean. Paper presented at the IX International Association of Caribbean Archaeology, San Juan, Puerto Rico.

Smith, R., D. Lakey, T. Oerthing, B. Thompson, and R. Woodward
1982 *Sevilla La Nueva: A Site Survey and Historical Assessment of Jamaica's First European Town*. Institute of Nautical Archaeology, Texas A&M University.

South, S.
1977 *Method and Theory in Historical Archaeology*. Academic Press, New York.

Stahl, A. B.
2001 *Making History in Banda: Anthropological Visions of Africa's Past*. New Studies in Archaeology. Cambridge University Press, New York.

Steffy, R.
1994 *Wooden Shipbuilding and the Interpretation of Shipwrecks*. Texas A&M University Press, College Station.

Stern, S.
1988 Feudalism, Capitalism and the World System in the Perspective of Latin America and the Caribbean. *American Historical Review* 93:829–72.

Stevens Arroyo, A. M.
1997 Canary Islands and the Antillian. In *La Sorpresa de Europa*, ed. A. T. Gaspar. Universidad de La Laguna, La Laguna, Tenerife, Islas Canarias.

Steward, J. H.
1948 Circum Caribbean Tribes: An Introduction. In *Handbook of South American Indians*, ed. J. H. Steward, pp. 1–43. Vol. 143. Bureau of American Ethnology, Washington, DC.

Stewart, J.
1823 *A View of the Past and Present State of the Island of Jamaica; with Remarks on the Moral and Physical Condition of the Slaves, and on the Abolition of Slavery in the Colonies*. Edinburgh.

Stewart, R. M.
1989 Trade and Exchange in Middle Atlantic Regional Prehistory. *Archaeology of Eastern North America* 17:47–78.

Stine, L. F., M. A. Cabak, and M. D. Groover
1996 Blue Beads as African-American Cultural Symbols. *Historical Archaeology* 30(3):49–75.

Styles, J., and A. Vickery
2006 *Gender, Taste, and Material Culture in Britain and North America, 1700–1830*. Yale University Press, New Haven.

Sutlive, V. H., M. D. Zamora, V. Kerns, and T. Hamada
1991 Resistance and Rebellion in Suriname: Old and New. Paper presented at the Studies in Third World Societies Conference, Williamsburg, VA.

Sweeney, K. M.
1994 High-Style Vernacular: Lifestyle of the Colonial Elite. In *Of Consuming Interest: The Style of Life in the Eighteenth Century,* ed. C. Carson, R. Hoffman, and P. J. Albert, pp. 1–58. University Press of Virginia, Charlottesville.

Tainter, F.
1995 Personal communication. Secondary Department of Forest Research, Clemson University.

Taylor, J.
1686–88 *Multum in Parvo or Taylor's Histori of His Life and Travels in America and Other Parts or Taylor's Life and Travels 1686–1688.* Manuscript on file at the National Library of Jamaica, Kingston.

Thomas, B. W.
1998 Power and Community: The Archaeology of Slavery at the Hermitage Plantation. *American Antiquity* 63(4):531–51.

Thomas, B. W., and L. Thomas
2004 Gender and the Presentation of Self: An Example from the Hermitage. In *Engendering African American Archaeology: A Southern Perspective,* ed. J. Galle and A. Young, pp. 101–31. University of Tennessee Press, Knoxville.

Thomas, J.
2002 Taking Power Seriously. In *The Dynamics of Power,* ed. Maria O'Donovan, pp. 35–50. Southern Illinois University Center for Archaeological Investigations, Carbondale.

Thomas, M.
1974 *Jamaica and Voluntary Laborers from Africa: 1840–1865.* Institute of Jamaica, Kingston.

Thompson, A.
2006 *Flight to Freedom: African Runaways and Maroons in the Americas.* University of the West Indies Press, Kingston, Jamaica.

Thorpe, W. A.
1927 *English and Irish Glass.* Medici Society, London.

Tomich, D.
[1990] 1991 The Other Face of Slave Labor: Provision Grounds and Internal Marketing in Martinique. In *Caribbean Slave Society and Economy: A Student Reader,* ed. V. Shepherd, pp. 304–18. New Press, New York.
1993 Une Petite Guinée: Provision Ground and Plantation in Martinique, 1830–1848. In *The Slaves' Economy: Independent Production by Slaves in the Americas,* ed. I. Berlin and P. D. Morgan. Frank Cass, London.

Torres, J. M., and R. Rodriguez Ramos
2008 The Caribbean: A Continent Divided by Water. In *Archaeology and Geoinformatics: Case Studies from the Caribbean,* ed. Basil A. Reid, pp. 13–29. University of Alabama Press, Tuscaloosa.

Towner, D.
1978 *Creamware.* Faber and Faber, London.

Trouillot, M.-R.
1988 *Peasants and Capital: Dominica in the World Economy.* Johns Hopkins Studies in Atlantic History and Culture. Johns Hopkins University Press, Baltimore.
Trussel, T. D.
2004 Artifacts of Ambition: How the 17th-Century Middle Class at Port Royal, Jamaica, Foreshadowed the Consumer Revolution. Ph.D. diss., Texas A&M University, College Station.
Turner, M., ed.
1995 *From Chattel Slaves to Wage Slaves: The Dynamics of Labour Bargaining in the Americas.* James Curry, London.
1998 *Slaves and Missionaries: The Disintegration of Jamaican Slave Society, 1787–1834.* University of Illinois Press, Urbana.
Ugan, A., and J. Bright
2001 Measuring Foraging Efficiency with Archaeological Faunas: The Relationship between Relative Abundance Indices and Foraging Returns. *Journal of Archaeological Science* 28:1309–21.
United Nations General Assembly
1948 Universal Declaration of Human Rights. In *10 December 1948,* Palais de Chaillor, Paris.
Upton, D.
1988 White and Black Landscapes in Eighteenth-Century Virginia. In *Material Life in America, 1680–1850,* ed. R. B. St. George, pp. 357–69. Northeastern University Press, Boston.
Van Velzen, H. U. E., and W. Van Wetering
1988 *The Great Father and Danger.* Foris Publication, Dordrecht, Netherlands.
Vanderwal, R. L.
1965 Jamaican Prehistory and History. *Bulletin of the Jamaican Historical Society* 4(4):64–70.
1967 The Prehistory of Jamaica: A Ceramic Study. Master's thesis, University of Wisconsin, Madison.
1968 Problems of Jamaican Prehistory. *Jamaica Journal* 2(3):10–13.
Vincentelli, M.
2003 *Women Potters: Transforming Traditions.* Rutgers University Press, New Brunswick, NJ.
Wadley, S.
2000 From Sacred Cow Dung to Cow "Shit": Globalization and Local Religious Practices in Rural North India. *Journal of the Japanese Association for South Asian Studies* 12:1–28.
Wallerstein, I.
1974 *The Modern World System.* Vol. 1: *Capitalist Agriculture and the Origins of the European World.* Academic Press, New York.
1979 *The Capitalist World Economy.* Cambridge University Press, Cambridge.
1980 *The Modern World System.* Vol. 2: *Mercantilism and the Consolidation of the European World Economy, 1600–1750.* Academic Press, New York.

1989 *The Modern World System*. Vol. 3: *The Second Era of Great Expansion of the Capitalist World Economy, 1730–1840*. Academic Press, San Diego.

Walsh, L.

1992 Fettered Consumers: Slaves and the Anglo-American "Consumer Revolution." Paper presented at the Annual Meeting of the Economic History Association, Williamsburg, VA.

1995a Work and Resistance in the New Republic: The Case of the Chesapeake, 1780–1820. In *From Chattel Slave to Wage Slave: The Dynamics of Labour Bargaining in the Americas*, ed. M. Turner, pp. 97–122. James Curry, London.

1995b Slave Life, Slave Society, and Tobacco Production in the Tidewater Chesapeake, 1620–1820. In *Cultivation and Culture: Labor and the Shaping of Slave Life in the Americas*, ed. I. Berlin and P. D. Morgan, pp. 170–99. University Press of Virginia, Charlottesville.

2000 Issues and Questions in African-American History. Paper presented at the Digital Archaeological Archive of Chesapeake's Slavery Steering Committee Workshop, Charlottesville, VA.

Watters, D.

1987 Excavations at Harney Slave Cemetery, Montserrat, West Indies. *Annals of the Carnegie Museum* 56:289–318.

Watts, D.

1987 *The West Indies: Patterns of Development, Culture, and Environmental Change since 1492*. Cambridge Series in Historical Geography No. 8. Cambridge University Press, Cambridge.

Weber, C. A.

1996 The Greenhouse Effect: Gender-Related Traditions in Eighteenth-Century Gardening. In *Landscape Archaeology: Reading and Interpreting the American Historical Landscape*, ed. R. Yamin and K. B. Metheny, pp. 32–51. University of Tennessee Press, Knoxville.

Weddle, R. S.

1985 *Spanish Sea: The Gulf of Mexico in North American Discovery, 1500–1685*. Texas A&M University Press, College Station.

Weitz, E. J.

1990 Vertebrate Fauna. In *The Old Village and the Great House: An Archaeological and Historical Examination of Drax Hall Plantation, St. Ann's Bay, Jamaica*, by D. V. Armstrong, pp. 212–27. University of Illinois Press, Urbana.

White, C. L.

2002 Constructing Identities: Personal Adornment from Portsmouth, New Hampshire, 1680–1820. Ph.D. diss., Boston University.

2005 *American Artifacts of Personal Adornment, 1680–1820: A Guide to Identification and Interpretation*. Rowman and Littlefield, Lanham, MD.

White, S., and G. White

1998 *Stylin': African American Expressive Culture from Its Beginnings to the Zoot Suit*. Cornell University Press, Ithaca.

Wilcoxen, C.

1992 Tin-Glazed Pottery from the Ina/Tamu Port Royal Project, 1981–1990: I. English and Dutch. Report on file, Department of Anthropology, Texas A&M University.

Wilkie, L. A.

1994 Archaeological Evidence of an African-American Aesthetic. *African-American Archaeology* 10:1–4.

1997 Secret and Sacred: Contextualizing the Artifacts of African American Magic and Religion. *Historical Archaeology* 31(4):81–106.

Wilkie, L. A., and K. M. Bartoy

2000 A Critical Archaeology Revisited. *Current Anthropology* 41(5):747–77.

Wilkie, L. A., and P. Farnsworth

1999 Trade and the Construction of Bahamian Identity: A Multiscalar Exploration. *International Journal of Historical Archaeology* 3(4):283–320.

2005 *Sampling Many Pots: An Archaeology of Memory and Tradition at a Bahamian Plantation.* University of Florida Press, Gainesville.

Willey, G. R.

1953 *Prehistoric Settlement Patterns in the Viru Valley, Peru.* Bulletin 155. Bureau of American Ethnology, Washington, DC.

Williams, E. E.

[1944] *Capitalism and Slavery.* University of North Carolina Press, Chapel Hill.
1994

1970 *From Columbus to Castro: The History of the Caribbean.* Vintage, New York.

Willis, R.

1976 The Archaeology of 16th Century Nueva Cadiz. Master's thesis, University of Florida, Gainesville.

Wilson, S. M.

1990 *Hispaniola: Caribbean Chiefdoms in the Age of Columbus.* University of Alabama Press, Tuscaloosa.

Winslow, D.

2000 Analysis of the Hollowware Pewter from Port Royal, Jamaica. Master's thesis, Texas A&M University, College Station.

Wolf, E., and S. Mintz

1957 Haciendas and Plantations in Middle America and the Antilles. *Social and Economic Studies* 6:380–412.

Wood, B., and M. Lynn, eds.

2002 *Travel, Trade and Power in the Atlantic, 1765–1884: Camden Miscellany Volume 35.* Cambridge University Press, Cambridge.

Woodward, R.

1988 The Charles Cotter Collection: A Study of the Ceramic and Faunal Remains. Master's thesis, Texas A&M University, College Station.

2006a Medieval Legacies: The Industrial Archaeology of an Early Sixteenth Century Sugar Mill at Sevilla La Nueva, Jamaica. Ph.D. diss., Simon Fraser University, Burnaby, British Columbia.

2006b Taino Artifacts from Post-Contact Jamaica. In *The Earliest Inhabitants: The Dy-*

namics of the Jamaican Taino, ed. L.-G. Atkinson, pp. 161–174. University of the West Indies Press, Kingston, Jamaica.

Wright, I.

1915 The History of Sugar—1. *Louisiana Planter and Sugar Manufacturer* 54:11, 125–26, 206–7, 302, 366–67.

1916 The Commencement of the Cane Industry in America. *American Historical Review* 21:755–80.

1919 The History of the Cane Sugar Industry in the West Indies—1 and 2. *Louisiana Planter and Sugar Manufacturer* 62:414–15, 63:14–15, 108–9, 222–23, 237–39, 414–15.

1921 The Early History of Jamaica (1511–1536). *English Historical Review* 36:70–95.

Wright, P., ed.

1966 *Lady Nugent's Journal: Of Her Residence in Jamaica from 1801 to 1805.* 4th ed. Institute of Jamaica, Kingston.

2002 *Lady Nugent's Journal of Her Residence in Jamaica from 1801 to 1805.* University Press of the West Indies, Mona, Kingston, Jamaica.

Wynter, S.

1983 *Report on Archival Materials Relating to Spanish Jamaica in Spain.* Jamaica National Heritage Trust, Kingston.

Yamin, R., and K. B. Metheny, eds.

1996 *Landscape Archaeology: Reading and Interpreting the American Historical Landscape.* University of Tennessee Press, Knoxville.

Zahedieh, N.

1986 The Merchants of Port Royal, Jamaica, and the Spanish Contraband Trade, 1655–1692. *William and Mary Quarterly,* 3rd ser., 43(4):570–93.

Contributors

Kofi Agorsah is originally from the Volta Region of Ghana in West Africa. He is Professor of Black Studies and International Studies at Portland State University. Since 1983, he has carried out major excavations and ethnographic studies on African and Maroon heritage. Current NSF-funded excavations in Ghana have been under way since 2009.

Douglas V. Armstrong holds Meredith and Maxwell professorships at Syracuse University. He is a historical archaeologist specializing in diaspora studies, GIS, and heritage site preservation in the Caribbean and New York. Armstrong's publications of findings from Drax Hall and Seville plantations in Jamaica examine community formation and cultural transformation within African Jamaican enslaved and free communities as well as comparisons of the material record of laboring and management classes. His more than thirty years of research in the Caribbean have ranged from studies of plantation slavery to transitions to freedom (St. John) and multiscalar social interaction in port towns (St. Thomas).

Maureen J. Brown holds a master's degree in archaeology from the University of Texas, San Antonio. A native of San Antonio, she currently is an archaeologist, artist, and educator.

Gregory D. Cook holds a master's degree in anthropology/underwater archaeology from Texas A&M and is completing his Ph.D. at Syracuse University. He is a research associate in the Archaeology Institute of the University of West Florida, where he teaches courses in maritime archaeology in the Division of Anthropology.

James A. Delle is Professor of Anthropology and Chair of the Department of Anthropology and Sociology at Kutztown University of Pennsylvania. As president of the Pennsylvania Archaeology Research Center (PARC), Delle has directed projects on African diaspora sites in and around Lancaster County, Pennsylvania. Primarily a Caribbeanist, Delle has worked on Jamaican coffee plantation sites since 1992, focusing on the analysis of space as a form of material culture. He has published numerous articles on the archaeology of Jamaican coffee plantations and is past editor of the *International Journal of Historical Archaeology.*

Marianne Franklin has a Ph.D. in underwater archaeology from Texas A&M University. Her dissertation analyzed a 1764 shipwreck site discovered near the coast of St. Augustine, Florida. She is currently president and director of Southern Oceans Archaeological Research, Inc., in Pensacola, Florida.

Jillian E. Galle is the project manager of the Digital Archaeological Archive of Comparative Slavery (*www.daacs.org*) at Monticello and is the codirector of the DAACS Caribbean Initiative. Her current research focuses on the evolutionary dynamics of slave villages and markets on the islands of Jamaica and Nevis. She has worked on sites throughout the Southeast and in the Caribbean. Galle is the editor of *Engendering African-American Archaeology,* and her research has appeared in several journals and edited volumes.

Candice Goucher is Professor of History at Washington State University in Vancouver (Washington). She has conducted archaeological and field research in Nigeria, Ghana, Togo, and the Caribbean. Currently she is on the board of editors for the *Cambridge History of the World* and series editor of *Issues and Controversies in World History* (Facts-on-File). She is coauthor of *World History: Journeys from Past to Present* (2008), which has been translated into Portuguese, Korean, and Chinese, and co-lead scholar on the Annenberg multimedia resource *Bridging World History.*

Mark W. Hauser is an Assistant Professor of Anthropolgy at Northwestern University, and specializes in the material culture of the African diaspora and social inequality and identity in the Caribbean. His work pays special attention to understanding the everyday life and material world of enslaved laborers. His first book, *An Archaeology of Black Markets: Local Ceramics and Economies in Eighteenth-Century Jamaica* (2008), explores these issues by focusing on yabbas. Hauser has published numerous scholarly articles and chapters on the archaeology of informal and unexpected economies; methodological considerations for understanding colonial landscapes and identity formation; and the centering of craft industries in Caribbean political economy. He coedited a special issue of the *International Journal of Historical Archaeology* on issues of scale in Caribbean archaeology.

Kenneth G. Kelly is Professor of Anthropology at the University of South Carolina, where he teaches historical archaeology and African archaeology. Kelly's longstanding research focus has been on developing a transatlantic perspective on the archaeology of the African diaspora and its impacts in both the Caribbean and West Africa. He has conducted long-term archaeological research in Jamaica, Guadeloupe, Martinique, Bénin, and Guinea and has published the results of his work in a variety of edited volumes and journals, including *American Anthropologist, World Archaeology, Journal of Archaeological Method and Theory, Archéologiques, Journal of Caribbean Archaeology,* and *Ethnohistory.*

Matthew Reeves is Director of Archaeology at James Madison's Montpelier in Orange, Virginia. His specialty is sites of the African diaspora including plantation and freedmen period sites, and Civil War sites. In his work over the past two decades, Reeves has maintained a focus on public archaeology, particularly involving descendant groups.

Amy Rubenstein-Gottschamer holds a master's degree in maritime archaeology from East Carolina University. Her thesis focused on an analysis of the artifacts recovered from the Readers Point Sloop in St. Ann's Bay, Jamaica. She is currently a real estate broker in Santa Fe, New Mexico, and Lawrence, Kansas.

Robyn P. Woodward has directed the excavations of Sevilla la Nueva since 2001. She completed her Ph.D. in archaeology at Simon Fraser University in 2007. Woodward lectures part-time on underwater archaeology and maritime history through the Department of Classical Studies and Continuing Education at the University of British Columbia and the Archaeology Department of Simon Fraser University. She is a governor of the Vancouver Maritime Museum and a director of the Society for Historical Archaeology and the Institute of Nautical Archaeology.

Index